HEALTH AND WELLNESS
IN 19TH-CENTURY AMERICA

"This volume admirably combines a wide-ranging overview of health in the 19th century with telling detail drawn from the lives of ordinary Americans. There is no better single volume available for learnedness, coverage, and sheer readability."

—Steven M. Stowe, Professor, Indiana University and
Author of *Doctoring the South: Southern Physicians
and Everyday Medicine in the Mid-Nineteenth Century*

"A crisp, synthetic account of nineteenth-century US medicine and healing... This is a skillful, smartly written survey, one attentive to the needs of both academic and popular audiences, and sure to be of use in the undergraduate classroom."

—Suman Seth, Associate Professor, Cornell University,
Department of Science and Technology Studies

Recent Titles in Health and Wellness in Daily Life

Health and Wellness in Antiquity through the Middle Ages
William H. York

Health and Wellness in Colonial America
Rebecca Tannenbaum

Health and Wellness in the Renaissance and Enlightenment
Joseph P. Byrne

Health and Wellness in the 19th Century
Deborah Brunton

HEALTH AND WELLNESS
IN 19TH-CENTURY AMERICA

JOHN C. WALLER

Health and Wellness in Daily Life
Joseph P. Byrne, Series Editor

 GREENWOOD

AN IMPRINT OF ABC-CLIO, LLC
Santa Barbara, California • Denver, Colorado • Oxford, England

Library of Congress Cataloging-in-Publication Data

Waller, John, 1972–
    Health and wellness in 19th-century America / John C. Waller.
        pages cm. — (Health and wellness in daily life)
    Includes bibliographical references and index.
    ISBN 978–0–313–38044–0 (hardback) — ISBN 978–0–313–38045–7 (ebook)
1. Medicine—United States—History—19th century. 2. Medical care—United States—History—19th century. 3. Public health—United States—History—19th century. I. Title.
R151.W35 2014
362.1—dc23   2014010742

ISBN: 978–0–313–38044–0
EISBN: 978–0–313–38045–7

18 17 16 15 14   1 2 3 4 5

This book is also available on the World Wide Web as an eBook.
Visit www.abc-clio.com for details.

Greenwood
An Imprint of ABC-CLIO, LLC

ABC-CLIO, LLC
130 Cremona Drive, P.O. Box 1911
Santa Barbara, California 93116-1911

This book is printed on acid-free paper (∞)

Manufactured in the United States of America

Charles Alexander Waller (June 15, 2008–December 5, 2013)

Contents

Series Foreword   xi

Acknowledgments   xiii

1. Factors in Health and Wellness   1

   The Disease Environment   1
   African American Cultures of Health, Disease, and Healing   4
   Native American Cultures of Health, Disease, and Healing   7
   Health, Disease, and Healing in the European Tradition   10

2. Education and Training: Learned and Nonlearned   27

   Identifying and Training African American Healers   27
   The Selection and Training of Native American Healers   31
   The Selection and Training of European-Style Healers   33

3. Faith, Religion, and Medicine   51

   Religion in European-Style Medicine   51
   Religion and African American Healing   60
   Religion and Native American Healing   63
   Religion in White, Black, and Native Medicine   67

4. Women's Health 73

Reproduction and Childbirth 73
The Politics of Reproduction 80
Doctors Writing about Women 84

5. The Health of Children and Infants 95

A Dangerous Time to Be Young 96
Coping with the Loss of a Child 105
Trying to Save Children's Lives 107
The Balance Sheet 111

6. Infectious Disease 115

The Specter of Infectious Disease 115
Infectious Disease and the Native Population 119
Slavery and Infectious Disease 120
The Culture of "Live and Let Die" 121
The Slow Beginnings of Sanitary Reform 123
Sanitary Reform Accelerates 124
Public Health in the Ascendant 127
The Recovery Begins 129
Reckoning Up 132

7. Occupational Health and Dangerous Trades 137

Slavery and Death 137
Sickness and Accidents on Farms 139
The Exploitation of Irish Men and Women 140
The Perils of Manufacturing 142
The Dangers of Mining 144
Death and Debility on the Railways 146
The Miseries of Prostitution 148
Child Labor 150
Unnecessary Deaths 151

8. Surgery, Dentistry, and Orthopedics 157

Pain, Infection, and Death 157
Rare Breakthroughs 159

Surgery and Slavery 160
The Birth of Anesthesia 161
Surgery and the Civil War 163
The Rise of Aseptic Surgery 163
The Transformation of the Hospital 165
The Flourishing of American Dentistry 166
The Limits of Surgical Advance 169

9. The Brain and Mental Disorders 173

Antebellum Ideas about Insanity 173
Insanity, Religion, and Morality 175
Medicine for the Insane 177
Moral Treatment and the Rise of the Asylum 179
The Rise of Neurology 184
New and Old Directions 186

10. The Pharmacopeia 191

Drugs in the European Medical Tradition 192
The Pharmacopeia of African American Medicine 199
The Pharmacopeia of Native American Medicine 201
The Three Traditions 203

11. War and Health 207

Military Medicine at the Start of the Century 208
The American–Mexican War and Its Aftermath 208
The Civil War Years 210
Sickness and the Spanish–American War of 1898 218
Military Medicine in Transition 221

12. Institutional Facilities 225

The Antebellum Hospital 226
The American Dispensary 230
The Transformation of the Hospital 231
Inventing the Professional Nurse 234
The Hospital and Medical Education 235
Institutional Care at the End of the Century 236

13. Disease, Healing, and the Arts   241

     Depicting Sickness and Death   242
     The Politics of Health   247
     Representations of Doctors and Surgeons   251

Bibliography   259
Index   279

Series Foreword

Communities have few concerns that are as fundamental as the health of their members. America's current concern for societal provision of healthcare is as much as political, ethical, economic, and social matter as it is a technical or "medical" one. Reflection on the history of health and medicine may help us to place our contemporary concerns in context, but it also shows how far humanity has come in being able and willing to provide for the highest levels of health and health care possible. It is a reminder, too, of the possibilities the future presents. Our culture believes in progress, but it is also aware that unforeseen challenges will continue to appear. Health and medicine are cultural as well as biological constructs, and we live each day with the constraints and opportunities that follow.

This series of seven monographs explores the courses that human health and medicine have taken from antiquity to the present day. Though far from being complete in their coverage, these volumes map out continuities and changes over time in a set of health and medical fields. Each author has taken on the same outline in order to allow the student of health, medicine and history to discover conditions, beliefs, practices, and changes within a given period, but also to trace the same concerns across time and place. With this in mind, each volume contains chapters on, for example, healers, children's health and healing, occupational and environmental threats, and epidemic disease. To the extent possible, we authors have attempted to emphasize the ways in which these have affected people in their daily lives, rather than viewing them through the lenses of the healers or their profession. Our hope is that these volumes constitute a small and very useful library of the history of health and medicine.

As editor, I have endeavored to bring on board authors who are medical historians as well as fine teachers who have the ability to transmit their knowledge in writing with the same enthusiasm they bring into the classroom. As an author, I am sharing the discoveries, the joys, and not least the challenges and frustrations that all of us encounter in producing this series.

Joseph P. Byrne
Honors Program
Belmont University

Acknowledgments

It is exceptionally hard in a short volume to do justice to the complex factors affecting the health and wellness of nineteenth-century Americans. The burgeoning cities of the East Coast, the arid plains of the Southwest, the makeshift settlements of a constantly-shifting frontier, the country towns of the Northeast, and the slave plantations of the South were all exposed to quite different disease burdens. The United States' diverse populations also developed a bewildering array of ideas about the cause and proper treatment of sickness ranging from the scientific to the supernaturalist and from the well-intentioned but ineffectual to the outright fraudulent. If I have managed to convey something of this complexity, it is due to the excellent scholarship of a number of historians: Charles E. Rosenberg, Paul Starr, John Harley Warner, Judith Walzer Leavitt, John Duffy, Gerald Grob, Susan Reverby, Todd Savitt, Steve Stowe, Virgil Vogel, Sheila Fett, Margaret Humphreys, Janet Golden, Mark Aldrich, Ira Rutkow, and many others. I am also deeply indebted to my friend and colleague David Bailey, whose knowledge of American history is extraordinarily broad; to Mike Waller for his wisdom and dedication; to Abigail and Esther Waller for their patience and love; to Steve Stowe, Walter Hawthorne, Suman Seth, and Susan Sleeper-Smith for helpful conversations about different aspects of health and medicine in the nineteenth century; and to series editor Joseph Byrne for the thoroughness of his comments on the manuscript.

My greatest debt of gratitude is to my son Charlie, who was diagnosed with terminal brain cancer shortly after I began writing this book. He passed away at the age of five shortly before its completion. Knowing that Charlie's days would be cut tragically short gave me a keener sympathy for the millions of sick children and grieving parents whose experiences this book seeks to capture. His prognosis ensured that I never lost sight of the terrible pain that lies behind the raw statistical data or the headstones that record the deaths of children. But my primary debt to Charlie is more personal. For it is due to his simple but wonderful qualities that I could write this book while caring for him during his slow decline. Charlie's happiness, ease of laughter, and precocious sensitivity to the feelings of others helped his family and friends to get through each day. This book is dedicated to an admirable and sorely missed young boy.

CHAPTER 1

Factors in Health and Wellness

THE DISEASE ENVIRONMENT

Suffering and premature death shadowed each of the achievements upon which white Americans of the nineteenth century looked with such conspicuous pride: the rapid growth of cities, the expansion of agriculture and industry, and the peopling of a vast land stretching all the way from the Atlantic seaboard through the Midwest, the Great Plains, and the Rocky Mountains, to the distant Pacific coast. The defining features of what Americans of European descent called with lofty optimism "Manifest Destiny" exposed all those living in North America to a brutal onslaught from old and new diseases. Many of these health hazards were unavoidable, the inevitable consequences of climate, geography, and the immunological history of the continent's peoples. Others were a consequence of collective human actions. Rapid urbanization exposed city dwellers to heightened risks of infection; the slave system subjected millions of African Americans to death and psychological distress; Native Americans suffered terribly through contact with whites; warfare cost hundreds of thousands of lives; and industrialization broke the bodies and stole the health of significant numbers of American workers.[1]

Climate and geography shaped the disease experience of many Americans. The warm moistness of the southern climate favored the multiplication of the pathogens that caused gastrointestinal illnesses

like dysentery, salmonella, and typhoid fever and provided a conducive environment for the breeding of both the flies that helped to propa-
gate diarrheal diseases and the mosquitos that spread malaria and
yellow fever. Mosquito-borne malaria also devastated populations in
the Midwest as people of European descent began to move west in
large numbers. In part due to the low drainage capacity of prairie soils,
there were plenty of pools of stagnant water in which mosquito larvae
could flourish. Climate and geography were no less important in promoting the spread of epidemics. Diseases like yellow fever and cholera
devastated North America because they could be carried for long dis-
tances along great navigable river systems like the Mississippi and the
Ohio.[2]

The extent to which a population had evolved immunity to different
pathogens exerted a considerable influence over whether or not they
succumbed to infection. Whites in the south lacked the innate immune
defenses against malaria possessed by many of West African descent.
Conversely, it may be that slaves were more susceptible to respiratory
infections like pneumonia and tuberculosis because their forebears
had not encountered them prior to the advent of the Atlantic slave
trade. Those of African origin also bore the excruciating burden of
sickle-cell anemia. Indigenous peoples were the most immunologically
vulnerable of all American populations. Their ancestors had not had
the opportunity to evolve resistance to most of the infectious diseases
common to European and African peoples, and so they were repeatedly devastated by maladies, like measles and influenza, from which
white and black children usually recovered.[3]

The actions of the white population dramatically increased the exposure and susceptibility of all Americans to disease through urbanization, westward expansion, warfare, and slavery. As a country of
hamlets and small towns transformed into a highly urbanized nation
of overcrowded and unsanitary cities, many more people succumbed
to potentially deadly infections like tuberculosis, dysentery, typhoid,
whooping cough, influenza, measles, scarlet fever, pneumonia, and
diphtheria. Not until the late 1800s, and even then only patchily, did
urban governments introduce the clean water supplies and adequate
sewage systems that could reduce the murderous onslaught of infectious disease.[4] The commercial revolution of the 1800s, tightly linked
to urbanization, facilitated the spread of bacteria and viruses. The
imperatives of trade drove an escalation in the number of foreign ships
entering American ports and an expansion of roads, canals, and later
railways. Improved communications brought material boons and economic opportunities but also allowed for the rapid propagation of

sickness from continent to continent, state to state, and coastal towns to interior settlements. Furthermore, the desire for profit and the fear of bankruptcy gave merchants and shopkeepers a vested interest in flouting or curtailing the quarantine measures that might have at least reduced the rate at which epidemics were propagated. Inclined to believe that sound medical policy coincided with their economic interests, tradesmen often warmly supported doctors who denied the contagiousness of disease and in some cases successfully joined forces with them to abolish quarantine restrictions.[5] The same urge to place profit before safety can be seen in how American politicians and industrialists responded to industrial deaths and accidents. For most of the century, miners, factory workers, and railway employees died at a considerably higher rate than their equivalents in the countries of western Europe.[6]

White American workers did not suffer on so vast a scale as African American slaves, whose welfare was sacrificed to the determination of slave owners to make money from cultivating sugar, rice, cotton, tobacco, and indigo. It gives some sense of the severe hardships of slavery that only about 40% of black boys and girls survived past their 15th birthday.[7] Those who perished were killed by a wide range of digestive and respiratory conditions related to poor nutrition, appalling housing, harsh work regimes, and physical abuse. In addition, slaves had to endure high levels of parasitic infection due to the nature of their labor, and they faced the unrelenting psychological burden of knowing that at any moment a master could break up their family, selling mothers, fathers, siblings, and children to new plantations often hundreds of miles apart.[8]

The colonization by white settlers of large areas of North America unleashed many more disease risks. Native American societies were devastated by the destruction of their traditional means of subsistence and their forced removal to reservations, where infectious disease spread with terrible ease.[9] White colonists also suffered as they moved into new lands. Many died of nutritional deficiencies, especially gold diggers who tried to survive on bread and bacon as they crossed plains and mountains. Those who settled in Midwest states like Ohio, Michigan, Wisconsin, Indiana, and Illinois perished in large numbers as a result of malaria, dysentery, and typhoid. Mosquitos bred copiously in the mill ponds dug by settlers, and they preyed easily on humans inhabiting cramped, dirty, dark, and damp cabins. The bacteria responsible for diarrheal diseases also throve where wells to collect effluence frequently overflowed and contaminated supplies of drinking water.[10]

In addition, warfare exposed white, black, and Native Americans to intense levels of infectious sickness. Maladies caused by overcrowding, poor sanitation, and poor nutrition always took more lives than artillery, bullets, or bayonets. Military camps acted as ideal breeding grounds for bacteria. Young men who had been raised in remote towns and had not been previously exposed to maladies that were common in urban areas sickened and died in large numbers.[11] Slaves who fled their plantations with nothing but the shirts on their backs frequently perished of cold, others of sickness in military camps, and many due to poverty and neglect after the war during the South's traumatic transition to a wage economy. Severe drought and crop failures in 1866–1867, magnified by the destruction of southern farms by Union troops, also triggered widespread hunger.[12]

Towards the end of the century the health of Americans did finally begin to improve. As we will see in later chapters, the abolition of slavery, the advent of sanitary reform, the provision of clean water, and improved housing, clothing, and nutrition all made important contributions to this recovery. The availability of vaccine matter dramatically reduced mortality to smallpox, and the rate at which malaria killed fell steadily due to the widespread use of quinine, a growing awareness that wetlands were best avoided during the summer, the improved drainage of fields, and the preference of mosquitos for the blood of the nation's vast cattle population. And although actual medical breakthroughs remained rare, the United States's healers formulated a wide variety of theories about the nature of disease and the ways in which it could be prevented and cured. The sections below will examine in turn the ideas and practices developed by African American, Native American, and European healers.

AFRICAN AMERICAN CULTURES OF HEALTH, DISEASE, AND HEALING

The Varieties of Slave Medicine

Slave healers on the plantations practiced according to either European-style medicine or a creole approach derived from African, European, and Native American traditions.[13] The slave known to us as Elsey is an example of the first category. The southern planter Alexander Telfair appointed her to be the "Doctress of the Plantation" and called in a white physician only in cases of "extraordinary illness."[14] Telfair was trying to save money, but he was also displaying a quite conventional belief that laypeople could diagnose a disease and prescribe a treatment without always requiring the physician's input. Healers like Elsey were frequently charged with giving sick slaves powerful cathartics like castor oil, calomel, and rhubarb or tartar emetic to induce vomiting and other forms of purge. Some enslaved doctors were retained even when white physicians were easily available for consultation. One Virginian physician complained bitterly about slave healers who were allowed to practice "on the same footing with the man who has spent time, wealth, and talents" in medical training. But experience taught many a master that slaves could often do the job every bit as well as their white counterparts. Like many other slave women, Elsey served as a midwife for the birth of children both black and white.[15]

A rival set of ideas about health and treatment flourished on the plantations because slaves tended to be hostile to the regimens of their masters. Out of skepticism about the efficacy of heroic medicines combined with a desire to maintain their own cultural traditions, slaves often preferred to dispose of white medicine and then call in a slave healer. Lizzie Chandler, a former Louisianan slave, felt sure that "quinines all right for white folks, but it ain't no good for black folks."[16] African Americans often implicated the quality of a patient's blood in him or her developing a sickness. The blood might flow too fast or too slow, be too hot or too cold, or too thick or thin due to the buildup of impurities. Most treatments involved making teas out of plants and herbs collected in forests, marshes, and meadows in the vicinity of the plantation. "Mostly, dey would use de herbs in de fields for dey medicine," explained South Carolina's Josephine Bacchus, having noted how little slaves had admired white doctors.[17] Many African Americans considered it vital to take sassafras tree root at various times of the year to purge the blood of impurities.[18] Other treatments, like garlic, asafetida, and nutmeg, were worn around the neck in the belief that their odors would deter the agents of sickness.[19]

Many of the healing practices developed on the plantations were based on overtly magical belief systems.[20] Conjurers or hoodoo men were often summoned to treat maladies that did not respond to the slaves' conventional herbal remedies or to European-style medicine. The practitioners of conjure or hoodoo were expected to identify afflictions reckoned to be caused by the casting of malicious spells or "fixes." They then had to remove the fix. This sometimes involved locating near the home of the victim a hoodoo bag containing such items as whisky bottles or animal parts that were said to carry the curse.[21] Having located the origin of the fix, the conjurer might then be expected to turn it back upon the perpetrator. Conjurors were believed to be equipped with such great powers that they sometimes stood alongside preachers as the most respected members of a slave community.[22] According to the former slave Henry Clay Bruce, slaves "believed and feared" their conjurors "almost beyond their masters."[23] The conjurer had to have plenty of charisma in order to convince fellow slaves of the reality of his powers, but his primary skill usually lay in understanding people. Given that the conjurer usually identified another member of the community as the source of the sick person's curse, he or she had to be skilled at discerning the covert loves, hatreds, and grudges that could be implicated as the motive for issuing of a fix.[24] Accusations had to be plausible, and so sharp judges of character and situation thrived in this role.[25]

The medical practices of the slave healer derived from multiple sources. Beliefs about the role of impure blood in causing sickness suggest the influence of both African and European traditions. Conjuring represents a clear case of continuity from the beliefs of West African societies like the Igbo, Yoruba, Bambara, and Kongo. "My mammy," remembered the ex-slave Harriet Collins of Texas, "larned me a lot of doctoring what she larnt from old folks from Africy."[26] A blend of African, Christian, and Native American ideas informed ideas about the sacred properties of plants; Harriet's mother also credited "de Indians" for teaching slaves about the properties of certain herbs. And, in a manner most obviously consistent with Christian theology, the plants and herbs believed to have therapeutic powers were also said to have been lovingly crafted by a benevolent creator.[27]

White society had a complex relationship with African American medicine. Some patients of European heritage borrowed recipes from slave doctors and consulted black healers for medical advice. The Virginian planter John Walker, having lost five of his seven children, did not scruple about sending a sickly slave to a nearby plantation to be treated with a "decoction of herbs" by a slave healer known as "Old Man Docr. Lewis."[28] The ex-slave Polly Shine recalled receiving the "best of care" when ill because "Master would get us a Negro mama, and she doctored us from herbs she got out of the woods."[29] Black healers could gain formidable reputations. Doctor John, a free black, practiced African American medicine with such success among both whites and blacks in pre–Civil War New Orleans that he could afford to buy a plantation complete with his own slaves.[30] Many other whites were hostile to black medicine and deeply wary of its practitioners. Owners were often fearful of slaves participating in cultural practices not sanctioned by the dominant white society. Others feared that slave herbalists and conjurers would use their skills to poison or otherwise harm their masters.[31] Nevertheless, owners and overseers were not always in a position to monitor what went on in slave quarters or in the fields and forests surrounding them. African American healing therefore flourished in spite of the massive curtailment of freedom on the plantations.

NATIVE AMERICAN CULTURES OF HEALTH, DISEASE, AND HEALING

Our knowledge of indigenous medicine in North America is limited by both the nature and the scarcity of surviving sources. Most of the accounts available to us were written by white observers who either did not understand the meaning and complexity of what they were observing or misrepresented native practices out of a contempt for indigenous cultures. Many more healing rituals are now forever lost so that we cannot grasp the full diversity of traditional practices. Some ancient ceremonies and remedies were forgotten with the forcible resettlement of native groups in new terrains with unfamiliar fauna and flora. Moreover, white agents were often successful in their deliberate suppression of indigenous cultures. Even so, we do have enough fairly sympathetic records to allow us to reconstruct some of the major belief systems and ceremonies. Many ancient rituals and techniques have also been preserved to the present. The variety in Native American medical systems is hardly surprising. Cultures that had been developing for at least 13,000 years within a landmass that stretched for over 2,000 miles east to west and across landscapes as starkly contrasting as the thickly forested Great Lakes region, the expansive grasslands of the Great Plains, and the parched terrain of New Mexico could hardly be expected to have settled on a single medical tradition. This section can only provide a basic introduction to some of the key themes in Native American medicine. Later chapters will explore the supernaturalist belief systems that underpinned diagnosis and healing in native communities and the extensive pharmacopeia employed by herbalists and shamans.[32]

Many native societies made rough-and-ready distinctions between natural and supernatural diseases and medicines. Snakebites, skin irritations, boils, bruises, fractures, and dislocations might be treated without reference to a spirit world by herbalists who would prepare poultices and herbal infusions from the local flora.[33] Nearly all native groups also developed effective techniques to staunch the loss of blood. Some peoples crammed open wounds with puffballs—fungi packed with microscopic spores—in order to arrest hemorrhage. The

Native American shaman treating a patient, after a watercolor by Seth Eastman, 1851, from *American Indians, their History, Condition, and Prospects* by Henry Rowe Schoolcraft. A geographer, ethnologist, and Indian agent, Schoolcraft learned much about the native societies living in northern Michigan, Minnesota, and Wisconsin. This picture shows a bowl and pestle for mixing medicines. The shaman is shaking a gourd rattle and may be singing a healing song. (National Library of Medicine)

Mohegans and Apaches achieved the same end by pressing spider webs into gashes, and the Kwakiutls of the Pacific Northwest used both spider webs and puffballs that they then covered with strips of bark and sealed with gum.[34] Especially impressive were indigenous techniques for promoting wound healing. The Ojibwas repaired torn ears by sewing them together using a needle and deer sinews. Others prepared sutures from human hair, deer tendons, and vegetable fibers like basswood. In an attempt to prevent infection, groups like the Illinois poured warm water containing special herbs into open wounds, and a number of societies employed turpentine and oily resins from trees. The Michigan Indians, Potawatomis, and Ojibwas made syringes from bladder and quills, which they used to wash out wounds and insert decoctions of vegetables. Michigan Indians also kept gunshot wounds open by inserting a "tent" made of the bark of slippery elm. By doing so they hoped that the ball would come out with the suppurating matter.[35]

Supernaturalist beliefs predominated in the diagnosis and treatment of internal or intractable maladies. For all the diversity of native medical theories and rituals, indigenous cultures all regarded sickness as a disruption to the harmony of a world in which every living thing had a life force or soul that could be disturbed or cause a disturbance to other forces.[36] Each culture had its own range of specific beliefs about how these disharmonies might arise and cause ill health. Some implicated particular spirits who were said to unleash sickness on people who violated moral taboos against activities like incest. Other cultures, like the Cherokee and Ojibwa, ascribed serious diseases to humans having slaughtered beasts for food without having shown the reverence expected by the celestial prototypes of the hunted animals that inhabited an upper world.[37] Those who broke hunting taboos could expect to sicken after the animal's ghost spirit entered their bodies.[38] In yet others, human spirits were believed to be capable of wreaking vengeance on their living enemies or returning from the afterlife in an attempt to bring family members along with them. Finally, diseases were widely believed to be caused by the evil powers marshaled by sorcerers and witches.[39]

The treatment of diseases said to be caused by offended spirits or malign magic usually called for the intervention of shamans known as medicine men or women. Dressed in distinctive garb and making use of bags, charms, sticks, and fetishes credited with magical powers, the shaman had first to identify the supernatural origins of a disease and then work out how to cure it. Discerning the role of sorcery or a vengeful spirit might require no more than observing the symptoms of the sick person, or it might demand the interpretation of his or her dreams in which a spirit might reveal itself. In other cases the shaman had to embark on a spiritual quest, entering a trance state in which his or her soul travelled into either the supernatural realm or the dream of the patient to learn which spirit or spirits were involved. Treatment could then take many different forms: the use of carefully selected and prepared herbs; the performance of special dances, chants, and songs to draw on the powers of healing spirits; elaborate rites designed to appease supernatural entities; rituals formulated to encourage spirits to leave the sick person's body; ceremonies to magically remove foreign objects magically inserted into the body; or the recovery of a lost soul by the shaman entering a trance and dispatching his or her own soul into the unearthly kingdom. The methods employed by the shaman or shamans differed dramatically from society to society.[40]

The white peoples of North America were not consistently dismissive of Native American healing practices. Benjamin Rush, professor of the theory and practice of medicine at the University of Pennsylvania from 1789 to 1813, may have scoffed that "We have no discoveries in the materia medica to hope for from the Indians in North-America."[41] In reality, white healers were quick to prescribe native plants to their patients. As a result, over 200 Native American plant medicines had been incorporated into regular medical practice by 1820.[42] Many white healers garnered extra custom by claiming that their medicines were of native origin, and large numbers of the sick bought patent remedies like Dr. Kilmer's Indian Oil in the belief that indigenous medicines were especially effective in combating the sicknesses of North America. Especially in frontier zones, where physicians were seldom available, native men and women were often called in to heal white settlers. One of the many tragedies of the treatment of Native Americans by white Americans is that they ultimately had to endure sustained attacks on their traditional healing practices as the government tried to assimilate them into white culture. These were blows aimed at the very heart of their cultural identity and dignity.[43]

HEALTH, DISEASE, AND HEALING IN THE EUROPEAN TRADITION

Lifestyle and Sickness

One of the most fundamental discoveries of modern medicine is that diseases often have their own specific causes. In striking contrast, those practicing medicine up until the late 1800s were firmly convinced that a collection of 20 people all suffering from a single malady such as tuberculosis, scarlet fever, pneumonia, or dysentery could have succumbed for as many different reasons. Smallpox alone seemed to have a specific cause with a predictable effect on the body. All other afflictions appeared to depend on idiosyncratic interactions among the individual's bodily "constitution," lifestyle, and mind-set. The term *constitution* referred to the power of an individual's body to resist sickness that could be compromised by either unhealthy living or a bad heredity.[44] The lifestyle factors believed to affect an individual's health included air quality, amount of exercise, quantity of sleep, the kinds of food and drink consumed, and the effectiveness with which a person excreted bodily impurities. Psychological factors were also considered to be essential to determining if a person stayed healthy or sank into disease. The famous nineteenth-century American doctor William Beaumont even concluded that more Americans died due to the fear of cholera in 1832 than to the "fatal tendency" of the disease itself.[45]

Within this general framework physicians divided the causes of disease into two separate levels: the predisposing and the exciting. Predisposing causes were responsible for rendering the bodily constitution susceptible to particular kinds of sickness. Hereditary predispositions, a poor diet, years of whiskey drinking, inadequate housing, excessive partying, and prolonged sadness were all identified as creating personal vulnerabilities to certain types of sickness. Phases of life such as infancy, puberty, and menopause were also associated with heightened risks of illness and debility.[46] The exciting cause was a trigger that tipped into an actual disease state someone whose resistance had been compromised. It might take the form of a sudden exposure to extreme weather, foul air, or food and drink that placed too much stress on the digestive system. Accordingly, doctors based their accounts of why patients became unwell on what they inferred or found out about their ancestry, habits, and state of mind. For instance, a poor Irish immigrant of Five Points in New York with tuberculosis would typically be assumed to have inherited a feeble body from her malnourished and immoral parents that she had further weakened through hard living, boozing, and depressed spirits. By contrast, a well-to-do young lady from Beacon Hill in Boston who developed the identical hacking cough might be told that she had been born with so sensitive a nature that the shocks of daily life had depleted the vitality needed to sustain her bodily health.

This system of explanation could also make sense of epidemic diseases that affected thousands of people at the same time. Cholera arrived in North America in the summer of 1832, generating shockwaves of terror and claiming as many as 150,000 lives. Contemporaries had no difficulty in identifying predisposing causes for cholera. The wretched inhabitants of slums perished disproportionately, and so physicians could chalk the disease up to constitutions wrecked by drinking, hardship, misery, and fornication. But why had this affliction appeared so suddenly?

Prior to the last third of the century most American doctors refuted the suggestion that cholera was a new disease that had spread from India by way of some kind of infectious material. Instead they depicted it as a form of normal diarrhea that had struck with concentrated rage due to a singular exciting cause in the form of a major disturbance to the quality of the air. Although opinions differed over the origin of this "choleraic distemperature," most argued that the normal constituents of air had somehow been changed. This might happen, they argued, if the putrid gases emitted by rotting matter, called "miasmas," had contaminated the air.[47] Although ultimately proven incorrect, at the time miasmatist physicians had good epidemiological grounds for regarding contagionism as the "vulgar prejudice" of the unschooled.[48] They pointed to the obvious fact that cholera nearly always raged in the most disagreeably smelly of urban areas. Why, then, look further for a cause than the stench of the slum? Doctors could also cite examples of diseases appearing among people in towns or cities who had had no apparent contact with other sufferers. Some physicians did argue that miasmatic particles could be transferred from person to person and thereby cause infection. But they were in a small minority and too few to be able to stop the majority of quarantine measures from being desultory and short-lived.[49]

Miasma theory also appeared to account for the incidence of devastating diseases like yellow fever and malaria. Yellow fever was blamed on the gaseous exhalations of filthy streets, damp cellars, overflowing privies, and the corpses rotting in graves dug within the city limits. Associated with marshy lowlands and the broken ground of new farms, malaria was typically attributed to the release of poisonous vapors into the surrounding air from rotting vegetation.[50]

Contemporary letters, diaries, and newspaper reports, in addition to medical texts, are replete with the notion that the body is under constant risk of being disrupted by improper living or the temperature and quality of the air. Even a brief change of temperature was believed to be capable of throwing the body into disequilibrium. "Clara had another slight attack" of illness, jotted the Arkansas planter John Brown in his diary in 1860, due to "an impudent change of garment." City dwellers avoided, if they could, foul and fetid places. Settlers in the rural West talked of landscapes that were inherently "healthy," "sickly," or "miasmatic." They knew that marshy areas were most dangerous in the summer. Hence many a southern planter abandoned his plantations during the hottest months: one said that he would rather serve as target practice for the "best Kentucky rifleman" than "spend a night on my plantation in summer." The denizens of settler towns also spoke of the bodies of new immigrants having to become acclimated or "seasoned" to their new environments if they were to survive.[51] Until at least the 1870s a majority of American doctors and patients concurred that disease was largely a matter of person and place. Physicians still accepted that any number of personal or environmental factors could cause in different people the same form of sickness. Conversely, they still asserted that a noxious miasma emanating from putrefying matter might cause malaria in one person, dysentery in a second, and typhoid in a third.[52] It would require a major conceptual reorientation for physicians and patients to accept that many diseases are discrete conditions with specific causes.[53]

Early Ideas about the Physiology of Disease

American physicians presented divergent theories about what happens inside the body when someone gets sick. Many subscribed to updated versions of the fourth-century BC Hippocratic system in which illness ensued when something unsettled the equilibrium or the flow of the body's four humours: yellow bile, black bile, phlegm, and blood. This general bodily disturbance then led to a specific ailment according to where the offending humor pooled or putrefied. By the nineteenth century, American physicians had added additional fluids to the ancient quartet. One typical medical encyclopedia noted that "any juice, or fluid part of the body" might lead to sickness, such "as the chyle, blood, milk, fat, serum."[54] The principles, however, remained the same. Take, for example, the theory about the cause of insanity presented in William Buchan's best-selling *Domestic Medicine*: "excessive cold," he explained, "especially in the lower extremities, will force blood into the brain, and produce symptoms of madness."[55] To widely read physicians such as Buchan, running noses, sweating, diarrhea, and vomiting were the body's means of trying to restore balance by getting rid of excess or corrupted liquids. The role of medicine was to help restore balance by regulating the patient's diet and hastening the excretion of the offending fluids.

A rival and increasingly dominant medical camp reduced sickness to abnormalities in the solid parts of the body. These "solidists" asserted that disease involves blood vessels or nerve fibers becoming irritated and inflamed as a result of pathological stimulation. Swelling inside the body then impeded the flow of liquids and in turn compromised the body's vital functions. These basic ideas took several specific forms as physicians jostled for patients and authority. Benjamin Rush explained *every* disease known to humanity in terms of the state of the blood vessels. In a lecture of 1796 he informed his students, "there is but one disease," a "Morbid excitement induced by capillary tension."[56] Francois J. V. Broussais, a famous French clinician whose influence extended far across the Atlantic Ocean, asserted that an over-stimulated gastroenteric tract becomes inflamed and, due to the inter-connectedness of the bodily system, gives rise to lesions and inflammation in other parts of the body. Dismissing both Rush and Broussais, Virginia's eminent physician John Esten Cooke argued that cold or noxious air weakened the heart, which led to a dangerous accumulation of blood in the vena cava and the liver.[57] Miasma theory could easily be made compatible with these different varieties of solidism. Physicians wrote of poisonous gases acting like chemical ferments or catalysts in causing tissues within the body to break down and organs to fail.

The view of sickness as involving the body's solid structures had secured considerable credibility by mid-century as more and more American physicians learned of the anatomical discoveries being made in postrevolutionary Paris.[58] Highly skilled French anatomists with access to boundless supplies of cadavers found that fatal ailments are often associated with specific lesions in the body's organs and tissues. Slicing open brains, hearts, lungs, spleens, intestines, kidneys, and livers revealed growths, swellings, and necroses that called into question Hippocratic notions of free-floating fluids causing sickness. The revelations of great French clinicians like René-Théophile-Hyacinthe Laennec and Pierre Louis thrilled the thousands of American physicians who traveled to the medical mecca of the Paris medical schools. "Merely to have a breathed a concentrated scientific atmosphere like that of Paris" enthused Dr. Oliver Wendell Holmes to his parents in 1833, "must have an effect on anyone who has lived where stupidity is tolerated, [and] where mediocrity is applauded."[59] Doctors like Holmes returned convinced that the phlegm, vomit, diarrhea, and sweat that their predecessors had considered to be the disease process itself were in fact mere side effects of lesions that affected the cells, tissues, and organs of the body.

For all their discord the humoralists and solidists shared some basic beliefs about treating disease. As Charles Rosenberg explains, medicine nearly always involved regulating the patient's intakes and outputs in order to restore bodily harmony: bleeding, diaphoretics to promote urination, cathartics to accelerate defecation, emetics to induce vomiting, and various dietary regimens.[60] The competing schools of thought simply provided different rationales for how the same therapies operated inside the body. A vomit might be given to a patient by a humoralist to "flush out unbalanced humors" whereas his solidist counterpart might do so in the belief that he was reducing the pathological friction between inflamed tissues and bodily fluids.[61] Especially in the early 1800s both humoralist and solidist physicians also favored heroic regimens, involving draining large quantities of blood or having patients ingest substantial quantities of harsh depletives like the element antimony, known as tartar emetic, and the element mercury, in the form of mercurous oxide, popularly known as calomel.[62] Physicians did realize that quinine, contained in cinchona bark or manufactured in the form of quinine sulfate, alleviated the symptoms of malaria, but they tended to believe that the malarial patient should first undergo a thorough vomit or bloodletting to ready his or her body for its administration.[63]

The theories and therapies of early nineteenth-century medicine were perfectly reasonable to an age innocent of what we have since learned from the sciences of physiology, biochemistry, bacteriology, histology, genetics, immunology, and endocrinology. Most maladies are associated with things like a fast pulse and the expulsion of vomit and diarrhea while recovery entails a return to normal patterns of respiration and excretion. The doctor merely had to see these symptoms as the attempts of the body to heal itself in order to conclude that his job was to help accelerate the depletion of blood, phlegm, sweat, feces, or bile in order to bring the fluids back into balance or lessen the irritation of nerves and blood vessels. Routine experience also buttressed the assumption that conventional therapies were effective. Like all persistent but flawed paradigms, humoralism and solidism could supply easy rationalizations when remedies failed. If a patient did not survive in spite of the doctor's ministrations, then the disease had presumably been too deeply ingrained to submit to drugs and dietary changes. All recoveries, however, could be simplistically interpreted as a vindication of both the particular medical theory and the clinical acumen of the physician.

Not that American medicine was resistant to change in the early decades of the century. On the contrary, by the 1830s the culture and practice of medicine had started to shift in important ways. Doctors became more and more convinced that many diseases are discrete entities and that their predecessors had been wrong to think that one disease can easily change into another. Studying the pathology of conditions like typhoid fever, typhus, and cholera from the bedside to the autopsy room persuaded a lot of clinicians that these were completely separate sicknesses. The investigation of disease at the cellular level by brilliant German researchers like Rudolf Virchow further undermined the belief that diseases are changeable and malleable. The possibility emerged that specific diseases might also have specific causes.[64] We can also chart a gradual decline in the appeal of heroic medicines accompanied by a growing conviction among physicians that nerves and tissues developed lesions and abnormal function due to becoming sapped of their vitality. The goals of medicine were therefore to fortify the body so that it could resist the forces of deterioration.[65] Many doctors by mid-century were withholding bleeding and calomel and instead giving patients rich diets and stimulants like quinine, alcohol, and iron compounds in the attempt to buttress their bodily systems.[66]

This shift occurred for a number of reasons. Perhaps most importantly, young American physicians who traveled to Paris to study with pioneers of medical statistics like Pierre Louis came back ready to believe that such therapeutic mainstays as bleeding and calomel were of questionable value. They came to the conclusion that they simply could not hope to defeat disease by their own efforts alone. Reluctant to arrive at the unappealing conclusion that medicine simply did not work, they opted for the claim that the body can heal itself but that it also often needs the hearty diets and stimulating drugs prescribed by the physician. In short, they had acknowledged limitations to the medical art without losing their faith in medicine. Although many physicians continued to give their patients large doses of depletives like mercury and antimony, staples of medical practice like bleeding had fallen almost entirely out of favor by the 1860s.[67] A second reason for the declining faith in heroic depletives is connected to the economic competition that orthodox physicians, trained in conventional medical theories, faced from rivals known as "irregulars." Many a "regular" physician could agree with the Cincinnati practitioner who declared in 1842 that the "inveterate" habit of "administering mercury" was "driving the community from regular physicians."[68] Given that patients often preferred the gentle herbal brews of alternative healers like homeopaths to the violent vomits of the regular doctors, many orthodox physicians slowly adapted their practice to the preferences of the market.[69]

Alternative Medicine in the United States

A diverse range of alternative practices and sects emerged in the nineteenth-century United States to challenge the authority of regular physicians. People often turned to alternative systems when they felt that conventional medicine had failed: the later pioneer of osteopathy, Andrew Jackson Still, lost faith in mainstream medical practice after physicians could not save three of his sons from disease. In addition, as just noted, many of the United States's sick preferred to call in an irregular because their remedies were often the least painful or uncomfortable on offer. Where irregular approaches appeared to work just as often as standard therapies, many a patient made the understandable decision to hire a healer whose drugs would not make him or her sweat, wretch, faint, or lose teeth and bowel control. Alternative practitioners were wise to this economic opportunity and drummed up trade by warning, like one Cleveland irregular, of the "murderous systems" of regular medicine.[70]

The most popular American medical sect of the early 1800s appealed strongly to the democratic sensibilities of ordinary citizens. The New England farmer Samuel Thomson cleverly marketed the system known as Thomsonianism as the expression of an unpretentious American wisdom that contrasted with the elitism and pomposity of the medical establishment.[71]Thomson presented himself as a medical egalitarian who offered simple, easily grasped truths in place of the regular's convoluted humbug. "It is as easy to cure disease, as it is to make a pudding," claimed one booster for the system.[72] The origins of Thomson's system were indeed distinctly humble. As a child he had become fascinated by herbs because he enjoyed making other boys swallow plants "merely by way of sport, to see them vomit."[73] In adulthood he developed a theory according to which blockages in the stomach prevent it from digesting food and generating the heat necessary for health and life. The healer's job was to restore body heat by removing the blockage through the administration of large doses of cayenne red pepper and lobelia to induce vomiting.[74] Followers bought the rights to Thomson's system for $20 apiece and organized themselves into "friendly botanic societies." An extraordinary 100,000 sets of rights to use his methods had been sold by 1839. So powerful did his egalitarian rhetoric prove that his followers were willing to take the kinds of heroic remedy that most alternative sects eschewed.[75]

Ultimately more enduring was the medical sect founded by the German doctor Samuel Hahnemann. Having received a medical degree in 1779 but failed to establish a successful practice, Hahnemann's intellectual wanderings led him to experiment with the bark of the cinchona plant used to treat malaria. Taking it in large doses gave him fatigue, a fast pulse, anxiety, trembling, and a terrible headache. From this he arrived at the view that drugs only work if they reproduce in milder form the diseases they are meant to cure. Cinchona treats malaria, he said, because it produces symptoms rather like it. From this idea he moved on to his second main principle: that the smaller the dose, the greater its therapeutic effect. Medicines had to be heavily diluted in order to work effectively. In various forms Hahnemann's homeopathic system spread across Europe and the United States. A Homeopathic College opened up in Cleveland in 1850 followed by the inception in the later 1800s of an American Institute of Homeopathy and an International Hahnemannian Association.[76]

Several other sects achieved high levels of popular support. The Eclectics, adherents of a New Yorker called Wooster Beach, condemned the heroic depletives of regular medicine, set up their own schools, and purveyed a range of botanical remedies. The Eclectics gained sufficient credibility that in 1849 one of their number was appointed head of Cincinnati's Board of Health.[77] U.S. naturopaths eagerly promoted hydrotherapy on the basis of the belief that sickness is caused by bad fluids inside the body that need to be flushed out, so they had patients consume large quantities of water and then wrapped them in wet or dry blankets to get them to sweat out their impurities. Hydropathy became extremely popular: as many as 213 centers were established in the United States between 1843 and 1900.[78] Naturopaths also railed against the dangers of tight corsets, masturbation, and sex, and they extolled the value of fresh air, exercise, and a proper diet. The leading American naturopath, Sylvester Graham, argued that all "kinds of

Sylvester Graham (1794–1851), one of the most vocal health reformers of the nineteenth century, explained death and debility within a highly moralistic framework. Graham believed that bodily excitement leads to sickness. Accordingly he extolled a bland vegetarian diet without any kind of seasoning, abstinence from alcohol, minimal sexual intercourse, and the complete avoidance of masturbation. Good health, said Graham, is the reward for right living. He attracted a wide following in the United States during the 1830s and 1840s. (Library of Congress)

stimulating and heating substances," such as "rich dishes," the "free use of flesh," and the excitement "of the genital organs," resulted in a potentially fatal overstimulation and inflammation.[79] His claims were quite consistent with those of regular doctors but were presented with a proselytizing zeal that set him apart.

Technology, Laboratories, and Germ Theory

The rise of laboratory science in countries like Germany and France had profound effects on how American doctors thought about disease. Traditional medicine had seen the body as an interconnected whole and sickness as the expression of a general state of imbalance. By mid-century this view was receding due to the findings of German and French scientists working in biological and chemical laboratories who made rapid advances in understanding digestive, neurological, neuro-muscular, and nutritional disorders. They also developed diagnostic technologies that allowed doctors to figure out the nature of a patient's ailment with unprecedented accuracy. In addition to the stethoscope, doctors in the United States gradually adopted the clinical thermometer, the sphygmomanometer for measuring blood pressure, the sphymograph for gauging the pulse, the spirometer for measuring the lungs' vital capacity, chemical urine analyses to detect Bright's disease or gout, and the X-ray machine. Highly trained clinicians were acquiring complex knowledge about disease that allowed them to make more accurate prognoses. With each of these advances the patient's narrative assumed less and less importance in the formulation of diagnoses.[80]

The discoveries made in European laboratories also led to one of the most profound conceptual innovations in modern medicine: the realization that many diseases are caused by microorganisms. Most of the research required to prove the validity of germ theory had been performed by scientists working in European laboratories, in particular those of Louis Pasteur in Paris and Robert Koch in Berlin. They revealed that distinctive germs could be extracted from the bodies of animals that had died from specific infections, grown in suitable media, and then injected into fresh laboratory animals, which then developed the identical disease. Few moments were as important as Robert Koch telling a meeting of Berlin's Physiological Society, on March 24, 1882, that he had identified the bacteria that cause tuberculosis. The next 10 years would see the discovery of the microbial causes of plague, scarlet fever, tetanus, typhoid fever, pneumonia, gonorrhea, and cerebrospinal meningitis. Building on research carried out in both Paris and Berlin, Koch's team also achieved the brilliant coup of saving the life of a young boy dying from diphtheria on December 25, 1891, by injecting him with serum containing antibodies against the deadly toxin released by diphtheria bacteria. Such singular achievements were complemented by the development of vaccines from weakened strains of bacteria and viruses. By the 1880s there was at last compelling evidence that many diseases were indeed caused by specific kinds of germ.[81]

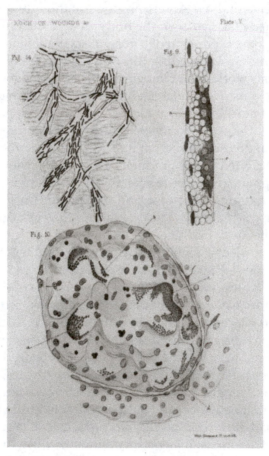

Illustration of bacteria from Robert Koch's *Investigations into the Etiology of Traumatic Infective Diseases*, 1880. A German physician and microbiologist, Koch was one of the foremost "microbe hunters" of the nineteenth century. Having developed important methods for the growth and identification of bacteria, he and his colleagues were able to discover the microorganisms that cause a number of deadly diseases. (Library of Congress)

Germ theory often proved a hard sell to American physicians in spite of the quality of the data amassed in European laboratories. There were many reasons to doubt the veracity of what bacteriologists were proposing: many physicians had no desire to accept a new theory that entailed an acknowledgement that they had been wrong for decades; others preferred not to have to accept that they had unwittingly spread infections on their hands, clothes, and instruments; some simply did not grasp the importance of laboratory research; others struggled to imagine how something as tiny as a germ could fell a human being; and plenty feared a loss of prestige if they were obliged to defer to laboratory technicians in making their diagnoses. As a result, recorded a contemporary, it was "well known" for physicians at prestigious medical meetings in the United States "to get up and leave the hall when medical papers were being read which emphasized the germ theory of disease."[82] Even some of those who accepted germ theory felt at liberty to pay only desultory attention to its implications. D. W. Cathell, whose *Physician Himself* was a best seller among new medical graduates for several decades, remarked in 1899 that dipping contaminated instruments in a glass of water or pressing them into a bar of soap was ample hygienic precaution.[83]

Fortunately, a few American physicians had kept an eager eye on developments in Europe and had studied in German or French laboratories and were quick to realize the significance of the work being carried out under Pasteur and Koch. Although American medicine lacked the funding and the facilities for doing cutting-edge laboratory research for most of the century, in 1894 some well-informed physicians wrote to Europe asking for vials of diphtheria antitoxin to be shipped across the Atlantic. Anticipating what American resources and business acumen were to achieve in the next century, institutes in several American cities were soon producing large quantities of the antitoxin from horses rendered immune to diphtheria. Around the turn of the new century, American bacteriologists also made their first major contribution to the understanding of human infections. Indebted to the earlier research of the Cuban physician Carlos Finlay, a team led by the bacteriologist Major Walter Reed proved that yellow fever is caused by a pathogen carried by the *Aedes aegypti* mosquito.[84]

But in several important ways the germ theory of disease had only a limited impact on American medicine prior to the twentieth century. First, bacteriology had provided only a single specific remedy: diphtheria antitoxin. Second, the recognition of the germ as a necessary cause for infectious diseases did not lead to an abandonment of the ancient emphasis on predisposing factors. Medical writers simply modified their language to talk about factors that reduced the individual's ability to fight off infection. Advocates of immigration restriction, for example, characterized eastern and southern Europeans as innately prone to contracting and spreading bacteria.[85] Third, older paradigms were still going strong at the end of the century. When President Ulysses S. Grant died of mouth cancer in 1885, it was widely said that it had been caused by the constant agitation of his soft palate by the smoking of cigars.[86] Physicians were still quite content to go on constructing speculative approaches to medicine that had no actual grounding in laboratory science.

Nor did the rise of the laboratory and the triumphs of bacteriology reverse the popularity of alternative medical practices. In fact, the later 1800s witnessed the rise of several new and powerful sects. Several traced major roots to the mesmerism of the Austrian physician Franz Mesmer, who argued that health depends on the free flow through the body of a poorly defined magnetic fluid. Magnetic healers in the United States were enthusiasts for anything that could deliver a current, including complex machines designed to dazzle the paying client. Mesmerism also fuelled the osteopathy of the Midwestern American physician Andrew Taylor Still. He set up practice on the basis of the claim that misplaced bones, especially in the spinal column, caused disease by impeding the flow of blood. By the 1880s he had gained a substantial reputation and established an osteopathic college in Missouri and an American School of Osteopathy.[87] Chiropractic also emerged in the United States when, in 1895, a magnetic healer called Daniel David Palmer claimed to have restored a man's hearing by thrusting an errant spinal segment back into place. Palmer built a school of chiropractic in Davenport, Iowa, and, with the help of his son, Bartlett Joshua Palmer, created a popular medical sect with about 7,000 practitioners by 1916.[88] In addition, mesmerism contributed to the resurgence of highly spiritualist medical sects. Mary Baker Eddy, the founder of Christian Science, asserted that there is nothing more to reality than the spirit or soul. Sickness and disability were therefore mere earthly delusions.[89]

And yet, in spite of the popularity of alternative medical sects, orthodox medicine had created the conditions necessary for the major curative breakthroughs of the twentieth century. Sanitary reforms would prevent more deaths than chemotherapy, and it would be a long time before medicine could identify specific treatments for killers like tuberculosis, but the growth of laboratory science would allow scientists to discover antibiotics to combat many bacterial infections, isolate insulin to save the lives of diabetics, develop vaccines against devastating disease such as typhoid fever and polio, and learn how to use radiation to treat cancers. Few living in the late nineteenth century anticipated quite how many life-saving treatments would become available. After all, the physician who asked rhetorically, "does this distinguishing the cancer cell cure our patient?" did have a point.[90] But by the late 1920s even he would surely have had to concede that laboratory science had transformed the power of medicine to explain and to heal.

NOTES

1. Gerald Grob, *The Deadly Truth: A History of Disease in America.* Cambridge, MA: Harvard University Press, 2002, pp. 119, 142.

2. John Duffy, *The Sanitarians: A History of American Public Health.* Urbana: University of Illinois Press, 1990.

3. Todd L. Savitt, "Black Health on the Plantation: Masters, Slaves, and Physicians," in Judith Walzer Leavitt and Ronald L. Numbers (eds.), *Sickness and Health in America: Readings in the History of Medicine and Public Health.* Madison: University of Wisconsin Press, 1985, pp. 351–68; and Russell Thornton, *American Indian Holocaust and Survival: A Population History since 1492.* Norman: University of Oklahoma Press, 1987, chapter 5.

4. Duffy, *The Sanitarians.*

5. Ibid., pp. 61, 105.

6. Mark Aldrich, *Safety First: Technology, Labor, and Business in the Building of American Work Safety, 1870–1939.* Baltimore, MD: Johns Hopkins University Press, 1997.

7. Janet Golden, Richard A. Meckel, and Heather Munro Prescott (eds.), *Children and Youth in Sickness and in Health: A Historical Handbook and Guide.* Westport, CT: Greenwood Press, 2004, p. 12.

8. Ira Berlin, *Generations of Captivity.*

9. Thornton, *American Indian Holocaust and Survival,* chapter 5.

10. Grob, *The Deadly Truth.*

11. Ibid., chapter 3.

12. Jim Downs, *Sick from Freedom: African-American Illness and Suffering during the Civil War and Reconstruction.* New York: Oxford University Press, 2012.

13. Sharla M. Fett, *Working Cures: Healing, Health, and Power on Southern Slave Plantations.* University of North Carolina Press, 2002; and Marie Jenkins Schwarz, *Birthing a Slave: Motherhood and Medicine in the Antebellum South.* Cambridge, MA: Harvard University Press, 2010.

14. Ibid., pp. 111–12.

15. Ibid., p. 47.

16. Wilkie, "Medicinal Teas and Patient Medicines," p. 122.

17. Herbert C. Covey, *African American Slave Medicine: Herbal and Non-Herbal Treatments.* Lanham, MD: Lexington Books, 2007, p. 75.

18. Fett, *Working Cures*, p. 75.

19. Ibid., p. 127.

20. Yvonne Chireau, "Conjure and Christianity in the Nineteenth Century: Religious Elements in African American Magic," *Religion and American Culture: A Journal of Interpretation* 7 (Summer, 1997), 225–46.

21. Fett, *Working Cures*, p. 105.

22. Charles Joyner, *Down by the Riverside: A South Carolina Slave Community*. Urbana: University of Illinois Press, 2009, p. 148.

23. Henry Clay Bruce, *The New Man: Twenty-Nine Years a Slave, Twenty-Nine Years a Free Man*. York, PA: P. Anstadt, 1895, p. 52.

24. Todd L. Savitt, *Medicine and Slavery: The Diseases and Health Care of Blacks in Antebellum Virginia*. Urbana: University of Illinois Press, 2002, p. 174.

25. Elliott J. Gorn, "Folk Beliefs of the Slave Community," in Ronald L. Numbers and Todd L. Savitt (eds.), *Science and Medicine in the Old South*. Baton Rouge: Louisiana State University Press, 1989, 295–326, p. 322.

26. Covey, *African American Slave Medicine*, p. 76.

27. Fett, *Working Cures*, p. 72.

28. Ibid., p. 61.

29. Ibid., p. 123.

30. Gorn, "Folk Beliefs of the Slave Community," p. 303.

31. Fett, *Working Cures*, p. 143.

32. Vogel, *American Indian Medicine*. Norman: University of Oklahoma Press, 1970; and Åke Hultkrantz, *Shamanic Healing and Ritual Drama Health and Medicine in Native North American Religious Traditions*. New York: Crossroad, 1992.

33. Hultkrantz, *Shamanic Healing*, chapter 1.

34. Vogel, *American Indian Medicine*, p. 224; and William Burk, "Puffball Usages among North American Indians," *Journal of Ethnobiology* 3, 1 (1983), 55–62.

35. Vogel, *American Indian Medicine*, p. 192, pp. 224–31.

36. Wade Davies, *Healing Ways: Navajo Health Care in the Twentieth Century*. Albuquerque: University of New Mexico Press, 2001.

37. Lee Irwin, "Cherokee Healing: Myth, Dreams, and Medicine," *American Indian Quarterly* 16 (Spring 1992), 237–57.

38. Vogel, *American Indian Medicine*, p. 15.

39. Ibid., p. 40.

40. Ibid., chapter 2; and Hultkrantz, *Shamanic Healing*, chapter 1.

41. Ibid., p. 63.

42. Ibid., p. 6.

43. Trennert, *White Man's Medicine*, chapter 5.

44. Charles Rosenberg, "The Bitter Fruit of Heredity: Heredity, Disease, and Social Thought," in Charles Rosenberg, *No Other Gods: On Science and American Social Thought*. Baltimore, MD: Johns Hopkins University Press, 1976, pp. 25–53; and John Waller, " 'The Illusion of an Explanation': The Concept of

Hereditary Disease, 1770–1870," *Journal of the History of Medicine and Allied Sciences* 57, 4 (October 2002), 410–48.

45. Charles Rosenberg, *The Cholera Years: The United States in 1832, 1849, and 1866*. Chicago: University of Chicago Press, 1987, p. 73.

46. Charles Rosenberg, "The Therapeutic Revolution: Medicine, Meaning and Social Change in Nineteenth-Century America," *Perspectives in Biology and Medicine* 20, 4 (1977), 485–506.

47. Ibid., p. 76.

48. Ibid., p. 79.

49. Ibid., p. 80.

50. Margaret Humphreys, *Malaria: Poverty, Race, and Public Health in the United States*. Baltimore, MD: Johns Hopkins University Press, 2001, chapter 2.

51. Grob, *The Deadly Truth*, p. 142. Conevery Bolton Valenčius, *The Health of the Country: How American Settlers Understood Themselves and Their Land*. New York: Basic Books, 2002, pp. 25, 76.

52. John Harley Warner, *The Therapeutic Perspective: Medical Practice, Knowledge, and Identity in America, 1820–1885*. Cambridge, MA: Harvard University Press, 1986, pp. 63, 144.

53. John Waller, *The Discovery of the Germ: Twenty Years that Changed the Way We Think about Disease*. New York: Columbia University Press, 2002.

54. Laurel Ulrich, *A Midwife's Tale: The Life of Martha Ballard, Based on her Diary, 1785–1812*. New York: Knopf, 1990, p. 51.

55. William Buchan, *Domestic Medicine, or, A Treatise on the Cure and Prevention of Diseases by Regimen and Simple Medicines*. London: A. Strahan, T. Cadell and W. Davies, 1798, p. 426.

56. Paul Starr, *The Social Transformation of American Medicine*. New York: Basic Books, 1982, p. 42.

57. John S. Haller, *American Medicine in Transition, 1840–1910*. Urbana: University of Illinois Press, 1981, pp. 70–85.

58. John Harley Warner, *Against the Spirit of the System: The French Impulse in Nineteenth-Century American Medicine*. Princeton, NJ: Princeton University Press, 1998.

59. Ibid., p. 3.

60. Rosenberg, "The Therapeutic Revolution."

61. Ulrich, *A Midwife's Tale*, p. 123.

62. Haller, *American Medicine in Transition*, p. 80.

63. Humphreys, *Malaria*, p. 36.

64. Ibid., p. 42.

65. Rosenberg, "The Therapeutic Revolution."

66. Warner, *The Therapeutic Perspective*, p. 144.

67. See Chapter 10 for a more detailed discussion.

68. Ibid., p. 51.

69. Ibid., pp. 51–52.

70. Warner, *Therapeutic Perspective*, p. 62.

71. Starr, *Social Transformation*, p. 51; and Ronald L. Numbers, "The Fall and Rise of the American Medical Profession," p. 187.

72. Warner, "The Laboratory Revolution in Medicine," p. 116.

73. John S. Haller, *Medical Protestants: The Eclectics in American Medicine, 1825–1939*. Carbondale: Southern Illinois University Press, 2013, p. 38.

74. John S. Haller, *The People's Doctors: Samuel Thomson and the American Botanical Movement*. Carbondale: Southern Illinois University Press, 2000, p. 23.

75. Starr, *Social Transformation*, p. 51.

76. James C. Whorton, *Nature Cures: The History of Alternative Medicine in America*. New York: Oxford University Press, 2002; and Naomi Rogers, *An Alternative Path: The Making and Remaking of Hahnemann Medical College and Hospital of Philadelphia*. New Brunswick, NJ: Rutgers University Press, 1998.

77. Warner, *The Therapeutic Perspective*, p. 127.

78. Susan Cayleff, *Wash and Be Healed: The Water-Cure Movement and Women's Health*. Philadelphia: Temple University Press, 1987, p. 3.

79. Sylvester Graham, *A Lecture to Young Men on Chastity*. Boston: George W. Light, 1840, p. 47.

80. Stanley Joel Reiser, *Medicine and the Reign of Technology*. New York: Cambridge University Press, 1978.

81. Waller, *The Discovery of the Germ*, pp. 80–145.

82. William G. Rothstein, *American Physicians in the Nineteenth Century: From Sects to Science*. Baltimore, MD: Johns Hopkins University Press, 1972, p. 265.

83. D. W. Cathell, *Physician Himself*. Philadelphia: F. A. Davis Co., 1899, p. 21.

84. Francois Delaporte, *The History of Yellow Fever: An Essay on the Birth of Tropical Medicine*. Translated by Arthur Goldhammer. Cambridge, MA: MIT Press, 1991.

85. Alan M. Kraut, *Silent Travelers: Genes, Germs and the "Immigrant Menace."* New York: BasicBooks, 1994, chapter 7.

86. David L. Gollaher, "From Ritual to Science: The Medical Transformation of Circumcision in America," *Journal of Social History* 28, 1 (Autumn 1994), 5–36, p. 14.

87. Whorton, *Nature Cures*, chapter 7.

88. Ibid., chapter 8.

89. Ibid., chapter 5.

90. Warner, *Therapeutic Perspective*, p. 272.

CHAPTER 2

Education and Training: Learned and Nonlearned

An extraordinary variety of healers practiced among the white, black, and Native American peoples of the nineteenth-century United States. Herbalists and conjurers provided medical care, often against the opposition of their masters, on the nation's slave plantations. Native societies relied on experts in herbal medicine as well as the spiritual powers of the shamans who worked alone in some cultures and as members of healing fraternities in others. Medical practice among people of European descent was strongly influenced by the fact that neither law nor custom dictated who could practice. White Americans drew from a glutted medical marketplace of regular and irregular physicians, neighbors, midwives, and itinerant healers who treated in accordance with long medical traditions, passing fads, or genuine scientific breakthroughs. This chapter explains how healers in white, black, and indigenous cultures were selected and trained and considers why lawmakers in the last decades of the century finally decided that physicians practicing European-style medicine ought to be well schooled before they commenced prescribing drugs, performing surgeries, and delivering babies.

IDENTIFYING AND TRAINING AFRICAN AMERICAN HEALERS

Although owners frequently overrode the preferences of their slaves in selecting healers to practice European-style medicine, this section is

largely concerned with how African American communities themselves decided who did or did not have the requisite knowledge and
abilities to serve as a healer. Traditions that included elements of both
African and European religion regulated who slaves trusted to treat
the sick. In many cases the skills needed to conjure, administer herbs,
and safely deliver babies were believed to be conferred by way of mysterious forces. The slave midwife Marie Campbell told of how, during
one especially difficult labor, she had received by supernatural means
a message from her deceased mentor about what to do.[1] In many cases
healers were said to have derived an innate healing prowess from
parents who had themselves treated the sick. For example, when
Frederick Douglass met a conjurer called Sandy in some woods while
fleeing a beating, he recorded that the man claimed to have "inherited"
his magical powers from his forebears.[2] Sometimes a child born with a
"caul"—a section of the amniotic sac—draped over his or her head was
assumed to have been marked out as having healing skills: the caul was
easily detached, yet such births were so rare that they seemed to por-
tend special abilities. Marie Jenkins Schwartz highlights the case of a
slave woman, Clara Walker, born with the amniotic veil on her face.
As a midwife later in life, she claimed to be able to "see spirits and foretell the spirits."[3] Many slave communities felt it to be just as auspicious
to be the seventh child or to be one of a pair of twins.[4]

Many African American healers also insisted that they had been
blessed by God with powers far beyond those of the ordinary being.
"When the Lord gives such power to a person, it just comes to 'em,' "
one conjurer told an interviewer.[5] Another explained that "There are
some things the Lord wants all folks to know, some things just the
chosen few to know, and some things no one should know."[6] The
wisdom and powers of the conjurer fell into the second category. At
pains to emphasize the devoutness of the conjurer's role, one contemporary explained that the ability to conjure was due to "special
revelations from God."[7] They spoke of being called to their profession
in the same way as a priest had apparently been divinely summoned
to his. The African American author and anthropologist Zora Neale
Hurston wrote about a conjuror in the post-Emancipation era who
was "one day plowing under the parching sun" when he suddenly
stopped and said, "Honey, I jes can't do dis yere work; I has a feelin'
God's done called his chile for higher tings. Ever since I been a boy I
done had dis yere feelin but I jes didn' obey." He then threw down
his plow and entered upon the career of a conjurer.[8]

Even a special calling had to be supplemented by training. As the
former slave Vinnie Brunson recalled, "we had de remedies dat wuz

handed down to us from de folks way back befo' we wuz born."[9] A parent who acted as a healer would often take on the role of teacher. The historian Sheila Fett gives the example of a slave from the South Carolina Sea Islands who recalled that "My moder taught me day way, started me day way, [I] keep up de way she started me."[10] The herbalist needed to know where to find the right flora, which parts were useful for curing, when in the year to gather them, how to dry the leaves and roots to stop them going moldy and losing their potency, and how to prepare teas, poultices, and salves. It took time to learn the art of herbal medicine.[11] Conjurers also underwent long periods of training during which they learned the prayers, incantations, charms, and amulets needed for removing or inflicting malicious curses. One conjurer known as "Ma" Stevens described a special cure called a "Hell Fire Gun" for counteracting evil charms. "Of course," she explained, "most people would be ignorant of how to concoct such a gun and would have to consult a root doctor [i.e., conjurer] who had knowledge of such things."[12] In some cases a period of hard study could be considered quite sufficient on its own for a slave to become a healer. Gus Feaster, born into slavery in South Carolina, remembered that those "too old to do any work" would often "take and study what to do fer de ailments of grown folks and lil' chilluns."· Gus explained that these elderly healers made a special point of learning how to make medicines for older men and women whose backs constantly ached from plantation labor: elderly healers had a vested interest in learning how to relieve sciatica and other chronic spinal conditions.[13]

Although African Americans frequently despised or feared white medicine on the plantation, a minority of free blacks acquired the resources to be able to train as regular physicians. Unable to overcome the hostility of most whites to African Americans exercising the status of a professional, the majority of these physicians treated only fellow blacks. The Virginian descendant of slaves, Alexander Augusta, MD, learned to his cost that his becoming a doctor was a direct affront to many a white practitioner. Born a free black in Virginia in 1825, Augusta received his MD in Toronto and then asked Abraham Lincoln if he might serve in the war as a surgeon "to my race." Having been appointed a full surgeon, his white colleagues refused to work beneath him, and he was eventually transferred to a role far from the action where his lowly rank could cause only himself offence.[14]

After Emancipation, the number of African Americans practicing European-style medicine rose significantly before dropping suddenly in the early twentieth century. Black medical schools started to appear in response to the barring of African Americans from state-supported schools in the South. Most of these institutions, like Meharry Medical College in Nashville, were set up with missionary funds. Elsewhere, black physicians, usually trained in the North, settled in the South and established proprietary schools. Some of these were purely commercial ventures, which, like their white-only equivalents, provided a substandard education in return for a modest fee and low expectations. Louisville National Medical College, however, achieved and maintained a higher level of professionalism. Opened in 1888 by three black physicians, including William Henry Fitzbutler, the first African American graduate from the University of Michigan College of Medicine, it reflected a widespread determination among educated African Americans to prove that with equal opportunities they could perform to the same standard as whites. The ability of medical colleges "managed entirely by colored men" to prosper, wrote one of the founders of the Louisville college, is "a crucial test of his ability."[15] Such

Louisville National Medical College. When opened in 1888 by three black physicians, this college achieved comparatively high academic and clinical standards. It continued to move with the times through the 1890s, as the demands of a medical education rose, but it closed in 1912 as fewer and fewer African Americans could afford the costs of a reformed medical training. The proportion of African American doctors plummeted as schools like Louisville National Medical College ceased to exist. (National Library of Medicine)

colleges produced a constant flow of black physicians into the market-place, who typically treated fellow African Americans.

Keeping these black medical colleges open became an increasingly arduous task toward the end of the century. As educational standards were forced up across the country by reformist physicians, fees inevitably climbed, and the sons and daughters of poorer families, including those of African American heritage, started to be priced out of the market. Louisville National Medical College did what it could to stay with the pack, but improvements to its facilities cost so much money that in 1912 the college permanently closed its doors.[16] Of the seven medical schools for blacks, only two—Howard and Meharry—survived the professionalization of medicine. The number of black doctors then fell substantially. It declined still further as colleges began to demand a year's hospital internship before allowing students to graduate. Hospitals in the North and the South habitually denied internship positions to African Americans. By 1930, only one in every 3,000 African Americans had an MD. Mississippi broke all the records: a paltry 1 in every 14,634 black men and women had managed to find a way to break through poverty and discrimination to become a doctor. As a result, black patients had even fewer means of avoiding the systematic neglect of Jim Crow medicine.[17]

THE SELECTION AND TRAINING OF NATIVE AMERICAN HEALERS

Identifying and training indigenous healers varied considerably from culture to culture. Most native populations assumed that only a minority had the shaman's magical ability to communicate directly with the spirit world. As among African American slaves, some considered this capacity to heal to be hereditary, descending in the male or the female line. In such cases, the heir to a parent's powers had to accept his or her role on pain of being punished by offended spirits.[18] Sometimes a future healer had to provide emphatic evidence of possessing special gifts in addition to lineal descent from a shaman. Here visions believed to be from the spirit world played an important role. Among the Eastern Shoshoni, buffalo hunters of the western Plains and the foothills of the Rocky Mountains, the child of a shaman had to have an appropriate spiritual vision to confirm his fitness for the role. Among the Ojibwas of the Lake Superior region, a young boy descended of healers would spend several days and nights alone in an isolated hut built by his father or grandfather. With his face darkened with charcoal, he would fast and then await the coming of a spirit. If the community could be persuaded that he had been visited by a spirit that conferred medical powers, he then became a shaman at a mature age. Such conventions reflected both the power of pedigree and the inseparability of medicine and supernaturalism within many indigenous cultures.[19]

Other methods of identifying healers could be highly physically demanding. The herbalists known as *wabeno* among the Ojibwas had to receive a vision, train as apprentices, and then endure an initiation process that involved holding burning coals and dipping their hands in hot water.[20] Some of the Plains cultures devised even more grueling methods of selecting their shamans. Young men would have to spend several days fasting and praying before existing shamans made cuts into the muscles of their chests and calves, through which they passed skewers. The aspiring healers were then either hung above the ground from cords strapped to the skewers or had heavy weights like buffalo skulls suspended from them. The Sioux devised a variant in which the skewer was tied to a young sapling that forced the prospective shaman to stand on tiptoes with his head thrown back so that he had to look directly at the sun. Only those who tolerated such trials without fainting were believed to have the virtue and courage necessary to practice spiritual medicine.[21]

In addition, all native practitioners had to undergo extensive periods of practical education. The herbalists who occupied the lower rungs of the medical hierarchy learned through apprenticeships how to heal wounds and broken bones and how to treat diseases with plant remedies. Herbalists were not usually deemed to have been spiritually inspired like the shaman, but they were believed to be able to harness supernatural agency by following prescribed ways of collecting, preparing, and administering plants.[22] The shamans in many cultures underwent long periods of training. Navajo shamans, for instance, had to spend years learning repertoires of chants and prayers where healing was felt to require the faultless delivery of several hundred songs over successive days.[23]

A number of native groups, especially the more settled agricultural societies of indigenous America, formalized the training of healers by preparing them for membership in "medicine societies" or "lodges." These were priesthoods of men or women specifically trained in a certain kind of ritualistic medicine. Aspiring healers among the Ojibwas had to find a preceptor, or apprentice master, who trained them in the woods during the day and in an empty wigwam late at night. Over the course of many weeks they learned the secret herbal lore entrusted to the medical society. At an annual ceremony initiates were inducted into the lodge and then permitted to treat particular sorts of disorder.

The Zunis of western New Mexico had several distinct lodges whose members were taught the formal knowledge of how to cure specific diseases: for instance, the Coyote society tackled illnesses induced by offended deer spirits, and the Cactus society treated bullet wounds and injuries from pointed objects like arrows. Crucially, these men and women were not said to have been directly inspired by the spiritual realm. The Zuni and Ojibwas regarded the members of lodges to be wholly reliant on the formal acquisition of secret knowledge.[24]

THE SELECTION AND TRAINING OF EUROPEAN-STYLE HEALERS

White Doctors in the Early 1800s

Only a minority of white physicians in the early nineteenth century could honestly be described as well schooled. In five counties of New England between 1790 and 1840, the proportion of doctors in possession of a medical degree never rose above a third.[25] At mid-century, a survey of doctors operating in eastern Tennessee revealed that out of a total of 201 practitioners a paltry 35 had diplomas.[26] Some American physicians had received a long and very expensive education at prestigious institutions. Those who travelled to Edinburgh, Leyden, and London and then later to the hospitals of Paris felt themselves to be the custodians of expert knowledge. A disgruntled nurse at New York's Marine House wrote in his diary of the members of this highest caste of physicians as "arrogant demigods" who demanded fawning deference from both nurses and patients.[27] Richer patients often preferred to hire physicians with their kind of decorous education, but most patients appear to have had much less regard for paper certificates. In fact, the mere aspiration to train one day to be a physician could be sufficient for a young man to gain a position as a doctor. One young New Englander who decided to go on a whaling voyage in an attempt to fend off tuberculosis was appointed as a ship's physician on the basis that he fully intended to study medicine on his return.[28]

Most American physicians in the early 1800s began to practice after completing between one and five years of apprenticeship to a doctor who served as a preceptor. The apprentice followed his preceptor from sickbed to sickbed, performed chores like grooming his horse and compounding medicines, and read whatever books the preceptor might chance to possess. Some preceptors in the South also allowed their apprentices to hone their skills on the bodies of slaves and poor Irish river boatmen. Even the most renowned physician expected to pass on his knowledge by way of this apprenticeship system. Pennsylvania's Benjamin Rush, who taught at the city's medical school and signed the Declaration of Independence, took on seven apprentices at one time. Americans of humbler means found preceptors who charged rather more modest fees than Rush and promised a conveniently hasty induction into the field. Thus, in 1846, a father from Gosport, Alabama, wrote to advise his son to become a doctor on the basis that "it is an easy profession to acquire." Medicine also has the advantage, this father added, that it would "not prevent" his son from "being a farmer."[29]

Only a minority of aspiring physicians attended medical school at the start of the nineteenth century. Just four colleges, located in Philadelphia, New Jersey, and New York, served a population of around 5 million people. Even so, some of these colleges were teetering on the verge of closure: Columbia Medical School granted a measly 34 degrees between 1792 and 1811.[30] These institutions were also in distinctly bad repute after a number of scandals involving students or hired middlemen raiding graves to procure corpses for dissection. In one notorious incident of 1799 known as the "Doctor's riot," a medical student in New York dangled a detached arm from a window in front of several young boys and joked that it belonged to one of their mothers. Since one of the boys had recently lost his mother, his father checked the grave and discovered that it had been plundered. A livid mob formed, destroyed the medical school's fledgling anatomical museum, and forced many of the students and faculty to hide quaking in the local jail.[31] The justified suspicion that medical colleges were procuring bodies from graveyards fueled popular distrust over the subsequent decades. In 1860 the dean of the Medical College of Georgia warned students that "no fragment of coffin nor of shroud" should be discoverable on the premises.[32]

Nevertheless, after 1812 American medical schools proliferated because aspiring doctors felt that they needed an extra credential if they were to gain a competitive edge. Ambitious doctors established new colleges, and 22 separate institutions were granting MDs by 1830. These proprietary schools were usually of a low caliber. Lacking both libraries and even rudimentary laboratory facilities, most could not even could offer pupils clinical instruction at the patient's bedside. In 1851 the reformer Dr. Nathan Davis calculated that nearly half of all students who graduated in the United States had received no "genuine bed-side instruction whatsoever."[33] Even the more exalted schools, such as Pennsylvania, Harvard, and New York's College of

Physicians, relied on lectures rather than clinical rounds. Where medical professors did wish for their students to receive practical instruction, they were usually blocked by lay trustees of hospitals horrified at the prospect of medical students being let loose on patients. Those students who gained access to the wards might be forbidden from actually talking to the sick.[34]

Nor did the lectures received by medial students make heavy demands on their intellects. The usual curriculum lasted just two years. Each year consisted of two terms of three to four months, and the second year merely repeated the content of the first. Not that students felt shortchanged by the brevity or repetitiveness of their education. Most could not afford a longer period of education, and many made full use of what opportunities to learn college provided. Others arrived at medical school with a distinctly cavalier attitude toward the importance of learning. The historian Steven Stowe tells of one William Whetstone, who was advised by his brother to go to medical college in order to occupy his mind and "take it off the *women*."[35] By the early 1800s medical colleges set the bar so enticingly low that they gained a reputation for recruiting those students "too stupid for the Bar or too immoral for the Pulpit."[36] When Charles Eliot became president of Harvard Medical School in 1869 and tried to introduce a written examination, it was pointed out to him that doing so would be a waste of time since only half the students could actually write.[37]

Obstacles to the Regulation of Medical Practice

Why did antebellum Americans not insist on their physicians acquiring a more rigorous education? A ramshackle assemblage of laws passed in the 1700s to limit medical practice to the formally educated was being erased from the statute books by mid-century. West of the Appalachians, demands by educated physicians for medical licensing were treated with contempt. Most Americans and many doctors simply failed to see the need for regulation based on an extended education. As a result, when the surgeon J. Marion Sims told his father that he planned to become a physician, he is said to have received the following stern objections to pursuing a career in medicine: "There is no science in it. There is no honor to be achieved in it; no reputation to be made."[38] Eventually medicine in the United States would become a highly regarded profession with its doors closed to anyone without the right educational accomplishments. In order to achieve this legal monopoly over medical practice, physicians had to be able to persuade the public that they had superior knowledge and skills. This crucial condition remained unmet in the first several decades of the century.

The basic limitations of the medical art prior to the late 1800s stood firmly in the way of regular medicine acquiring high prestige and legal protection. Where regular doctors and their patients shared the same basic ideas about health and sickness, physicians could not lay claim to a complex body of knowledge that took years to acquire. When Rebecca Butterworth, an emigrant to the Ozarks of Missouri, wrote in 1846 that a thunderstorm "scared me and threw the blood to my head," she was using standard medical language.[39] In consequence there was relatively little to set doctors apart from the untrained. Egalitarian physicians hardly helped their brethren by emphasizing the accessibility of medical concepts and skills. The Tennessee doctor John C. Gunn's best-selling *Domestic Medicine*, for instance, insisted that anyone could perform an amputation so long as he was not "an idiot or an absolute fool" and had access to a carving knife, penknife, and shoemaker's awl.[40] Nor was it clear that the therapies administered by elite physicians were any better than those provided by other types of healer. This is not to say that patients were necessarily skeptical of learned doctors but that a medicine unable to provide the unequivocal benefits of modern drugs like antibiotics, steroids, and insulin could not expect to inspire unanimous approval or confidence. People apparently got better or went to the grave in similar proportions regardless of the particular healer's level of training, so even the most expensively educated physician had to devote a lot of attention to looking respectable and seeming competent. The Louisiana physician David Raymond Fox told how he worked hard to maintain a genteel bearing that would impress clients. He assiduously changed his trousers and shirt every day and his underwear once or twice a week.[41]

American doctors might have raised the status of learned medicine by carrying out original scientific work, but very few actually did so. At the launch of the American Association for the Advancement of Science in 1848, only 11% of its leadership positions were occupied by physicians.[42] In fact, the sons of doctors were no more likely than the offspring of farmers to undertake formal scientific research. Such was the competition for patients that few physicians actually had the time or the energy to do medical science. "You will lose a patient for every experiment you make in the laboratory," warned one professor.[43] In striking contrast to Germany, where the science of physiology had made rapid progress in state-sponsored laboratories, there were no medical professorships in the United States that came with a stipend to carry out research. William Beaumont was one of very few

American physicians to conduct scientific investigations in the early 1800s, publishing highly original work on the nature of digestion. He could only afford to do so because he was a salaried surgeon in the U.S. army with spare time and a soldier with a gaping stomach wound on his hands.[44]

Learned doctors hardly helped their cause by being so openly fractious. Inveterate disagreements were fostered by uncertainties about the causes of diseases and by the economic imperative for each doctor to try to discredit his business rivals and purloin his patients. These public spats and bedside quarrels undermined faith in the veracity of what doctors said. Everyone could tell stories of doctors coming to blows, waging wars in newspapers, and even fighting duels. The inability of orthodox physicians to agree on the cause and treatments for major and terrifying killers like cholera and yellow fever did further damage to their credibility. Were these diseases contagious or due to atmospheric corruption? Was quarantine really worthwhile? Did the medicinal benefits of calomel outweigh the severe discomfort of mercury poisoning? And why did some doctors suddenly abandon the old staples in order to prescribe tobacco-smoke enemas, electric shocks, injections of saline solution, and anal plugs of beeswax? As these remedies were no more effective than what had gone before, it seemed obvious to many a citizen that a majority of medical theories about epidemic diseases were unruly conjectures.[45]

The medical profession also struggled to elicit the deference of the public because its members found it hard to make enough money to maintain the genteel lifestyle that commanded respect. Lacking the aristocracy or gentry of a nation like Britain, most American physicians had to see a wider range of patients who could not usually afford high fees. An elite of doctors based largely in East Coast cities did enjoy lucrative practices with plenty of genteel patients. But in the early 1800s a majority worked in rural areas where it was much harder to make ends meet. Since most of the sick lived in far-flung rural settlements, these physicians had to spend a lot of their time on horseback. The doctor was said to spend "half his life in the mud and the other half in the dust," enduring the routine dangers of snakes and falling tree limbs, the loneliness of long night rides, and the indignities of getting soaked on the road, being attacked by swarming insects, and having to swim across roads engulfed by swollen rivers.[46] With so much time spent traveling, the country doctor could only see a few patients in a day. Not surprisingly, then, medicine was among the worst remunerated of the professions, and few men born into wealth and high social status were willing to train as

doctors. Far more lucrative and therefore prestigious careers beck-
oned for most men of good birth.

Intense economic competition made it even harder for most doctors
to earn decent incomes. Many a newly trained physician grumbled that
"There are so many physicians so little business & so much competition."[47] The proprietary schools and apprenticeship systems were
churning out far more doctors than there were fee-paying patients to
go around. With an average of one physician for about 550 people, they
had to fight doggedly for virtually every client. Some neophytes could
not help but wish for the premature demise of their rivals. "There is
not much chance of either of those physicians dying," lamented one
Maryland practitioner in 1828.[48] Many a male doctor tried to resist the
entry of women into the field of medicine because they too represented
inconvenient competition. After mid-century they had increasingly
strong economic reasons to be alarmed. Not only were 17 women's
medical colleges been established but as many as 10% of the students
in 19 coeducational schools had female by 1893–1894. An absence of
regulation and the unwillingness of proprietary colleges to turn away
income meant that far more women could become doctors than in
countries like England and France.[49]

Then there were the irregulars to contend with. By 1860 it is estimated that about 2,400 homeopaths competed against 60,000 regulars.
Add in the Thomsonians, hydropaths, naturopaths, and Eclectics, and
the regulars were facing a seriously overcrowded medical market.[50]
The sick, explains Conevery Valenčius, "exercised a pragmatic eclecti-
cism about their health care."[51]

The popularity of self-dosing did at least equal harm to the wallets
and pride of regular doctors. Many families were fully confident in
their diagnostic abilities and had easy access to popular medical
guides. Valenčius tells of how the settlers of regions like Arkansas and
Missouri relied on family and neighbors to pull their rotting teeth, lance
their boils, and burst their abscesses. If they needed quinine to treat a
fever, they could also purchase without prescription as many boxes of
Sappington's Anti-Fever Pills as they desired.[52] A lot of households
were obliged to self-treat because they could not afford to call in a
physician. Not only were medical fees of necessity quite high, but prospective patients had to cover the costs in time and money of sending
someone to fetch a doctor. In such circumstances it was not feasible
for physicians, with or without college degrees, to become the automatic recourse for the sick.[53]

Ambitious physicians tried various ways of boosting their incomes.
They developed new specializations such as psychiatry and steadily

elbowed out the traditional female midwife from the birthing room. Others juggled medicine with another career. In both North and South, doctors coming from well-established families might be primarily politicians at the state or federal level. Lower down the social scale, they worked farms or set up drug stores. In the southern states they hired themselves out for a fee to plantation owners to inspect slaves before purchase as well as contracting with masters to treat all of their slaves in return for a yearly fee.[54] Those who were especially hard up were obliged to treat horses and cattle as well as humans.[55]

Attempts to raise the prestige of medicine by improving educational standards were doomed to failure prior to the last two decades of the century. In 1830 the Medical College of Georgia decided to extend its terms to six months in order to provide a superior reputation. The attempt did not last long. When no other medical school followed suit and the college found its applicant numbers to be falling, it quickly rescinded the policy.[56] Few young doctors could afford the extra time spent not earning that a longer semester entailed, and if they did not enroll, then the colleges closed down because they were dependent on the fees that students paid. Nor could intellectual levels easily be raised where the bulk of a student's fee only became payable after he had passed his oral examination. Failing grades were in the interests of neither colleges nor students, and the colleges became mere diploma mills.[57] Not that longer terms would necessarily have meant better medical practitioners. Given that no one system of therapeutics appeared obviously superior, it is easy to see why the public was not insistent on the reform of regular medical education.

The pressure to improve the standards of education came largely from among sections of the medical profession itself. These were the "younger, more active, and, perhaps, more ambitious" doctors who founded the American Medical Association in New York City in 1846.[58] Their motives combined social responsibility and pure self-interest. They were genuinely appalled at the poor quality of care provided by some of the worst educated and least skilled. These physicians also knew, however, that they could lessen an oversupply of doctors that forced down their incomes if they used a lack of education as a means of driving many of their competitors out of practice. Thus, Nathan Smith Davis, who twice served as president of the AMA, having insisted on the need to protect the public from the venal incompetence of the uneducated, went on to make the additional point that "by adding to the standard of requirements" the numbers of doctors would be slashed, to the benefit of those left in practice.[59] As Mark Twain shrewdly joked, "The physicians think they are moved by regard for the best interest of the public. Isn't there a little touch of self-interest back of it all? ... The objection is, people are curing people without a license and you are afraid it will bust up business."[60] The AMA's argument for regulation met strident opposition both from ordinary citizens and from the owners of proprietary schools and the thousands of doctors who carried their diplomas.

Many Americans also had strong social and political objections to restricting the practice of medicine just to those with degrees from respectable colleges. Any attempt to create a privileged monopoly could be seen as a violation of the spirit of a revolution which they saw as having been fought against the stranglehold of privileged elites. This egalitarian mind-set resonated with the belief of many poorer citizens, however unrealistic in practice, that they might in the future be in a position to rise up the ranks. They were not about to allow the erection of professional barriers that one day might stand in the way of their own possibilities of ascent. Businessmen echoed their mantra of a "fair field and no favor." Allowing one group of doctors to create a monopoly offended the capitalist egalitarianism of large numbers of American people. Alexis de Tocqueville recorded one irregular healer disparaging "King-craft, Priest-craft" in the same breath as "Doctor-craft."[61] The Thomsonians capitalized on this fervent populism, boasting that their system brought medicine to everyone's "fireside" in language "so plain and simple" that it became as "easy to cure disease, as it is to make a pudding."[62] And so the old licensing laws were eagerly struck down with only a minority of frustrated healers to bemoan their demise.[63]

Organized Medicine Comes of Age

The opposition to medical licensing began to recede in the later 1800s due in part to economic and technological factors that served to make doctors more accessible, affordable, and apparently necessary. Urban migration, explains Paul Starr, played a key role in increasing the demand for professional medical help. City living meant that more people fell sick without the kin or neighborly supports of the rural settlement or the country town. They were often therefore obliged to consult physicians and to enter the hospital if they became seriously unwell. At the same time urbanization was making seeing doctors less costly as journey times became shorter and shorter. It cost patients and their families much less in terms of time and money to fetch a physician in a built-up area than it did in a rural landscape of dirt roads, swollen or frozen rivers, and far-flung homesteads. Likewise, where country doctors had to charge patients roughly 25 cents for every mile covered to visit them, in towns and cities doctors could lower their fees and make their services more widely available. Physicians in urban areas also more often arrived in time to help, or at least be seen to help, their fee-paying patients.[64] Transport improvements had the same positive effect on the demand for physicians' services. Canals, steamboats, railroads, and later automobiles allowed them to receive a summons and get to a patient more quickly than ever before. Just as important were the telecommunications that doctors began to use in the 1870s. Before long patients were using the telephone to call in physicians who could be on the road within minutes. These factors helped to make the physician a more obvious go-to person when someone fell sick.[65]

The status of educated physicians then rose as the American public came to regard them as possessing new and sophisticated knowledge. To a large extent this happened as a result of real medical advances. By the later 1800s clinicians and laboratory scientists in Europe had seriously undermined the credibility of the common pool of medical ideas from which both doctors and patients had long drawn. As many as 15,000 young physicians returned to the United States with cutting-edge experience from the medical laboratories of Vienna, Berlin, Göttingen, and Heidelberg between the 1850s and World War I.[66] These doctors had acquired complex information about a range of digestive, neurological, neuromuscular, and nutritional disorders. Inspired by European example, the gradual uptake of the stethoscope, the ophthalmoscope, and the laryngoscope in the post–Civil War era enhanced the accuracy of diagnosis and helped to establish the educated doctor's credentials as an expert who alone could make sense of the body's subtle interior signs. Indeed, the stethoscope exemplifies the growing division between the sick and the trained doctor, for only the latter could hear the symptom and had the knowledge of pathological anatomy to interpret it. The hard-to-acquire scientific knowledge and skills were now available that could set apart the physician from his or her patient.[67]

Medical scientists from the 1860s onwards also made strides in understanding infectious disease. By the last decade of the century, American doctors were coming to appreciate the quality of the evidence gathered by Louis Pasteur, Robert Koch, and other European scientists to the effect that microorganisms are the cause of many common diseases. Bacteriology more than any other branch of medicine made both the sick person and the civil authorities feel dependent on the expertise of physicians educated in laboratory science. New York City set up the first diagnostic laboratory in 1893, and a number of states and cities followed its lead. By the century's end, American scientists were beginning to make their first major contributions to medical science. In 1900, building on the work of the Cuban physician Carlos Finlay, a team led by Walter Reed established the role of the *Aedes aegypti* mosquito in spreading yellow fever. Outstandingly successful public health campaigns rapidly reduced the burden of this devastating disease.[68]

Reed's career illustrates how and why American medicine gained in credibility around the turn of the new century. As a young man, Reed had benefited from major reforms taking place in the country's top medical schools. Around mid-century the better colleges had begun to provide access to patients on wards. In the 1840s Harvard University Medical School started a new trend by hiring physicians to train students in palpation, auscultation, and percussion at the bedside. After the Civil War, the better colleges began to raise their entrance requirements, provide regular bedside instruction, and lengthen the period of required study. The introduction of proper laboratories came next. Harvard, Pennsylvania, and Michigan medical schools led the way by introducing a less didactic form of instruction involving the hands-on study of anatomy, histology, chemistry, materia medica, and pathology in the laboratory. But Johns Hopkins brought the modern medical education to fruition. At this pioneering university medical school, Reed had studied under William Welch, one of the driving forces for change in American medical education. Welch had returned from the medical laboratories of Europe determined to make the laboratory a central component of acquiring a medical degree in the United States. His opportunity came with the $7 million bequest of the Baltimore merchant Johns Hopkins to set up a new hospital. Inspired by the German model of combining hospitals with universities, Johns Hopkins allowed for both clinical and laboratory instruction. Students who attended this medical school after its opening in 1893 had to have gained a bachelors degree before applying, and they were instructed by highly talented teachers and researchers who had been headhunted to work there.[69] Moreover, aspiring doctors at Johns Hopkins had to undertake four years of study and pass every course. They followed a demanding program comprising two years of instruction in the basic sciences that included extensive laboratory work followed by two years of training at the bedside in clinical subjects. In these last two years, students were assigned patients, and under the guidance of attending physicians, they were assigned to take patient histories, carry out physical exams, test blood and urine, insert catheters, and apply dressings. Formal lecturing had taken a back seat. The student was no longer, says Kenneth Ludmerer, merely a "passive observer."[70] Inspired by the high standards of Hopkins, unwilling to fall too far behind, and with fewer of the old guard alive to oppose them, physicians at other schools introduced similar reforms. Within a few years all the most prestigious colleges were turning out graduates after three or four years of study who were well versed in chemistry, histology, and pathology. Hopkins also accelerated the establishment of original research programs. By 1911, 60 American colleges had at least one salaried medical scientist.[71]

Hospitals emerged at the same time as flagships of advanced medical practice. Throughout the early 1800s most Americans had looked upon the hospital with horror. Indelibly linked with desperate poverty, contagion, vermin, and filth, no one with an alternative consented to enter one. After the Civil War the hospital then emerged as a symbol of medical progress, managed by highly trained clinicians, staffed by new corps of professional nurses, and equipped with the latest diagnostic technologies. Perhaps most importantly, the safety of surgery improved dramatically in the tightly controlled environment of the hospital surgical theater. By the 1890s surgeons had adopted the rigorous standards of hygiene that allowed them to perform highly invasive operations in the abdomen, chest, and skull. The middle classes now began to see the urban hospital as an obvious place to receive care for serious illnesses. Here the skills and knowledge of the physician and surgeon far outstripped their own.[72]

Science and Expertise

Medicine's stock also climbed due to its general association with the scientific enterprise. Gains in the efficacy of medical care were actually very modest during the nineteenth century, and not all doctors accepted important scientific discoveries. The classic 1880s medical handbook, D. W. Cathell's *Physician Thyself*, insisted that having a clean-shaven face and a command of a few Latin tags mattered just as much as knowledge of histology or bacteriology.[73] But what often counted for more than being able to cure people was a growing public willingness to regard medicine as scientific at a time when American society was acquiring a new belief in the value of science in general. Physicians who had learned about the mysterious workings of the human body at medical schools were able to cast themselves as practical men of science. They were now more often seen to be in possession of specialized knowledge, and those with inferior or nonexistent degrees were at a heavy disadvantage as education came to count for something.

A growing confidence among Americans in the value of expertise enhanced the prestige of medical science.[74] Many had come to feel that the policy of leaving things alone and hoping that social evils would eventually just right themselves had demonstrably failed. Technocrats alone appeared to have the potential to rectify the ills of society by amassing data and then devising rational solutions.[75] Public health now became a key area in which Americans were willing to accept a role for experts who could lay claim to specialized knowledge.[76] The management of human health was to be placed in the hands not of amateurs, politicians, or dilettantes but of qualified physicians, sanitary engineers, chemists, statisticians, and microbiologists. The better medical colleges rose to the challenge of producing men of the necessary caliber. At the Massachusetts Institute of Technology in the 1880s, William T. Sedgwick began teaching sanitary science and public health. In the same decade the University of Michigan offered a course on bacteriology. Before long Michigan's State Board of Health had established examinations in medicine, physical science, sanitary engineering, sanitary inspection, and sanitary law by which to select the best qualified to undertake public health programs.[77]

Medical initiatives aimed at improving the welfare of ordinary people enhanced the public's willingness to accept the claims of educated physicians. The AMA launched a major assault on the purveyors of useless and dangerous nostrums and in the process cultivated a public image of the doctor as fundamentally civic-minded.[78] The AMA's campaign led to the Pure Food and Drug Act of 1906 that stipulated that many medicines could only be obtained with a prescription. In consequence, patients were often safer while doctors gained control over what drugs could be produced and prescribed and how much they cost. Licensed physicians also extended their authority over the regulation of the public's health. Medical societies collected health statistics and promoted laws to introduce proper sanitation and clean water supplies, ensure the quality of milk, and improve the health of school children.[79] Never before had the American public been so eager to defer to the expertise of educated physicians.

The Rebirth of Medical Licensing

In a Supreme Court decision of 1888, Justice Stephen Field articulated the new confidence in doctors as practitioners of applied science:

"Few professions require more careful preparation," he said, "than that of medicine." Only qualified physicians, he explained, have an understanding of the "subtle and mysterious influences upon which health and life depend."[80] Field's judgment put out of business a healer with a degree from an Eclectic college in Cincinnati that was felt to be of dubious quality. The assault on doctors who were deemed to be poorly trained continued apace from the 1870s as states once again began to introduce licensing to restrict the use of the title "doctor" to those judged to have received an adequate medical education. Few of these laws carried much punch at first, but they were steadily strengthened so that the graduates of cheap proprietary schools were no longer guaranteed the right to practice. In 1900 every American state had some kind of legislation to uphold the university-trained physician's claims to superior ability. Those who wished to start out practicing medicine had to show the right kind of degree certificate or pass an examination set by a board of well-trained, discriminating, and self-interested physicians.

Gaining control over medical practice had required that educated physicians start acting collectively instead of simply relying on the rising status of medical science. They had won over legislatures by showing a new ability to collaborate and not just compete. Their willingness to make common cause can be traced to a number of factors. First, doctors were now more able to form broader networks of professional ties because a higher proportion worked in close proximity to one another in towns and cities. Second, the creation of hospitals encouraged cooperation because hospital specialists depended on referrals from obliging general practitioners. Third, a steep rise in malpractice suits in the late 1800s provided a powerful impetus for physicians to unite in mutual defense. Hundreds of local medical societies were created in order to achieve greater legal protections for their members. The Michigan Medical Society, for instance, agreed in 1887 that its members would never give voluntary evidence against another member. Some explicitly argued that mistakes must be covered up by medical societies for the collective good of the profession. Once these local societies had come into being, they were able to lobby state lawmakers while the AMA coordinated their efforts on the national stage.[81]

A pragmatic decision to ally with irregulars strengthened the hand of the medical societies. The AMA had spent decades maligning homeopaths and Eclectics as dangerous quacks, even to the point of expelling one Connecticut physician for speaking with a homeopath who happened to be his wife.[82] Now they arrived at a mutually beneficial arrangement. Graduates from the more demanding regular *and* irregular schools lobbied state legislatures together to exclude those from cheaper colleges of *either* persuasion. In this way they presented a larger and more united front to state lawmakers. As one exponent of medical licensing put it, "Let the medical practitioner be a homeopath, allopath, or no path at all. Only see to it that he is an educated man."[83] In joining with their old enemies, orthodox practitioners had only to give up a modest amount of ground given that the best Eclectic and homeopathic schools now incorporated medical science in their curricula. As a result, licensing laws targeted just the least literate and the scientifically ill-informed. Before long only those schools offering extended programs, ward experience, and laboratory facilities were still in existence. Although medicine was not transformed overnight, within the first two decades of the twentieth century it had emerged as an exclusive profession of the highly trained.

The advent of medical science and the growing rigor of medical education created conditions in which those who could afford it would receive more appropriate and more effective care. But in closing, we also need to acknowledge downsides to the fact that doctors were now graduating from far superior medical schools. Now that only the children of the wealthy could aspire to a medical career, medicine was to be ever more dominated by the sons of the elites. The proportion of physicians who were women, nonwhite, or of lower-class origin fell precipitously. This development had negative consequences. A serious shortfall of doctors in remote areas emerged as highly educated doctors seldom wished to work outside of major towns or cities. Furthermore, the services of physicians who now tended to be expensively educated were usually beyond the pockets of the working poor.[84]

NOTES

1. Marie Jenkins Schwarz, *Birthing a Slave: Motherhood and Medicine in the Antebellum South*. Cambridge, MA: Harvard University Press, 2010, p. 147.

2. Frederick Douglass, *Narrative of the Life of Frederick Douglass, an American Slave*. London: H. G. Collins, 1851, p. 65.

3. Schwartz, *Birthing a Slave*, p. 61.

4. Schwarz, *Birthing a Slave*, p. 147.

5. Sharla M. Fett, *Working Cures: Healing, Health, and Power on Southern Slave Plantations*. University of North Carolina Press, 2002, p. 53.

6. Yvonne Chireau, "Conjure and Christianity in the Nineteenth Century: Religious Elements in African American Magic," *Religion and American Culture: A Journal of Interpretation* 7 (1997), 225–246, p. 231.

7. Jeffrey E. Anderson, *Conjure in African American Society*. Baton Rouge: Louisiana State University Press, 2007, p. 95.

8. Yvonne Patricia Chireau, *Black Magic: Religion and the African American Conjuring Tradition*. Berkeley: University of California Press, 2003, p. 23.

9. Schwartz, *Birthing a Slave*, p. 61.

10. Fett, *Working Cures*, p. 131.

11. Laurie A. Wilkie, "Medicinal Teas and Patient Medicines: African-American Women's Consumer Choices and Ethnomedical Traditions at a Louisiana Plantation," *South-eastern Archeology* 15, no. 2 (1996), 119–31, p. 122.

12. Patrick Minges, *Far More Terrible for Women: Personal Accounts of Women in Slavery*. Winston-Salem, NC: John F. Blair, 2006, p. 105.

13. Fett, *Working Cures*, p. 130.

14. Margaret Humphreys, *Intensely Human: The Health of the Black Soldier in the American Civil War*. Baltimore, MD: Johns Hopkins University Press, 2008, p. 62.

15. Todd Savitt, "Four American Proprietary Medical Colleges: 1888–1923," *Journal of the History of Medicine and Allied Sciences* 55 (July 2000): 203–55, p. 212.

16. Ibid., p. 218.

17. Paul Starr, *The Social Transformation of American Medicine*. New York: Basic Books, 1982, p. 124; and Thomas J. Ward, *Black Physicians in the Jim Crow South*. Fayetteville: University of Arkansas Press, 2003, p. 160.

18. Dary, David. *Frontier Medicine: From the Atlantic to the Pacific, 1492–1941*. New York: Alfred A. Knopf, 2009, p. 23.

19. Åke Hultkrantz, *Shamanic Healing and Ritual Drama Health and Medicine in Native North American Religious Traditions*. New York: Crossroad, 1992, p. 94.

20. Ibid., p. 36.

21. Virgil J. Vogel, *American Indian Medicine*. Norman: University of Oklahoma Press, 1970.

22. Hultkrantz, *Shamanic Healing and Ritual Drama*, p. 19.

23. Wade Davies, *Healing Ways: Navajo Health Care in the Twentieth Century*. Albuquerque: University of New Mexico Press, 2001.

24. Hultkrantz, *Shamanic Healing and Ritual Drama*, p. 119.

25. Starr, *Social Transformation*, p. 64.

26. John Duffy, *From Humors to Medical Science: A History of American Medicine*. Urbana: University of Illinois Press, 1993, p. 140.

27. Charles E. Rosenberg, *Care of Strangers: The Rise of America's Hospital System*. New York: Basic Books, 1987, p. 45.

28. Sheila M. Rothman, *Living in the Shadow of Death: Tuberculosis and the Social Experience of Illness in American History*. New York: Basic Books, 1994, p. 55.

29. John Harley Warner, *Against the Spirit of the System: The French Impulse in Nineteenth-Century American Medicine*. Princeton, NJ: Princeton University Press, 1998, p. 19. See also Steven M. Stowe, *Doctoring the South: Southern Physicians and Everyday Medicine in the Mid-Nineteenth Century*. Chapel Hill: University of North Carolina Press, 2004.

30. Duffy, *Humors to Medical Science*, p. 131.

31. Ibid., p. 131.

32. Stowe, *Doctoring the South*, p. 60.

33. Edward C. Atwater, "Touching the Patient: The Teaching of Internal Medicine in America," in *Sickness and Health in America: Readings in the History of Medicine and Public Health*. Madison: University of Wisconsin Press, 1985, 129–47, p. 133.

34. Ibid., p. 134.

35. Stowe, *Doctoring the South*, p. 17.

36. Anonymous, "Practical Essays on Medical Education and the Medical Profession, in the United States," *The Western Journal of the Medical & Physical Sciences* 3 (April, May, and June, 1829), p. 14; and Ronald L. Numbers and John Harley Warner, "The Maturation of American Medical Science," in *Sickness and Health in America: Readings in the History of Medicine and Public Health*. Madison: University of Wisconsin Press, 1985, 113–28, p. 114.

37. Duffy, *Humors to Medical Science*, p. 205.

38. James Marion Sims, *The Story of My Life*. D. Appleton and Company, 1888, p. 116.

39. Conevery Bolton Valenčius, *The Health of the Country: How American Settlers Understood Themselves and Their Land*. New York: Basic Books, 2002, p. 62.

40. John C. Gunn, *Gunn's Domestic Medicine: Or, Poor Man's Friend; Describing, in Plain Language the Diseases of Men, Women, and Children*. J. Edwards & J. J. Newman, Pittsburgh, 1839, p. 696.

41. Schwartz, *Birthing a Slave*, p. 38.

42. S. E. Shortt, "Physicians, Science, and Status: Issues in the Professionalization of American Medicine in the Nineteenth Century," *Medical History* 27 (January 1983), 51–68, p. 57.

43. Numbers and Warner, "The Maturation of American Medical Science," p. 115.

44. William Beaumont, *Experiments and Observations on the Gastric Juice and the Physiology of Digestion*. Edinburgh, Scotland: Maclachlan & Stewart, 1838.

45. Charles E. Rosenberg, *The Cholera Years: The United States in 1832, 1849, and 1866*. Chicago: University of Chicago Press, 1987, p. 68.

46. Stowe, *Doctoring the South*, p. 137.

47. Warner, *Against the Spirit of the System*, p. 19.

48. Stowe, *Doctoring the South*, p. 20.

49. Starr, *Social Transformation*, p. 117.

50. Ronald L. Numbers, "The Fall and Rise of the American Medical Profession," in *Sickness and Health in America: Readings in the History of Medicine and Public Health*. Madison: University of Wisconsin Press, 1985, 225–37, p. 227.

51. Valenčius, *The Health of the Country*, p. 57.

52. Ibid., p. 82.

53. Starr, *Social Transformation*, Chapter 4.

54. Stowe, *Doctoring the South*, p. 86.

55. Starr, *Social Transformation*, p. 85

56. Stowe, *Doctoring the South*, p. 23.

57. Starr, *Social Transformation*, p. 44.

58. Ibid., p. 90.

59. Samuel Haber, *The Quest for Authority and Honor in the American Professions, 1750–1900*. Chicago: University of Chicago Press, 1991, p. 109.

60. K. Patrick Ober, "Mark Twain and Medicine: 'Any Mummery Will Cure.' " Columbia: University of Missouri Press, 2003, p. 13.

61. John Harley Warner, "The Fall and Rise of Professional Mystery in Cunningham and Williams," in *The Laboratory Revolution in Medicine*. New York, NY: Cambridge University Press, 1992, p. 13.

62. Warner, "The Fall and Rise of Professional Mystery," p. 116.

63. Haber, *The Quest for Authority*, p. 99.

64. Starr, *Social Transformation*, Chapter 4.

65. Ibid.

66. W. F. Bynum, *Science and the Practice of Medicine in the Nineteenth Century*. New York: Cambridge University Press, 1994, p. 115.

67. Stanley Reiser, *Medicine and the Reign of Technology*. New York: Cambridge University Press, 1978.

68. Mariola Espinosa, *Epidemic Invasions: Yellow Fever and the Limits of Cuban Independence, 1878–1930*. Chicago: The University of Chicago Press, 2009.

69. Rothstein, *American Physicians*.

70. Kenneth Ludmerer, *Learning to Heal: The Development of American Medical Education*. New York: Basic Books, 1985, pp. 60, 65.

71. Ibid., p. 103.

72. Rosenberg, *Care of Strangers*, p. 149.

73. Rothstein, *American Physicians*, p. 280.

74. John Duffy, *The Sanitarians: A History of American Public Health*. Urbana: University of Illinois Press, 1990, p. 130.

75. Burton J. Bledstein, *The Culture of Professionalism: The Middle Class and the Development of Higher Education in America*. New York: Norton, 1976.

76. Starr, *Social Transformation*.

77. Duffy, *The Sanitarians*, p. 151.

78. Starr, *Social Transformation*, p. 128.

79. Duffy, *The Sanitarians*, p. 227.

80. Starr, *Social Transformation*, p. 106

81. Duffy, *The Sanitarians*, p. 222.

82. Starr, *Social Transformation*, p. 98.

83. Haber, *The Quest for Authority*, p. 330.

84. Starr, *Social Transformation*, pp. 123–25.

CHAPTER 3

Faith, Religion, and Medicine

Supernaturalist beliefs deeply influenced how Americans thought about and responded to disease throughout the nineteenth century. Communities of European, African, and native descent all ascribed certain kinds of sickness to the violation of religious taboos. Members of these three broad cultural traditions also believed that plant and mineral medicines had been placed on Earth by a benevolent deity or deities and that supernaturalist rituals were essential for curing the sick. Toward the end of the century, physicians working in the European medical tradition became more and more critical of this conflation of religion with healing. Well versed in new discoveries about the physical workings of the body and eager to assert a professional identity separate from the church, they increasingly described and treated sickness without reference to a Creator. And yet, as leading white physicians severed their professional ties with religion, new quasi-medical sects like Christian Science were sweeping the country, attracting adherents to a set of ideas about disease inspired by a theology of the most esoteric kind. At the end of the century, religion continued to play a basic role in how many white, black, and indigenous healers practiced medicine.

RELIGION IN EUROPEAN-STYLE MEDICINE

Although the phenomenon of the "pastor-physician" had declined significantly since the revolutionary era, in the early 1800s people of

European descent still prayed to stay healthy, prayed even harder to get better, and sought comfort for their pain and bereavement in the promise of a disease-free afterlife during which they would be reunited with deceased loved ones.[1] Both lay and professional healers were also convinced that the herbs that could be gathered in forests, fields, and marshes were all part of God's beneficent bounty of cures.[2] In addition, they routinely explained death in terms of the workings of divine will.[3] Two alternative models of the role of God in sickness jostled for supremacy. The most traditional view stipulated that maladies are divine scourges, the result of a direct intervention from a righteous and punitive Creator unable to tolerate inveterate sinners. The second model, favored by most physicians by the nineteenth century, asserted that God had so designed the laws of human physiology that sin led to sickness without the need for his direct intervention. In this formulation God was the designer of a clockwork universe, a master craftsmen who created organic laws of health and then left them to operate in perpetuity. We should not be surprised that physicians spliced together theology and physiology. As Jonathan B. Imber has stressed, for much of the century medicine did not have enough intellectual credibility for the profession to cut its ties to organized religion. Far from dispensing with religion, practitioners instead sought to take on the mantle of the priest by marshaling medical arguments in favor of avoiding sin. Many a physician took pride in regarding medicine as a sacred vocation.[4]

Implicating the Creator in the onset of sickness allowed bodily and mental health to be held up as a measure of a person's moral worth. Doctors and lay writers joined together in preaching that longevity depended on "right living."[5] Adam and Eve never got sick before the Fall, Dr. Elizabeth Blackwell asserted, and so we can trace the accumulation of disease to "the neglects, the excesses, and the abuses" committed over the succeeding millennia.[6] Drawing on voguish medical theory, physicians often said that satisfying base pleasures dissipated the body's nervous energies or caused excess stimulation of the tissues that resulted in dangerous levels of irritation and inflammation. These ideas were preached to a wide audience by a health reform movement that flourished in New England during the first half of the century. Men and women who had renounced the old Calvinist insistence on the depravity of humankind preached an uplifting gospel according to which through reason and self-restraint any man or woman could learn how God meant us to live. William A. Alcott of Connecticut wrote dozens of books of pious physiology arguing that good Christians had a duty to God to stay healthy by observing divine laws of health.

Writers like Alcott regarded themselves as trying to recover a pre-Flood state of pristine health. "Whose heart does not beat high," he enthused, "at the bare possibility of becoming the progenitor of a world, as it were, of pure, holy, healthy, and greatly elevated beings—a race worthy of emerging from the fall."[7]

Cholera and God's Flail

Responses to the arrival of cholera in the United States clearly reveal the extent to which religion, fused with self-interest, conditioned popular and professional views of disease. As tens of thousands perished of this horrifying disease during the summer of 1832, bankers, doctors, priests and statesmen were quick to characterize it as an expression of God's contempt for sinners. Realizing that the disease always took its heaviest toll amid the squalor and vice of city slums, New York City's governor insisted that "an infinitely wise and just God had seen fit to employ pestilence as one means of scourging the human race for their sins, and it seems to be an appropriate one for the sins of uncleanliness and intemperance."[8] Epidemics, announced a New York pastor from the pulpit, are a just God's attempt to "drain off the filth and scum which contaminate and defile human society." It seemed nothing less than proof of divine justice that the death rate in the wretched Five Points area of New York City stood at three times the level for the rest of the city.[9]

Physicians shared with laymen the basic perception that sin had played a critical role in allowing cholera to thrive. Even if few American doctors during the three epidemics of 1832, 1849, or 1866 identified God as the direct cause of cholera, they still considered immorality to have facilitated its lightening spread. The poor were dying from cholera in their thousands, physicians explained, because they had slipped into poverty due to idleness and low moral fiber, because they lacked the self-respect to keep clean, and because they had worn out their constitutions by indulging in unmentionable vices. So, in the aftermath of the 1832 epidemic, the moral regeneration of the tenement dweller appeared to many to be the best defense against further outbreaks. One Connecticut physician demanded that the Board of Health "change the habits of the sensual, the vicious, the intemperate." Those who correctly pointed out that drunkards appeared to die less often, presumably because alcohol killed the cholera vibrio, earned few plaudits.[10]

Harsh religious judgments based on a complete absence of imaginative sympathy for the lower classes were often fatally

A political cartoon, ca. 1870, illustrating the unsanitary health conditions of New York City with Boss Tweed welcoming a cholera epidemic. Notoriously corrupt city bosses like Tweed were major obstacles to proper sanitary reform. It took the concerted efforts of public health campaigners to overcome their intransigence. (Bettmann/Corbis)

counterproductive. The sanitary horrors of American cities could never be tackled at the level of improving individual morality. Nor did it help that many citizens placed their trust in further divine intervention to turn back epidemics. In 1832 the governor of Pennsylvania imposed a day of fasting and prayer to "mitigate the afflictions of the epidemic."[11] And many citizens were incensed when President Andrew Jackson refused to mandate a nationwide day of repentance but gratified when the White House of President Taylor ordered fasting and prayer during the 1849 wave of cholera.[12] By insisting that cholera be understood in moral and religious terms, doctors and wealthier citizens were ignoring the fact that keeping clean was all but impossible for the slum dwellers where profit-hungry landlords built squalid tenements in which as many as 20 families had to share two or three overflowing privies. Wealthier citizens invoked theological explanations for economic as much as for religious reasons. The claim that the victims of epidemics were being punished for sin was an appealing rationalization because it absolved healthy tax payers of any moral responsibility to pay out for expensive public health reforms. Old Testament punitiveness offered the perfect cover for the pursuit of self-interest at the expense of a wider community of unfortunates.[13]

Other members of the higher social classes found in religion an impetus to act to mitigate the sufferings of the poor. Where state and city authorities were paralyzed by graft and inertia, hastily formed committees of "Christian gentlemen" stepped in to provide food, clothing, and disinfectants to slum dwellers.[14] A belief in the Christian duty to care for the weak played an equally key part in driving the public health movement that eventually helped to conquer epidemic killers like cholera. John H. Griscom, a Quaker physician who submitted a highly critical report on the sanitary condition of New York in 1844, regarded it as a *"religious* duty" to advocate for clean water and proper drains.[15] Although he believed that "Indulgence in a vicious or immoral course of life is sure to prove destructive to health," Griscom argued that those born into the misery of the slum could not possibly maintain a moral existence. Living in a cellar, he wrote, inevitably depresses the "moral tone." Robert Hartley, who in 1842 founded the New York Association for Improving the Condition of the Poor, shared Griscom's evangelical inspiration to make cities more salubrious. Hartley's association succeeded in opening dispensaries that provided medicines and health advice to the poor and established a Bath and Wash House in 1852 where the impoverished could bathe and wash their clothing. In 1862 Hartley spearheaded the passage of a law to regulate the quality of milk.[16] Evidently, the fusion of religion and medicine did not always lead to pious inaction.

Religion, Sickness, and Sex

The fierce medical campaign waged against masturbation and non-procreative sex provides another striking example of the tight relationship between physiology and theology. By the 1830s a widespread fear had developed among Americans and Europeans that by committing the vice of "self-abuse" they would rapidly expend the limited

quantities of vital energy with which they had been born and in consequence reap the rewards of feeble constitutions, impaired vision, physical disability, insanity, and eventual death. The naturopath Sylvester
Graham terrified generations with his warning that the masturbator
grows up "with a body full of disease, and with a mind in ruins, the
loathsome habit still tyrannizing over him, with the inexorable imperi-
ousness of a fiend of darkness."[17] Psychiatrists were especially insistent
on the dire consequences of masturbation. The superintendent of the
Massachusetts State Asylum claimed in 1848 that 32 percent of his
wards had reduced themselves to madness through this act.[18] Many
doctors and laypersons agreed that God deemed nonprocreative sexual
activity to be iniquitous. He had therefore ensured that the inveterate
masturbator suffered for his or her sins. Even at the turn of the twentieth century, the leading psychologist G. Stanley Hall could say in a lecture: "If a boy in an unguarded moment tries to entice you to
masturbatic experiments he insults you. Strike him at one and beat
him as long as you stand."[19] Nor did the uptake of bacteriology in the
1880s eliminate this kind of moralism from medicine. If a person fell
ill after exposure to bacteria, then doctors could still argue that he or
she had been weakened by "vicious" activities like masturbation.[20]

Treatments for self-abuse were designed to be painful and humiliating because masturbators were guilty of sin as well as potentially
deadly behavior. The doctor, sanatorium owner, and Seventh-Day
Adventist John Harvey Kellogg advocated genital cups that cut into
the testicles, chastity belts, leeches applied to the inner thighs, scalding
water poured on the penis, electrodes inserted into the rectum or ure-
thra, and toothed urethral rings that were attached to an electrical
alarm that would sound if a chronic masturbator had an erection
during the night and risked nocturnal emission. Some American doctors prescribed circumcision to cure the urge. Kellogg said that the
"operation should be performed by a surgeon without administering
an anesthetic, as the brief pain attending the operation will have a salu-
tary effect upon the mind." For females he preferred "the application of
pure carbolic acid to the clitoris."[21] This was obviously strong medicine. But physicians were acting on the conviction that even the slightest deviation from Christian morality could have fatal consequences.

It is tempting but misleading to characterize writers like Graham and
Kellogg as asexual or sexually frustrated prudes. In fact, their warnings
about sexual activity gained wide currency for a very good reason: they
lived at a time when sexual desire entailed considerable risks. A young
woman becoming pregnant out of wedlock could trigger a series of
tragedies because the biological father frequently absconded. Families

might sink into extreme poverty if they tried to feed another mouth with no extra income and had to bear the odium of a daughter's moral crime. In order to lessen the ignominy and the financial burden of an illegitimate grandchild, parents often felt the need to force their pregnant daughter to leave home. Not surprisingly, rates of early death among illegitimate offspring were terribly high. Illicit sex could also be extremely dangerous for all ages because of the potential for contracting venereal disease. Women who caught syphilis from a partner could pass it on to offspring, who were liable to grow up with skeletal defects, facial abnormalities, and deafness. Masturbation might have been tolerated as a safer outlet for sexual desire, but parents usually felt it safer to suppress anything that excited or awakened the animal passions. This applied especially to middle-class families who were determined to distance themselves from those beneath them in the social scale, whom they associated with a lesser ability to control base urges.[22]

The Secularizing Turn

Historians often talk of the last decades of the century as witnessing the decline in the cultural authority of religion as Americans became more secular in outlook. We can detect this drift away from theology in the growing defensiveness of the clergymen who gave commencement addresses at medical schools. Having once celebrated the harmonious union of medicine and theology, in the postbellum period their tone betrayed an increasing fear of theology losing its relevance. In 1866 the Reverend Abram Newkirk Littlejohn sought to drag doctors back from the brink of the "the mire of blank materialism" that he warned would lead them to see the human body as merely a "plaster statue of nucleated cells."[23] Littlejohn identified a genuine gap between theology and medicine. Charles Rosenberg has also shown that Americans in the second half of the century were more inclined to insist that epidemics like cholera be combated with practical initiatives like the building of sewers and the laying of water pipes than with days of fasting and prayer. The "civilized morality" of the Victorian age also came under attack by doctors no longer so beholden to Christian taboos. One physician from Montana exclaimed in 1896: "Great God! The Creator of all Nature, it is a crime to possess a penis or a vagina? Or possessing one, is it a crime to feel the natural desire to put it to its intended uses?"[24]

The growing secularism of the physician formed part of a much broader nineteenth-century trend that arose in complex ways due to urbanization and industrialization. As David Martin pointed out, "religious practice declines proportionately with the size of an urban concentration."[25] There is not an exact correspondence between urbanization and secularism: one need only think of the immigrants who did so much to revitalize U.S. urban churches. Nevertheless, there is a rough-and-ready correlation between city life and lower levels of religiosity. The clergyman in a rural parish might exercise stern authority over a static social hierarchy that his doctrines were designed to uphold, but the city's individualism and anonymity often eroded the intellectual authority of the urban pastor. In addition, because economically successful cities could produce a financial surplus to support "cadres of scientific and technological personnel," experts gained the opportunity to demonstrate that problems that had once seemed intractable or providential were in fact soluble given people with the right kind of training and experience.[26] This attitude is well summed up in the words of Arthur Guerard, a bacteriologist in New York's Department of Health, who announced: "Tuberculosis ... is not an inevitable decree of fate, not an unavoidable dispensation of Providence, but, like many other ills ... the remedy for it exists to a great extent in ourselves."[27] Men like Colonel George E. Waring Jr. received summonses from the White House because they were known to possess the technical knowledge to effectually tackle epidemic disease. Few could be unimpressed by the sanitary plan Waring implemented in Memphis after the 1878 yellow fever epidemic or his achievement in transforming the streets of New York from among the nation's filthiest to the cleanest.[28] That contemporaries dubbed Waring the "scourge of dirt" in quasi-Biblical fashion is highly revealing. They were now inclined to see human activity as the most potent form of agency.

Furthermore, well-educated physicians of the later 1800s were more than ever motivated to distance themselves from the church because they no longer felt that they had to be subservient to another profession. They preferred to be seen as champions of science over doctrine and as objective seekers after the truth who could provide far better explanations and treatments for mental and bodily ills than any pastor or priest. Of course, a lot of medical claims to scientific competency were no more than triumphalist rhetoric. But there is no question that the rising prestige of science had freed the learned physician from a reliance on the borrowed kudos of the religious establishment.[29]

Sects, Science, and Spirituality

In spite of the newfound confidence of the physician, there were limits to the secularizing trends of American medicine. John Harvey Kellogg's training as a Seventh-Day Adventist highlights the degree to which the United States's diverse religious movements adopted the formula that the laws of health are divinely ordained. Kellogg had been inspired by Ellen White, the spiritual leader of the Seventh-Day Adventists, who claimed to have received in visitations from angels, Christ, and God a set of clear instructions on the holy rules of right living. These boiled down to a conventional but highly charged set of moral strictures about how to eat, drink, and dress. As a young man, Kellogg took charge of the Battle Creek sanitarium in Michigan where he taught the "right mode of living" as it had apparently been revealed to Ellen White. The sanatorium became a major success, attracting an impressive list of politicians and celebrities including Warren G Harding, Amelia Earhart, Henry Ford, and Mary Todd Lincoln.[30]

Christian Science developed out of a parallel tradition that stressed the central role of the mind or soul in human health. Under the

The Battle Creek Sanitarium in Michigan. First opened in 1866, the doctor and Seventh-Day Adventist John Harvey Kellogg took charge in 1878. The sanitarium enforced strict dietary regimens and purveyed a variety of "healing" techniques including vigorous enemas, hydrotherapy, and electrotherapy. Although many regular physicians disavowed the dogmatism of Kellogg's denunciations of fat, protein, and masturbation, the sanitarium proved extremely popular. (Library of Congress)

leadership of New Hampshire's Mary Baker Eddy, this movement drew on several prior ways of thinking about disease. Doctors had long regarded the mind as exerting power for good or ill over the body. A number of popular sects, including mesmerism, spiritualism, and magnetic healing, had also implicated vaguely defined spirits and energies in the onset of sickness. Mary Baker Eddy combined these beliefs with Oriental and Judeo-Christian traditions and the idealist philosophy of the eighteenth-century Swedish mystic Emanuel Swedenborg. This eclectic mixture informed her 1875 work *Science and Health* in which she argued that disease and death are mere illusions because nothing actually exists except for pure emanations from God. Diseases and death cannot be real, she reasoned, because there is no such thing as a physical world. We only think that we are sick, declared *Science and Health*, because our senses sustain false beliefs. Recovering one's health therefore involved coming to the realization that corporeal complaints are just imaginary.[31] From these core principles sprung a number of rival school of Christian Science, and the movement spread rapidly from coast to coast. Regular doctors were becoming more secular in their outlook, but many of their patients were evidently not satisfied by ways of thinking about illness that left no room for the Almighty.

RELIGION AND AFRICAN AMERICAN HEALING

African American medical theory attached profound importance to the divine realm. Herb doctors spoke of having been born with the "gift" to heal, threats to bodily health were often deemed to be supernatural, and treatments were understood to act through spiritual mechanisms. Black healers treated those deemed to have corrupted blood using botanical remedies gathered from forests and wetlands that were thought to be alive with nonphysical forces. God had apparently scattered the earth with health-giving plants, like sassafras root, butterfly root, red shank root, and bull tongue root, that contained a "vital force" for the purpose of bringing about healing.[32] Sometimes the herb doctor was expected to ask for divine assistance in identifying the plant with the right spiritual properties to cure a particular affliction. Aunt Darkas of Georgia, for example, was said to be quite blind, "but she could go to the woods and pick out any kind of root or herb she wanted" because she was guided by "the Lord."[33] George White, a healer whose enslaved father had been a herb doctor, later stressed: "you have got to talk wid God an' ask him to help out."[34] One ex-slave told of how "Doctor Jesus" had healed her when white doctors had given up hope. The "doctors said I should not live beyond a certain time," she recalled, "but every time they said so Doctor Jesus said she shall live."[35]

The healers known as hoodoos, rootmen, voodoo priests, or conjurers based their entire medical practice on a magical belief system. Conjure assumed the world to be alive with spirits and divine powers that could be used for good or ill. As noted in Chapter 1, the conjurer's primary task was to identify "unnatural" diseases assumed to have been caused by a curse or a "fix." Having worked out the origin and nature of the fix, the conjurer was then expected to either neutralize it or turn it back upon the perpetrator. This often involved using magic to locate a "hoodoo bag" containing things like whisky bottles or animal parts near the victim's cabin. In other cases, conjurers determined that the fix had involved the magical insertion of snakes and lizards inside the victim's body. Music, songs, and massage with supernatural effects were then employed to expel them. Conjurers also routinely prepared charms to protect their clients against evil magic or from harsh treatment at the hands of owners and overseers. The belief in the conjurer's power to protect and to harm was pervasive in slave societies of the nineteenth-century South. Walking with a crooked cane, carrying his conjure bag, and often filing his teeth and reddening his eyes, the conjurer elicited reverence and fear. Even some white masters were sufficiently impressed to call upon their services. Indeed, in one unusual case, a South Carolina slaveholder hired a conjurer to first treat his slaves and then to kill his wife.[36]

Some of the roots of African American conjuring can be traced back to the religions of Africans societies like the Igbo, Yoruba, Bambara, and Kongo. Although the slave regimes in North America made it impossible to maintain religious traditions exactly as practiced in Africa, individual conjurers acting covertly were able to uphold many of the basic supernaturalist beliefs of their African forebears. Archaeological digs in recent years on the sites of old southern plantations have uncovered hundreds of objects used by conjurers to divine the nature of illnesses, invoke the powers of spirits, repel fixes, or foretell the future. These include crystals, gnarled roots, pieces of iron, metal, wooden rings, crab claws, pieces of glass, buttons, and human hair and nails.[37] Some of these items of material culture were clearly used by conjurers in similar ways to how they would have been employed by priests and priestesses in central and western Africa. This kind of cultural continuity represents more than the power of tradition. Keeping alive aspects of their African heritage provided some slaves with a gratifying and psychologically important means of challenging the dominance of white cultural authority.[38]

Christian theology also deeply influenced conjure as practiced in North America. By the nineteenth century, conjurers frequently invoked the powers of the Christian God and the devil to inflict or lift curses and to confer spiritual properties to charms. In fact, conjurers were often insistent that their powers were derived from God. "I tricks in the name o' the Lord" said one conjuring woman from Alabama, "It's a spirit in me that tells—a spirit from the Lord Jesus Christ."[39] The convergence of Christianity and conjure took multiple forms. Some conjurers considered the Bible itself to be a powerful charm. Jacob Stroyer, once a slave in South Carolina, recounted how a conjurer on his plantation had been asked to identify the culprit of a theft. He held the Bible on a piece of string before the hut of each of the most likely perpetrators. The spontaneous movement of the Bible magically identified the criminal.[40] Conjurors also named and used a wide range of plant materials said to receive their powers from heaven or hell, including angel's root, devil's shoestring, bowels-of-Christ, and blood-of-Jesus leaf. Most slave conjurers saw no contradiction between their attendance at Christian churches and their practice of conjure. This coexistence continued into the early twentieth century when famous conjurers like Jimmy Brisbane also held weekly Christian prayer meetings.[41]

The supernaturalism of conjure explains much of its appeal to African Americans before and after Emancipation. The belief in evil magic reflected the acute sense of being powerless in the face of malign forces that paralleled the realities of both slavery and the debt bondage that for many African Americans followed on the heels of abolition. In addition, the conjurer presented the uplifting possibility of bringing to bear powerful spiritual forces that could ease the life of the slave and sharecropper. An incident on Josh Hadnot's Texas plantation conveys a sense of how desperate many slaves were to believe that conjure could restore some of the dignity of which slavery had stripped them. One of Hadnot's slave women felt so "safe" wearing a small bag of sand given to her by a conjurer that she went so far as to "sass de master." The slaveholder whipped her "so hard he cut dat bag of san' plumb in two."[42] From the bags of sand, soil, bones, coins, and other objects that they kept upon their persons, many other slaves derived a sense of control and safety that was comforting if often illusory.

The worldly success of some conjurers after Emancipation in 1863 serves as a measure of the ongoing importance of a distinctively African American tradition of religious healing. The conjurer Jimmy Brisbane owned a house, extensive land, and several cars. When the black senator from North Carolina William H. Moore apparently quit his seat in 1878 in order to become a conjurer, one of his white enemies snarled that he had thereby been able to afford a "handsome horse and buggy." Indeed, it was said that good conjurers easily outearned white physicians in the South. Demand remained strong for spiritual medicine where so many African Americans still craved the feelings of safety and control.[43]

RELIGION AND NATIVE AMERICAN HEALING

Disease as Spiritual Disharmony

In the indigenous societies of North America medical ideas were just as tightly woven into religious belief systems. Every Native American society accepted that some conditions, especially superficial injuries, wounds, and skin conditions, had natural causes, but they also took for granted that most serious maladies are a consequence of disharmonies within a world replete with spiritual presences and sacred forces. The word "medicine" itself often carried strongly supernaturalist connotations. It can perhaps best be translated as "mysterious" in the sense of something having an ill-understood effect.[44] Medicine men and women, or shamans, were said to be able to heal because their connections with the spirit world gave them mysterious powers. Their apparent ability to communicate with deities also meant that they were called upon to help their people win victory in battle. Such were the perceived powers of the shaman that some rose to become dominant decision makers within their communities.[45]

Different native cultures had contrasting beliefs about how spiritual order and harmony came to be disrupted.[46] Violating taboos that disturbed the functioning of native communities was widely considered to elicit punishment from the spirit world in the form of disease. The Navajos of the Southwest, for example, believed that committing incest with a member of one's own clan would bring on the anxiety, rage, and uncontrolled behavior of "moth sickness." Other societies imagined sickness to arise out of inevitable tensions between humans and the spirit world. Among the Ojibwas spirits were believed to have fallen out with humans after too many animals had been needlessly killed. In revenge the spirit world sent disease down via mosquitos.[47] A number of the peoples living in southeastern woodland areas warned of the harmful effects of being a wasteful fisherman or of killing a muskrat or beaver without saying the right prayer for permission or offering up tobacco to their spirits.[48] To the eastern Cherokee disease had come into existence because humans slaughtered beasts in order to live

without having shown the reverence expected by the celestial prototypes of animals that inhabited an upper world. In retaliation, the spiritual forms of bear, fish, deer, fishes, and snakes as well as birds and
insects had devised illnesses to punish errant and ungrateful human
beings. If a hunter failed to show gratitude, then he might be made to
suffer illness by way of the animal's ghost spirit entering his or her
body. Sometimes humans suffered even if they were unaware of breaking taboos. Boils and skin irritation could be attributed to ghost spirits
who entered the body after a person killed an insect or a worm without
knowing it.[49]

Most native peoples identified human spirits as additional sources of
disease. The recently deceased were reckoned to be especially dangerous. The spirits of young children were felt to be a threat as they were
believed to have the power to drag grieving loved ones with them to
the "darkening land" of the west.[50] The Navajo were intensely wary
of the spirits of those who had died at the prime of life. The spirits of
the dead were thought to be guided to an underworld to the north,
but if the body were not properly buried the spirit could return. Those
involved in the burial might also come into contact and be sickened
by the ghost of the deceased. Navajo families often abandoned the huts
of loved ones in case the deceased returned.[51] Similarly, the Alabamas
were wary of anyone who might have been invaded by a ghost spirit
while present at a graveside. The Hurons were more fearful of the
power and rage of the ghosts of enemies who had been captured and
tortured to death.[52]

Other diseases were believed to arise out of the evil powers marshaled by sorcerers and witches. A number of cultures taught that the
wicked could magically place something tangible inside a person's
body where it would cause a painful disturbance. The object might be
a bone fragment, stone, thorn, hair, tiny worm, or a small animal. In
1833 the German explorer Prince Maximilian of Wied-Neuwied
recorded a medicine dance performed by the Minnetaree people of
the Minnesota region in which one man claimed to have "three live lizards in his inside" that had been magically inserted into his body.[53] The
Cherokee said that witches prey on people at night by stealing and
spoiling their saliva, a fluid with deep significance as it was considered
to be an analogue to spiritually important rivers and pools. The
Cherokee implicated night-goers when a person developed a sickness
that changed "the mind to a different condition."[54] Beliefs in witchcraft
were especially popular among the native cultures of the Southwest.
Among the Zunis of New Mexico persistent diseases were routinely
ascribed to sorcery.[55] According to the Czech-born American

anthropologist Aleš Hrdlička, those identified as witches who confessed were "simply exiled." Any who refused to confess might be tortured or killed.[56]

The Shaman and Spiritual Healing

Serious illnesses that did not respond to the ministrations of the herbalist were usually considered to require the intervention of one or more shamans. In most cultures the shamans were expected to rely on special costumes and medicine sticks to call on the spirit realm or to channel their powers. Most shamans also made use of a "medicine bundle" made of animal skin, often of a totemic animal, that contained charms or fetishes like a deer tail, bone, bird feather, dried fingers, or the stomach of an animal.[57]

Like any healer, the shaman began by trying to diagnose the source and nature of a person's complaint. Some were expected to be able to deduce the cause of the sickness on the basis of visible symptoms. Others entered trance states in which they were said to leave their bodies and visit unearthly kingdoms. In many cultures shamans relied upon dreams to give them knowledge of the spirit that had inflicted the disease. If a sick person dreamed of deer or snakes, the shaman could deduce that the patient had somehow offended the deer or snake ghosts spirits. The Wabanaki peoples of New England, Quebec, and the Maritimes of Canada believed that the shaman sent a spirit helper into the dream of the sufferer to determine the spiritual cause of his or her sickness.[58] The Ojibwas adopted quite different rituals of diagnosis. Their shaman knelt on the ground next to the patient and shook his rattle while singing a song taught to him by a guardian spirit. A dull thud would announce the appearance of helpful spirits in the rattle, and they would allow him to "see" into the body and identify a disease object that had to be removed. The Ojibwas also developed an elaborate means of diagnosing a person who had fallen sick after having unwittingly killed an animal. The patient was taken to the "shaking tent" where the shaman summoned spirits who could identify the offended animal spirit so that the person could apologize for his or her violation.[59]

The nature of healing varied enormously from culture to culture but usually involved religious ceremonies. The healing practices of the eastern Cherokee give us a good sense of the inseparability of medicine and supernaturalist beliefs. If a dream revealed the negative agency of deer or snake to a Cherokee shaman, he would seek "deer's eye" or "snake's tongue" because these plants were associated with the sacred powers of the offended animal spirits. The shaman next had to select individual specimens of the plant that seemed most likely to have a potent magical effect while performing appropriate rituals. For example, the shaman might have to gather fresh herbs with roots travelling in an easterly direction while offering up prayers to the female Sun.[60] Administering the plant cure required an equally keen attention to magical ritual. On the basis of the belief that rivers have the power to take away illness, the Cherokee shaman put the gathered herbs in a sacred cloth and placed the bundle in a river while reciting specific prayers. In the case of conditions imputed to night-goers, special plants were ground up and then blown through a tube over the victim's head, breast, and other affected areas.[61]

Healing ceremonies in which healers publicly sought to elicit the help of kindly spirits were integral to most indigenous cultures. The Eastern Shoshoni held an annual religious dance during which the shaman brushed an eagle feather against a sacred cotton tree before stroking it across the bodies of the sick in order to convey a positive spiritual force to the patient.[62] The Iroquois held festivals in which they asked the Great Spirit and his entourage to protect them from evil spirits. A different kind of ritual developed in societies of the Pacific Northwest such as the Kwakwaka'wakw of British Columbia. Where a patient entered a coma the shaman deduced that his or her soul had left the body and become lost. The healer had then to master special rites in order to recover these lost souls, entering a trance state to send his own spirit to hunt down the missing soul or to beseech a guardian spirit to carry out the search.[63]

Indigenous populations of the Southwest developed the most elaborate healing ceremonies. These often lasted for several days and involved plants remedies, amulets, songs, the laying on of hands, dances, and the creation of sand paintings. All of these practices had the aim of placating or expelling evil spirits from the body. Apache rituals would include the entire community, under the guidance of the shaman, in drumming, singing, and chanting incantations.[64] Navajo ceremonies could last up to nine days and nights as medicine men or women sought to restore health and harmony with chants selected according to the nature of the sickness. These rituals often took place in a traditional home, or hogan, that was held to be a microcosm of the universe and was oriented to the four sacred directions with a doorway facing east.[65] Sand paintings were especially important in Navajo healing. The shaman would produce a complex sand painting, often on the floor of the sick person's hogan, using a variety of colors of sand mixed with gypsum, ochre, charcoal, flower pollen, and other substances. These were not freestyle paintings. Rather, they conformed to set patterns, and their accuracy and symmetry were believed to be necessary for effective healing. The shaman then used the painting, and specific chants, to summon the "Holy People." Once completed, the patient would sit on the painting, absorbing its spiritual powers, and the spirits would carry away his or her sickness.[66]

A number of native rituals were designed to make the patient's body an uncongenial place for the spirits or small animals that made people sick. The merchant and naturalist Josiah Gregg described in the 1830s how the Comanches maintained "an irksome, monotonous singing over the diseased person" using rattles and drums so as "to frighten away the evil spirit which is supposed to torment him."[67] Herbs could also be crushed up and swallowed by patients on the basis that their bitter flavors would drive out animals causing pain and illness. Alternatively a shaman might try to suck out the offending animal or object, sometimes after having made a tiny incision with the point of a feather. Shamans among the Cree of Canada, for instance, were described as placing their mouths on parts of the body into which snakes were believed to have invaded through magical means and sucking hard to bring them out.[68] Once the offending entity had been extracted, the shaman would then burn, swallow, or bury it or send it down a river. The Ojibwas had a similar ritual during which the shaman, having identified the nature and location of an object inside the patient's body, used a hollow bone to suck out the offending material and vomited it into a bowl of water.[69]

It is because Native American ideas about sickness were inseparable from their fundamental beliefs about the nature of the cosmos that white Americans intent on assimilating them did what they could to stamp out traditional healing rituals. They sought to discredit shamans and deployed European-style medicine in an attempt to demonstrate the putative advantages of white civilization: the Department of the Interior, responsible for native health after 1849, explicitly extolled regular medicine's value as a "civilizing tool."[70] Corralled onto reservations and in many cases forced into lands with unfamiliar flora, many native populations found it hard to maintain their ancient healing rituals. That knowledge of many ceremonies and remedies has survived to the present testifies to their determination to hold on to their cultural separateness.

RELIGION IN WHITE, BLACK, AND NATIVE MEDICINE

It is useful in concluding to remind ourselves of the many overlaps among the medical traditions of the nineteenth-century United States.

White doctors poured scorn on native medical practices as "supersti-tious, inert, and absurd" and regarded the African American conjurer as the practitioner of superstitious nonsense.[71] And yet, in terms of effi-cacy, Europeans actually had few effective remedies and borrowed, usually without acknowledgment, a large number of herbal drugs from native peoples. Nor were white communities obviously less supersti-tious in their views of sickness. Throughout the century, people of European descent prayed in church and in private for good health and for the recovery of themselves and others. Even the most sophisti-cated doctors resorted to moral judgments linked to Christian moral doctrines in explaining why some people got sick. In all three sets of cultures, magical beliefs provided a comforting sense of control over disease. At the same time we must avoid exaggerating the similarities between European-style medicine and those of African American or Native American societies. For a complex range of social, demographic, and economic reasons, a small number of Europeans and white Americans were developing methods of inquiry from which real advances in understanding the body and disease could be made. Medicine shorn of its traditional connections with religion had become a clear possibility. This was a major step forward in the human capacity to heal. And yet the current popularity among Americans of all ethnic-ities of practices that claim descent from Native American medicine underscore how many people regret biomedicine's tendency to strip disease of spiritual meaning.

NOTES

1. Paul Starr, *The Social Transformation of American Medicine*. New York: Basic Books, 1982, p. 75.

2. Laurel Ulrich, *A Midwife's Tale: The Life of Martha Ballard, Based on Her Diary, 1785–1812*. New York: Knopf, 1990, p. 6.

3. Nancy Schrom Dye and Daniel Blake Smith, "Mother Love and Infant Death, 1750–1920," *The Journal of American History* 73, No. 2 (September 1986), 329–53, p. 335.

4. Jonathan B. Imber, *Trusting Doctors: The Decline of Moral Authority in American Medicine*. Princeton, NJ: Princeton University Press, 2008, p. 71.

5. Edward Jarvis, "Depreciation of Life," *The Journal of Health and Monthly Miscellany* 1 (1846), p. 78.

6. Charles Rosenberg, "The Bitter Fruit of Heredity: Heredity, Disease, and Social Thought," in Charles Rosenberg, *No Other Gods: On Science and American Social Thought*. Baltimore, MD: Johns Hopkins University Press, 1976, pp. 25–53.

7. James C. Whorton, "Patient, Heal Thyself: Popular Health Reform Movements as Unorthodox Medicine," in Norman Gevitz (ed.), *Other Healers: Unorthodox Medicine in America*. Baltimore, MD: Johns Hopkins University Press, 1988, pp. 52–81, p. 66.

8. Charles Rosenberg, *The Cholera Years: The United States in 1832, 1849, and 1866*. Chicago: University of Chicago Press, 1987, p. 42.

9. Rosenberg, *Cholera Years*, p. 96.

10. Ibid., p. 96. See also John Duffy, *The Sanitarians: A History of American Public Health*. Urbana: University of Illinois Press, 1990.

11. Ibid, p. 83.

12. Rosenberg, *Cholera Years*, p. 149.

13. Gert H. Brieger, "Sanitary Reform in New York City," in Judith Walzer Leavitt and Ronald L. Numbers (eds.), *Sickness and Health in America: Readings in the History of Medicine and Public Health*. Madison: University of Wisconsin Press, 1985, 185–96.

14. Rosenberg, *Cholera Years*, p. 139.

15. Duffy, *The Sanitarians*, p. 95.

16. Charles Rosenberg, "Pietism and the Origins of the American Public Health Movement: A Note on John H. Griscom and Robert M. Hartley," *Journal of the History of Medicine and Allied Sciences* 23 (1968), 16–35.

17. Sylvester Graham, *A Lecture to Young Men on Chastity*. Boston: George W. Light, 1838, p. 92.

18. Peter Lewis Allen, *The Wages of Sin: Sex and Disease, Past and Present*. Chicago: University of Chicago Press, 2000, p. 97.

19. Allen, *Wages of Sin*, p. 97.

20. Rosenberg, "Bitter Fruit of Heredity."

21. John Harvey Kellogg, *Plain Facts for Young and Old*, p. 384.

22. Charles E. Rosenberg, "Sexuality, Class and Role in 19th-Century America," *American Quarterly* 25 (May 1973), 131–53.

23. Imber, *Trusting Doctors*, p. 71.

24. Nathan Hale, *Freud and the Americans; the Beginnings of Psychoanalysis in the United States, 1876–1917*. New York: Oxford University Press, 1971, p. 251.

25. See Christian Smith (ed.), *The Secular Revolution: Power, Interests, and Conflict in the Secularization of American Public Life*. Berkeley: University of California Press, p. 22.

26. Peter L. Berger, *The Sacred Canopy: Elements of a Sociological Theory of Religion*. Garden City, NY: Doubleday, 1967, p. 132.

27. Sheila M. Rothman, *Living in the Shadow of Death: Tuberculosis and the Social Experience of Illness in American History*. New York: Basic Books, 1994, p. 185.

28. James H. Cassedy, "The Flamboyant Colonel Waring," *Bulletin of the History of Medicine* 36 (March and April 1962), 163–68, p. 166.

29. Imber, *Trusting Doctors*, Chapter 3.

30. Ronald L. Numbers, "Sex, Science, and Salvation: The Sexual Advice of Ellen G. White and John Harvey Kellogg," in Charles E. Rosenberg (ed.),

Right Living: An Anglo-American Tradition of Self-Help, Medicine and Hygiene. Baltimore, MD: Johns Hopkins University Press, 2003, pp. 206–226.

31. Norman Gevitz (ed.), *Other Healers: Unorthodox Medicine in America.* Baltimore, MD: Johns Hopkins University Press, 1988.

32. Sharla M. Fett, *Working Cures: Healing, Health, and Power on Southern Slave Plantations.* Chapel Hill: University of North Carolina Press, 2002, p. 72.

33. Patrick Minges, *Far More Terrible for Women: Personal Accounts of Women in Slavery.* Winston-Salem, NC: John F. Blair, 2006, p. 105.

34. Fett, *Working Cures*, p. 79.

35. Gretchen Long, *Doctoring Freedom: The Politics of African American Medical Care in Slavery and Emancipation.* Chapel Hill: University of North Carolina Press, 2012, p. 17.

36. Fett, *Working Cures*, p. 50.

37. Mark P. Leone and Gladys-Marie Fry, "Conjuring in the Big House Kitchen: An Interpretation of African American Belief Systems Based on the Uses of Archaeology and Folklore Sources," *The Journal of American Folklore* 112 (Summer 1999), 372–403, p. 38.

38. Charles Joyner, *Down the Riverside: A South Carolina Slave Community.* Urbana: University of Illinois Press, 1984.

39. Paul Harvey, *Freedom's Coming: Religious Culture and the Shaping of the South from the Civil War through the Civil Rights Era.* Chapel Hill: University of North Carolina Press, 2005, p. 122.

40. Yvonne Chireau, "Conjure and Christianity in the Nineteenth Century: Religious Elements in African American Magic," *Religion and American Culture: A Journal of Interpretation* 7 (Summer 1997), 225–46, p. 236.

41. Yvonne Chireau, *Black Magic: Religion and the African American Conjuring Tradition.* Berkeley: University of California Press, 2002, p. 24.

42. Martha B. Katz-Hyman and Kym S. Rice (eds.), *World of a Slave: Encyclopedia of the Material Life of Slaves in the United States.* Santa Barbara, CA: Greenwood Press, 2011, p. 337.

43. Chireau, *Black Magic*, p. 24.

44. Virgil J. Vogel, *American Indian Medicine.* Norman: University of Oklahoma Press, 1970, p. 25; and David Dary, *Frontier Medicine: From the Atlantic to the Pacific, 1492–1941.* New York: Alfred A. Knopf, 2009, p. 5.

45. Ibid., p. 13.

46. Wade Davies, *Healing Ways: Navajo Health Care in the Twentieth Century.* Albuquerque: University of New Mexico Press, 2001.

47. Åke Hultkrantz, *Shamanic Healing and Ritual Drama Health and Medicine in Native North American Religious Traditions.* New York: Crossroad, 1992, p. 29.

48. Vogel, *American Indian Medicine*, p. 15.

49. Lee Irwin, "Cherokee Healing: Myth, Dreams, and Medicine," *American Indian Quarterly* 16 (Spring 1992), 237–57.

50. James Mooney, "Cherokee Theory and Practice of Medicine," *The Journal of American Folklore* 3, no. 8 (1890), 44–50, p. 46.

51. Davies, *Healing Ways*, p. 7.

52. Vogel, *American Indian Medicine*, p. 19.

53. Ibid, p. 17.

54. Irwin, "Cherokee Healing," p. 240.

55. Marc Simmons, *Witchcraft in the Southwest: Spanish and Indian Supernaturalism on the Rio Grande*. Lincoln: University of Nebraska Press, 1980, p. 124.

56. Vogel, *American Indian Medicine*, p. 15.

57. Vogel, *American Indian Medicine*, pp. 27–28.

58. Ibid., Chapter 2.

59. Hultkrantz, *Shamanic Healing*, p. 34.

60. Irwin, "Cherokee Healing," p. 242.

61. Ibid., p. 242.

62. Hultkrantz, *Shamanic Healing*, p. 19.

63. Vogel, *American Indian Medicine*, p. 15.

64. Hultkrantz, *Shamanic Healing*, Chapter 1.

65. Davies, *Healing Ways*, p. 4, and Trennert, *White Man's Medicine*, p. 8.

66. Ibid., p. 6.

67. Vogel, *American Indian Medicine*, p. 34.

68. Ibid., pp. 16–17.

69. Hultkrantz, *Shamanic Healing*, p. 34.

70. Robert A. Trennert, *White Man's Medicine: Government Doctors and the Navajo, 1863–1955*. Albuquerque: University of New Mexico Press, 1998, p. 6.

71. Vogel, *American Indian Medicine*, p. 108.

CHAPTER 4

Women's Health

The topic of women's health in the nineteenth century encompasses several quite different themes. This chapter starts by looking at the dangers associated with pregnancy and childbirth: all parturient women risked serious complications and faced a terrifying possibility of death due to sepsis, but the burden fell most heavily upon slave and indigenous women who suffered appallingly high rates of miscarriage, stillbirth, and infection. It goes on to chart the role of the traditional midwife and the success enjoyed by white physicians and later obstetricians who sought to exclude them from the birthing room. It then explores the attempts by middle-class women of European descent to control their own fertility and the fierce backlash by social purity campaigners that culminated in the criminalization of both abortion and trading information about contraception. It concludes by examining how doctors used the language of medicine to characterize women as less intelligent than men and as naturally fitted for the domestic sphere. We will see that the male physician's misogynistic understanding of female physiology inspired a range of unhelpful and sometimes dangerous medical interventions.

REPRODUCTION AND CHILDBIRTH

Pregnancy and Childbirth

Depending on the mother's circumstances, pregnancy has always been associated with emotions as diverse as joy, relief, ambivalence, shame, and fear. Women knew to expect discomfort when pregnant, excruciating pain during delivery, the risk of death due to infection or blood loss, and a fair chance of losing their child before he or she reached the age of five. Most African American women considered childbirth an essential rite of passage, but they also knew that many of their pregnancies would end in miscarriage or stillbirth.[1] The conditions of slavery prevented a shocking number of their fetuses from surviving to full term. In the late 1830s the British actress Fanny Kemble spent a winter living on her husband's rice plantations in Georgia. Fanny asked nine slaves about their histories as mothers. She found that they were worked so hard when pregnant and soon after parturition that among them they had experienced 12 miscarriages and 5 stillbirths as well as the deaths of 24 children.[2] One South Carolinian slave reported in 1862: "You neber 'lowed you hoe till labor 'pon you, neber! No matter how bad you feel, you neber 'lowed to stop till you go in bed, neber!"[3] In consequence, an extraordinary 15% of slave pregnancies may have resulted in stillbirth. This is double the frequency of stillbirths among babies born to white women in the United States.[4] And we can tell that overwork was the primary factor in killing these fetuses because women who entered labor during the arduous periods of preparing and planting crops were the most likely to give birth to dead babies.[5]

Native American women suffered just as egregiously at the hands of the white population. Prior to falling under the authority of white populations, indigenous peoples had developed a variety of practices in the attempt to reduce the potential risks and traumas of childbirth. They adopted detailed rules about what a birthing woman could eat and drink, the positions she could assume while giving birth, and the words that had to be recited during labor. Eastern societies used plants from the crowfoot family to stimulate labor, made tea made from blue cohosh to lessen its duration, and took decoctions of plants like hemlock to eliminate the afterbirth.[6] The Micmacs of eastern Canada were described as attaching birthing women to poles to keep them upright while others pressed hard on their sides to try to push the baby out. Many other societies developed techniques of abdominal massage to place babies in the correct position for birth. Not putting hands inside the vagina almost certainly reduced levels of septicemia. In New England, rates of postbirth infection may have been lessened by pregnant women leaving the village to give birth and spending nights in special huts for some days after birth. The tendency in many groups to space out births also meant that women's bodies had longer to recover from the stresses of gestation and parturition. Unfortunately, white demands for their land and labor made it virtually impossible for native peoples to maintain many of these practices.[7]

When forcibly removed to missions and reservations, native women were at far greater risk of abuse and infection. Rates of sterility and miscarriage were strikingly high among the indigenous women gathered into the Catholic missions of California under Spanish rule. The missionaries, dependent on Native Americans for labor, accused them of deliberately avoiding parenthood. One enraged and probably voyeuristic priest of the mission in Santa Cruz in the early 1800s ordered one infertile couple to have sex in his presence. When they refused, he had the woman given 50 lashes and forced her to carry around a small wooden doll that represented the unborn child.[8] The United States authorities likewise commented on the low birth rates and high levels of miscarriage among native peoples on reservations. The doctor responsible for the Navajo interned at Bosque Redondo in New Mexico during the 1860s concluded that they must be practicing family limitation on a large scale.[9] Neither the Catholic Church in California nor the U.S. Army Medical Department could allow themselves to see that fetuses were dying because of the conditions in which their mothers lived. At Bosque Redondo, as on most Native American reservations, birth rates were low for two main reasons. First, indigenous peoples inhabiting cold, damp, and cramped reservations were susceptible to tuberculosis at a rate more than 10 times higher than that for the average white person, and genital tuberculosis caused sterility in many women. Second, fetuses were killed in utero by the syphilis spirochete, usually contracted from U.S. soldiers stationed at nearby outposts. This link between reduced fertility and white contact is epidemiologically apparent across the United States: native groups with the highest levels of infectious disease contracted from settlers and soldiers also had the worst rates of miscarriage and stillbirth.[10]

Women in the best of social and economic circumstances also had much to fear at a time when an average of 2% of white women died during or after delivery.[11] The southern lady Anne Davis spoke of parturition as "the most severe trial of nature."[12] Birthing women might suffer fatal hemorrhages or the often deadly seizures of eclampsia. They might be left with serious perineal tears, prolapsed uteri, and vesico-vaginal or recto-vaginal fistulas. Mothers with narrow pelvic openings, due to youth or rickets, might labor for days until they or their babies died of exhaustion or a physician crushed the skull of the baby in order to bring it out.[13] Some new mothers developed postpartum depression. Many more fell victim to childbed fever. Caused by streptococcal bacteria invading the body via uterine and vaginal tissue

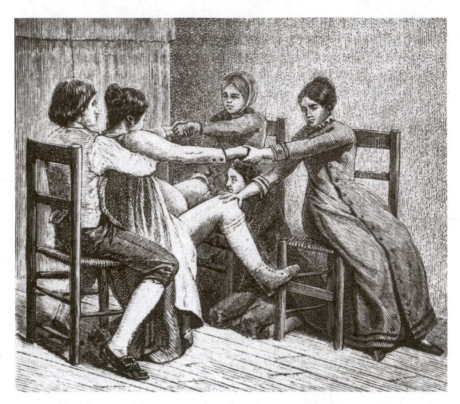

A childbirth scene ca. 1800. Female midwives delivered a large proportion of the babies born to all ethnicities in the early 1800s. Female friends often accompanied the birthing mother and midwife. Sometimes the birth would also be attended by the new mother's husband. In addition, male physicians were increasingly participating in deliveries. (© Bettmann/Corbis)

damaged during childbirth, childbed or puerperal fever developed between the second and seventh days postpartum. This infection haunted the larger lying-in hospitals. Mothers would spike a fever, develop a severe headache, and begin to vomit and have diarrhea. If the condition appeared on days two or three, the fatality rate was as high as 80% or 90%. If symptoms appeared later, the mother had on average a 35% chance of leaving her child motherless. "Epidemics of puerperal fever are," aptly wrote one French doctor, "what war is to men."[14]

There were several competing theories in the first half of the nineteenth century as to the origin of puerperal fever. Most doctors and midwives favored the idea of "self-infection" according to which some kind of infective matter is already present in the vagina or uterus before birth and wreaks havoc only afterwards. Evidence for the contrary claim that puerperal fever is passed from mother to mother on the hands of physicians and other attendants had been building for some decades in spite of strong opposition. In an 1855 book, Harvard's Dr. Oliver Wendell Holmes noted that childbed fever had the habit of picking individual practitioners and then "following their footsteps with the keenness of a beagle."[15] Holmes implored physicians to wash their hands between deliveries. Charles Meigs, Philadelphia's professor of obstetrics and diseases of women, penned an angry rebuttal. He could not understand how childbed fever could be contagious when mothers who gave birth in filthy conditions usually did not get it. There was also reluctance on the part of physicians and midwives to acknowledge that they had been the unwitting agents of so many deaths. The theory of self-infection, sagely remarked Dr. Theophilus Parvin in 1884, "is a doctrine full of comfort to the obstetrician."[16]

It took the triumph of bacteriology from the 1880s to persuade most physicians that germs really are responsible for all cases of puerperal fever. The staff of many lying-in hospitals now started to take obvious precautions to keep deadly bacteria away from birthing women. "Everything and everybody in the house is clean and jealously kept so," remarked Dr. Joseph Price of the Preston Retreat in Pennsylvania in 1889, with the result that he and his staff had delivered 540 babies over five years without a single maternal death.[17] Lives were unquestionably saved by the use of clean aprons and disinfectant to wash hands as well as the hospital's insistence on maintaining scrupulously clean floors and bed linen. Unfortunately, physicians elsewhere did not maintain such high standards and took hygienic shortcuts to save time. Moreover, in 1900 about 90% of births were still taking place in the far-from-sterile private bedrooms of clients.[18]

The Traditional Birth Attendant

In most American communities female attendants were expected to be present during childbirth. The diaries of Martha Ballard, a midwife and healer who worked amid the forests, lakes, and rivers of Maine from 1785 to 1812, convey a rich sense of the communal and co-operative nature of childbirth before the modern age. Martha delivered as many as 40 babies a year, often having to ford turbulent streams and rivers and row across half-frozen lakes in order to reach a woman in labor. On arrival she orchestrated the events of the labor and delivery. Allowing nature to take its course as much as possible, Martha would provide comfort and advice before the baby emerged, and then she would tie the umbilical cord. Sometimes midwives would be a little more interventionist: manually checking on the dilation of the cervix, turning around improperly positioned fetuses, and administering small doses of ergot to hasten the contractions.[19] Throughout the process, the birthing mother also drew comfort from being surrounded by female family members, friends, and neighbors who had already undergone the pains and dangers of delivery. What Carroll Smith-Rosenberg called "social childbirth" helped to bind together the women of white communities.[20]

Within indigenous societies women played an equally central role in delivering babies and conducting the rituals considered necessary to gain the support of spirits and reduce the risks of malevolent magic. Although women in some cultures gave birth in isolation, in many other cases they were accompanied by a few female helpers.[21] Such attendants might be responsible for completing a number of rituals following birth: washing the mother and child, wrapping the baby in bear skin, feeding it oil from a seal or bear, and hanging a section of the umbilical cord around the baby's neck.[22] Among the Zunis of New Mexico, female attendants massaged the abdomen of the mother, made drinks with special herbs, and bathed the child in water infused with the twigs of the juniper tree.[23]

On slave plantations midwives were usually fellow slave women.[24] Some slaves, like Clara Walker of Arkansas, were so competent that their owners hired them out to attend the births of both fellow slaves and white babies.[25] Accordingly, physicians in the South sometimes expressed outrage at their business going to "mere" slaves: the slave-midwife Mildred Graves recalled arriving to assist with a white woman's delivery and being confronted by two white doctors who "laugh at me an' say, 'Get back darkie, we mean business an' don' won't any witch doctors or hoodoo stuff." Slave midwives were also able to deliver babies in a culturally sanctioned manner. They could provide reassurance to expectant slave mothers by prescribing traditional herbs and roots that were believed to ease pain and strengthen their contractions. In addition, they knew how to perform the appropriate religious rituals such as ensuring the proper treatment of the placenta. Even at the end of the century, most black women had their babies delivered by the hands of an African American midwife.[26]

The Decline of the White Midwife

During the 1800s the experience of giving birth for women of European heritage underwent a radical change. At the end of the century midwives were attending on average only half of all births: only among African Americans, some Native American groups, and immigrant populations from eastern and southern Europe did female birth attendants continue to predominate. This shift involved a highly controversial medicalization of childbirth. And, for all the bold claims made by doctors and obstetricians, it remains unclear to what extent birthing mothers actually benefited from the eclipse of the traditional midwife.[27]

In the decade before the Revolutionary War, male physicians were already performing a minority of deliveries. Rudimentary classes on midwifery became available to doctors in Boston and New York in the early 1800s, with instructors making use of manikins and women too impoverished to afford the luxury of dignity. With each passing decade doctors, especially those working in cities, brought childbirth further under the control of the medical profession. They were able to do so because expectant mothers were increasingly willing to invite them into the birthing room.[28] The appeal of the physician, especially among the higher classes, lay in his training in the use of innovative equipment and chemicals that made him seem more scientific. Physicians in Martha Ballard's day already gave opium and laudanum and used forceps in difficult cases to remove the child. During the second half of the century they made far greater gains in scientific stature. After the introduction of nitrous oxide, ether, and chloroform during the mid-1840s, pregnant women eagerly sought them out in order to have the benefits of anesthesia during labor. They were also often impressed by doctors who experimented with disinfecting the vagina with bichloride of mercury or by administering intramuscular or intravenous injections of formalin to lessen the risk of puerperal fever. These interventions did a lot more harm than good, but they had the virtue for the physician of looking unmistakably cutting-edge. Furthermore, by relentlessly emphasizing the dangers of parturition, physicians steadily redefined childbirth as a pathological process demanding medical intervention.[29]

The conflict between midwives and doctors sparked major controversy. Critics of the traditional midwife were absolutely correct in pointing out that midwives often did not follow hygienic principles. A New York study of 1906 stated that 90% of them were "hopelessly dirty, ignorant, and incompetent." And yet regular physicians were not obviously better. A U.S. Department of Labor report revealed that midwives had superior mortality records to physicians.[30] This is not surprising given that even the best medical schools arranged for students to see no more than four deliveries.[31] Physicians could also be overzealous and clumsy in using forceps and were less likely to encourage breast-feeding, partly due to their discomfort at showing mothers how to massage the nipple to stimulate milk flow. Nor did it help that until late in the century male physicians, out of a strong sense of the woman's modesty, were still being trained to carry out much of the business of delivering babies without looking at the vagina. Avoiding inflicting damage with the forceps therefore required that the doctor insert his hand into the vagina and run his fingers round the blades. This often led to the transfer of the bacteria causing puerperal fever. Judith Walzer Leavitt highlights the example of Dr. H. Whitcomb of Pennsylvania, who in 1886 cared for a patient with scarlet fever and then passed on her deadly germs to 33 birthing women.[32]

Nor did the specialty of obstetrics, first taught in medical schools in the 1840s and gathering momentum in hospitals by the end of the century, offer a workable alternative. Although obstetricians argued loudly that the job of delivering babies ought to be their exclusive preserve, there were not enough of them to go around, and a large proportion of the population simply could not afford their services. Moreover, no obstetrician would provide the extensive aftercare for mothers that was an essential aspect of the midwife's role among the immigrant communities of cities like New York and Boston. In calling for the complete abolition of midwifery, obstetricians were being just as disingenuous as regular physicians who insisted that they were superior to female midwives at delivering babies. A better approach might have been to provide more training for midwives: where states did introduce training and licensing for midwives, mortality rates sometimes dropped below the national average.[33] But in many states this option was vehemently resisted by doctors and obstetricians who rightly feared a loss of business. And so, by 1900, white midwives found themselves in headlong retreat.[34]

THE POLITICS OF REPRODUCTION

Family Limitation

In a variety of contexts women in the nineteenth-century United States sought to exercise control over when and how often they bore children. Native American societies had long practiced techniques to prevent conception or terminate pregnancies. The women of some indigenous cultures ingested plants like *Lithospermum rudedrale* in an attempt to achieve at least temporary sterility; they took the herbs horehound, silk tassel bush, and mistletoe in trying to induce abortion; and they continued breast-feeding for several years to reduce the likelihood of conception. In some cases native peoples resorted to infanticide where an additional child could not be supported without risking the survival of his or her siblings.[35] Native Americans corralled into missions had a different reason to take abortifacients or to kill their newborns. Hugo Reid, a Scotsman who settled in the Los Angeles area, wrote in 1852 of how women who had been sexually assaulted by Spanish priests and soldiers felt such "disgust and abhorrence" that "every white child born among them for a long period was secretly strangled and buried."[36]

On plantations some female slaves tried to avoid bringing new generations of slaves into the world. They had no desire to put their wombs to the service of masters who regarded them as breeding stock. Mary Gaffney of Texas proudly said that in having no children when enslaved she had "cheated Master."[37] Slave women could reduce the chance of conception by breast-feeding till their children were as old as three. Chewed cottonwood may also have served as an effective contraceptive.[38] Moreover, women raped by masters or overseers took what they hoped to be abortifacients in an attempt to rid themselves of the resulting fetuses.[39] But masters were often on the lookout for slaves who did not reproduce and were willing to use coercion to get them to do so. One ex-slave called Rose later explained that her new master told her to live with a male slave called Rufus. Not liking him, she refused. Threatened with a "whipping," Rose complied with his wishes.[40] Other masters were more subtly coercive. Major Wallon rewarded slaves on his plantation with a new dress and a silver dollar at every birth.[41] Slave women who did not provide their masters with babies were liable to be sold as "unsound."[42]

In very different circumstances the white middle classes of the nineteenth-century United States showed a new determination in regulating their family size. This is not to say that they were striving to avoid parenthood entirely. Many women felt that they had failed to do their duty to their husbands and to God if they failed to reproduce. Sally Bliss of Massachusetts, for instance, confided to her diary that if the Almighty did not grant her a child in the next year, he might as well end her life so that she did not uselessly "cumber the ground."[43] The point is that fewer conceptions were taking place than at any previous time in the nation's history: the average rate of fertility fell from 7.04 in 1800 to just 3.56 in 1900. The trend began in the urban and commercial regions of New England, particularly among the white Protestant middle and upper classes, and soon spread to rural and frontier areas of the Northeast and then to the West and to some extent to the South.[44]

There are several probable reasons as to why large families became less desirable. Economic factors were the most significant motivations to have fewer children. As the available supply of high-quality agricultural land dried up, many American parents realized that they could not bequeath enough to justify having more than a few offspring. Having lots of children made even less sense in the new conditions created by the expansion of urbanization and the growth of an industrial economy. In urban settings in which women were more reliant on wage labor outside of the home, children were far harder to look after than in the countryside. Offspring were also becoming more expensive because there was an expectation that middle-class children should be moderately well-educated. This meant that parents had to pay for schooling as well as forfeit the income they would have derived in earlier periods from their young children working. At the same time, large families were becoming less important for the middle classes as security for old age now that wages were rising and money could be saved in banks. In addition, an awareness of the cost of maintaining a family with any degree of gentility encouraged young men and women to delay marriage by several years. This had a significant effect on the number of children they had time to produce.[45]

How did men and women of the nineteenth century control their fecundity? The valorizing of abstinence as a sign of bourgeois respectability encouraged some husbands and wives to master their sexual urges. Others clearly had to take precautions.[46] Explicit texts like Charles Knowlton's 1833 *Fruits of Philosophy* offered them advice on how to practice contraception. Couples could learn about family limitation from their physicians, women exchanged contraceptive information with one another in their private letters, and plenty of men learned how to lessen the risks of conception from visiting prostitutes.[47] The most common contraceptive techniques among American whites were the continuation of breast-feeding to postpone ovulation, coitus interruptus, and the rhythm method. Rubber condoms could also be procured for the male, and diaphragms were sold for women with coyly euphemistic names like "womb veils." In addition, women relied on douching with water or astringents. When a gynecologist writing in the *Michigan Medical News* of 1880 boldly asked his colleagues to inquire of their female patients as to whether they would "douche the engorged uterus and vagina with cold water?" he learned that a considerable number did so.[48]

Where contraception failed, women frequently fell back on abortion. For the first several decades of the century, state laws in the United States did not recognize abortion as a crime until the fetus had first moved, a stage known as quickening, usually before the fourth or fifth month of pregnancy. James Mohr has estimated that as Protestant wives of the middle and upper classes tried to avoid multiple pregnancies, the abortion rate shot up from around 1 for every 25–30 live births in 1800 to 1 for every 5–6 births by the 1850s and 1860s.[49] Some abortionists became very wealthy. Madame Restell, an English immigrant, started to provide abortions in 1830 in New York City, operating on Fifth Avenue close to St. Patrick's Cathedral. Later she established spin-off offices in Boston and Philadelphia and a booming mail-order business. Abortionists like Restell thrived in an age that held bourgeois privacy in high regard.[50]

Anglo-American Opposition to Family Limitation

Around mid-century the practice of family limitation sparked a major backlash from social purity campaigners led by the firebrand Anthony Comstock, funded by the YMCA, and lent scientific kudos by the American Medical Association. A crusade of middle-class social conservatives, they argued that intercourse unredeemed by the possibility of conception violated divine laws, that women have a God-given duty to procreate, and that the white elites were jeopardizing the future of the Anglo-Saxon "race" by having fewer offspring than poor immigrants from Ireland or southern and eastern Europe.[51] Prominent doctors assisted the purity campaign by supplying apparently scientific arguments against both abortion and contraception. Physicians said that terrible numbers of women suffered at the hands of unskilled abortionists practicing uterine surgery. More dubiously, Harvard's professor of obstetrics, Dr. Horatio Storer, claimed that contraception gave women vaguely-defined conditions like "lame backs," "neuralgic breasts," "obscure abdominal aches and pains," and "impatient bladders."[52] Harvard's Dr. Charles Bigelow added that if men practiced coitus interruptus, they denied the womb the therapeutic benefits of semen. This resulted in what he called "pelvic congestion."[53]

The alliance of clergymen, physicians, and assorted conservatives against family limitation enjoyed astonishing success. A wave of state and federal legislation from the 1860s onwards criminalized both contraception and abortion. Women who had abortions risked criminal prosecution while the abortionist could be charged with second-degree homicide. The Comstock Law of 1873 then made it illegal to sell, send, lend, or receive printed literature on abortion and contraception. Obtaining a copy of Knowlton's *Fruits of Philosophy* could condemn a person to five years of hard labor. In 1880 Comstock proudly totted up the results of a purge that had grown to Reformation proportions: 24,225 pounds of books and sheet stock dealing with sexual matters had been seized and destroyed along with 64,094 "rubber articles for immoral use" and 4,185 boxes of pills and powders for abortion.[54] These laws forced abortion underground, but doctors in urban areas could still be found to perform the procedure. Studies of the 1930s revealed a considerable number of physicians who in effect ran abortion clinics. They operated in hygienic conditions and relied on networks of doctors for referrals.[55] Advice about contraception also continued to circulate in private among female friends and between doctors and married couples.[56]

DOCTORS WRITING ABOUT WOMEN

The Trouble with Wombs

Doctors predicted for middle-class women short lives of disease and debility if they did not conform to their roles as wives and mothers. They couched this belief in the weakness of womankind in fashionable physiological terms. The chief dangers to women were said to lie in their reproductive apparatus. "Women's reproductive organs are pre-eminent," said one American physician at mid-century; "They exercise a controlling influence upon her entire system, and entail upon her many painful and dangerous diseases. . . . Everything that is peculiar to her, springs from her sexual organization." Or as another put it: "Ovulation fixes woman's place in the animal economy." In keeping with the popular theory of reflex action, too much irritation to the nerves around the uterus and ovaries was believed to have negative effects both locally and in remote parts of the body. When a woman falls sick, one physician elaborated, the condition "will be found . . . to be in reality, no disease at all, but merely the sympathetic reaction or the symptoms of one disease, namely, a disease of the womb."[57] The causes were easily identified: overly rich food, menstrual irregularities, inappropriately tight clothing, and excessive stimulation of the vagina or clitoris. The Chicago professor of gynecology Henry Byford concluded in 1860s, "it is almost a pity that a woman has a womb."[58]

Physicians differed on how much sexual intercourse a woman's system could safely bear. Standard medical opinion said that too much genital friction was a leading culprit of female maladies. This excess irritation might be caused by intercourse or masturbation or even by erotically rhythmic jolts from travelling on steam trains, operating sewing machines, or riding horses and bicycles. Moreover, condoms, diaphragms, and prophylactic sponges inserted into the vagina were said to cause uterine irritation and excite lasciviousness, which in turn led to more sex and a more extreme state of nervous prostration. In 1887 the surgeon William Hammond offered the standard but welcome reassurance that leaving "prostitutes out of consideration," only about "one-tenth of the instances of intercourse" involved the woman experiencing even "the slightest pleasurable sensation." As a result they were mostly uninterested in sex and safe from the effects of overexcitation.[59]

Female physiology also required that women avoid anything that might deplete their limited store of vital energy. Most male doctors thought women to be innately more emotional and less rational than males, fitted for mothering rather than governing. As a result, mind work could easily become a heavy tax on their health. Such dangers were said to be especially acute during puberty. Serious damage could apparently be inflicted when the ovaries and uterus were forming. Edwin C. Clarke stated in a widely read book of 1873 that if women devoted themselves to education between the ages of 12 and 20 they would permanently impair their health. The weaker female body, he explained, cannot do "two things well at the same time." Clarke tried to prove that higher education was bad for women by citing cases of flat-chested and barren consumptives who had gone to college rather than staying at home waiting on husband and babies.[60] Those who deviated from the roles apparently assigned to them by God and nature were also believed to run a terribly high risk of developing "hysteria."

Hysteria: The Female Malady

The catch-all term *hysteria* comprised not only anxiety and depression but more elaborate presentations that included twisting, cramping, difficulty breathing and swallowing, and muscular contractions, often accompanied by rigidity of the trunk and limbs. While some "hysterical" patients had organic conditions like neurosyphilis or frontal-lobe epilepsy, many of the symptoms recorded are likely to have been physical manifestations of acute distress. Like their classical forebears, nineteenth-century doctors believed that women were far more likely than men to develop hysteria. "Hysteria," said one, "is second Nature to them."[61] In the later 1800s American doctors adopted the term "neurasthenia," minted by the Connecticut physician Charles Beard, to describe the varied presentations of hysteria. Beard believed these symptoms to arise from actual lesions to the nerves caused by the excessive strains of modern life caused by such inventions as steam engines, the telegraph, the printing press, and the education of women. The Civil War surgeon Silas Weir Mitchell quickly emerged as the leading specialist in treating neurasthenia. In accordance with conventional medical theory, he found most of his clients among the ranks of wealthy women. By virtue of their sex they apparently had the most sensitive and easily damaged of nervous systems.[62]

A number of historians have theorized about why more women than men were diagnosed as suffering from hysteria. Scholars like Phyllis Chesler argue that more middle-class white women were in fact breaking down and that they did so due to the constrictive nature of their lives. Hysteria offered an escape route from the routine drudgery of Victorian domesticity.[63] There seems little doubt that what Chesler called a "half-life" of submission and dependence did drive some women into despair. But, as Nancy Tomes has stressed, men and women both suffered psychological anguish due to the stiflingly strict gender codes of the age.[64] Although men might have broken down in less flamboyant ways, they too often had to cope with severe anxiety and depression. Moreover, women diagnosed with hysteria were not always the highly creative victims of insufferable boredom. In her book *Shattered Nerves*, Janet Oppenheim pointed out that women had many other reasons to slip into a disordered mental state. In particular, the repeated loss of children and unhappy relationships could make their lives utterly intolerable.[65] Lydia Buck Gates of Nanticoke Valley in rural New York lost two sons to diphtheria during the Civil War and then her two daughters within the same week. Not surprisingly, her granddaughter was later told she "just about lost her mind." In desperation, she and her husband sold their home and moved to a new state. Lydia later returned, with a baby boy, but "very depressed."[66] Simple, terrible hardship explained why many women broke down.

Treating Women's Disorders

The New England advocate of the water cure Russell Thacher Trall felt obliged to acknowledge his indebtedness to "frail woman" because, he said, these fragile beings represented nearly three-quarters of his business.[67] Many medical interventions and recommendations for women were predictably designed to reduce irritation of the uterine system. In order to avoid overexcitation and to control their sexual desire they were advised to eat only bland food and abstain from meat and brandy.[68] From the 1870s Silas Weir Mitchell's "milk and rest cure" enjoyed remarkable popularity. Neurasthenic women came to his clinic for a period of seclusion, bed rest, and a diet mostly comprising fatty milk to restore the nerve fibers. Across the country entrepreneurial neurologists set up private nerve clinics where they enforced the same regimen of inactivity and full-fat dairy products.

More heroic methods of quelling the irritation of the genital nerves were also readily available. Some physicians applied electricity, bled the vulva, or gave intrauterine injections. In 1843 William Potts Dewees, professor of midwifery at the University of Pennsylvania, recommended placing bloodsucking leeches on the neck of the uterus, though he felt the need to caution his colleagues to count how many they inserted because if any were left behind the patient would suffer "acute pain."[69] The Georgia surgeon Robert Battey popularized the "normal oviarotomy," involving the excision of healthy ovaries in women with symptoms of anxiety, depression, or backache. Mortality rates sometimes reaching 22% did not lessen the determination of surgeons like Battey. He personally removed the perfectly healthy ovaries of several hundred women.[70] Women diagnosed with nymphomania or a chronic urge to masturbate might have their ovaries removed or be subject to clitoral cauterizations using nitrate of silver or the cautery iron. Seldom did anyone suggest removing the penis or testicles of a melancholic, anxious, or philandering male.[71]

Nineteenth-century doctors also induced orgasms in their female patients as a treatment for hysteria. They did so by aiming streams of water at the vagina, by using their hands, and, after the 1880s, with the use of the first electromechanical vibrators. Although this practice might seem paradoxical, the historian Rachel Maines has shown that most doctors did not see the intervention as in any way sexual. Women were believed to be suffering from a dangerous build-up of nervous energy that had to be purged by the sudden release of a "hysterical paroxysm." The vibrator became the choice means because doctors apparently found genital massage by hand to be tedious and tiring.[72]

Medicine as Misogyny

In characterizing women as deficient in reason and prone to hysteria, most male doctors were articulating in the language of biology the basic misconceptions of their time and place. They were reading into nature an idealized relationship between middle- and upper-class husbands and wives. The woman's role, said one Victorian writer, is to "rear the offspring and ever fan the flame of piety, patriotism and love upon the sacred altar of her home."[73] Moreover, males were inclined to accept erroneous assumptions about sex and gender where most women did conform to classic gender stereotypes because they had few chances to prove their intellectual potential. Few male physicians bothered to notice when the Massachusetts Labor Union found

American college women to be mostly in fine health and many to be more robust than they had been at home.[74]

But male doctors who wrote about alleged female limitations were not entirely innocent in using biological arguments against the women who quit the domestic sphere. It is surely no coincidence that

Elizabeth Blackwell (1821–1910). Photomechanical print by Swaine. Blackwell was the first woman to receive a medical degree in the United States. Born in England, her family immigrated to the United States in 1832. She was admitted to the Geneva Medical College in New York in 1847. Having gained her medical diploma in 1849, Blackwell undertook further studies in Paris and London. She practiced medicine in both the United States and Britain, helping to establish the New York Infirmary for Indigent Women and Children and later the London School of Medicine for Women. Blackwell's career was defined in important ways by her gender. Male physicians were often hostile to her ambitions and refused to cooperate with her; she seriously contemplated dressing as a man in order to gain access to the Paris teaching schools. Conversely, some physicians argued that her gender perfectly qualified her for certain kinds of medicine. Blackwell herself concurred with the latter sentiment, insisting that women brought an invaluable "spiritual power of maternity" to the bedside that allowed them to care for the sick with compassion, understanding, and patience. (Wellcome Library, London)

they stepped up their scientific critiques of female ambition just as more women were trying to gain access to professional careers including medicine. In 1849 Elizabeth Blackwell became the first female doctor in the United States, having trained at Geneva Medical College in upstate New York, and in 1868 she opened the Women's Medical College of the New York Infirmary. Nearly 50% of colleges accepted women in 1870, and this number shot up to 73% in 1910.[75] Having been virtually banned from medicine before 1860, women constituted about 5% of the profession nationwide by the end of century.[76] Although some physicians deemed female physicians to be usefully adept at treating fellow women, others regarded them as unwelcome competition. Now they had a vested interest in shoring up and refining old claims about the intellectual inferiority of womankind. In this context many championed Edwin Clarke's convenient claim that women were mentally and physically unsuitable for medical careers.

Sex and Suffering

American women in the nineteenth century faced most of the same health risks as their male contemporaries in addition to those associated with pregnancy and childbirth. The health gains that were achieved for women in the nineteenth century were not evenly distributed. The advent of obstetric anesthesia relieved substantial numbers of white women from pain, and the recognition by at least some doctors and midwives that they had to wash their hands to avoid transmitting the germs of puerperal fever significantly reduced the likelihood of their babies being left motherless. In contrast, African American and Native American women gained very little from medical advances. African American women achieved greater longevity as a result of the abolition of slavery, but they and their children still sickened and died at a much higher rate than those of white women. The fortunes of Native American women plummeted in crowded reservations established on poor land and where they had to subsist on meager government-supplied rations. Tuberculosis and syphilis sapped their capacity to survive and produce offspring. Women's health remained a function of the unequal distribution of power. So too did the way male physicians described their bodies and minds. Troubled by the number of women going to college and aspiring to professional careers, doctors were quick to furnish speculative physiological claims about the weakness of their nerves, the smallness of their brains, and the fragility of their ovaries.

NOTES

1. Deborah G. White, *Ar'n't I a Woman? Female Slaves in the Plantation South*. New York: Norton, 1999, p. 108.

2. William Dusinberre, *Them Dark Days: Slavery in the American Rice Swamps*. New York: Oxford University Press, 1996, pp. 236–37.

3. Diane Price Herndl, "The Invisible (Invalid) Woman: African American Women, Illness, and Nineteenth-Century Narrative," in Judith Leavitt (ed.), *Women and Health in America: Historical Readings*. Madison: University of Wisconsin Press, 1999, 131–45, p. 134.

4. Richard H. Steckel, "A Dreadful Childhood: The Excess Mortality of American Slaves," *Social Science History* 10 (1986): 427–65, 431.

5. Ibid., p. 433.

6. Janet Farrell Brodie, *Contraception and Abortion in Nineteenth-Century America*. Ithaca, NY: Cornell University Press, 1994, p. 51; and Virgil Vogel, *American Indian Medicine*. Norman: University of Oklahoma Press, p. 235.

7. Ann Marie Plane, "Childbirth Practices among Native American Women of New England and Canada, 1600–1800," in Leavitt (ed.), *Women and Health in America*, 38–47, p. 42.

8. Antonia I. Castañeda, "Engendering the History of Alta California, 1769–1848: Gender, Sexuality, and the Family," *California History* 76, no. 2/3 (Summer–Fall, 1997), pp. 230–59; and Robert H. Jackson and Edward Castillo, *Indians, Franciscans, and Spanish Colonization: The Impact of the Mission System on California Indians*. Albuquerque: University of New Mexico Press, 1997, p. 82.

9. Nancy Shoemaker, *American Indian Population Recovery in the Twentieth Century*. Albuquerque: University of New Mexico Press, 1999, pp. 49, 32.

10. Ibid., p. 54. See also Sherburne Friend Cook, *The Conflict between the California Indian and White Civilization*. Berkeley: University of California Press, 1976, pp. 28–30; and David S. Jones, "The Persistence of American Indian Health Disparities," *American Journal of Public Health* 96, no. 12 (December 2066), 2122–34.

11. Janet Golden, *A Social History of Wet Nursing in America: From Breast to Bottle*. New York: Cambridge University Press, 1996, p. 45.

12. Elizabeth Fox Genovese, *Within the Plantation Household: Black and White Women of the Old South*. Chapel Hill: University of North Carolina Press, 1988, p. 277; and Elaine Tyler May, *Barren in the Promised Land: Childless Americans and the Pursuit of Happiness*. New York: BasicBooks, 1995, p. 51.

13. Irvine Loudon (ed.), *Childbed Fever: A Documentary History*. New York: Garland, 1995, p. 131.

14. Loudon (ed.), *Childbed Fever*, pp. xxxvi, 159.

15. Oliver Wendell Holmes, *Puerperal Fever as a Private Pestilence*. Boston: Ticknor and Fields, 1855, p. 47.

16. Judith Walzer Leavitt, *Brought to Bed: Childbearing in America, 1750 to 1950*. New York: Oxford University Press, 1986, p. 156.

17. Leavitt, *Brought to Bed*, p. 159.

18. Leavitt, *Brought to Bed*, p. 161.

19. Laurel Ulrich, *A Midwife's Tale: The Life of Martha Ballard, Based on Her Diary, 1785–1812.* New York: Knopf, 1990, p. 12.

20. Carroll Smith-Rosenberg, "From Puberty to Menopause: The Cycle of Femininity in Nineteenth-Century America," in Mary Hartman and Lois Banner (eds.), *Clio's Consciousness Raised.* New York: Harper & Row, 1974, p.16.

21. Plane, "Childbirth Practices," p. 39.

22. Ibid., p. 41.

23. Scott M. Camazine, "Traditional and Western Health Care among the Zuni Indians of New Mexico," *Social Science and Medicine* 14 (1980), 73–80, pp. 75–76.

24. Gertrude Jacinta Fraser, *African American Midwifery in the South: Dialogues of Birth, Race, and Memory.* Cambridge, MA: Harvard University Press, 1998.

25. Schwartz, *Birthing a Slave*, p. 148.

26. Sharla M. Fett, *Working Cures: Healing, Health, and Power on Southern Slave Plantations.* University of North Carolina Press, 2002, p. 51.

27. Leavitt, *Brought to Bed.*

28. Catherine M. Scholten, *Childbearing in American Society, 1650–1850.* New York: New York University Press, 1985.

29. Leavitt, *Brought to Bed*, p. 116.

30. F. E. Kobrin, "The American Midwife Controversy: A Crisis of Professionalization," *Bulletin of the History of Medicine* 40, no. 4 (1966), 350–63, p. 351.

31. Ibid., *Brought to Bed*, p. 63.

32. Ibid., p. 57.

33. Samuel H. Preston and Michael R. Haines, *Fatal Years: Child Mortality in Late Nineteenth-Century America.* Princeton, NJ: Princeton University Press, 1991, p. 15.

34. Charlotte G. Borst, *Catching Babies: The Professionalization of Childbirth, 1870–1920.* Cambridge, MA: Harvard University Press, 1995, p. 67.

35. Brodie, *Contraception*, p. 51.

36. Jackson and Castillo, Indians, Franciscans, and Spanish Colonization, p. 82.

37. Marie Jenkins Schwarz, *Birthing a Slave: Motherhood and Medicine in the Antebellum South.* Cambridge, MA: Harvard University Press, 2010, p. 147, p. 93.

38. Liese M. Perrin, "Resisting Reproduction: Reconsidering Slave Contraception in the Old South," *Journal of American Studies* 35 (2001), 255–74; and Schwartz, *Birthing a Slave*, p. 95.

39. Jacqueline Jones, *Labor of Love, Labor of Sorrow: Black Women, Work and the Family, from Slavery to the Present.* New York: Basic Books, 2010, p. 35.

40. May, *Barren in the Promised Land*, p. 56.

41. White, *Ar'n't I a Woman?* p. 100.

42. Todd L. Savitt, *Medicine and Slavery: The Diseases and Health Care of Blacks in Antebellum Virginia.* Urbana: University of Illinois Press, 2002, p. 116; and May, *Barren in the Promised Land*, p. 55.

43. May, *Barren in the Promised Land*, p. 42.

44. Michael Grossberg, *Governing the Hearth: Law and the Family in Nineteenth-Century America*. Chapel Hill: University of North Carolina Press, 1985, pp. 156, 170.

45. Michael R. Haines and Richard H. Steckel, *A Population History of North America*. New York: Cambridge University Press, 2000, pp. 326–29.

46. Carl N. Degler, "What Ought to Be and What Was: Women's Sexuality in the Nineteenth Century," *The American Historical Review* 79 (December 1974), 1467–90.

47. Brodie, *Contraception*, p. 5.

48. Ibid., pp. 88–89.

49. Grossberg, *Governing the Hearth*, p. 170. See also Estelle B. Freedman, "Sexuality in Nineteenth-Century America: Behavior, Ideology, and Politics," *Reviews in American History* 10, no. 4 (December 1982), 196–215.

50. Grossberg, *Governing the Hearth*, p. 160.

51. Carroll Smith-Rosenberg and Charles Rosenberg, "The Female Animal: Medical and Biological Views of Woman and Her Role in Nineteenth-Century America," *The Journal of American History* 60, no. 2 (September 1973), 332–56.

52. Brodie, *Contraception*, p. 271.

53. Rachel P. Maines, *The Technology of Orgasm: "Hysteria," the Vibrator, and Women's Sexual Satisfaction*. Baltimore, MD: Johns Hopkins University Press, 1999, pp. 51–53.

54. Brodie, *Contraception*, p. 281.

55. Leslie J. Reagan, *When Abortion Was a Crime: Women, Medicine, and Law in the United States, 1867–1973*. Berkeley: University of California Press, 1997, p. 133.

56. Freedman, "Sexuality in Nineteenth-Century America," p. 200.

57. Rosenberg, "Female Animal," p. 336.

58. Ann Douglas Wood, " 'The Fashionable Diseases': Women's Complaints and Their Treatment in Nineteenth-Century America," *The Journal of Interdisciplinary History* 4, no. 1 (Summer 1973), 25–52, p. 29.

59. Manier, *Technology of Orgasm*, p. 61.

60. Rosenberg, "Female Animal," p. 341.

61. Athena Vretto, *Somatic Fictions: Imagining Illness in Victorian Culture*. Stanford, CA: Stanford University Press, 1995, p. 92.

62. Elaine Showalter, *The Female Malady: Women, Madness, and English Culture, 1830–1980*. New York: Pantheon Books, 1985.

63. Phyllis Chesler, *Women and Madness*. Garden City: Doubleday, 1972.

64. Nancy Tomes, "Feminist Histories of Psychiatry," in Micale and Porter (eds.), *Discovering the History of Psychiatry*. New York: Oxford University Press, 1994.

65. Janet Oppenheim, *"Shattered Nerves": Doctors, Patients, and Depression in Victorian England*. New York: Oxford University Press, 1991.

66. Nancy Grey Osterud, *Bonds of Community: The Lives of Farm Women in Nineteenth-century New York*. Ithaca, NY: Cornell University Press, 1991, p. 121.

67. Maines, *Technology of Orgasm*, p. 90.

68. Carol Gronenman, "Nymphomania: The Historical Construction of Female Sexuality," *Signs* 19, no. 2 (Winter 1994), 337–67.

69. Wood, "Fashionable Diseases," p. 29.

70. Ian R. Dowbiggin, *Keeping America Sane: Psychiatry and Eugenics in the United States and Canada, 1880–1940*. Ithaca, NY: Cornell University Press, 1997, p. 84.

71. Gronenman, "Nymphomania," p. 350.

72. Maines, *Technology of Orgasm*, p. 11.

73. Regina Markell Morantz, "The Connecting Link: The Case for the Woman Doctor in 19th-Century America," in Ronald Numbers and Judith Leavitt (eds.), *Sickness and Health in America: Readings in the History of Medicine and Public Health*. Madison: University of Wisconsin Press, 1985, p. 214.

74. Vern Bullough and Martha Voght, "Women, Menstruation, and Nineteenth-Century Medicine," *Bulletin of the History of Medicine* 47, no. 1 (1973), 66–82, p. 72.

75. Patricia D'Antonio, *American Nursing: A History of Knowledge, Authority, and the Meaning of Work*. Baltimore, MD: Johns Hopkins University Press, 2010, p. 31.

76. Morantz, "The Connecting Link," p. 164.

CHAPTER 5

The Health of Children and Infants

In Grafton, Vermont, there stands a tombstone dated 1803 bearing the mute but terrible inscription:

IN Memory of
Thomas K. Park Junr
And thirteen Infants,
Children of Mr.
Thomas K. Park and
Rebecca his wife.[1]

Only a minority of families suffered as grievously as the Parks, but mothers and fathers could consider themselves highly fortunate if they did not lose at least one of their offspring in early childhood to a diarrheal or respiratory disease. Many of those who did survive had to endure severe disabilities: skeletons distorted by childhood rickets, scoliosis, or tuberculosis; deafness and blindness caused by infections; and hearts severely damaged by diphtheria or scarlet fever. Not until the last decades of the century did the mortality and morbidity of infants and children begin to decline. This chapter looks at why infancy and childhood were so terrifyingly dangerous, how Americans coped with the demise of their offspring, and the factors that laid the basis for the rapid improvement in the health of infants and children during the early twentieth century.

A DANGEROUS TIME TO BE YOUNG

A few stark statistics convey some sense of the horrors of infant and child mortality in the nineteenth century. Richard Steckel arrived at a rough calculation of child mortality rates by working out the proportion of children in various areas who appeared in the 1850 household census but were absent from the 1860 census. This method revealed that in the American northeast around 13% of children who reached the age of one were destined to die before reaching their fifth birthday. In the frequently squalid frontier zones of Minnesota, Iowa, Texas, and regions further to the west, about a fifth of infants perished before the age of one and at least another quarter between the ages of one and four. The southern states were healthier but still deadly for large numbers of the young: about a quarter of infants died and 16% of those aged one to four. The odds were much worse for the offspring of slaves. Over a third of African American infants in the antebellum era were dead before the age of one, nearly a half had perished before the age of five, and almost 60% were buried before reaching 15. These figures can be hard to comprehend when currently fewer than 0.6% of American infants die per year.[2]

Gastrointestinal, respiratory and infectious diseases cut short most of these young lives. Samuel H. Preston and Michael R. Haines calculate that about 25% of all infant deaths were due to gastrointestinal infections and a fifth of all fatalities between the ages of 0 and 14. Respiratory illnesses like pneumonia and bronchitis claimed around 19% of the infants who died and nearly a third of those who succumbed between the ages of one and four. Measles, scarlet fever, diphtheria, whooping cough, and smallpox were together responsible for another 11.5% of young deaths until late in the century. Meningitis claimed an additional 5% of young deaths. Physicians in the 1800s identified tuberculosis as the cause of death in only about 2% of fatalities, although this may well have been a significant underestimate due to the underdeveloped diagnostics of the age. Moreover, we know that the children of tuberculous mothers were more likely to die at a young age and that the adult incidence of tuberculosis was very high.[3] Finally, accidents and injuries were responsible for approximately 3% of infant and child mortality, a figure partly to be explained by the fact that as late as 1900 about a sixth of children aged 10–15 were employed, often in dangerous trades like textile manufacturing and mining.[4] The risk of premature death varied from country to city, from North to South, and from desert or plain to forest and mountain range, but very few regions of the nineteenth-century United States could be considered healthy by modern standards.

We need also to remember the suffering caused by a multitude of nonfatal afflictions. Hookworms also attached themselves to the intestinal mucus and induced lethargy and stunted growth.[5] Hookworm was endemic to much of the rural South. Tapeworm and roundworm also passed from wild or domesticated animals to human hosts.[6] In addition, children suffered from a variety of discomfiting conditions: rotting teeth, abscesses, ulcers and boils, and the kind of fungal infection that the St. Louis schoolgirl Mary E Smith described in her diary of 1836 as having "obliged" her "to leave Church on account" of her "feet itching very much."[7] Whether deadly, severe, or merely irritating, disease was a fundamental component of the lived experience of the nineteenth-century child.

The Death of Children in the City

Rapid urbanization from the 1830s onwards placed in danger the lives of millions of American babies and children. With the influx of rural migrants and then wave after wave of immigrants from the poorer regions of Europe, death rates for the young shot up in all towns and cities. Infants and children born and raised in large urban areas were usually more likely to die in childhood than those living in either small towns or rural sites with long-established communities.[8] They died because they drank water contaminated with dangerous bacteria, ate food on which flies had deposited lethal germs, lived in close proximity to family and neighbors with infectious maladies, and were often so badly nourished that their immune systems were unable to withstand pathogens. At the end of the century one wretched tenement block in New York's Lower East Side contained 2,781 residents with just 264 toilets and no bathtubs.[9] These conditions made it virtually impossible for even the most scrupulous and hygienically informed parent to keep a newborn or infant clean. Infections also propagated in the filthy, crowded factories and sweatshops in which hundreds of thousands of American children toiled from a young age. Those abandoned or orphaned by parents lacking the kin supports of the rural world had a still smaller chance of survival. "The high mortality among the foundlings is not to be marveled at," wrote Jacob A. Riis in his brilliant expose of 1890 entitled *How the Other Half Lives*, "The wonder is, rather, that any survive."[10]

Social class could exert a powerful effect on the likelihood of an infant or child living or dying. The relationship between status and

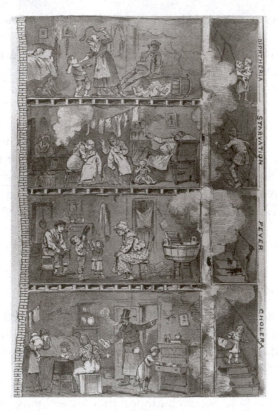

Cross section through a slum dwelling in lower New York, showing children living amid poverty and disease. Lithograph created in 1880. (© Bettmann/Corbis)

mortality is not straightforward: before the advent of horse-drawn streetcars and trams, the rich of U.S. cities often lived in fairly close proximity to the pestilential tenement districts and succumbed to the same maladies.[11] Social class did make a large difference where the wealthier classes had a safe water supply. The public health pioneer Charles Chapin discovered in 1865 that the infants of parents too impoverished to pay tax in Rhode Island died at roughly twice the rate of those of taxpayers. Chapin explained that infants were especially vulnerable to gastrointestinal diseases, and those in poor areas of Rhode Island suffered terribly due to the contamination of the public water supply with fecal matter. Towards the end of the century, as richer citizens were able to commute from a greater distance and leave the tenements far behind each evening, the social disparity in health inevitably widened.[12]

Death of Children on the Frontier

Belying the romantic image of covered wagons rumbling west and rugged families staking and defending their claims, the most deadly places for white children to be born and raised were often the scattered settlements of the American frontiers. The historian Richard A. Meckel highlights a graveyard in Leavenworth, Kansas, containing 354 graves from the year 1875. Almost a half of these graves were dug for infants and children. The problems of inadequate sanitation, water supply, and nutrition that blighted the lives of the urban young were exacerbated by the primitiveness of frontier existence. Early homesteaders dwelt in damp, dark, and insect-infested huts, eating deficient diets, and drinking water often contaminated by overflowing privies. John Mack Faragher's account of life on the Illinois prairie tells vividly of the "warring with mosquitos" of early settlers and the life-threatening bacilli that thrived in dung and stagnant pools.[13] Quite apart from the high risks of death from dysentery, typhoid, and malaria, large numbers of infants and children also had to grow up motherless due to high rates of childbed fever.

The children of the native peoples with whom white settlers and soldiers came into contact in frontier zones were even worse hit by illness. Indigenous groups were ravaged by deadly epidemics to which they were exposed at drinking spots polluted by whites heading to the West to farm, trade, or prospect and by the soldiers who violently drove native peoples into new and unfamiliar lands. An Indian subagent among the Pawnees at Council Bluffs recorded in 1849 that "two hundred and fifty men and nine hundred women and children have fallen victims of cholera." Nearly a quarter of the community had died during this second cholera epidemic. There were so many fatalities to infectious disease among the western Sioux in the 1850s that survivors were said to talk about little other than the dead.[14] Ecological disaster also drastically lowered the capacity of native children, and their parents, to resist infections like cholera, smallpox, or tuberculosis. Virtually all indigenous groups were subject to forced migration to reservations on which they could no longer maintain the traditional forms of subsistence that had provided them with excellent diets for millennia. Most notoriously, the Plains Indians were devastated by the calculated destruction of buffalo herds by a government determined to eliminate native ways of life.[15] "Formerly when the buffalo roamed the prairies in great numbers," noted an author for a Catholic publication on the Sioux in 1906, "the Indians had plenty of meat. This accounts for the fact that the old Indians are like giants in physical stature, while the younger generation is weak and sickly."[16] When Sioux prisoners were taken to a reservation in 1881, one observer noticed tuberculous youths with "fleshless limbs" who were "looking on wistfully at the dances of the warriors in the summer twilight" whose "magnificent physique and a boundless vitality . . . contrasted cruelly" with their own feeble sickliness.[17]

The thousands of native boys and girls who were sent far from home to government boarding schools to be "civilized" escaped the guns of the U.S. cavalry only to be exposed to increased risks of infectious disease. In crowded establishments, Native American children succumbed to tuberculosis, measles, mumps, and influenza. Those who survived suffered the psychological trauma of being separated from their families for long periods of time. Few of their parents could have known how difficult it would be to get their sons and daughters back, and letters home tell of the terrible loneliness of their children. The superintendents who ran these schools showed little understanding of the emotional needs of those under their care, and their commitment to breaking native culture bred callousness towards them. Take, for instance, the 1906 note sent to the father of a girl who had been sent to the Flandreau School in South Dakota for Lakota and Chippewa children. Explaining that his "daughter Lizzie" had died, the school's superintendent implied that the greatest shame was not her demise in itself but the fact that she had "improved very much since you let her come here with me."[18]

Slavery and the Health of Children

African Americans were at constant threat of premature death due to the savagery of the slave system. Even before birth they faced a grueling battle to survive in the womb as many masters made expectant mothers work in the fields and usually did not increase their dietary intake. Those offspring who survived gestation entered the world at a considerable biological disadvantage by being born at an abnormally low birth weight. Masters then made the situation worse by making the mother return quickly to the plantation.[19] Many an owner instructed the mother to leave her infant in the slave cabin and then rush back for a short period a few times a day to provide milk. One woman recalled that she had had to "nus my chil'n four times a day and pick two hundred pounds of cotton besides."[20] Some mothers were not given adequate time. They simply could not reach their cabins, nurse their infants, and return to work in the allotted 15 minutes. Those who tried to sneak away to give extra feedings faced whipping.

Encouraged by their owners, slave mothers frequently gave up trying to breast-feed and weaned their infants before they were six months old. One physician, W. C. Daniell, provided a new medical spin to the master's preference for getting slave women back out into the fields. He declared the milk of slave women to be so often poisonous that it made better sense to feed their babies with "sweet oil and molasses" and have the "mother's breasts freely drawn and daily emptied of their milk" by a nurse or even by "a puppy."[21] Spending their days away from their parents in "chillun's houses," young slave children were usually fed "pap and gruel," a diet seriously lacking in protein, iron, and calcium.[22] They would have to wait till early adolescence, when they could be sent into the fields to labor all day, to start receiving a reasonable diet. As a result they grew up badly undernourished. By examining the shipping manifests kept by ship and train companies that transported slaves, Richard Steckel found slave children to have been on average shorter than those in even the poorest African countries today.[23] The unsanitary surroundings of the slave barracks and the dirty bottles and spoons used to feed infants also ensured that they were exposed to the germs causing diarrheal and parasitic infections. The same filthy living conditions caused higher rates of neonatal tetanus due to bacteria getting into the umbilical stump. It is no wonder that slave women lost their infants at more than twice the rate of other American women.[24]

Nor could a slave mother protect her children from the pain and humiliation of maltreatment. "During slavery," an ex-slave from Virginia called Caroline Hunter remembered, "it seemed lak you' chillum b'long to ev'ybody but you. Many a day my ole mama stood by an' watched massa beat her chillum 'till they bled an' she couldn' open her mouf."[25] If a mother did intervene she risked either herself or her children being sent to the slave market. One ex-slave explained that the "cruel separation" of being sold and never again seeing his mother "brought on a fit of sickness from which they did not expect I would recover." He may have regained his bodily health, but his emotional wounds had obviously never healed.[26]

The Civil War unleashed further dangers on African American infants and children. Many of those families who fled to Union lines endured terrible suffering from exposure and hunger en route. Tragically, the northern states were neither free from the virulent racism of the South nor equipped with adequate infrastructure to receive, clothe, or feed these escaped slaves. The story of the ex-slave Joseph Miller is far from atypical. He arrived with his wife and four children at the military's Camp Nelson in Ohio along with hundreds of other escapees from the slave plantations. Joseph was obliged to stay in the camp to train as a soldier while the army moved his family under armed guard to an old boarding house where dozens huddled around a small fire and received little to no food. In these conditions his wife and children soon passed away. Joseph followed them into the grave. The Union army repeatedly said that it would take care of the families of male ex-slaves so long as they took up arms against the Confederacy. In the event, it frequently lacked the resources or motivation to make good on its promise.[27]

At least the proslavery camp's claim that slaves would not be able to survive freedom was quickly refuted in the decades after the Civil War. Free black families found themselves trapped by the sharecropping system into a state of debt bondage, but they could at least make crucial decisions that affected the welfare of family members. Many ex-slave women were now able to leave the fields in order to focus on raising their children. This allowed them to breastfeed infants and thereby lessen the dangers of infection and malnutrition. They were also able to save their offspring from the devastating trauma of being taken away to be sold. Those African Americans who migrated to urban areas after the Civil War, especially to the large cities of the North, suffered higher death rates than their rural counterparts. But even they enjoyed a longevity superior to their slave forebears. For all the high-sounding cant of those who extolled slavery, the system had condemned hundreds of thousands of infants and children to pain, misery, and premature death.

Feeding White Babies

The health of infants and children depended to a significant degree on the quality of the nutrition they received. The sons and daughters of slaves suffered grievously by being denied the nutrition and antibodies contained in a mother's milk. In Native American societies mothers frequently breast-fed until a child had reached the age of three.[28] The nutritional value of their milk presumably declined when they were driven onto reservations and forced to subsist on poor farmland combined with paltry government handouts. But indigenous babies would have been far worse off had they been weaned early. Within white societies babies were much less likely to be fed at the breast of their own mothers, and this often had catastrophic consequences for the infant or young child.

There was nothing new in white offspring not being fed at the maternal breast. Mothers died from blood loss in childbirth or succumbed days after from conditions like puerperal fever. New mothers might also be too weak to nurse, unable to supply sufficient milk, or suffer from mastitis that made breast-feeding intolerably painful. In addition, white working-class women frequently had to forgo breast-feeding as they had to get back to work soon after giving birth in order to keep their positions in factories, mills, or sweatshops. At the other end of the social spectrum, some wealthier ladies were committed to public causes or hectic social lives that left no time for punctual breast-feeding. In such circumstances babies were often given the milk of animals or were rapidly weaned with honey, butter, mashed bread, or chopped meat. Due to a widespread feeling that these substitutes were inadequate and that many children wasted away if weaned too early, wet nurses were frequently hired by those who could afford the expense. Although there were risks involved, at least babies suckled by wet nurses stood a fair chance of receiving appropriate nutrition and maternal antibodies.

Unfortunately, during the 1800s many urban well-to-do families turned against the idea of wet nurses. In rural areas a baby could be deposited with a wet nurse who lived close by in perfectly adequate conditions. In the burgeoning urban areas of the nineteenth-century United States, wet nurses had to be drawn from among the female inhabitants of tenement districts. Unwilling to allow a treasured child to be taken into such noxious environments, families instead had to accommodate the wet nurse in their own homes. Typically incapable of empathizing with the urban poor, many middle- and upper-class parents felt as if they had brought a dangerous stranger into their private domestic world, a sentiment intensified by most wet nurses being of a despised Irish descent. So a ready market lay open for any innovation that would allow women to avoid breast-feeding without requiring either early weaning or the use of a wet nurse.[29]

In the 1860s these women's prayers seemed to be answered with the inception of the commercial production of milk substitutes. Chemists like Justus von Liebig in Germany had worked out the proportion of proteins, fats, carbohydrates, and various minerals in breast milk. Invoking Liebig's name, entrepreneurs marketed powders, like Mellin's and Nestlé's formulas, that could be added to water or to diluted cow's milk. A couple of technological innovations then made formula feeding easier: better nursing bottles and nipples made out of plastic rather than pewter, ivory, or silver. For decades parents and many doctors considered substitute milk to be scientifically beyond reproach. In consequence, it became an enormous commercial success. A barrage of shameless advertising heralded the introduction of these milk substitutes. "No More Wet Nurses" declared one from 1869 composed by men who clearly understood their product's niche. Although producers were reluctant to claim that formula food was better than breast milk, they went as close as they could to saying so.[30] Hence there was nothing unusual in a mother writing to *Babyhood* magazine in 1887 explaining, "We have just welcomed our sixth baby, and, as our babies need to be fed after the third month, we are feeding this baby after the second week from its birth."[31]

Enthusiastic claims made about the virtues of formula feeding were to prove tragically mistaken. Mothers who turned to bottle feeding, whether giving their infants straight cow's milk or substitute formula, unwittingly deprived them of a healthy and nutritious diet. Poorer women who opted for the bottle were obliged to mix formula into fluids often contaminated with dangerous bacteria from filthy dairies or polluted water pumps. The impoverished also diluted the powder to save money, with the result that their infants were undernourished. In a study of late-1800s Baltimore, Samuel Preston and Michael Haines found that infants whose mothers worked outside the home and so were probably reliant on breast-milk substitutes perished at a rate about 59% above the average.[32] Rose A. Cheney's analysis of mortality in Philadelphia provides further evidence for the devastating effects of mothers not breast-feeding their babies. She showed that the survival chances of one-year-olds in the later 1800s were significantly better than those of infants. The difference, she explains, lies partly in the fact that if a child survived its first year on formula feed it had almost certainly acquired a reasonable degree of immunity to bacterial or viral assaults. In contrast, babies died at a high rate because they lacked developed digestive systems and immunities to infection.[33] Public health experts were correct in trying to persuade mothers not to turn to milk substitutes and to delay weaning at least until the child's second summer.[34]

The "Scientific" Feeding of Babies

The medical profession from the 1860s onwards was divided on the safety of substitute milk products. Many strongly supported the use of formula whether or not a woman could breast-feed. Opposition arose from doctors and public health advocates who feared that it caused higher rates of rickets and diarrhea. Some regarded formula as intolerable for a less admirable reason. Having come to regard themselves as the chief guardians of human health, learned doctors complained that medical wisdom had been by-passed. "The position occupied by the physician in comparison with that of the vendors of patent foods is very humiliating," complained one doctor.[35] Most aggrieved were the members of the rising specialty of pediatrics who regarded infant feeding as their own domain. The "proper authority for establishing rules for substitute feeding," opined Dr. Thomas Morgan Rotch of Harvard University Medical School, "should emanate from the medical profession, and not from non-medical capitalists."[36] Rotch emerged as the leading exponent of what came to be called "scientific feeding."

Conveniently for the profession of pediatrics, Dr. Thomas Rotch "found" that milk substitute had to be precisely tailored to the individual child. The doctor, he announced, has to constantly adjust the percentages of protein, fat, and sugar in the milk. To provide all of these different varieties of milk, Rotch began by establishing the Walker-Gordon Milk Laboratory in Boston in 1891 and then branched out by building new laboratories from Philadelphia to Grand Rapids, Michigan. His lab's technicians, dressed in the white coats of the scientist, received prescriptions from doctors, prepared bottled milk according to the perceived needs of individual children, and then had bottles delivered directly to mothers in well-heeled neighborhoods. Many doctors were unconformable making complex calculations about feeding infants at the bedside, but they appreciated Rotch for enabling them to fight back against the monopoly of "non-medical capitalists." Some physicians even began to assert that scientifically prepared milk was better than the real thing. This kind of hubris, understandable in a time of soaring confidence in laboratory science, cost the life of many a newborn and child.[37]

COPING WITH THE LOSS OF A CHILD

The death of a child has nearly always brought acute suffering to parents and siblings, but the expression of grief varies according to what each culture permits. Where strict Protestantism was a powerful cultural force in the Northeast, those who lost a child were encouraged to calmly accept bereavement as an expression of God's higher if often inscrutable will.[38] Failing to mourn with moderation could be interpreted as doubting the superiority of divine fiat. The doctrines derived from earlier Puritan theologians further intensified the pain of a child's loss because they insisted that most children are born stained with the sin of Adam and Eve and might end up in Hell. Many parents secretly fulminated against God for taking their children without apparent cause and mourned without moderation in private. But there seems little doubt that the prevailing culture of emotional restraint limited their ability to elicit succor from friends and neighbors.[39]

The nineteenth century saw a strong reaction against Puritan views of the child in life and death. As the traditional Protestant church progressively lost its monopoly over worship, men and women were able to adopt beliefs about sin and the afterlife that were far more congenial to their emotional needs. In place of the innately wicked child who died and suffered damnation there arose a view that children who perished had been too pure for a tawdry world. Books, diaries, and letters of the period are replete with descriptions of the deceased as "pretty innocents," "harmless creatures," and "little doves."[40] Most mothers felt sure that children would be saved and strove to provide an uplifting explanation for their loss. Evangelical authors satisfied a thriving market in tracts in which the death of a sweet, innocent child was shown to have the beneficial effect of inspiring others to lives of the same moral purity. Mary Louisa Alcott's *Little Women* epitomizes the urge to see the demise of the young as ultimately beneficent. When Beth dies after a long period of suffering, her family see her departure as that of a "benignant angel."[41] Of course, expecting to be reunited with a deceased child could provide only limited comfort. Nothing changed the awful fact, conveyed by one Illinois mother, that the child had gone:

> Sleep, little baby, sleep,
> Not in thy mother's arms or cradle bed,
> But in the grave forever with the dead.[42]

In spite of the retreat of hardline Protestant dogmas, callous rationalizations of the misery and death of children still flourished. This is exemplified by the depth of naiveté among southern planters about the capacity for suffering among their slaves. One escaped slave recounted how he had received an aggrieved letter from his ex-mistress, saying: "You know that we reared you as we reared our own children." One wonders how she responded to his apt reply: "Woman, did you raise your *own children* for the market? Did you raise them for the whipping-post?"[43] Most slave owners, lacking any incentive to empathize with their slaves, were oblivious to the terrible suffering of infants, children, and bereaved parents. The ex-slave Fannie Moore of Asheville in North Carolina recalled how her mother was refused permission to leave the field to see her son when he was dying of a fever.[44] We encounter much of the same cold indifference in middle- and upper-class attitudes towards mortality among the offspring of white slum dwellers. Consider the remark of the ex-mayor of New York, Philip Hone, during the 1849 cholera epidemic that boys and girls in the Orange Street district were so revolting that "pigs were contaminated" by them.[45] The respectable classes preferred to regard the heavy burden of death placed on young tenement dwellers as either an unavoidable fact of life or as a judgment on the wickedness of their type. Making cities safer for the young required the overthrow of this brutally pessimistic attitude.

TRYING TO SAVE CHILDREN'S LIVES

In the last two decades of the nineteenth century infant and child mortality finally entered the long period of decline that culminated in today's high levels of survival.[46] Even once-filthy New York City enjoyed a decline in the infant death rate from 273 per 1,000 live births in 1885 to a much more modest 94 per 1,000 live births by the year 1915.[47] These decreases are highly significant. A number of different explanations have been offered for the gradual reduction in the rate at which infants and children were dying by the end of the century.

Medical factors played a valuable but secondary role. Infants and children gained access to more and more dispensaries that provided dental care and basic surgical services and that distributed disinfectants in times of epidemics. The dispensaries were especially important in making smallpox vaccinations easily available to the poor. On a smaller scale, diphtheria antitoxin also had a positive impact from the late 1890s, bringing thousands of children back from the brink of death. William H. Park's New York laboratory tested swabs in order to diagnose the disease and then provided the antitoxin free of charge to needy patients. The fatality rate from diphtheria among admissions to Boston City Hospital plummeted from 47% in 1888 to just 10% in 1899.[48] At the same time, doctors and nurses working for municipal agencies or private charities were going into the worst urban slums to discourage early weaning and instruct mothers in how to feed, clean, and clothe their infants. They also provided basic medical care, in particular placing drops of silver nitrate in the eyes of babies to prevent or cure blindness caused by gonorrhea bacteria.

In other respects medical treatment had little to offer. Children's hospitals were too small to treat more than a minority of youngsters while orphanages, foundling hospitals, and Native American boarding schools guaranteed a heightened risk of infectious disease. In 1897 Luther Emmett Holt, superintendent of the Babies Hospital of New York City, had the candor to note that many of his patients picked up acute infections during their stay.[49] Not even the new specialty of pediatrics initially saved many young lives. What gains were made in understanding the particular ills of childhood were more than offset by the failure of pediatricians to vigorously promote breast-feeding. Nor could pediatricians do much for their young patients. Not until the 1920s and 1930s would they make the key discovery that children with diarrheal diseases ought to be given fluid and electrolytes.[50]

Public health interventions funded by cities and states were considerably more important than any kind of therapeutic institution. Richard Meckel has shown how a growing concern about infant mortality provided a key part of the motivation for the civic authorities to begin to introduce sanitary reform.[51] New initiatives were mounted to supply fresh water that had passed through sand filtration plants, to install sewers to take effluence away, to more efficiently dispose of garbage, and to prohibit hogs in city streets. Laypersons and doctors also set up more milk stations that dispensed free or low-cost milk that had not been watered down. The philanthropist Nathan Strauss opened the most famous of these stations in New York's Lower East Side in 1893. In its first year of operation alone, 34,000 bottles were handed out.[52] These measures significantly reduced the rate at which infants and children contracted diarrheal diseases from contaminated water and food. They may have saved further lives because children who avoided intestinal infections like typhoid and dysentery were then less vulnerable to the microorganisms causing secondary respiratory infections such as tuberculosis, pneumonia, and bronchitis.[53] That sanitary reforms did not safeguard the lives of more babies and children is largely due to the fact that so much remained to be done. Millions of households still did not have access to clean water or drains at the end of the century. Moreover, most milk inspectors did not start to test for bacterial contamination until the early 1900s, and as late as 1911 only 15% of New York's milk supply was being pasteurized.[54]

A number of scholars have argued that by the close of the century economic growth had also started to save the lives of large numbers of infants and children. The British epidemiologist Thomas McKeown claimed that only improvements in nutrition and living standards made possible by rising household incomes could explain overall mortality declines in Britain. More recently, Robert Fogel and Hans Waaler have shown that mortality falls when people achieve adequate diets as reflected by their body mass index. A low body mass index, they assert, is associated with fatal disease because the resilience of the immune system is depressed by chronic malnutrition.[55] In understanding the gradual improvement in the health of young Americans, it may therefore be relevant that late in the century food prices dropped

dramatically with the result that more children could be fed the relatively nutritious diets that help to withstand infections. Technological
changes linked to the expansion of the economy may have complemented improving diets. The invention of electric trolleys reduced the
reliance on horses and the quantity of manure scattered across city
streets. Rose A. Cheney also notes that the greater longevity of children
from around the 1860s coincides with the mechanization of ice cutting.
By the early 1880s, when ice boxes had been adopted by all but the very
poor, food could be kept fresher for much longer than before, and the
chances of contamination went down.[56]

Conflict and Compromise

Although sanitary reform and economic growth were probably the
most important factors in reducing infant and child mortality by 1900,
the medical profession certainly had a lot of potential to improve the
health prospects of poor children. The difficulty lay in the fact that the
provision of free medical care and advice to the lower social classes
conflicted with the financial interests of doctors in private practice.
This tension is obviously apparent in the attitude of many doctors to
the dispensary. They complained bitterly that many of those who
received free care at the dispensary were quite capable of affording
the doctor's fees.[57] In fact, the vast majority of the dispensary's clients
could not possibly have afforded to pay for a consultation with a
doctor. Moreover, the closure of dispensaries that many doctors advocated would have deprived large numbers of families of the benefits
of free smallpox vaccination and the provision of disinfectants.[58]
Private practitioners were similarly furious when New York's municipal laboratory started to provide free diphtheria antitoxin to the poor.
This kind of paternalism deprived doctors of the profits from administering life-saving drugs. They retaliated by declaring the state's generosity to be a form of "municipal socialism." In 1902 over a thousand
New York physicians and druggists signed a petition demanding that
no more antitoxin be given away. No one denied that most patients
would struggle to afford to buy the antitoxin, but many doctors did
not feel that they enjoyed the economic security that allowed them to
be generous.[59]

The most serious and damaging conflicts over the health of poor
children concerned the role of the school health inspector. Public
health officials realized that schools were both primary sites of contagion and the perfect sites in which to diagnose and treat the ills of
the young. Private practitioners had a very different perception of

the state sending practitioners into schools to diagnose and treat children for free. They saw instead the loss of the business from parents who could meet the costs of taking their children to the physician. So they fought the public health authorities into making major concessions. Health inspectors could do no more than to go into schools, perform physical exams, and send a note home with sick children strongly recommending that their parents consult a physician. The many boys and girls whose parents' incomes were too small therefore simply went untreated. In subsequent decades, as the efficacy of medicine increased, this compromise would be a significant obstacle to providing adequate medical care to the children of low-income families.[60]

A mother and her children succumb to yellow fever. Epidemics of yellow fever, usually spread by *Aedes aegypti* mosquitos, regularly devastated southern cities like New Orleans. In 1878 the disease spread up the Mississippi River and then as far north as Cincinnati. In Memphis alone yellow fever killed around 5,000 people. Only in 1900 did American medical scientists demonstrate the role of mosquitos as vectors in transmitting the disease. (© Bettmann/Corbis)

THE BALANCE SHEET

By the end of the century, white infants and children were on average healthier than those born before the Civil War. The beginnings of the large-scale installation of clean water pipes and sewage systems, improved nutrition, and the greater cleanliness of public areas had started to bring down the horrendous mortality rates of previous decades. Many states and cities had accepted responsibility for the health of their citizens, even if a lot still had to be accomplished to make water and milk safe to drink. The gains for the children of African American and Native American populations were far more modest. Although black American health did improve as a result of the abolition of slavery, appalling health disparities persisted. In 1900 they had an average life expectancy at birth of only just over 30 years compared to the nearly 50 years of the average white person.[61] Native Americans fared as badly once they had been corralled onto reservations. Census data suggests that the roughly 237,000 surviving native people could expect to live somewhere between 20 and 35 years at birth.[62] The figures for Native Americans and Africans Americans are shockingly low in part because these populations had to endure terrible rates of infant and child mortality. Poverty and discrimination ensured that nonwhite infants and children entered the new century with the odds stacked very heavily against them.

NOTES

1. Peter Gregg Slater, *Children in the New England Mind in Death and in Life*. Hamden, CT: Archon Books, 1977, p. 68.

2. See Richard A. Meckel, "Levels and Trends of Death and Disease in Childhood, 1620 to the Present," in Janet Golden, Richard A. Meckel, and Heather Munro Prescott (eds.), *Children and Youth in Sickness and in Health: A Historical Handbook and Guide*. Westport, CT: Greenwood Press, 2004, pp. 11–12.

3. Samuel Preston and Michael Haines, *Fatal Years: Child Mortality in Late Nineteenth-Century America*. Princeton, NJ: Princeton University Press, 1991, pp. 3–6.

4. Ibid., pp. 31–32.

5. Gerald Grob, *The Deadly Truth: A History of Disease in America*. Cambridge, MA: Harvard University Press, 2002, p. 140.

6. Ibid., p. 139.

7. Conevery Bolton Valenčius, *The Health of the Country: How American Settlers Understood Themselves and Their Land*. New York: Basic Books, 2002, p. 6.

8. Grob, *The Deadly Truth*, Chapters 5 and 6.

9. Howard Markel, "For the Welfare of Children," in Alexandra Minna Stern and Howard Markel (eds.), *Formative Years: Children's Health in the United States, 1880–2000*. Ann Arbor: University of Michigan Press, 2002, pp. 47–65, p. 52.

10. Jacob Riis, *How the Other Half Lives: Studies among the Tenements of New York*. New York: Charles Scribner's Sons, 1914, p. 188.

11. Meckel, "Levels and Trends of Death and Disease in Childhood," p. 10.

12. Grob, *The Deadly Truth*, p. 117–8.

13. John Mack Faragher, *Sugar Creek: Life on the Illinois Prairie*. New Haven, CT: Yale University Press, 1986, pp. 88–89.

14. Ramon Powers and James N. Leiker, "Cholera among the Plains Indians: Perceptions, Causes, Consequences," *The Western Historical Quarterly* 29, no. 3 (Autumn 1998), 317–40, p. 323.

15. Richard White, *The Roots of Dependency: Subsistence, Environment, and Social Change among the Choctaws, Pawnees, and Navajo*. Lincoln: University of Nebraska Press, 1983.

16. Marilyn Irwin Holt, *Indian Orphanages*. Lawrence: University Press of Kansas, 2001, p. 39.

17. David S. Jones, "The Persistence of American Indian Health Disparities," *American Journal of Public Health* 96, no. 12 (December 2006), 2122–34, p. 2127.

18. Brenda Child, "Homesickness, Illness, and Death: Native-American Girls in Government Boarding Schools," in Barbara Bair and Susan E. Cayleff (eds.), *Wings of Gauze: Women of Color and the Experience of Health and Illness*. Detroit, MI: Wayne State University Press, 1993, p. 178.

19. Marie Jenkins Schwarz, *Birthing a Slave: Motherhood and Medicine in the Antebellum South*. Cambridge, MA: Harvard University Press, 2010, p. 90.

20. Jacqueline Jones, *Labor of Love, Labor of Sorrow: Black Women, Work and the Family, from Slavery to the Present*. New York: Basic Books, 2010, p. 60.

21. Gretchen Long, *Doctoring Freedom: The Politics of African American Medical Care in Slavery and Emancipation*. Chapel Hill: University of North Carolina Press, 2012, p. 11.

22. Priscilla Ferguson Clement, *Growing Pains: Children in the Industrial Age, 1850–1890*. New York: Twayne Publishers, 1997, p. 67.

23. Steckel, "A Dreadful Childhood," p. 430.

24. Todd L. Savitt, *Medicine and Slavery: The Diseases and Health Care of Blacks in Antebellum Virginia*. Urbana: University of Illinois Press, 2002, p. 122.

25. Clement, *Growing Pains*, p. 68.

26. Heather Munro Prescott, "Stories of Childhood Health and Disease," in Golden et al., *Children and Youth*, p. 29.

27. Jim Downs, *Sick from Freedom: African-American Illness and Suffering during the Civil War and Reconstruction*. New York: Oxford University Press, 2012, p. 21.

28. Ann Marie Plane, "Childbirth Practices among Native American Women of New England and Canada, 1600–1800," in Leavitt (ed.), *Women and Health in America*, pp. 38–47, p. 42.

29. Janet Golden, *A Social History of Wet Nursing in America: From Breast to Bottle*. New York: Cambridge University Press, 1996, Chapters 1–3.

30. Golden, *Social History of Wet Nursing*, pp. 78, 134; Rima D. Apple, *Mothers and Medicine: A Social History of Infant Feeding, 1890–1950*. Madison: University of Wisconsin Press, 1987; and Harvey Levenstein, " 'Best for Babies' or 'Preventable Infanticide'? The Controversy over Artificial Feeding of Infants in America, 1880–1920," *Journal of American History* 70, no. 1 (1993), 76.

31. Jacqueline Wolf, "Low Breastfeeding Rates and Public Health in the United States," *American Journal of Public Health* 93, no. 12 (December 2003), 2000–2010.

32. Preston and Haines, *Fatal Years*, p. 27.

33. Rose A. Cheney, "Seasonal Aspects of Infant and Childhood Mortality: Philadelphia, 1865–1920," *The Journal of Interdisciplinary History* 14, no. 3 (1984), 561–85.

34. Jacqueline H. Wolf, *Don't Kill Your Baby: Public Health and the Decline of Breastfeeding in the 19th and 20th Centuries*. Columbus: Ohio State University Press, 2001, p. 104.

35. Richard A. Meckel, *Save the Babies: American Public Health Reform and the Prevention of Infant Mortality, 1850–1929*. Baltimore, MD: Johns Hopkins University Press, 1990, p. 55.

36. Apple, *Mothers and Medicine*, p. 24.

37. Levenstein, " 'Best for Babies' or 'Preventable Infanticide'?"

38. Slater, *Children in the New England Mind*, p. 15.

39. Nancy Schrom Dye and Daniel Blake, "Mother Love and Infant Death, 1750–1920," *The Journal of American History* 73, no. 2 (September 1986), 329–53, p. 339.

40. Slater, *Children in the New England Mind*, p. 70.

41. Heather Munro Prescott, "Stories of Childhood Health and Disease," in Golden et al., *Children and Youth*, p. 31.

42. Faragher, *Sugar Creek*, p. 95.

43. Howard Zinn, *A People's History of the United States*. New York: The New Press, 2013, p. 136.

44. Sharla M. Fett, *Working Cures: Healing, Health, and Power on Southern Slave Plantations*. Chapel Hill: University of North Carolina Press, 2002, p. 31.

45. Charles Rosenberg, *The Cholera Years: The United States in 1832, 1849, and 1866*. Chicago: University of Chicago Press, 1987, p. 107.

46. Michael R. Haines, "The Population of the Unites States, 1790–1920," in Stanley L. Engerman and Robert E. Gallman (eds.), *The Cambridge Economic History of the United States*. Cambridge, England: Cambridge University Press, 2000, p. 153; and Michael R. Haines and Richard H. Steckel (eds.), *A Population History of North America*. New York: Cambridge University Press, 2001.

47. Gretchen and Crimmins-Gardner, "Public Health Measures and Morality in US Cities in the Late Nineteenth Century," *Human Ecology* 6, no. 1 (1978), 27–54.

48. Preston and Haines, *Fatal Years*, p. 13.

49. Ibid., p. 12.

50. Ibid., p. 17.

51. Meckel, *Save the Babies*.

52. Stern and Markel (eds.), *Formative Years*, p. 5.

53. Simon Szreter, "Rethinking McKeown: The Relationship between Public Health and Social Change," *American Journal of Public Health* 92, no. 5 (2002), 722–25.

54. Preston and Haines, *Fatal Years*, pp. 23–24.

55. David Cutler and Grant Miller, "The Role of Public Health Improvements in Health Advances: The Twentieth Century United States,"*Demography* 42, no. 1 (2005), 1–22; and R. W. Fogel, "Economic Growth, Population Theory, and Physiology: The Bearing of Long-Term Principles on the Making of Economic Policy," *American Economic Review* 84 (1994), 369–95.

56. Cheney, "Seasonal Aspects," pp. 580, 584.

57. Paul Starr, *The Social Transformation of American Medicine*. New York: Basic Books, 1982, p. 83.

58. Ibid., p. 183.

59. Ibid., p. 187.

60. Ibid., p. 188.

61. Thomas A. LaVeist, *Minority Populations and Health: An Introduction to Health Disparities in the U.S.* San Francisco, CA: John Wiley & Sons, 2011, p. 69.

62. Nancy Shoemaker, *American Indian Population Recovery in the Twentieth Century*. Albuquerque: University of New Mexico Press, 1999, p. 9.

CHAPTER 6

Infectious Disease

The road leading to the modern prosperity of the United States is covered with the corpses of long-forgotten men, women, and children who died of infectious disease. They perished in high numbers for several reasons: the ease with which certain microorganisms and disease vectors reproduced and spread in the American climate; the appalling sanitary conditions of slave plantations, burgeoning cities, native reservations, frontier settlements, and army encampments; and the damage wrought to the immune systems of slaves, indigenous peoples, white settlers, and the urban poor by severe dietary deficiencies. Only in the last decades of the century did the vulnerability to infectious disease of some sections of American society begin to decline. Sanitary reform, economic growth, and the abolition of slavery all contributed to a sustained fall in the incidence of diarrheal and respiratory infections. Even so, rates of death due to contagious maladies remained extremely high by modern standards. Chronic poverty, discrimination, and policies of systematic oppression also ensured that African Americans and Native Americans died on average significantly younger than members of the white population.[1]

THE SPECTER OF INFECTIOUS DISEASE

Americans were at the mercy of the interplay between pathogens and prevailing climate. Heat played an especially important role in

promoting bacterial and viral infections. The semitropical South provided a congenial incubator for typhoid and intestinal disorders like
dysentery. Yellow fever also thrived in the warm moistness of the
South, repeatedly devastating cities located, like New Orleans, on
the sweltering Gulf Coast. So many Louisianans died in the 1853 epidemic that newspapers spoke of "a feast of horror" during which
coffins burst open due to the build-up of putrefaction inside.[2] In
addition, the heat of the South sustained high levels of malaria.
With the *Anopheles* mosquito able to survive year-round, South
Carolina became notorious for malarial fever. The toll taken by this
infection obliged the South Carolinians to abandon two of their early
state capitals. Only the cooler Northeast managed to escape the routine depredations of yellow fever and malaria. The port communities
of the Middle Atlantic and New England were struck hard by yellow
fever between 1793 and 1822, but thereafter their more tepid weather
held it at bay. A relatively cool climate also kept New England
largely free of malaria.[3]

The rapidly colonized Midwest was not so fortunate. The vast and
rugged lands in which those of European descent settled during the
great western migration contained no shortage of biological hazards.
Following the arduous overland trails from Independence, Missouri,
to California, migrants were hit by diarrheal diseases caused by
protozoans native to where they camped or settled. Migrants also
brought along their own agents of disease and death. In the early
1800s they carried west the malaria-bearing *Anopheles* mosquito. In
the Midwest its larvae flourished in countless streams, rivers, and
ponds fed by melting snows and in the stagnant pools formed due
to the poor drainage capacities of prairie soils. Settlers in states like
Ohio, Michigan, Wisconsin, Indiana, and Illinois then constructed
mill ponds in which mosquito larvae grew. Their small, filthy, damp,
and windowless cabins provided ideal environments for adult mosquitos to infect human hosts. Many people lived with the chronic
anemia induced by the malarial parasite, weakened by the destruction of their hemoglobin, and left prey to deadlier maladies by the
weakening of their immune systems. Rates of infant mortality from
dysentery and typhoid were also tragically high, in part because digging wells was so time-consuming that drinking water often became
contaminated with feces long before new wells could be excavated.
Those heading further west introduced malaria to areas like Oregon
where the *Anopheles* mosquito vector was already present but which
had been free of the malarial parasite. Deadly diarrheal diseases soon
joined the migration. White gold-seekers inadvertently discarded

The smallpox troubles in Milwaukee. Basic disagreements about the safety of smallpox vaccination in Milwaukee were exacerbated by political and ethnic divisions within the city. When smallpox struck in 1894–1895 many among Milwaukee's Polish and German populations felt that the attempt to quarantine sufferers was the act of an arbitrary Health Department that had no regard for immigrant culture or individual rights. Furious and frightened mobs attacked police officers with clubs and stones and hurled scalding water at ambulance horses to prevent the infected being taken away to the isolation hospital. Drawing by G. A. Davis from a sketch by Fred Doughtery, 1894. (© Bettmann/Corbis)

millions of lethal bacilli in pools of water that later prospectors had no choice but to drink. Native American populations suffered terribly as a result.[4]

Rapidly expanding trading networks enhanced the ability of migrants and traders to convey infectious disease. Courtesy of the Erie Canal, cholera marched swiftly west, having reached New York City in 1832. The faster steamboats and railroads of the post–Civil War period enabled the *Aedes aegypti* mosquito to carry yellow fever deep into Tennessee and Ohio. The 1878 epidemic was carried so far up the Mississippi river valley that it killed 10% of the populations of Vicksburg and Memphis.[5] Entrepots were naturally the hardest hit by diseases arriving from overseas. Merchant ships from the West Indies regularly delivered yellow fever to New Orleans. The cholera bacillus appears to have undergone a genetic mutation in Jessore, India, near Calcutta in about 1817 that increased its virulence and launched it as a pandemic. From India it made its way, via major trade routes, into Russia and western Europe and then across the Atlantic. As many as 150,000 Americans perished in the first and deadliest of the continent's four cholera epidemics.[6] At the end of the century a fear of contagion prompted California to maintain relatively stringent quarantine policies. These were not enough to keep out a ship that arrived in San Francisco in 1900 and caused the deaths of about 100 people from bubonic plague.[7] A more interconnected world brought with it heavy risks of contagion.

So did the rapid urbanization of the nineteenth century United States. In 1790 there were only six urban areas with over 3,000 people. By 1850 this number had leaped to 85, and commercial centers like New York, Boston, and New Orleans were expanding at a breathless pace. Unregulated and therefore almost entirely haphazard, this phase of urbanization triggered a rapid upswing in death rates.[8] The heavy concentration of people in towns and cities inevitably led to heightened death rates. High population density made it possible for pathogens to become endemic by providing bacteria and viruses with a constant supply of fresh hosts. Yellow fever became an ongoing threat to the inhabitants of New Orleans after 1800 when a population of just 10,000 swelled to 27,000 within 20 years after the influx of rural migrants, immigrants from Europe, and French refugees fleeing the slaughter of the Haitian Revolution.[9] Overcrowding then allowed for the easy transmission of respiratory diseases. While the average Bostonian dwelling in 1800 had contained 8.3 persons, by 1845 a claustrophobic 10.6 were typically crammed together. Between 1820 and 1850 the population density of Manhattan almost doubled.[10] Hundreds of thousands of people now lived in what Cincinnati's Bishop Purcell described as "filthy and disgusting hovels."[11] City dwellers were constantly assailed by airborne germs contained in the breath, mucus, and sputum of the sick. Tuberculosis, that "great destroyer of human health and human life," in the words of the sanitarian Lemuel Shattuck, now took "the first rank as an agent of death."[12] Influenza, pneumonia, diphtheria, scarlet fever, measles, and whooping cough spread just as rapidly in poorly ventilated tenements, workshops, and factories. So too did the lice that bore typhus and travelled easily among the unwashed clothes of the urban poor.

Almost as devastating as respiratory maladies were the intestinal diseases caused by abysmal sanitary conditions. As urban areas engulfed the outlying countryside, people were increasingly forced to collect drinking water from city wells often polluted by nearby sewers. Public health advocates decried the proliferation of overflowing privies, stagnant pools of fetid water, and piles of rotting garbage. New Yorkers are said to have been amazed in 1832 when a long-overdue sweeping revealed that there were cobblestones beneath the thick muck of the city's streets.[13] In 1853 another delayed clean-up of New York City led to the removal of 439 large animal carcasses, as well as 71 dogs, 93 cats, 17 sheep, 4 goats, and 19 hogs. These were ideal conditions for Asiatic cholera to take hold. Far more devastating, however, were the diarrheal infections that never went away. An appalling 25.1 out of every 1,000 people in New York between 1840 and 1845 died each year due to drinking contaminated water or eating food laced with bacteria.[14]

As a result of urbanization, migration, and trade, Americans were dying sooner and getting sick more often in the mid-1800s than they had at the start of the century. Between the years 1800 and 1809, a white American male or female alive at the age of 20 could expect to live for an additional 46.4 or 47.9 years respectively. These figures had sunk to just 40.8 and 39.5 between 1850 and 1859.[15] The disease risks of urban areas, prairies, and plains explain one of the most striking aspects of the nineteenth-century American experience: people were on average significantly shorter of stature than their colonial-era predecessors. Whites who fought in the Revolutionary War were about as tall as their counterparts in World War II. Those born in 1860 were over an inch shorter. Their growth had almost certainly been impaired by the dangerous disease environments of their childhoods.[16]

INFECTIOUS DISEASE AND THE NATIVE POPULATION

Native Americans bore a terrible burden of infectious disease due to a combination of immunological susceptibilities and the white man's determination to seize their traditional lands. English, German, and Scottish immigrants began moving into western Pennsylvania and Tennessee during the late 1770s. They then pushed further into the Midwest and by mid-century were pouring across to the Pacific Coast in search of gold and land. After 1869 white migrants could travel the entire distance to San Francisco Bay by railroad. This mass movement of peoples and the growing integration of the U.S. economy endangered the lives of hundreds of thousands of indigenous people. They were repeatedly hit by lethal epidemics to which most of the white and black population had acquired immunity. The 1801–1802 smallpox pandemic virtually destroyed the Omaha, the Ponca, the Oto, and the Iowa and badly affected the Crow and the Sioux. When smallpox reached the Pawnees in the early 1830s as much as half of their population died. A witness spoke of bodies everywhere, "laying about in the river, lodged on sand-bars, in the hog-weeds ... and in their old corn caches; others again were dragged off by the hungry dogs of the prairie, where they were torn to pieces by the more hungry wolves and buzzards." A few years later smallpox descended on the native societies of the Upper Missouri and cut the Mandan down from a population above 1,600 to a mere 100 souls. The same epidemic also shattered the Arikara, the Minnetaree, and the Assiniboine.[17] Largely due to the depredations of infectious diseases the numbers of Native Americans fell from around 600,000 in 1800 to a mere 237,000 by 1900.[18]

Native people suffered especially badly from contagious maladies caught while being driven by soldiers into new and unfamiliar territories. The Choctaws lost about 15% of their population during their removal. Roughly half of the Creeks and Seminoles perished as they were forced to the west, and about 4,000 out of 16,000 Cherokee men, women, and children did not survive the Trail of Tears of the late 1830s as disease and exposure took their toll. Several decades of Indian wars west of the Mississippi subsequently left native peoples struggling to obtain the nutrition required to fight off infection. The deliberate destruction of the bison herds in order to break native resistance also led to widespread malnutrition and a heightened susceptibility to diseases like smallpox and tuberculosis. Equivalent episodes of the destruction of native ways of life occurred across the Americas. In 1892 white hunters in Alaska almost eliminated the sea otter and thereby reduced indigenous hunters to near starvation.[19] Government policy continued to have a murderous effect on Native Americans as they were moved onto reservations. By never staying in one place for long, plains Indians had not allowed filth to accumulate or parasites to flourish.[20] Now they were forced to farm inferior land and dwell in crowded and airless cabins. These conditions resulted in rates of tuberculosis up to five times the level endured by the white population.[21]

SLAVERY AND INFECTIOUS DISEASE

Chattel slavery added most to the lot of suffering and death in the Americas of the nineteenth century. Even though some people of African descent had genetic advantages in combating malaria and yellow fever, their biological heritage could offer limited defence against the appalling living and working conditions on plantations.[22]

A comparison of data on ex-slaves who volunteered to fight for the Union and southern whites who fought for the Confederacy tells of a heavy burden of disease: black adult recruits were on average about two inches shorter than whites. African American slaves succumbed in terrible numbers to respiratory diseases like tuberculosis, pneumonia, whooping cough, measles, chicken pox, and mumps to which their ancestors had not been regularly exposed. Forced to live in cramped, drafty, and damp quarters heightened the risks of being exposed to these maladies. The filth amid which they were obliged to reside also provided breeding grounds for the mosquitos that caused malaria and yellow fever and the flies that spread cholera, salmonella, and dysentery.[23]

Plantation labor rendered slaves still more susceptible to infectious diseases. Backbreaking work, frequent beatings, and diets lacking in several amino acids and vitamins reduced the slaves' resistance to infection.[24] Depleted immunity gave rise to endemic elephantiasis around Charleston in South Carolina: grotesque scrotal, labial, or leg and foot swellings caused by mosquito bites. Many slaves also had to endure hookworm, which attached to the intestinal mucus, sucked blood, and caused the sufferer lethargy and stunted growth. Those toiling knee-deep in water on the rice plantations of South Carolina and coastal Georgia were at especially high risk of acquiring debilitating parasitic infections.[25] After Emancipation, African Americans continued to die younger than the average white. Heavily indebted to white landowners, those who toiled as sharecroppers experienced hard and usually truncated lives. The many thousands who preferred to find work in the cities of the North or South lived for even shorter periods. But the average lifespan for both rural and urban African Americans after the Civil War was still higher than during the period of slavery.[26]

THE CULTURE OF "LIVE AND LET DIE"

Many of the diseases that sickened and killed urban Americans could have been tackled early in the century if the authorities had taken concerted action. Several obstacles stood in the way of an effective response. Few towns were able to draw on traditions of sanitary intervention, and most churches focused on individual piety rather than obviating the causes of social distress.[27] Moreover, reaching any degree of consensus as to the most appropriate public health policies proved extremely hard where the epidemiological data were so confusing and physicians disagreed so much about the causes of epidemics: involving doctors in health boards, noted one New Yorker, would just lead to "interminable disputes."[28] Other key deterrents to doing something about the sanitary horrors of the age were firmly rooted in economics. Effective quarantine laws were notoriously hard to get past state legislatures when inspections and long delays cost powerful merchants and traders money.[29] The anticontagionist lobby could also count on sympathetic physicians such as Dr. J. McNulty of New York, who, during a convention on public health, dubbed quarantine to be nothing but a "commercial curse."[30] Even when quarantine measures were adopted they were maddeningly hard to enforce. Captains often bribed enforcement personnel, and sometimes the officers on board trading vessels who had no desire to be delayed ferried cholera sufferers to the shore and dumped them on beaches before entering port.[31]

Economics played an equally important role in blocking sanitary reforms. Most tax-payers were averse to forking out to clean up cities, secure clean water supplies, and install adequate systems of sanitation. The vast social inequalities that had opened up in the decades after the Revolution combined with the rapid pace of urbanization nurtured a profound a lack of sympathy among the elites for the plight of the underclass. The lowest classes had been transformed into a faceless and nameless mass whose sufferings did not prick the consciences of wealthier citizens as they might have done in rural areas in which rich and poor often knew one another by name. Hence Dr. George Shrady, editor of the *Medical Record*, declared that the public health movement threw away money on "worthless and undeserving persons."[32] The influx of Irish immigrants in the 1840s and 1850s intensified the indifference of Protestant tax-payers, who mostly regarded Hibernians as innately inferior heretics.[33] With self-serving inaccuracy, the propertied insisted that most slum dwellers were merely lazy when in fact they were more often young, aged, or infirm. Such attitudes were not expressions of republican individualism but sprang from a timeless human selfishness. As the Providence-born sanitarian Charles V. Chapin explained, "Our business leads us to the depletion of men's pockets and the restriction of their liberty. We cannot expect the thanks of those who might feel themselves aggrieved."[34] A high-sounding credo of individual moral improvement issued from the pulpits and assemblies of the early nineteenth-century United States. But it was no substitute for fresh water and decent drains.

Self-interest in the form of the notorious corruption of city officials created an additional barrier to public health reform. New Yorkers dubbed the filth collecting in their city's streets as "corporation pie" in sarcastic reference to the graft at Tammany Hall. One Wisconsin chronicler, appalled by the inaction of his city's authorities, wryly observed that "human nature predominates in an Alderman."[35] During epidemics the inaction of city authorities drove at least some concerned citizens to take action. In southern states, the Howard Association organized young businessmen in the wake of the 1837 yellow fever epidemic to provide medicines, housing, and food for victims. Cholera outbreaks also moved private citizens to act where city governments remained supine. But the efforts of philanthropists were insufficient to bring about lasting sanitary improvements.[36]

THE SLOW BEGINNINGS OF SANITARY REFORM

At the start of the century sanitation remained primarily the responsibility of individual citizens. In 1804 New York appointed a city inspector to try to ensure that residents obeyed the law and kept the streets clean outside of their houses. The law had little effect because it failed to equip the inspector with the power to punish violators. Like every American city, New York swiftly found itself losing the battle against filth as more and more people from overseas and rural regions flooded into its tenement districts. When hit by epidemics of yellow fever or cholera, city authorities created or revived health boards to implement *ad hoc* measures: cleaning the streets, draining fetid pools, pouring disinfectants into gutters, emptying overflowing privies, and maybe knocking down a few of the worst slums over the outraged cries of the slumlords. A few cities made a more determined effort to combat the rising pollution of air, streets, and rivers. Philadelphia had by far the most advanced system by 1801 that involved using a steam engine to pump water through wooden pipes from a clean water source outside of the city. A few states and cities also took on the threat of smallpox by promoting vaccination using fresh cowpox matter.[37] But a weak sense of collective identity in American towns and cities meant that such efforts were exceptions to a general rule of neglect, indifference, or opposition. Nearly all health boards became effectively defunct with the passing of the immediate disease threat. The few that were made permanent were all poorly funded. In 1848 the city of Washington's Health Board had a derisory annual budget of $15.[38]

In most cities residents prioritized convenience and economic self-interest over the health of their neighbors. New York had to pass a law to try to stop people installing their privies within 30 feet of public drinking wells. New laws to stop residents allowing their hogs and cows to roam the streets were routinely flouted. In Pittsburgh, Pennsylvania, quickly emerging as a town of conspicuous filth, the

authorities responded to the failure of citizens to keep their streets clean
by strapping groups of eight or a dozen of the elderly poor to scrapers
and making them walk the streets pushing the dirt before them.
Nothing else seemed to work.[39] Even those paid to keep cities clean
typically put profit first. The collectors assigned to gather up the dirt
in several cities left behind everything but the manure that they could
sell. In another demonstration of the power of self-interest to stymie reform, in 1816 Madison, Indiana, installed a system of wooden pipes
with plugs that people could remove in order to fill their buckets with
clean water. The men who had once made a living by carting inferior-
quality water around town for sale took axes to the pipes. It would take
three decades before Madison replaced the wreckage.[40]

SANITARY REFORM ACCELERATES

Around mid-century a number of cities began to undertake serious
public health programs. Chicago is a good example of the new spirit
of activism. With its flat terrain and nonporous soil, the city became a
quagmire in heavy rain. Citizens also had to draw their water from
the mouth of Lake Michigan in which the city's garbage and feces collected. So hard was the city's ground that the existing sewers comprised brick tunnels running above the streets, with the result that
they were unable to carry away the filthy rainwater that collected
during storms. In the 1850s the city fathers appointed Ellis Sylvester
Chesbrough as the chief engineer for a comprehensive sewage system.
The son of an impoverished businessmen, Chesbrough had had to start
work at the age of nine but rose with little formal training to the post of
chief engineer of the Boston Water Works' West Division. His solution
to Chicago's drainage problem was a model of ingenuity. He had the
downtown buildings raised up as much as 10 feet above the level of
his new sewers using a complex array of jacks, and he then had the
Chicago River dredged in order to be able to pack earth around the
pipes to create a new ground level. Filth and groundwater now poured
into underground sewers. Chesbrough, it was said, had "pulled
Chicago out of the mud."[41] The main shortcoming of his design was
that the city's effluence still ran into Lake Michigan. After having visited the sanitary systems of over a dozen European cities, Chesbrough
returned to Chicago to plan another brilliant engineering feat. He had
workmen dig a tunnel running for two miles under Lake Michigan connecting the city to a crib in the lake into which fresh water flowed. The
quality of workmanship and planning were so high that the two teams
of tunnel diggers, one starting out from the city and another excavating

Construction of a sewage system in Nebraska, ca. 1889. By the late 1800s, the devastating and terrifying toll of epidemic and endemic diseases like typhoid, yellow fever, cholera, and dysentery forced cities to create active health departments. Bringing in supplies of clean water and carrying away effluence demanded large-scale civil engineering projects. (Library of Congress)

towards them from out in the lake, met in the middle only a millimeter away from a perfect fit.[42]

Several other cities showed a similar willingness to improve sanitary conditions. After 1844 some New York residents had the benefits of fresh water from the Croton Reservoir channeled into the city over the Croton Aqueduct. Soon after, Boston completed the construction of the Cochituate Aqueduct and enjoyed a plentiful supply of clean water.[43] With death rates still remaining high, popular pressure grew in New York City for the creation of a health office that actually did the job assigned to it. During the 1860s Dr. Stephen Smith led the charge against what he dubbed "the most corrupt and corrupting municipal government in the civilized world." The existing Health Department, he stormed, "does little for health, but much for disease and death." The city inspector tried to brush him off by blaming its problems on immigrants. Twice in 1865 the New York legislature rejected public health bills. A year later the Municipal Health Bill passed and New York acquired a new health department for the metropolitan area with genuine powers to make and enforce sanitary laws.[44] It was the first comprehensive piece of public health legislation in the United States. Unfortunately, not everywhere followed New York's example. Newark, New Jersey, formed a health board in 1857 that proceeded to do absolutely nothing for two decades.[45]

But levels of health activism were unquestionably on the rise. The main impetus to reform was the fact that urban growth had become a problem that all social classes confronted every day as they walked amid the debris of city streets and breathed in the malodorous air. The population of Boston had grown by a factor of seven between 1800 and 1860, Philadelphia had expanded eightfold in the same period, and Chicago had exploded from a mere 5,000 residents in 1840 to well over 100,000 twenty years later. The full horrors of life in the tenement districts were also being forcefully brought to the attention of lawmakers and citizens by the detailed reports published by men like Lemuel Shattuck in New England and Stephen Smith in New York. Shattuck's 1850 *Report of the Sanitary Commission of Massachusetts* stood as a model of the careful statistical analysis of health data. With brutal precision it revealed the alarming facts of the nation's losses to infectious disease.[46] In the following decade Stephen Smith organized teams of young physicians to document the sights, smells, and sicknesses of New York's slums. Smith's inspectors described a litany of sanitary sins, including countless privies spilling out on to floors and streets, animal blood draining into rivers from the slaughterhouses of Thirty-Ninth Street, and children raised in tenements adjacent to stinking stables and bone-boiling establishments. Sanitarians like Shattuck and Smith pressed home the vital point that disease in the slums had much less to do with individual vice than with the dreadful conditions in which people were forced to live.

For the respectable classes, feeling that something had to be done usually meant that they were being personally affected by declining sanitary conditions. Rich and poor residents of Chicago had both been troubled by their streets regularly turning into swamps. New Yorkers of the highest social class had good reason to fear contracting cholera and typhoid when they had to pay young boys to sweep paths for them through the garbage of Broadway in order to get to their offices.[47] Even if many of the well-to-do could leave the city for less malodorous suburbs in the evening, they had to return the next day to filth and foulness. The concerns of wealthier citizens for their own health increased around mid-century as the theory of contagion gained credence after the research of European physicians and scientists like John Snow, William Budd, and Max von Pettenkofer. Decades before germ theory took hold, wealthier Americans had calculated that it might be safest to support public health initiatives even if the greatest benefits would probably fall to the urban masses. After all, there was no telling what fatal contagions a lower-class servant might bring from the slums to the house of her genteel employer.[48]

Merchants and businessmen also became more inclined to think that preventing epidemics might ultimately save them money. When yellow fever struck Memphis in 1878, half the population escaped the city, desperately trying to find temporary accommodation in spite of the barricades swiftly erected by well-armed residents in outlying towns. Most of those who stayed behind caught the disease, and about 5,000 of them died. In these brutal months yellow fever had paralyzed trade and business. After this disaster the Memphis business leaders who had once been so obdurately opposed to health boards demanded a sanitary survey which, as John Duffy relates, found 6,000 homes with overflowing toilets and hundreds of shallow wells a short distance from seeping privies. Terrified of another catastrophic blow to business, they called in one of the most brilliant exponents of public health reform, Colonel George E. Waring Jr., who oversaw a complete sanitary makeover.[49] When this apostle of cleanliness had finished, only two wards lacked sewers, and the annual death rate had fallen from a scandalous 46.6 per 1,000 to a much more respectable 21.5 per 1,000.[50]

Businessmen in other cities now came to see that cleanliness and low death rates were useful for projecting a favorable urban image to potential investors. When the city council of New Orleans failed to support public health initiatives in the 1870s, local business owners set up their own society to tackle sanitary hazards under the motto, "Public Health is Public Wealth."[51] They knew that few people wanted to invest in notoriously sickly cities. Furthermore, many recognized that infectious disease hindered economic growth by killing or incapacitating workers, so the exponents of sanitary laws emphasized the massive waste to the economy caused by sickness. They knew that such arguments appealed to pragmatic minds where loftier talk of charity or duty failed to register.[52] In the last decades of the century, enough people had a vested interest in promoting the healthfulness of towns and cities that they were willing to put their trust and at least some tax dollars into funding new cadres of public health experts and engineers.

PUBLIC HEALTH IN THE ASCENDANT

In the last three decades of the century more cities and states accepted the need for sanitary reform. By 1878, 50 U.S. cities had set up health departments and 16 states had appointed boards of health. Chicago once again led the way in improving the quality of drinking water. Taking up an idea proposed by Chesbrough, sanitary engineers in the 1890s set about stopping filthy water flowing into Lake Michigan by constructing a canal that reversed the flow of the Chicago River so that it now carried polluted water away to the south. Other cities quickly followed suit. In 1870 only about 17% of Americans had access to public water supplies. This number leaped to 42% in 1896. Most of these programs had been inspired by a belief that airborne or waterborne miasmas caused infectious disease. But by the 1880s sanitarians were refining their approach in light of germ theory. Sanitary engineers now introduced sand filtration to significantly reduce the bacterial content of drinking water. Filtered public water had barely existed in the United States in 1870, but 310,000 city dwellers had access to it in 1890 and 1,860,000 by 1900.[53]

Reducing the transmission of the tuberculosis bacillus became another overriding concern of health workers. Schools drilled students in the importance of not spitting and of always coughing into a handkerchief. New York health officials distributed a pamphlet translated into German, Italian, and Yiddish that explained how to avoid passing the disease on to loved ones and neighbors in cramped tenements. New York also introduced a compulsory registry of the tuberculous in 1893, and the laboratory set up by Hermann M. Biggs and William H. Park offered a 24-hour turnaround on swabs sent to it by physicians. The fear of contagion also inspired the construction of sanitaria for quarantining the tuberculous. By 1900 there were already 34 sanatoriums with 4,485 beds available in the United States, to which consumptives went hoping for a cure and to avoid infecting loved ones. In 1903 New York City also opened a custodial hospital at Riverside for those who refused to observe strict guidelines about preventing transmission.[54] Not that these measures were always welcomed or adopted. Many physicians preferred to reject the germ theory of tuberculosis because they feared losing clients if they gained a reputation for reporting tuberculous patients to the authorities.[55]

Germ theory also underpinned new initiatives to treat the diseases of the poor. Park's New York laboratory provided free diphtheria antitoxin to impoverished patients after 1894. Dispensaries also proliferated in many states, offering free vaccinations and minor surgery to members of the lower classes who could not afford to consult private practitioners. Likewise, health boards and volunteer organizations sent doctors and nurses to the homes of immigrant families to instruct them in how to maintain a semblance of hygiene in spite of the appalling conditions of the slums. In 1876 Dr. Charles F. Chandler of New York founded the Summer Corps, hiring 50 physicians to visit tenements and give state-of-the-art advice on health and hygiene. Such endeavors were complemented by the work of school health inspectors who examined pupils and informed parents when they needed medical treatment.[56]

Health boards turned their efforts to improving milk safety once sanitary experts realized that a bottle of milk might smell fine and yet carry bacteria that caused fatal diarrhea or tuberculosis from infected cows. Against strident opposition from dairy farmers, in 1889 the City Council of Philadelphia appointed a milk inspector with the power to ensure that milk was not only nutritious but also produced by healthy cows. Laboratories in Philadelphia, New York, and Chicago were soon inspecting batches of milk for bacterial contamination and in 1897 Chicago mandated the pasteurization of milk.[57] At the same time, U.S. public health authorities were launching hard-hitting public information campaigns to persuade mothers to feed their infants at the breast. Correctly identifying the fall in rates of breast-feeding as a major cause of infant and child mortality, they implored mothers to delay weaning until at least the infant's second summer.[58]

The knowledge of germs as well as a new mandate to tackle environmental health hazards on a large scale converged to produce the first major achievement of the United States in medical science. Physicians had long believed yellow fever to be caused by poisonous airborne miasmas. In order to reduce the risk of yellow fever spreading to North America, in 1898 the redoubtable Colonel Waring had been sent to Havana in Cuba to oversee the installation of a sewage system and proper garbage collection. Waring implemented his plan. He then perished of yellow fever as rates of the disease remained devastatingly high. Encouraged by the work of the Cuban scientist Carlos Finlay to examine the possible role of mosquitos rather than filth, Walter Reed and his colleagues managed to prove that the disease is spread by the mosquito species *Aedes aegypti*. They then dispatched engineers to eliminate almost every imaginable breeding ground. Levels of yellow fever rapidly fell.[59]

THE RECOVERY BEGINS

Annual mortality levels were about 21–23 per 1,000 in the 1850s and roughly 20 per 1,000 in 1880. Between 1890 and 1900 they had fallen to 17.6 and were getting better with each passing decade. New York,

Boston, Philadelphia, and New Orleans lost 25.7 out of every 1,000 residents between 1864 and 1888 and then only 18.9 per 1,000 between 1889
and 1913.[60] Chicago underwent a dramatic rise in healthfulness with its
annual death rate dropping nearly 38% from 24.24 to 15.09 per 1,000
between 1870 and 1900. Not everywhere did as well as Chicago: San
Francisco's death toll fell just 10% from 21.79 to 19.60 per 1,000. But few
states or cities bucked the general trend towards achieving longer lives
for their citizens.[61] Major diseases were in retreat by 1900. Deaths to scarlet fever fell by two-thirds; diphtheria and typhoid fatalities halved; and
smallpox and yellow fever almost disappeared.[62]

There is no question that public health programs sponsored by city
and state governments played a vital part in bringing about these falls
in mortality. There are clear correlations between the installation of
well-designed systems of water supply and sewage outtake, on the
one hand, and reductions in levels of morbidity and mortality, on the
other. In many towns and cities, the severity of epidemics declined dramatically in the immediate aftermath of the construction of sewers and
the provision of filtered water. Not only did rates of intestinal disease
fall, but so too did the deadly respiratory maladies that often exploited
bodies weakened by typhoid and diarrhea.[63]

And yet, although sanitarians in the late 1800s had made a good
start, much still had to be achieved. Some waterworks were so badly
designed that they managed only to diffuse dirty water to more neighborhoods.[64] In many cities rank corruption and the flouting of laws
marred attempts to create healthier environments: one New York con-
tractor made a pretense of preparing the ground near his tenement
block for the laying of sewer pipes and then quietly filled them in
empty.[65] In most cities sanitary projects were also incomplete or inadequate. Only towns and cities that introduced water filtration could
expect a significant decline in mortality, and only about 2.5% of the
nation's population had benefited from this innovation by 1900.
Moreover, a majority of households remained unconnected to the main
sewer pipes. In 1890 cities that had new sewage pipes had on average
connected them to just half of all households.[66] Inadequate expendi-
tures stood in the way of more rapid progress. The amount of cash
health boards had at their disposal seldom rose above a modest 20
cents per capita in large cities. The Missouri board received exactly $0
between 1885 and 1887.[67] Some city councils appear to have slowed
down the construction of sewers and waterworks once the needs of tax-
payers had been satisfied. The economist Werner Troesken's analysis of
the higher rates of death to typhoid among blacks than whites in the
Jim Crow South suggests that segregation allowed city governments

to delay or avoid extending service to African American neighborhoods.[68]

As noted in the previous chapter, deliberate human actions like the building of sewers were complemented by other developments that served to lower levels of mortality. Rising wages probably allowed more city dwellers to afford the improved nutrition that could raise the capacity of their immune systems to destroy invading bacteria and viruses.[69] The introduction of refrigeration and the gradual replacement of horses with electric trolleys also reduced the sources of dangerous bacteria. At the same time economic and technological developments significantly lessened the threats posed by mosquitos in the upper Mississippi Valley. Railroad construction allowed settlers to establish communities away from the poorly drained lowlands; a growth in income allowed for the construction of drier cabins with windows to keep out swarms of flies and mosquitos; and it is possible that the attention of mosquitos was drawn away from humans by the availability of millions of grazing livestock.[70]

In some cases medical knowledge and interventions made a difference. A growing awareness of the high rates of fever in marshy regions encouraged the building of settlements in regions less conducive to the growth of malarial larvae. Large numbers of people also managed to control malarial infections by taking quinine. One economically savvy Missouri physician alone sold almost 6 million boxes of his quinine-containing "Dr. Sappington's Anti-Fever Pills" between the early 1820s and the 1840s.[71] Furthermore, the ease of obtaining free vaccinations late in the century did much to vanquish smallpox from American towns and cities. After a pitiful start, the Bureau of Indian Affairs had particular success in vaccinating the members of indigenous societies. In 1832 Congress had provided funds for a vaccination program, but over the following five years up to 150,000 Native Americans had died of smallpox. Only in the 1880s, with Native Americans largely confined to reservations and looked upon as "objects of national charity," did the government step up its efforts. Outbreaks of smallpox, shows David S. Jones, were met by doctors imposing quarantine, fumigation, and vaccination. One reservation doctor, James Walker, talked of trekking in snow shoes through a Chippewa reservation in northern Minnesota in the bitter winter of 1883, quarantining the sick and administering vaccinations to the healthy. Although the smallpox pathogen may have lost some of its virulence in the later 1800s, the efforts of doctors like Walker certainly helped to contain smallpox epidemics and to prevent new ones from starting.[72]

RECKONING UP

Urbanization and industrialization, the expansion of slavery, and the great westward migration condemned millions of Americans to premature death. Only in the last decades of the century did longevity for some sections of American society begin to improve as levels of nutrition were raised and as cities and states took greater responsibility for the quality of drinking water, the purity of milk, and the cleanliness of streets. In the early 1900s, as millions more gained access to filtered water and public health authorities began to chlorinate water supplies, American life expectancy substantially increased. But data on the distribution of infectious disease reveal some ugly facts. Poor whites in American cities were still more prone to die young than their well-heeled counterparts. African Americans in towns and rural areas sickened at elevated rates through overwork and poverty, and Native Americans driven onto reservations were dying on average between 15 and 30 years younger than the white population. Although the nineteenth-century battle against infectious disease had laid the basis for the longevity enjoyed by most twentieth-century Americans, it also established patterns of health inequality that persist to the present day.

NOTES

1. Thomas A. LaVeist, *Minority Populations and Health: An Introduction to Health Disparities in the U.S.* San Francisco, CA: John Wiley & Sons, 2011, p. 69; and Nancy Shoemaker, *American Indian Population Recovery in the Twentieth Century.* Albuquerque: University of New Mexico Press, 1999, p. 9.

2. Jonathan B. Pritchett and Insan Tunali, "Strangers' Disease: Determinants of Yellow Fever Mortality during the New Orleans Epidemic of 1853," *Explorations in Economic History* 32, no. 4 (1995), 517–39, p. 518.

3. Gerald Grob, *The Deadly Truth: A History of Disease in America.* Cambridge, MA: Harvard University Press, 2002, p. 102.

4. Ibid., chapter 6.

5. John Duffy, "Social Impact of Disease in the Late Nineteenth Century," *Bulletin of the New York Academy of Medicine* 47, no. 7 (July 1971), 797–810.

6. Charles Rosenberg, *The Cholera Years: The United States in 1832, 1849, and 1866.* Chicago: University of Chicago Press, 1987.

7. Alan Kraut, *Silent Travelers: Germs, Genes, and the "Immigrant Menace."* New York: Basic Books, 1994, chapter 7.

8. Grob, *Deadly Truth*, chapter 5.

9. Grob, *Deadly Truth*, p. 111.

10. Martin V. Melosi, *Garbage in the Cities: Refuse, Reform, and the Environment.* Pittsburgh, PA: University of Pittsburgh Press, 2005, p. 14.

11. Rosenberg, *Cholera Years*, p. 146.

12. Sheila M. Rothman, *Living in the Shadow of Death: Tuberculosis and the Social Experience of Illness in American History*. New York: Basic Books, 1994, p. 13.

13. Rosenberg, *Cholera Years*, p. 88 and Grob, *Deadly Truth*, p. 114.

14. John Duffy, *The Sanitarians: A History of American Public Health*. Urbana: University of Illinois Press, 1990, p. 88 and Grob, *Deadly Truth*, p. 114.

15. Grob, *Deadly Truth*, p. 149.

16. Ibid.

17. Marilyn Irwin Holt, *Indian Orphanages*. Lawrence: University Press of Kansas, 2001, pp. 39–40. David S. Jones, *Rationalizing Epidemics: Meanings and Uses of American Indian Mortality*. Cambridge, MA: Harvard University Press, 2004, p. 75.

18. Russel Thornton, *American Indian Holocaust and Survival: A Population History since 1492*. Norman: University of Oklahoma Press, 1987, p. 133.

19. Holt, *Indian Orphanages*, p. 38.

20. Richard H. Steckel and Joseph M. Prince, 'Tallest in the World: Native Americans of the Great Plains in the Nineteenth Century,"*The American Economic Review* 91, no. 1 (March 2001), 287–94.

21. David S. Jones, *Rationalizing Epidemics*, p. 128.

22. Grob, *Deadly Truth*, p. 142; and Todd L. Savitt, *Medicine and Slavery: The Diseases and Health Care of Blacks in Antebellum Virginia*. Urbana: University of Illinois Press, 2002.

23. Grob, *Deadly Truth*, pp. 142–43.

24. Ibid., chapter 6.

25. Grob, *Deadly Truth*, p. 140.

26. Ira Berlin, *Many Thousands Gone*.

27. Duffy, *The Sanitarians*, p. 65.

28. Ibid., p. 62.

29. Ibid., p. 61.

30. Ibid., p. 105.

31. Duffy, "Social Impact of Disease," p. 417.

32. Paul Starr, *The Social Transformation of American Medicine*. New York: Basic Books, 1982, p. 182.

33. Rosenberg, *Cholera Years*, p. 181.

34. Rothman, *Living in the Shadow*, p. 188.

35. Rosenberg, *The Cholera Years*, p. 139.

36. John Duffy, "Social Impact of Disease," p. 420.

37. Duffy, *The Sanitarians*, p. 54.

38. Ibid., pp. 80–85.

39. Ibid., p. 70.

40. Ibid., p. 75.

41. Louis P. Cain, "Raising and Watering a City: Ellis Chesbrough and Chicago's First Sanitation System," in Judith W. Leavitt and Ronald L. Numbers (eds.), *Sickness and Health in America: Readings in the History of Medicine and Public Health*. Madison: University of Wisconsin Press, 1985, pp. 531–41.

42. Ibid., p. 538.

43. Duffy, *The Sanitarians*, p. 91.

44. Gert H. Brieger, "Sanitary Reform in New York City: Stephen Smith and the Passage of the Metropolitan Health Bill," in Leavitt and Numbers (eds.), *Sickness and Health in America*, pp. 437–50, p. 445.

45. Duffy, *The Sanitarians*, p. 142.

46. Ibid., p. 98.

47. Rosenberg, *The Cholera Years*, p. 191.

48. Ibid., p. 196.

49. Duffy, *The Sanitarians*, p. 145. James H. Cassedy, "The Flamboyant Colonel Waring," *Bulletin of the History of Medicine* 36 (March and April 1962), 163–68, p. 165.

50. Duffy, *The Sanitarians*, p. 147.

51. Steven J. Hoffman, *Race, Class and Power in the Building of Richmond, 1870–1920*. Jefferson, NC: McFarland & Co., 2004, p. 87.

52. Duffy, "Social Impact," p. 420.

53. Samuel Preston and Michael Haines, *Fatal Years: Child Mortality in Late Nineteenth-Century America*. Princeton, NJ: Princeton University Press, 1991, p. 23.

54. Rothman, *Living in the Shadow of Death*, p. 188.

55. Ibid., p. 189.

56. Duffy, *The Sanitarians*, p. 141.

57. Ibid., p. 200; and Gretchen A. Condran, Henry Williams, and Rose A. Cheney, "The Decline of Mortality in Philadelphia from 1870 to 1930: The Role of Municipal Services," in Leavitt and Numbers (eds.), *Sickness and Health in America*, pp. 422–38.

58. Jacqueline H. Wolf, *Don't Kill Your Baby: Public Health and the Decline of Breastfeeding in the 19th and 20th Centuries*. Columbus: Ohio State University Press, 2001.

59. Cassedy, "Flamboyant Colonel Waring," p. 457.

60. "Sickness and Health in America: An Overview," in Leavitt and Numbers (eds.), *Sickness and Health in America*, p. 5. See also Edward Meeker, "The Improving Health of the United States, 1850–1915," *Explorations in Economic History* 9, no. 4 (1972), 353–70.

61. Robert Higgs, "Cycles and Trends of Mortality in 18 Large American Cities, 1871–1900," *Explorations in Economic History* 16, no. 4 (1979), 381–408, p. 394.

62. Meeker, "Improving Health," p. 365.

63. David Cutler and Grant Miller, "The Role of Public Health Improvements in Health Advances: The Twentieth-Century United States,"*Demography* 42, no. 1 (February 2005), 1–22.

64. Gretchen A. Condran and Eileen Crimmins-Gardner, "Public Health Measures and Mortality in U.S. Cities in the Late Nineteenth Century," *Human Ecology* 6, no. 1 (March 1978), 27–54.

65. Duffy, *The Sanitarians*, p. 78.

66. Condran and Crimmins-Gardner, "Public Health Measures," p. 30.

67. Duffy, *The Sanitarians*, p. 176.

68. Werner Troesken, *Water, Race, and Disease*. Cambridge, MA: MIT Press, 2004, p. 135.

69. Robert W. Fogel, "Health, Nutrition, and Economic Growth," *Economic Development and Cultural Change* 52, no. 3 (April 2004), 643–58.

70. Grob, *The Deadly Truth*, p. 133.

71. Conevery Bolton Valenčius, *The Health of the Country: How American Settlers Understood Themselves and Their Land*. New York: Basic Books, 2002, p. 82.

72. David S. Jones, *Rationalizing Epidemics*, p. 120.

CHAPTER 7

Occupational Health and Dangerous Trades

Chattel slavery and the absence of worker safety laws made the nineteenth-century United States a dangerous place to labor. Slavery obviously inflicted physical and psychological suffering on the most tragic scale, but many other categories of worker were also treated with utter contempt. The rise of the factory, the proliferation of workshops and sweatshops, the construction of vast interlocking railroads, the deepening of coal and metal mines, and the burgeoning of cheap brothels entailed heavy loads of disease, distress, and mortality. As the United States emerged as a developed capitalist nation, one person's profit often came to depend on another's severe exploitation or premature demise. This chapter examines the underbelly of the United States' emergence as a major economic power in order to explain why a significantly higher proportion of Americans than western Europeans suffered death or disability in the workplace.

SLAVERY AND DEATH

From cradle to grave the lives of black Americans were defined and circumscribed by a system that sought to extract profit by abolishing freedom. Although for a brief period in the late 1700s it had seemed that slavery might wither away, the invention of the cotton gin and the opening up of vast new lands in the South and West provided an enormous incentive to create new and larger slave plantations. Between

1790 and 1830 alone the slave population of the United States tripled, and by 1860, 4 million black slaves toiled in the United States.[1] They constituted in 1850 nearly a quarter of the nation's labor force over the age of nine.[2] Some historians have suggested that masters recognized the humanity of their slaves to the extent that they accepted moral limits to the degree of suffering they were justified in inflicting. A paternalistic spirit, wrote Eugene Genovese, became integral to the southern gentleman's sense of honor.[3] But talk of the white man's sense of stewardship usually amounted to no more than high-sounding cant. Raw statistics give the lie to the self-serving mythologies of the southern planter. Infants born to slave mothers were as much as four times more likely to die than their white counterparts.[4]

These men, women, and children, classified as mere property to be inventoried alongside tools, cattle, and household possessions, suffered due to the gruelling demands of masters who could with impunity inflict upon them extreme hours, dangerous jobs, and horrendous whippings; house them in the most squalid and cramped conditions; and count their gains as slave sons, daughters, husbands, and wives were handed over to itinerant traders to be sold to new masters maybe hundreds of miles away. The diaries of southerners and the recollections of freed slaves are replete with heart-breaking accounts of petty tyranny, systematic violence, and a coldly calculating mind-set that wrecked hundreds of thousands of lives.[5] The breaking up of families induced distress of an especially acute kind. "The white people thought in slave-time we poor darkies had no soul, and they separated us like dogs," recalled Fannie Moore of North Carolina. With the decline of tobacco growing in the Chesapeake coinciding with a massive demand for slaves on cotton plantations, at least 875,000 of the enslaved were sent in manacles between 1820 and 1860 to states like Florida, Alabama, Mississippi, and Louisiana, where they were put to work in punishing conditions transforming the landscape into new plantations.[6] A significant number of those in this "mighty torrent" had been torn from their families in the upper South. Wanting only the young and fit, planters spoke of buying "none in families."[7]

The hardness of daily life on the plantation is well documented. Slaves on cotton plantations had to sustain a demanding pace if they were to avoid being whipped by master, driver, or overseer. If "one falls behind or is a moment idle," recalled Solomon Northup in 1841, "he is whipped." Each night their pickings were weighed and, Northup added, "a slave never approaches the gin-house with his basket of cotton but with fear."[8] Rice cultivation, concentrated in the South Carolina and Georgia tidewater, involved an arduous yearly cycle of growing and harvesting the crop as well as maintaining a complex irrigation system. Sugar plantations, especially in Louisiana, were the most notorious as they involved hard work all year round in addition to the risks of injury and death from the sharp tools used to hack down cane, heavy rollers used to squeeze out the juice, and boiling copper vats for reducing the juice. The psychological stresses of slavery also placed relationships under strain and resulted in abundant "distress and discord" between spouses and between parents and their children.[9]

That some slave masters were less vicious than others says more about their business acumen than their capacity for empathy. Especially after the official closure of the international slave trade in 1808, many masters came to realize that slaves were a major capital investment and that it made no sense to work them to an early death. They were also aware that if pushed too far slaves were liable to work slowly, break tools, feign sickness, or even flee the plantation. When slaves did perish from overwork or maltreatment, the rationalizations offered up by the master class reveal an extraordinary capacity for self-delusion. People of African American descent were said to be naturally prone to sickness, controllable only through force, and unable to feel the same intensity of pain or emotions as the white race.[10] Treating a few slaves in the "Big House" comparatively well made it easier for slave owners to persuade themselves that they were Christian gentlemen and to ignore the sufferings of the majority in the fields. Most lived wretched and short lives.[11]

SICKNESS AND ACCIDENTS ON FARMS

The free men, women, and children who worked on farms were exposed to a wide variety of hazards, even if most were subject to far fewer horrors than the slave. The United States may have been undergoing rapid industrialization from the 1830s onwards, but as many as 40% of Americans, or nearly 30 million people, still worked on farms in 1900.[12] In consequence, the risks of sickness and injury were shared by a large proportion of the population. John Mack Faragher describes the terrible levels of malaria that debilitated farm workers in malarial regions. During harvest time, laborers who had contracted malaria found that they lacked the energy to work efficiently: in 1821 one man from rural Illinois lamented that his life was "at least fifty percent below par in the months of August and September."[13] Others were cut down by epidemics of diseases like typhoid fever spread by flies that carried bacilli from the "stagnant pools, rotting offal, or open sewage" that were nearly always to be found on farms.[14]

Not least due to the scale of the agricultural sector, more people were seriously injured on farms than in either factories or mines. Adults and children were killed or maimed by falls, runaway wagons, drownings, kicks from animals, cuts from blades, overturned carts, blocks of ice falling from silos, snakebites, and hunting accidents. As a young man Abraham Lincoln was kicked so hard in the head by a horse that neighbors assumed he would die.[15] Thousands of other incidents were recorded by local newspapers. During the harvest season of 1858, for instance, a 14-year-old Stephen Bilbee of Carthage died after a friend's scythe pierced his abdomen.[16] Nor did competent doctors tend to be around when such accidents occurred on remote farms and homesteads. The Wyoming homesteader Elinore Stewart told of one laborer with a cut in his finger that had turned gangrenous. One of her neighbors luckily had the knowledge and confidence to give him morphine and whiskey and then "chipped off the black, swollen finger."[17] Many were far less fortunate and simply perished from infection, leaving little if any trace on the historical record.

THE EXPLOITATION OF IRISH MEN AND WOMEN

The treatment of the Catholic Irish provides another example of the subjection of the ethnically vulnerable to soul-destroying and sometimes deadly labor. From 1815 to 1845, a million Irish men, women, and children, sailed from Dublin to Liverpool, crossed the Atlantic, and settled in North America. They were followed by the hundreds of thousands of refugees from the catastrophic Irish potato famine who settled in the tenement districts of the East Coast's cities or fanned across the nation in desperate search of work. Poor and usually despised, Irish immigrants set up what were pejoratively called Paddytowns or Little Dublins on the outskirts of towns in the West. The huts they built were hardly better than the primitive, damp, and tumbledown cottages they had been forced to leave behind. The majority performed jobs in the lowest reaches of the economy. They served as unskilled laborers, loggers, dockhands, miners, ditch-diggers, and construction workers, and they built the roads, canals, and railroads upon which the rapid growth of the American economy depended.[18]

Everywhere they went, from seaport Boston to frontier Denver, the Irish took on the most risky and degrading jobs. "It is a well-established fact," observed one Irish immigrant in a letter back to County Cork, "that the average length of life of the emigrant after landing here is six years, and many insist it is much less."[19] Those of

Anglo-American stock frequently placed the Catholic Irish on a racial par with the African slave. The Irish, noted the escaped slave and abolitionist Frederick Douglass, shared in the black's "degradation."[20] Irishmen were sometimes made to do jobs on which a prudent master would not risk his slaves. The historian Dennis Clark writes, "When the builders of canals wanted a labor force to build the Chesapeake Canal in Virginia, they went to the local plantation owners and said, 'Rent us your slaves.' But the planters replied. 'No way, these slaves are worth money. Get Irishmen instead. If they die, there's no monetary loss.'"[21] The Irish were white and technically free, but they could be deprived of basic rights and paid a mere pittance.

Desperate for work, the Irish were terribly vulnerable to the trickery of the native born. Irish miners and laborers on canals, railroads, or building sites were often remunerated in overpriced goods or not paid at all. Patrick Walsh from County Cork recalled that the contractors for railroads would promise "the finest terms to the working men." When they had enough workers they would then reduce the wages, knowing that their desperate laborers had no money to get back to Boston or New York and would have to accept the new terms. If the outraged laborers did go on strike, the army was poised to drive them away. One immigrant visited a settlement where the rail company had reneged on its promises. "I went to see the condition of those that remained," he wrote, "in their 'shanties', with the fierce wind howling through them, a scene of suffering presented itself which made the heart sick. All along for miles was one continued scene of anguish and suffering, as if some curse was chasing the unfortunate people of Ireland. Yet these things were noticed as mere items of news in the paper."[22] Elsewhere, Irishmen who complained too much were simply replaced by Chinese labourers. There is "no love" for the Irish, lamented one immigrant, "no protection of life. He can be shot down, run through, kicked, cuffed, spat on—and no redress, but a response of 'Serves the damn son of an Irish bitch right, damn him'."[23] Racist anti-Irish sayings like, "It's as natural for a Hibernian to tipple as it is for a pig to grunt" abounded.[24] It is hardly surprising that many Irish men, arriving in the United States damaged and defeated, turned to drink or became perpetual drifters.

The hundreds of thousands of Irish women who became maids and cooks confronted fewer physical dangers than most of their male counterparts but had to endure decades of contempt from middle- or upperclass employers.[25] By 1855, after the rapid influx of famine Irish, they constituted three-quarters of all domestic servants in New York City. Although most Protestant families would have preferred a native-born cook or maid, with the expansion of the middle class these were in short supply. Poor Irish were deemed to be better than nothing, but the relationship could only be fraught. These Irish women arrived in the United States so poor that it was virtually unthinkable for a master and mistress to treat them with anything but disdain and distrust. Few employers could have contemplated speaking to an Irish maid or cook on terms of familiarity without feeling that they had compromised their social standing. The Catholicism, poor education, and strong accents of the immigrant compounded the social gulf between employer and employee. It was a dispiritingly lonely existence for women who, although well fed and housed, were virtual strangers in a family home. Not surprisingly, the Irish domestic often complained of being treated like a "machine."[26] The letters and diaries of employers as well as newspapers and popular magazines bear witness to the hostility of the upper and middle classes towards their Irish maids and cooks. Native-born families expected deference because their servants had been "born and bred in a mud-hovel." The Irish domestic, in contrast, had come to the United States expecting a land of opportunity and often rebelled in subtle or not-so-subtle ways. In response, employers fashioned a stereotypical figure of Irish servants as crude, ill-mannered, and savage in disposition.[27]

Conditions for Irish men and women gradually improved, even if they were not fully embraced by mainstream Anglo-American culture until the decades after World War II. Irish women increasingly became schoolteachers as they managed to save enough money to go to college and prove their intellectual worth. Political savvy and sheer weight of numbers also allowed the Irish to take control of the Democratic Party in most northern cities. Before long there were enough Irishmen in political office for them to start to relieve the poverty of some of their brethren by using state taxes to funnel money to Irish contractors. The "Boston of the Endicotts and the Winthrops," remarked an observer in 1885, has become "the Boston of the Collinses and the O'Briens."[28] Eventually the Irish would achieve levels of upwards social mobility into safer and better-paid jobs that would have been unimaginable in the 1850s. But even at the end of the century, poor Irish men and women were overrepresented in the most demanding and poorly paid industrial occupations.

THE PERILS OF MANUFACTURING

Manufacturing industry transformed the United States as it did European states. In the 1820s cities like New York already had a few industrial-scale enterprises such as ship building and sugar refining. Over the following decades thousands of textile mills producing ready-made clothing from slave-harvested cotton sprung up in both the larger cities of the Northeast and smaller towns like Holyoke and Lawrence, in Massachusetts, and Poughkeepsie, New York. Levels of industrial production soared after the Civil War. In New York in 1860, 594 clothing, millinery, and laundry establishments employed 30,158 people. The equivalent numbers in 1906 were 10,189 and 235,565. By then the shores of Manhattan were crowded with iron works, ship yards, abattoirs, soap-making plants, engine works, and brass foundries. Across the water in Brooklyn, chemical and paint factories jostled for space. Factories were also growing rapidly in size. A few monstrous industrial sites employed as many as 10,000 workers by the century's end. The same kind of industrial growth, if seldom as breathless as in New York, occurred across the country.[29]

Industrialization significantly increased the risks of labor. Factory production brought a tremendous rise in the level of force used to drive wheels, cogs, gears, pulleys, shafts, and belts. Workers rendered clumsy by fatigue or who momentarily lost concentration could receive terrible bruising, broken limbs, smashed bodies, and severed fingers, hands, or arms. The hard teeth of uncovered cogwheels could shred sinew and bone in seconds.[30] Woodworking machines were especially treacherous. The boss of one local branch of the Carpenters Union is said to have asked men to vote by holding up their stumps. In large factories accidents were commonplace. Factory workers were expected to navigate narrow gaps between moving equipment and unguarded walkways suspended high above. A shocking 9 per 1,000 operatives in the Pennsylvania Railroad workshops were seriously injured due to accidents every month![31] Arthur H. Young, later an advocate of better personnel relations, recalled the horror of being asked to climb a ladder to oil a spinning shaft on his first day at work at the Joliet steel works of Illinois. Young commented that "no thought" was ever "given to safety." Big factories also meant giant boilers that were prone to explode if owners put safety second. One study found that between 1883 and 1907, 7,000 Americans had been killed in boiler explosions compared to 700 in Britain and 400 in Germany.[32]

Then there were the dangers of the noxious air and toxic chemicals to which workers were exposed. When the New York doctor Allan McLane Hamilton visited local factories in 1873, he discovered large numbers of adults and children suffering from varying degrees of lead poisoning. Others were sickly or dying as a result of the ease with which deadly bacteria and viruses spread in windowless buildings.[33]

The transmission rate was just as high in the squalid sweatshops in which many thousands of poor natives and immigrants from Ireland and from southern and eastern Europe labored. In poorly ventilated and unsanitary workshops located in tenement basements, operatives sewed together cloth produced in nearby factories. Germs were spread from residents to workers and from workers to the clothes and then to those who bought and wore them. The legislature stepped in during the 1890s to regulate sweatshops, partly because customers were also voters.[34]

So unimportant did manufacturing bosses consider safety that one historian has called the United States the "land of disasters." Each year around 700,000 workers were disabled in industrial accidents for one month or more. It is estimated that around the year 1900 as many as a third of the homeless had been disabled in their places of work.[35] Late in life factory and sweatshop operatives then faced heightened risks of chronic disease. Industrial workers aged 65 and over were about five times more likely to die of respiratory maladies than those aged 15–29, in part due to decades of breathing in noxious chemicals, dust, and fumes.[36]

THE DANGERS OF MINING

Few occupations could rival the treacherousness of mining as the soaring demand for coal and metals placed a premium on extracting raw material as fast as possible. Coal mining, concentrated largely around Pennsylvania, had always involved a fair degree of danger. From the 1850s, however, the level of risk escalated. With the exhaustion of surface deposits, the shafts became ever deeper, and the threats of roof falls, explosions, fire, electrocution, and haulage accidents all rose concomitantly. Most of those killed were crushed or asphyxiated by falling rock, whether through avalanches at the workface or tunnels collapsing due to insufficient supports. Accidents were common occurrences because managers incentivized risk-taking by remunerating workers on a piece-rate system: taking home more cash the more coal they extracted, they erred too often on the side of recklessness. Flawed safety protocols cost additional lives. Miners were expected to wear safety lamps only in sections of the mine known to contain explosive gases like methane. As a result they often used naked flames and black powder in tunnels thought to be safe but that in fact contained dangerous build-ups of methane or explosive concentrations of coal dust.[37]

The air miners breathed carried its own severe risks. Coal miners were constantly inhaling the dust that might one day cause them to

Young boys working in a Pennsylvania coal mine in 1895, before the introduction of child labor laws. Over a quarter of the 87,000 coal miners in Pennsylvania in 1882 were 15 or younger. (© Bettmann/Corbis)

develop black lung and various forms of cancer. Those who mined the silver lodes of the Comstock mine of western Nevada and the base metal ores of Eureka in Nevada, Leadville in Colorado, Butte in Montana, and Coeur d'Alene in Idaho were at a terribly high risk of toxic poisoning. The introduction of machine drilling and dynamite as a blasting agent increased the quantities of silica or quartz in the air of the mine. As many as half of hardrock miners at any one time developed fibrous nodules in their lungs that caused difficulty in breathing. Those drilling into the silver–lead ores of places like Leadville and Coeur d'Alene also experienced severe lead poisoning, sometimes having to spend weeks at a time in hospitals consuming high doses of magnesium chloride.[38] Children as young as eight years of age, made to work underground for 10 to 12 hours a day, were exposed to these hazards alongside adults.[39]

The overall toll of death and disability from American mining is staggering. A study carried out in 1858 revealed that the average miner had less than a 50% chance of surviving for a dozen years.[40] Nearly 6,000 miners were killed in major accidents alone between 1878 and

1910. A still higher number perished from minor incidents that were beneath the notice of newspapers and judges. The historian Richard Lingenfelter calculates that an appalling one in eighty hardrock miners died each year.[41] Realizing that the mine owners were indifferent to their deaths and disabilities and that judges nearly always interpreted legislation in ways that favored companies over workers, some fraternities of miners took safety into their own hands. In the 1880s and 1890s hardrock mining unions oversaw the building of 20 hospitals in the western United States and Canada providing care for injured miners out of member dues.[42]

DEATH AND DEBILITY ON THE RAILWAYS

No other sector of the economy employed as many people as the million men and women who worked for the railroads by 1900. Nor did any other business in the United States give rise to anything like the 12,000 accidental deaths of workers and others recorded annually on the railways by 1907.[43] Railmen perished in three main ways. First, engine boilers exploded and instantly killed the engine driver. Managers obviously knew of the risk of explosions, and so in the early days of the railways they placed carriages stuffed with sandbags between the cab and the first passenger carriage so that only the drivers would die in the event of an explosion. Second, brakemen were liable to fall to their deaths because they had to clamber on top of the cars and turn the brake wheels in all weathers.[44] Third, brakemen were often injured or killed when trying to couple rail cars. They had to wait between moving cars to drop a metal pin into position when the link on one car had slotted into the socket on the other. The difficulty of the task and the mighty forces involved meant that "old time" brakemen were recognizable by their shattered fingers and hands. Many were killed instantly when, fatigued after long shifts, they did not step back sufficiently quickly.[45]

Technologies to prevent these deaths and injuries were developed long before they were universally installed. The 1869 Westinghouse Air Brake, obviating the need for brakemen to scramble across the roofs of cabs, appeared in 1869, and in 1873 Eli Janney introduced an automatic coupler. Managers agreed to pay for these innovations to be fitted to passenger trains but were much less concerned about preserving the lives of brakemen who worked on freight trains. When a modified version of the Westinghouse Air Brake suitable for freight trains appeared in 1881, few rail companies put in orders. Although states were beginning to demand better worker safety, as late as 1889 about 1 out of every 100 engineers, firemen, conductors, and brakemen

In 1869 George Westinghouse introduced the Westinghouse Air Brake, which obviated the need for brakemen to climb dangerously across the roofs of train cabs in order to operate manual brakes. The managers of rail companies soon agreed to pay for their installation on passenger trains. But they were much slower to adopt the modified version of the Westinghouse Air Brake for use on freight trains because they were rather less concerned about the lives of brakemen. (Library of Congress)

were killed every year. Fewer than half as many fatalities were reported among the workers on English railways.[46] When it was put to Vice President Perkins of the Chicago, Burlington & Quincy railroad company that a worker's compensation fund be set up, he scoffed at what he considered to be giving "something for nothing."[47] So unconcerned were the managers of American railroad companies for the welfare of employees that they paid out far more for cattle killed on their lines than they did to disabled workers or widows of the dead. In 1893, Congress finally passed the Safety Appliance Act, albeit by a slim margin, which mandated that all trains be equipped with air brakes and automatic couplers. Many lives could have been saved had this legislation been passed earlier.[48]

THE MISERIES OF PROSTITUTION

Most of the women who turned to prostitution in the nineteenth century did so for the timeless reasons identified by one New York prostitute, known as M. T., interviewed in 1855: "I had no work, no money, and no home."[49] Desperation had driven them into a dangerous and psychologically demanding trade. The level of disease and violence to which individual prostitutes were exposed varied according to their place in a hierarchy stretching from the highest-paid courtesan to the humblest street walker. Among the most vulnerable were the thousands of young Chinese women brought over to California to work in brothels.[50] Some of these women were kidnapped from rural districts and shipped to the United States. Others were the children of poor parents who effectively sold their daughters to procurers in the expectation of them one day returning. Some were lured over on false pretences of receiving good jobs and an education. Having been off-loaded into barracoons on arrival, they were split into two groups. Those considered to be most attractive were sold to high-class brothels where they might become the concubines to rich Chinese immigrants. The rest were despatched to brothels where they had to have sex with any customer. Physical appearance also determined the conditions in which a white prostitute received clients. The less alluring ended up in lower-class dives and cribs. The more desirable worked in high-class establishments but knew that if they did not marry or find an alternative living they would eventually lose their looks and be dismissed. Chinese prostitutes were considered to be "useful" for just four years, after which they would be thrown out or possibly find work as a cook or laundress. The sick were sometimes just left to die. Californian newspapers reported the finding of the discarded corpses of young Chinese women in Chinatown. Nobody troubled to send their bodies home to China.[51]

Women working the streets or in cheap brothels were the most likely to be beaten or contract disease. Chinese prostitutes were subject to severe chastisements if they failed to perform adequately or if they refused to pay the taxes imposed on them by the gangs that controlled the trade. Many thousands of miles from home, they could be whipped, subjected to torture by fire, dispatched to the notorious brothels next to gold mines, or shot dead. Lower-end prostitutes of all ethnicities were also the most prone to contracting venereal diseases. Whereas a high-class prostitute might see four men a day, her lowlier counterpart might see anywhere between 13 and 30. A study of New York City prostitutes in the early 1900s found that more than a fifth had clinical manifestations of syphilis. Malnutrition also increased the susceptibility of poor prostitutes to deadly diseases like tuberculosis.[52]

Many prostitutes were broken by psychological strains as much as the immediate threats of sickness and violence. Although red-light districts could offer companionship and camaraderie, prostitutes had every day to tolerate physical disgust for their clients, the fear of being beaten, and the sense of having been permanently ostracised by polite society. Most women changed their names when entering the brothel, a customary acknowledgment of the shame that accompanied their profession. They were well aware that "civilized society" cared nothing for their ills: a prostitute who developed the "loathsome disease" of syphilis was believed to have reaped the wages of sin and deserved neither protection nor sympathy. A significant proportion of prostitutes also had to bear the grinding sadness of having had to give up newborns to baby farms. One study found that over 10% had tried to take their own lives at least once. The prostitute Maimie Pinzer, who lost an eye to syphilis and later wrote eloquently about her experiences, spoke of the "smallness of her life" as a prostitute.[53] Many relied on opium, morphine, or cocaine to ease the sapping indignities of life. But not all prostitutes were equally humiliated by the piteous disdain of the social purity campaigner. One girl from New Orleans's Storyville red-light district, the daughter of a prostitute, told of how she had her virginity auctioned for $7.75 at the age of five. Asked what she thought of her early life she replied, "I ain't ashamed of what I did, because I didn't have much to do with it." She was just "like a kid whose father owns a grocery store," she went on: "He helps him in the store. Well my mother didn't sell groceries." Many a prostitute spoke contemptuously of "nosy" reformers and claimed to pity the factory workers who worked long hours for derisory pay.[54]

Calls to regulate prostitution on health grounds were heard increasingly after the 1860s from doctors and citizens who feared that too many patrons were becoming infected with syphilis. Some of those who did not think that prostitution could ever be stamped out proposed systems of compulsory inspection and treatment. The registration and medical examination of prostitutes was mooted in New York, Pennsylvania, and Maryland, but only in St. Louis, Missouri, did the authorities take concerted action. In 1870 the city passed the Social Evil Ordinance. Prostitutes were licensed and inspected by doctors, and those infected with venereal disease were sent to a Social Evil Hospital. In an attempt not to offend ratepayers, the city paid for the program by levying fees on brothels and individual prostitutes. But local church members were outraged because the city was seen to be condoning vice and regulating "bawdy houses." In 1874 the legislature bowed to public pressure and repealed the act.[55] It is not clear how many prostitutes mourned the nullification of the Social Evil Ordinance. The inspections must have been demeaning, and enforced quarantines prevented them from making money. They were also fully aware that their own interests were not being considered.[56]

CHILD LABOR

Children worked in many of the worst-paid and most physically demanding occupations. The 1880 U.S. census data indicate that more than a million children between 10 and 15 were gainfully employed, though this figure is an underestimate because it does not include the hundreds of thousands who were toiling long before they reached the age of 10. In frontier regions the young had for generations helped in the arduous task of clearing land for agriculture and building. On farms, children as young as eight spent long hours picking berries and apples, gathering cranberries from acidic bogs, milking cows, fetching water, feeding cattle, and harvesting corn, tobacco, and cotton.[57] Others worked gruelling shifts in fruit and vegetable canneries located close to the farm. In fact, in 1880 two-thirds of working children were employed in the agricultural sector. Others were employed by mining companies. In Pennsylvania, for instance, over a quarter of the 87,000 coal miners in 1882 were 15 or younger. Factories were another significant employer of the young. As early as 1820 children comprised 43% of the labor force of textile mills in Massachusetts. After the Civil War, textile manufacturing boomed in the South, where poverty-stricken sharecroppers and tenant farmers gladly delivered themselves and their children up to work in the mills of the Carolinas, Georgia, and Alabama.[58] In towns and cities across the nation children also toiled in tenement sweatshops, delivered heavy bundles of newspapers, peddled cheap goods, and acted as messengers. Along the coastlines, they shucked oysters and picked shrimp from as early as five years of age.

The physical and mental health of children clearly suffered as a result of these labor demands. In nearly all trades and industries hours were long, and excessive demands were placed on growing bodies. Mining was especially hazardous for boys rendered careless by fatigue. Children hired to extract slate and rock from moving chutes without gloves ended up with cracked hands and missing fingers and ran the risk of asthma and black lung disease due to the constant inhalation of coal dust. Children in mines were also killed by runaway carts, rock

falls, and explosions.[59] In factories the young were at risk of having dig-
its and limbs crushed or severed by fast-moving machinery during
working weeks as long as 84 hours.[60] A 1902 report commissioned by
the American Federation of Labor observed of southern textile mills:
"It is a common sight to see children of cotton operatives stretched on
the bed dressed as they come from the mills in the morning, too weary
to do anything but fling themselves down to rest."[61] Exhaustion and
crowded working conditions also increased the risk of contracting
tuberculosis and pneumonia. A number of organizations did try to
ameliorate the conditions in which children labored. The American
Federation of Labor, General Federation of Women's Clubs, and the
Consumers' League of the City of New York all campaigned for legisla-
tive protections. In 1903, 5,000 textile workers in Kensington,
Pennsylvania, including thousands of children, participated in a strike
demanding, among other things, an end to child labor. They enjoyed
some success. During the course of the century many states did institute restrictions on the hours a child could work and the age at which
they could enter factory or mine. But these laws did not apply to street
trades or to farm or domestic labor. Nor did they decrease the number
of working children: roughly one in six, or 1,500,000, children aged
10–15 were working in 1900.[62]

UNNECESSARY DEATHS

Americans in the nineteenth century died as a result of working conditions considerably more frequently than those in other industrializing
nations like Britain and Germany. This is in large part due to the
obvious fact that western European nations did not practice domestic
slavery. People of African descent were not, however, the only
Americans to suffer more grievously than the workers in other industri-
alized countries. By way of example, one out of every 357 railroad
employees were annually killed in service, and one out of every 35
injured. In England the comparable statistics were one worker in every
875 killed and one in 158 injured.[63] By 1908 American miners were
dying at 300% the frequency of their British counterparts.[64]
Legislators and courts in the United States accepted with singular alac-
rity the logically absurd claim that men who agreed to perform dangerous jobs had accepted the risks and deserved no pay-outs in the event
of injury or death.[65]

How did American owners and managers get away with maintaining such low standards of worker safety and welfare? It is not that
major businesses went unopposed: disaffected and desperate workers

set up unions, organized strikes, and created their own support systems for injured workers and their families. But workers in low-skilled industries were in a very weak bargaining position in relation to their employers. The owners and managers of factories, mines, and railroad companies could readily recruit new able-bodied laborers to replace the dead and injured from among the average of 375,000 immigrants who by mid-century were passing through port cities desperate for work each year. Existing workers were expendable. Moreover, the fact that immigrants were of diverse ethnicities meant that bosses could exploit a lack of worker solidarity. If one set of employees complained about brutal conditions, managers could threaten to replace them with members of a more desperate and therefore biddable ethnic group. Where many employees were obliged to live in "company towns," this meant that those who were fired forfeited their homes and schooling for their children in addition to their jobs. Most deemed it better just to accept conditions as they were. The welfare of workers and their families could therefore be largely disregarded because most managers had few inducements to be concerned.[66] Moreover, business leaders by the end of the century were stronger—and more resistant to outside interference—than ever before. In the 1890s and early 1900s companies like the US Steel Corporation and Standard Oil took over or put out of business thousands of smaller firms to create massive trusts. These giant corporations had unprecedented power to face down labor opposition and attempts by the government to regulate the treatment of workers. There were few barriers to them using intimidation and violence to suppress the complaints of their workers.[67]

NOTES

1. Ira Berlin, *Many Thousands Gone: The First Two Centuries of Slavery in North America*. Cambridge, MA: Belknap Press of Harvard University Press, 1998.

2. David Montgomery, *Citizen Worker: The Experience of Workers in the United States with Democracy and the Free Market during the Nineteenth Century*. New York: Cambridge University Press, 1993, p. 13.

3. Eugene D. Genovese, *The World the Slaveholders Made: Two Essays in Interpretation*. Middletown, CT: Wesleyan University Press, 1988; Robert William Fogel and Stanley L. Engerman, *Time on the Cross: The Economics of American Negro Slavery*. Boston: Little, Brown, 1974; and Elizabeth Fox-Genovese, *Within the Plantation Household: Black and White Women of the Old South*. Chapel Hill: University of North Carolina Press, 1988.

4. Kenneth F. Kiple and Virginia Himmelsteib King, *Another Dimension to the Black Diaspora: Diet, Disease and Racism*. Cambridge: Cambridge University Press, 1981, p. 192.

5. David Brion Davis, *Inhuman Bondage: The Rise and Fall of Slavery in the New World*. New York: Oxford University Press, 2006.

6. Ira Berlin, *Generations of Captivity: A History of African-American Slaves*. Cambridge, MA: Belknap Press of Harvard University Press, 2003, p. 163.

7. Sharla M. Fett, *Working Cures: Healing, Health, and Power on Southern Slave Plantations*. Chapel Hill: University of North Carolina Press, 2002, p. 30. David Brown and Clive Webb, *Race in the American South: From Slavery to Civil Rights*. Gainesville: University Press of Florida, 2007, p. 121.

8. Solomon Northup, *Twelve Years a Slave: Narrative of Solomon Northup, a Citizen of New-York*. New York: Miller, Orton & Mulligan, 1855, p. 167.

9. Brenda E. Stevenson, "Distress and Discord in Virginia Slave Families, 1830–1860," in Carol Bleser (ed.), in *Joy and in Sorrow: Women, Family, and Marriage in the Victorian South, 1830–1900*. New York: Oxford University Press, 1991, p. 42.

10. Jeffrey Robert Young, "Ideology and Death on a Savannah River Rice Plantation, 1833–1867: Paternalism amongst 'a Good Supply of Disease and Pain,' " *Journal of Southern History* 59, no. 4 (November 1993), 673–706.

11. Michael Tadman, "Class and the Construction of 'Race': White Racism in the American South," in Melvyn Stokes (ed.), *The State of US History*. Oxford, England: Berg, 2000.

12. James C. Williams, "The American Industrial Revolution," in Carroll Pursell (ed.), *A Companion to American Technology*. Malden, MA: Blackwell Pub., 2005, pp. 20–35, 24.

13. John Mack Faragher, *Sugar Creek: Life on the Illinois Prairie*. New Haven, CT: Yale University Press, 1986, p. 90.

14. Ibid., p. 89.

15. Ibid., p. 88.

16. Susan Sessions Rugh, *Our Common Country: Family Farming, Culture, and Community in the Nineteenth-century Midwest*. Bloomington: Indiana University Press, 2001, p. 69.

17. Mary Ellen Jones, *Daily Life on the Nineteenth Century American Frontier*. Westport, CT: Greenwood Press, 1998, p. 201.

18. Kerby A. Miller and Paul Wagner, *Out of Ireland: The Story of Irish Emigration to America*. Niwot, CO: Roberts Rinehart Pub., 1997, p. 40; and Kerby A. Miller, *Emigrants and Exiles: Ireland and the Irish Exodus to North America*. New York: Oxford University Press, 1985.

19. Miller and Wagner, *Out of Ireland*, p. 41.

20. Noel Ignatiev, *How the Irish Became White*. New York: Routledge, 1995, p. 129.

21. Quoted in Miller and Wagner, *Out of Ireland*, p. 43.

22. Ibid., pp. 52–53.

23. Miller, *Emigrants and Exiles*, p. 332.

24. Malcolm Campbell, *Ireland's New Worlds: Immigrants, Politics, and Society in the United States and Australia, 1815–1922*. Madison: University of Wisconsin Press, 2008, p. 28.

25. Carol Groneman, "Working-Class Immigrant Women in Mid-Nineteenth-Century New York: The Irish Woman's Experience," *Journal of Urban History* 4 (May 1978): 257–71.

26. Andrew Urban, "Irish Domestic Servants, Irish Domestic Servants, 'Biddy' and Rebellion in the American Home, 1850–1900,"*Gender & History* 21, no. 2 (August 2009): 263–86, p. 273.

27. Urban, "Irish Domestic Servants," p. 264.

28. Ronald Takaki, *A Different Mirror: A History of Multicultural America*. New York: Little, Brown, and Co., 2008, p. 150.

29. George Rosen, "Urbanization, Occupation and Disease in the United States, 1870–1920: The Case of New York City," *Journal of the History of Medicine and Allied Sciences* 43, no. 4 (1988): 391–425.

30. Mark Aldrich, *Safety First: Technology, Labor, and Business in the Building of American Work Safety, 1870–1939*. Baltimore, MD: Johns Hopkins University Press, 1997, p. 78.

31. Aldrich, *Safety First*, p. 80–82.

32. Ibid., pp. 78–82.

33. Rosen, "Urbanization, Occupation and Disease," p. 395.

34. Ibid., p. 418.

35. K. L. Kusmer, "The Homeless Unemployed in Industrializing America, 1865–1930: Perception and Reality," *Amerikastudien* 40, no. 4 (1995), 667–94, p. 678.

36. Susan I. Hautaniemi, Alan C. Swedlund, and Douglas L. Anderton, "Mill Town Mortality: Consequences of Industrial Growth in Two Nineteenth-Century New England Towns," *Social Science History* 23, no. 1 (Spring 1999), 1–39, pp. 23–27.

37. Jacqueline Corn, "Protective Legislation for Coal Miners, 1870–1900: Response to Safety and Health Hazards," in David Rosner and Gerald E. Markowitz (eds.), *Dying for Work: Workers' Safety and Health in Twentieth-Century America*. Bloomington: Indiana University Press, 1987, pp. 67–82; and Gerald Grob, *The Deadly Truth: A History of Disease in America*. Cambridge, MA: Harvard University Press, 2002.

38. Richard E. Lingenfelter, *The Hardrock Miners: A History of the Mining Labor Movement in the American West, 1863–1893*. Berkeley: University of California Press, 1974, p. 16.

39. Corn, "Protective Legislation for Coal Miners," pp. 67–82.

40. Grob, *The Deadly Truth*, p. 167.

41. Lingenfelter, *The Hardrock Miners*, p. 23.

42. Licht, *Working for the Railroad*, pp. 8, 80.

43. Mark Aldrich, *Death Rode the Rails: American Railroad Accidents and Safety, 1828–1965*. Baltimore, MD: Johns Hopkins University Press, 2006, p. 2.

44. Aldrich, *Safety First*, p. 186.

45. Walter Licht, *Working for the Railroad: The Organization of Work in the Nineteenth Century*. Princeton, NJ: Princeton University Press, 1983, pp. 177, 191.

46. Licht, *Working for the Railroad*, p. 190.

47. Ibid., p. 209.

48. Aldrich, *Safety First*, pp. 9, 109.

49. Groneman, "Working-Class Immigrant Women," p. 261.

50. Lucie Cheng Hirata, "Free, Indentured, Enslaved: Chinese Prostitutes in Nineteenth-Century America," *Signs* 5, no. 1 (Autumn 1979), 3–29.

51. Hirata, "Free, Indentured, Enslaved," p. 20.

52. Ruth Rosen, *The Lost Sisterhood: Prostitution in America, 1900–1918*. Baltimore, MD: Johns Hopkins University Press, 1982, p. 98.

53. Rosen, *Lost Sisterhood*, p. 100.

54. Ibid., p. 165.

55. Jeffrey S. Adler, "Streetwalkers, Degraded Outcasts, and Good-for-Nothing Huzzies: Women and the Dangerous Classes in Antebellum St. Louis," *Journal of Social History* 25, no. 4 (1992), pp. 737–55.

56. John C. Burnham, "Medical Inspection of Prostitutes in the Nineteenth Century: The St. Louis Experiment and Its Sequel,"*Bulletin of the History of Medicine* 45, no. 3 (May–June 1971), 203–18.

57. Chaim M. Rosenberg, *Child Labor in America*. North Carolina: McFarland and Company, 2013, p. 104.

58. Ibid., p. 37.

59. Ibid., p. 90.

60. Walter I. Trattner, *Crusade for the Children: A History of the National Child Labor Committee and Child Labor Reform in America*. Chicago: Quadrangle Books, 1970, p. 24.

61. Rosenberg, *Child Labor in America*, p. 21.

62. Trattner, *Crusade for the Children*, p. 42.

63. Licht, *Working for the Railroad*, p. 191.

64. Grob, *Deadly Truth*, p. 167.

65. Licht, *Working for the Railroad*, p. 199.

66. James M. Bergquist, *Daily Life in Immigrant America, 1820–1870*. Westport, CT: Greenwood Press, 2008, pp. 9–13; and Charles J. McClain, *In Search of Equality: The Chinese Struggle against Discrimination in Nineteenth-Century America*. Berkeley: University of California Press, 1994.

67. Laurie Collier Hillstrom. *The Muckrakers and the Progressive Era*. Detroit, MI: Omnigraphics, 2010, p. 52.

CHAPTER 8

Surgery, Dentistry, and Orthopedics

Surgery in the nineteenth century advanced more dramatically than any other branch of American medicine. In the early decades of the Republic, pain, shock, and the risk of infection restricted most physicians to minor and superficial surgical interventions. During the 1840s the discovery of anesthetic chemicals like ether and chloroform at last mitigated the problem of surgical pain. Then from the late 1870s surgeons started to accept the veracity of the germ theory of infection and began to perform operations in relatively sterile conditions. Skilled operators could now risk surgeries in the abdomen and behind the chest wall. Dentistry also made substantial advances. Having made breakthroughs in pain relief and the design of fillings and dentures, American dentists were able to persuade large sections of society to have their rotting teeth repaired or replaced instead of allowing them to slowly disintegrate and then fall out. At century's end, dentists were far more educated and effective than their predecessors. But it was the highly trained surgeon, operating in the state-of-the-art hospital, who had become the most esteemed member of the medical profession.

PAIN, INFECTION, AND DEATH

In the first four decades of the century surgery in the United States barely advanced from the practices of the colonial era. Most operations

were carried out in the home of the physician or patient, few practitioners had specialized training, hygienic conditions were abysmally
low, and interventions remained relatively few and very risky. Even
as late as 1876 the famous surgeon Samuel Gross, professor of surgery
at the Jefferson Medical College in Philadelphia, lamented that "there
is not a medical man on this continent who devotes himself exclusively
to the practice of surgery."[1] A small minority of physicians became
adept at tying off aneurysms caused by syphilis, trauma, or cancer
and at removing easily accessible tumors and cancerous breasts.[2] But
the majority never attempted anything beyond extracting teeth, draining ulcers and abscesses, managing difficult births, setting broken
bones, and perhaps treating gunshot wounds, bladder stones, cataracts,
and hernias.[3]

Reading New York surgeon Valentine Mott's 1847 account of an
operation, one can easily see why surgery still conjured up images of
the abattoir. Mott told of "individuals praying in mercy that we would
stop, that we would finish, thus imploring and menacing us, and who
would not fail to escape if they were not firmly secured."[4] Family and
friends would have to hold down the surgical patient to prevent him
or her fleeing once the blade began tearing into flesh and bone. One
woman described undergoing a mastectomy in 1814 as involving
"suffering ... beyond expression, my whole being absorbed in pain."[5]
It took some time for most surgeons to become inured to the suffering
and screams of their patients. Nor was it easy to perform complex surgery on a writhing subject.[6] Furthermore, patients were understand-
ably loathe to serve as surgeons' guinea pigs. Most doctors of the
early 1800s therefore preferred to treat serious conditions like breast
cancer with depletives and a low diet rather than resorting to "so
terrible a measure" as the mastectomy.[7]

Surgical patients who survived the initial blood loss and shock
faced a tough battle against bacteria contracted from dirty operating
rooms, filthy instruments, and the unwashed hands of the surgeon
and his staff. The "surgical fevers" of tetanus, erysipelas, hospital
gangrene, and pyemia took a heavy toll. Ignorant of the role of
germs in causing infection, surgeons proudly sported aprons caked
in dried blood and surgical detritus and used saliva to aid in thread-
ing sutures. Philadelphia's Samuel Gross could be seen sharpening
his scalpel on the heel of his boot. Another eminent surgeon
described removing a cyst by clawing at it with a fingernail. Nor
did it help that surgeons regarded pus to be an essential part of the
healing process and so left it to accumulate until the wound became
obviously foul.[8]

RARE BREAKTHROUGHS

A few significant advances were made in spite of the agony and complications that dogged surgical innovation. Where the patient's death seemed imminent, surgeons were sometimes willing to inflict greater pain, undertake risky operations, and experiment with new ones. Dr. Physick earned fame for the successful removal of agonizing bladder stones: he safely extracted a thousand from Chief Justice John Marshall alone. Doctors Wright Post of Long Island and Valentine Mott of New York became skilled at tying off major arteries affected by aneurysms, and Dr. Warren Stone of New Orleans introduced silver wire for ligating arteries and demonstrated how to lessen the risk of hemorrhage by not pulling the ligature too tight.[9]

Several of the United States' greatest surgical achievements lay in the fields of gynecology and obstetrics. Ephraim McDowell, who had trained in the United States and Britain and practiced in Danville, Kentucky, achieved the remarkable feat in 1809 of saving the life of a young woman, Jane Crawford, who was believed to be carrying twins but whom McDowell showed to have a large ovarian tumor. Once he had agreed to perform a highly dangerous operation to remove the mass, Crawford rode 60 miles to Danville on horseback with the tumor supported by her saddle's pommel. He sliced open her abdomen, ligated the fallopian tubes, and cut out a 20-pound tumor. She lived another 31 years, and McDowell performed another 13 ovariotomies with just a single death.[10] J. Marion Sims, who practiced in Alabama, became an innovator after a 17-year-old slave girl called Anarcha sustained a vesico-vaginal fistula during childbirth that left her with complete urinary and rectal incontinence. It took him four years of operating on slave women with the same kind of fistula to develop a reliable method of repairing a condition that was not only exquisitely humiliating but gave rise to regular infections. Sims had his patients kneel down; he then dilated their vaginas and used a special kind of speculum to make the tear visible. Next he repaired the tear using silver sutures to reduce the risk of sepsis and fitted a catheter to keep the bladder empty while the fistula healed.[11] Several American physicians also carried out caesarean sections on women enduring life-threatening labor. Eschewing the conventional method of crushing the baby's skull and extracting a corpse, Louisiana's Francois Marie Provost performed caesareans a staggering 79 times between 1822 and 1877.[12]

These advances should not obscure the fact that there were hundreds of inept and mediocre practitioners for every successful

innovator. Genuine breakthroughs were also slow to be dissemi-
nated. Sims bemoaned how little most doctors of his day knew about
the treatment of gynecological problems. Classes on gynecology,
wryly observed the female doctor Elizabeth Blackwell, were a source
of dirty jokes more than useful instruction.[13] In any case, most of
those practicing surgery in the first decades of the century learned
by watching their preceptor and then embarked on their own careers
with little guidance and few formal opportunities to improve. Nor
should we overlook the key role played by coercion in the development of surgery.

SURGERY AND SLAVERY

One of the most important revelations of modern historical scholarship
has been the extent to which surgical greats like McDowell, Sims, and
Provost were dependent on the institution of slavery. Accounts of
new surgical procedures, as Todd Savitt has shown, disproportionately
involved blacks. Having elected to take on the challenge of correcting
vesico-vaginal fistulas, Sims later recalled, he "ransacked the country
for [black] cases and set up an eight-bed infirmary" in which to house
them.[14] Raised in slave societies in which they were forced to obey the
white man's word, women like Anarcha did not have to be overtly
coerced into putting their lives at risk for uncertain gain. They were
accustomed to submitting. Indicative of the power relationship that
underpinned his achievements, Sims only tried his operation on white
women once he had perfected it on slaves.[15] Ephraim McDowell may
have performed his first oviarotomy on a desperate white woman, but
he then honed his technique on four black patients. Similarly, all of
Prevost's early cases were slaves because he would not take the chance
of opening up the abdomen of a white client. Slavery and surgical
experimentation went hand in hand, and only occasionally did the
subject benefit.[16]

Plenty of far more obscure physicians casually sacrificed the interests
of vulnerable men and women for purposes of medical education or
therapeutic research. Many thousands of the poor had to relinquish
control over their own living or dead bodies in return for access to a
hospital bed. Medical schools thrived in areas with large populations
of the indigent who could be dissected for anatomical instruction.
White drifters, retired sailors, and poor immigrants often ended up on
the slab in northern cities and in southern port towns. Slaves were the
most defenseless group of all and hence the most systematically
abused. In 1834 Harriet Martineau noted that the bodies of "coloured

people" in Baltimore were regularly taken for dissection "because the whites do not like it, and the coloured people cannot resist it."[17] About 65% of cadavers dissected by medical students at Johns Hopkins between 1898 and 1904 were those of black men and women.[18] Similarly, an analysis of skeletons found beneath the basement floor of the Medical College of Georgia found that 79% were African American in spite of the fact that only a third of the people living in the area had been black. They were being singled out because white doctors did not believe them to warrant the same dignity as whites in life or in death.[19]

THE BIRTH OF ANESTHESIA

The introduction of anesthesia removed one of the primary restraints on surgical progress. Laughing-gas parties and "ether frolics" inspired a handful of Americans to see if nitrous oxide or ether might obviate the pain of surgery. Having participated in a number of ether parties when an undergraduate in Rochester, New York, in 1842 William E. Clarke appears to have been the first to give ether to a patient. A young woman painlessly had a tooth removed, but Clarke took the discovery no further. At about the same time, Dr. Crawford Long administered ether to a young man and then excised a tumor from his neck. Although Long went on to use anesthesia for operations for several years, he made no attempt to broadcast his discovery. In 1844 the Connecticut dentist Horace Wells, who had witnessed a public demonstration of nitrous oxide during which a participant sustained an injury but felt no pain, began to use it on his patients. He agreed to give a demonstration at Massachusetts General Hospital but administered too little gas; the patient screamed in pain, and Wells lost credibility. His business partner, William Morton, had better luck.

With the assistance of the Harvard professor Charles Jackson, Morton switched to the use of ether and, in October 1846, gave it to a patient at Massachusetts General before the removal of a neck tumor. "Gentlemen," the surgeon John Collins Warren famously announced at the completion of the procedure, "this is not humbug."[20] A year later the Scottish physician James Young Simpson introduced chloroform as an alternative. Subsequently American surgeons made important contributions to the development of local analgesics. Building on Viennese physician Carl Koller's realization that cocaine has local anesthetic effects, in the mid-1880s William Halsted experimented by injecting it into his own nerve trunks. Halsted ended up with a severe

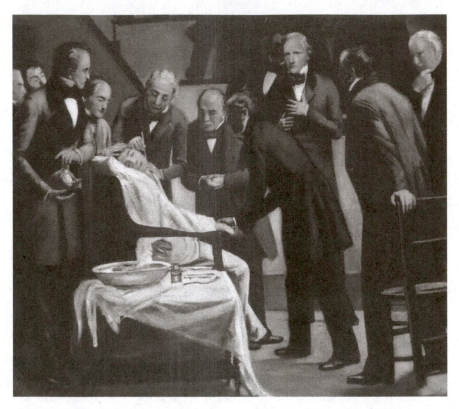

An illustration showing the first administration of ether during surgery in 1846. The scene at Massachusetts General Hospital shows William T. G. Morton, at left, administering anesthesia to Gilbert Abbot while John Collins Warren operates. Anesthesia relieved a vast amount of human suffering and made more radical surgeries possible. In the short run, however, more invasive surgeries frequently led to increased rates of death due to postoperative infection. (© Bettmann/Corbis)

cocaine addition but helped to create alternatives to general anesthesia.[21]

Now that patients could be sedated, surgeons were able to cut and probe deeper inside their bodies. They could try out surgeries that would have been out of the question on screaming, writhing, terror-stricken patients. Unfortunately, as a result of a lack of awareness of bacteria, this increased adventurousness caused rates of postoperative death to infection to shoot up. Not until asepsis had been combined with anesthesia would surgery start to become safe. Even so, ether and chloroform spared humanity a vast amount of suffering during surgery and childbirth.[22]

SURGERY AND THE CIVIL WAR

The deficiencies of even the best medical education for imparting surgical skills were brutally revealed in the early months of the American Civil War. When William Williams Keen, the new assistant surgeon for the Fifth Massachusetts Infantry, was confronted by the blood and chaos of the Bull Run battlefield in 1861, he saw immediately that the operating surgeon, who was busily removing a young man's arm at the shoulder, knew virtually nothing about limb anatomy. This was typical of the staggering rate of incompetence and ignorance that condemned large numbers of soldiers on both sides to premature death. Keen was conscious of his own shortcomings in 1861 because he had been a student at Philadelphia's Jefferson Medical College just two weeks earlier and knew that a few months of book-learning were poor preparation for battlefield operations. Keen's preceptor replied to his anxious letter with the less than reassuring words "It is perfectly true that you know very little." But he did offer one consolatory thought. Keen knew "a good deal more than" than the hopeless man he had been sent to replace.[23]

Doctors and civilians did eventually rise to the challenge of lessening the burden of human suffering, and the Civil War had an enduring impact on the quality of surgery carried out in the United States. Courtesy of the efforts of a large number of dedicated men and women, by the end of the war the Union side had developed a system of ambulances and hospitals that were to stand as models for the efficient care of military casualties. Thousands of physicians gained unrivaled experience in the ligation of arteries and amputation of limbs. Just as importantly, experience revealed the importance of keeping the operating area and the convalescent hospital as clean as possible: medical staff rarely suspected the involvement of germs in causing infection, but they did come to appreciate that fewer postoperative patients died in well-washed and ventilated wards. Finally, the essential duties performed by nurses in assisting surgeons, cleaning hospitals, and taking care of patients contributed to the postbellum emergence of nursing as a career for skilled and educated professionals.[24]

THE RISE OF ASEPTIC SURGERY

The efficacy and prestige of surgery obviously depended on surgeons conquering the timeless problem of infection. Some progress had been made before the acceptance of the germ theory of disease. In Europe and the United States physicians had gradually come to appreciate the virtues of general hygiene in hospitals. In an attempt to prevent the release of the "poisonous miasmas" implicated in hospital infections, by the 1840s the staff in many American facilities were making real efforts to keep wards clean. They regularly emptied bed pans, washed linen, and confined infectious patients to separate wards.[25] To the same end, the hospitals of the Civil War became models in the postwar era. A number of antebellum practitioners had also experimented with means of fighting infection. In an essay of 1835 the Harvard physician Oliver Wendell Holmes encouraged his obstetric colleagues to wash their hands in calcium chloride before participating in childbirths. Civil War surgeons sometimes poured acidic solutions on suppurated wounds to fight sepsis, and one team of Confederate surgeons discovered that wounds healed better if maggots were allowed to eat away necrotic flesh.[26]

But these early advances fell far short of making surgery hygienic. Only some physicians heeded the evidence provided by Oliver Wendell Holmes. Furthermore, a majority of Civil War surgeons wrongly concluded that disinfectant was a waste of time because they did not try it until gangrene had become well established, by which time it could not arrest the infection. Even the postsurgical utility of maggots was quickly forgotten after the war. Into the 1870s American surgeons still carried out operations in bloody aprons with unwashed hands. When the British surgeon Joseph Lister announced in the 1860s the efficacy of using carbolic acid as a spray during operations, other surgeons in Britain and the United States declared his system to be scientifically unjustified. One New York medical journal surmised that Lister must have a "grasshopper in his head" for so tirelessly boosting the use of carbolic acid.[27] Most were content to operate so long as the surroundings were well aired and clean to the eye. Looking back to this time, one surgeon recalled a colleague who "amputated the limb of a corpse and a limb of the living on the same forenoon, on the same table, in the same purple gown."[28] Nor did the discoveries of Louis Pasteur and Robert Koch have an immediate effect on how surgeons went about their business. Many considered it simply absurd to imagine a microscopic organism felling a human being; few relished the prospect of having to admit their own role in the spread of devastating infections; and, in any case, the idea that chemical ferments or miasmas cause infection seemed quite sufficient to account for the incidence of postoperative infection.

But from the mid-1870s onwards a minority of American surgeons did start to take germ theory seriously. A German physician working in New Orleans, Dr. Moritz Schuppert, adopted Lister's methods and wrote an article in 1879 recommending that others do the same. Although the system was promptly abandoned when Schuppert quit New Orleans soon after, surgeons at the New York Hospital also decided to add the "free use of carbolic acid" to their existing approaches to tackling infection. In 1886 Massachusetts General Hospital created an operating room where strict antiseptic principles were enforced. "Hospital gangrene," the managers of the hospital declared "has been stamped out."[29] By the mid-1880s the scientific evidence for germ theory had become still stronger. Copious reports arriving from German hospitals told of very low levels of infection because they kept operating theaters virtually free from germs. Germany's "aseptic surgery" now began to transform hospital surgery in the United States. The Midwestern surgeons William and Charles Mayo led the field in exploiting the enticing new freedom that aseptic surgery gave them to open up the body's cavities. They carried out 54 abdominal surgeries between 1889 and 1892 and then a spectacular 612 in 1900 alone. The Mayos gained an international reputation for their inventiveness and skill.[30] The enhanced safety of operating in the abdomen also allowed J. Marion Sims to pioneer gallbladder surgery, and John B. Murphy of Northwestern University developed an important method for reuniting sections of the intestinal tract.[31]

THE TRANSFORMATION OF THE HOSPITAL

These advances provided the basis for the transformation of hospitals into sites of surgical excellence to which even members of the upper and middle classes increasingly went for operations. Well-heeled Americans slowly came to appreciate that only in the hospital's operating theater could surgeons create the sterile fields that made operations relatively safe. In the best hospitals, patients could also benefit from the ever-widening range of procedures made possible by aseptic surgery. It is important to avoid overstating how rapidly surgeons grasped the full implications of germ theory: some were stubbornly resistant to the new techniques (it took over a decade after the invention of latex gloves for surgeons to begin wearing them on a regular basis), and a lot of surgeries were still performed in private homes or offices where the complex rituals of asepsis were out of the question.[32] Nevertheless, Americans of all social classes were coming to appreciate that nowhere compared in terms of safety to the hospital's pristine operating theater. Hospitals had the additional advantage to surgical patients of being able to afford the expensive X-ray machines, introduced into the United States in late 1895, that were making it so much easier to identify when surgery was called for and where surgeons needed to cut.[33]

The emergence of hospital surgery as a prestigious specialty also depended on social and economic factors. Until the later 1800s most American physicians had been obliged to practice both medicine and surgery in order to make a living. This situation changed because the heavy concentration of people in urban areas meant that at any one time there were substantial numbers of patients living in close proximity requiring the same type of procedure. In this context it was economically viable for some practitioners to devote themselves exclusively to surgery. By having patients come to the hospital, surgeons also saved the wasted time and income of having to travel from patient to patient. As several American cities grew to contain hundreds of thousands of residents, many surgeons were able to go a step further and focus on treating a single organ or condition. The rise of clearly defined surgical specializations was marked by the inception of a series of professional organizations: the American Ophthalmological Society in 1864 and the American Gynecological Society in 1876, followed by the American Association of Genito-Urinary Surgeons in 1886 and the American Orthopedic Association a year later. The prestige of surgery and the hospital specialist rose in unison.[34]

THE FLOURISHING OF AMERICAN DENTISTRY

Dentistry progressed more swiftly in the nineteenth-century United States than in any other nation. John Duffy plausibly argues that this is because most physicians were economically obliged to practice dentistry as well as conventional medicine. As a result the trade did not become indelibly associated in the public mind with itinerant quacks and hucksters as it did in Europe. Prominent dentists were able to build on this foundation by creating a caste of properly trained and credentialed dental practitioners.[35] In 1825 Horace H. Hayden began to offer a course of lectures on dentistry in the medical school of the University of Baltimore. In 1867 Harvard University gave the specialty a boost by opening its own dental department. Hayden and Chapin A. Harris had by then already set up the Baltimore College of Dental Surgery, and 12 more dental colleges had been established by 1880. The poor state of American teeth also assisted in the development of dentistry as a respectable profession. Americans by mid-century were consuming more refined sugars and fresh rather than the salted meats of old, with the result that rates of decay were climbing fast. One archaeological dig at a Confederate army burial site in Glorietta, New Mexico, found that out of the 30 men buried there, 5% had lost teeth from abscessing, a third actually had abscesses at the time of death, and just four had teeth free from decay. These figures are likely to have been better than those of the general population since volunteers with bad teeth were supposed to be sent back home.[36] So the demand for dentists was growing swiftly and with it the economic pay-offs for those able to offer a high level of care.

American dentists had strong financial incentives to innovate, and they did so with consummate success. Perhaps the greatest gains of nineteenth-century dentistry lay in the field of anesthesia, in which dentists like Horace Wells and William Morton developed the use of ether and nitrous oxide to reduce the pain and therefore the deterrence against people undergoing dental surgery. American dentists

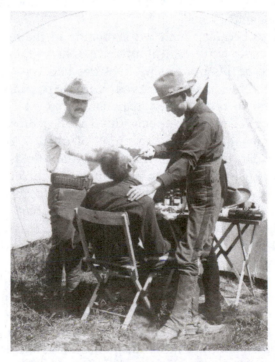

A dentist at work in a U.S. Army camp during the Spanish–American War of 1898. Dentists in the United States had made significant advances by the last years of the century courtesy of the development of anesthesia, high-quality false teeth, crowns, amalgam fillings, and effective dentures. (Library of Congress)

were also responsible for a series of improvements to the quality of false teeth and fillings. From his supply house in Philadelphia, Samuel Stockton White became well known for the high quality of the porcelain teeth he sold. Manufacturers like Stockton White made significant improvements to false teeth design by finding ways to imitate the shades and translucency of natural teeth. In 1849 the Ohio-born dentist Chapin Harris introduced the first crown that could be applied to the root of a natural tooth. At about the same time, dentists were starting to employ amalgam fillings, an alloy of mercury combined with metals like silver, tin, and copper that performed much better than traditional fillings made of tin or gold. Amalgam had been brought to the United States from France in 1833 by the shamelessly profiteering Crawcour brothers, who had used impure materials which expanded and fractured their clients' teeth. American dentists like Dr. J. Foster Flagg, professor of dental pathology and therapeutics at the Philadelphia College of Dental Surgery, labored to work out the best combinations of metals to make up amalgam fillings.[37]

Dentures also became much more reliable in the nineteenth century due to a basic technological advance. One of the major impediments to more people purchasing dentures had been that they had to be fitted into bases made of carved ivory or pounded gold or silver. These were so prohibitively expensive that into the Civil War era many poorer clients were being fitted with dentures made from animal bones or stolen from the gums of dead soldiers. In 1839 Charles Goodyear, of Woburn, Massachusetts, found that he could create hard and elastic, or vulcanized, rubber by mixing natural rubber with sulfur. His brother, Nelson, patented the vulcanizing process, and in 1844 Charles developed it as a base material for dentures. Vulcanite denture bases were durable, easy and cheap to produce, and could be molded to conform to the unique ridge pattern of the individual patient's mouth. Unfortunately, the price of dentures did not immediately drop because dentists had to pay royalties to the Goodyear Dental Vulcanite Company for each and every denture they made through vulcanization. The patent soon came into the hands of one Josiah Bacon, who was determined, regardless of the animosity of dentists and the public, to reap a vast fortune. Bacon was eventually shot dead by a dentist whom he was prosecuting in San Francisco. Finally, in 1881, the Goodyear patent came to an end and the mass production of porcelain teeth with vulcanized bases could begin.[38] Dentistry had become not only highly effective but also affordable to a large section of American society.

THE LIMITS OF SURGICAL ADVANCE

Although surgery in the United States had largely shed its ancient association with butchery by the end of the century, in many ways it had to yet to become truly scientific. The nation's premier surgeons were now medical heroes, and those trained in university medical schools like Johns Hopkins considered surgery in the days of Benjamin Rush to be almost unbelievably primitive. Yet even the very best surgeons remained prone to the speculative flights that had defined medicine in the days of Rush. Some new procedures could be carried out cleanly, skillfully, and with a minimum of pain but remained wedded to either unproven theories about the human body or the same moral sensibilities that fuelled the antimasturbation panic. We can illustrate this point by briefly considering the advent of one of the most popular of all modern surgical procedures: male circumcision.

This operation, explains David L. Gollaher, began its ascent in 1870 when J. Marion Sims called in a New York surgeon, Lewis A. Sayre, to see a boy who could not walk properly and who also had a painfully contracted foreskin. Sayre removed the offending foreskin with scissors. Soon after, he reported, the boy started to walk without difficulty. Sayre concluded that he had relieved the boy's paralysis by "quieting" a nervous system that was in a state of unhealthy agitation due to the pressure on the boy's penis. As resident surgeon of New York City Hospital, Sayre zealously promoted circumcision for the next three decades until his death.[39] Fellow surgeons argued that even if the foreskin did not cause irritation in early youth it must still be removed because the tissue of the glans could then harden and thereby lessen the enjoyment and appeal of both onanism and sexual intercourse. There is no better prophylactic against "the vile habit of masturbation," explained the 1896 book *All about the Baby*, than snipping off the foreskin. During the 1890s, vaguely inspired by bacteriology, surgeons gradually reframed the operation as a "sanitary precaution." As so often in the history of medicine and surgery, an intervention became extremely widespread on the basis of a mixture of rationalism, speculation, and hubris.[40] Surgery had come a very long way within a century, but surgeons were sometimes better at performing operations than at working out whether or not they were actually necessary.

NOTES

1. Ira M. Rutkow, *Surgery: An Illustrated History*. St. Louis, MO: Mosby-Year Book Inc. and Norman, 1993, p. 448.

2. John Duffy, *From Humors to Medical Science: A History of American Medicine*. Urbana: University of Illinois Press, 1993, p. 97.

3. Ibid., p. 95.

4. Ibid., p. 97.

5. Robert A. Aronowitz, *Unnatural History: Breast Cancer and American Society*. New York: Cambridge University Press, 2007, p. 15.

6. Martin S. Pernick, *A Calculus of Suffering: Pain, Professionalism, and Anesthesia in Nineteenth-Century America*. New York: Columbia University Press, 1985, p. 99.

7. Aronowitz, *Unnatural History*, p. 33.

8. Duffy, *From Humors to Medical Science*, chapter 7.

9. Ibid., p. 99.

10. Ibid., p. 100.

11. Deborah Kuhn McGregor, *From Midwives to Medicine: The Birth of American Gynecology*. New Brunswick, NJ: Rutgers University Press, 1998.

12. Duffy, *From Humors to Medical Science*, chapter 5.

13. Ann Douglas Wood, " 'The Fashionable Diseases': Women's Complaints and Their Treatment in Nineteenth-Century America," *The Journal of Interdisciplinary History* 4, no. 1 (Summer 1973), 25–52, p. 46.

14. Todd L. Savitt, "The Use of Blacks for Medical Experimentation and Demonstration in the Old South," *The Journal of Southern History* 48, no. 3 (August 1982), 331–48, p. 334.

15. Duffy, *From Humors to Medical Science*, chapter 7.

16. Ibid., p. 106.

17. Savitt, "The Use of Blacks," p. 337.

18. Stephanie P. Browner, *Profound Science and Elegant Literature: Imagining Doctors in Nineteenth-Century America*. Philadelphia: University of Pennsylvania Press, 2005, p. 185.

19. Judith M. Harrington and Robert L. Blakely, "Bones in the Basement: Bioarcheology of Historic Remains in Nonmortuary Contexts," in Anne L. Grauer (ed.), *Bodies of Evidence: Reconstructing History through Skeletal Analysis*. Wiley-Liss, 1995, pp. 105–19.

20. Duffy, *From Humors to Medical Science*, chapter 7.

21. Rutkow, *History of Surgery*, p. 287.

22. Ibid., p. 123.

23. Ira M. Rutkow, *Bleeding Blue and Gray: Civil War Surgery and the Evolution of American Medicine*. New York: Random House, 2005, p. 4.

24. Rutkow, *Bleeding Blue and Gray*.

25. Charles E. Rosenberg, *Care of Strangers: The Rise of America's Hospital System*. New York: Basic Books, 1987, chapter 5.

26. Duffy, *From Humors to Medical Science*, p. 165.

27. Rosenberg, *Care of Strangers*, p. 143.

28. Ibid., p. 148.

29. Rosenberg, *Care of Strangers*, p. 148.

30. Paul Starr, *The Social Transformation of American Medicine*. New York: Basic Books, 1982, p. 157.

31. Duffy, *From Humors to Medical Science*, p. 194.

32. Ibid., chapter 7.

33. Bettyann H. Kevles, *Naked to the Bone: Medical Imaging in the Twentieth Century*. Reading, MA: Addison-Wesley, 1998.

34. Rutkow, *Surgery*, p. 450.

35. Duffy, *From Humors to Medical Science*, pp. 195–8.

36. John M. Hyson, *A History of Dentistry in the US Army to World War II*. Washington, DC: Borden Institute, Walter Reed Army Medical Center, 2008, p. 29.

37. Hyson, *A History of Dentistry*, p. 18.

38. Wallace W. Johnson, "The History of Prosthetic Dentistry," *The Journal of Prosthetic Dentistry* 9, no. 5 (1959), 841–46.

39. David L. Gollaher, "From Ritual to Science: The Medical Transformation of Circumcision in America," *Journal of Social History* 28, no. 1 (Autumn 1994), 5–36.

40. David Gollaher, *Circumcision: A History of the World's Most Controversial Surgery*. New York: Basic Books, 2000, pp. 85, 90, 104.

CHAPTER 9

The Brain and Mental Disorders

The treatment of the mentally ill in the United States during the nineteenth century blended kindness, tragedy, cruelty, and vast indifference. The period opened with a steady growth in the belief that insanity could be cured, which promoted the building of scores of public and private asylums run by medical superintendents. It came to an end in an atmosphere of dark pessimism about the capacity of medicine to treat the severely mentally ill and with the asylum system buckling under the pressures of overcrowding and underfunding. As the dreams of the asylums' founding fathers withered, a confident young fraternity of neurologists preached a gloomier gospel according to which extreme mental illnesses were signs of hereditary degeneracy that no existing treatments could abate. By the beginning of the twentieth century, neurologists were doing a thriving business in treating clients with less severe forms of mental illness while a majority of state asylums had become warehouses for the chronically insane.

ANTEBELLUM IDEAS ABOUT INSANITY

Psychiatry came to exist as a distinct specialty in the nineteenth century under the leadership of doctors who rejected claims that madness is caused by either God or Satan. The idea that insanity is a physical disorder was actually far from new: since classical antiquity healers and laypersons had frequently preferred naturalistic to supernatural explanations for mental illness.[1] Physicians of the early 1800s merely denounced demonological views of mental illness with greater consistency. Their dominant theory of insanity depended on a classic distinction between body and mind. To most antebellum doctors, "mind" was synonymous with the immortal soul, and this meant that it could never itself be harmed.[2] So they inferred that insanity ensues when the body or brain suffers some kind of somatic damage or irregularity that leads to distorted information being delivered to the mind. The soul was not itself altered, but the individual behaved according to the false information it received. Psychiatrists attributed damage to the physical brain to a combination of "physical" and "moral" causes. Physical causes, wrote New England's Dr. Edward Jarvis, produce "their primary effect on the physical structure of the brain or some other organs, and disturbing the cerebral actions, produce their secondary effect on the mental operation." Examples included "a blow on the head, epilepsy, or a disordered stomach." Moral causes, in contrast, were stressors that acted "directly on the mind itself" such as "excessive study, disappointment, grief, trouble, &c." Upsetting the mind unleashed physiological effects that compromised brain function. For instance, shock, trauma, worry, and grief were said to sap the body of energy, weaken its nerves, send the blood flow awry, and injure the delicate tissues of the brain. The malfunctioning brain then caused the mind to develop the fears, delusions, and hallucination of insanity.[3]

Psychiatrists also applied the standard medical distinction between predisposing and exciting causes. They argued that men and women could be predisposed to insanity by heredity, a bad upbringing, or climatic influences operating on their bodily fluids. Exciting causes included bodily disease, trauma to the brain, excessive bouts of physical or mental effort, traumatic brain injury, or the extreme emotions caused by bereavement, a failed love affair, or financial disaster.[4] The category of predisposing causes allowed psychiatrists to import social and ethnic prejudices into their beliefs about the insane.[5] One of the few things that brought together the native-born of all classes in the United States was a visceral distaste for immigrants from Ireland. Many an asylum director articulated this kind of chauvinism in his theories about the causes of insanity. Ralph L. Parsons, superintendent of the asylum on Blackwell Island in New York, estimated that the Irish in his care had "imperfectly developed brains" and could not be treated as effectively as trueborn Americans.[6] A few psychiatrists also claimed that African Americans were subject to specific varieties of insanity. A decade before the Civil War, the physician Samuel Cartwright, who practiced in Louisiana and Mississippi, coined a new psychiatric diagnosis. "Drapetomania" denoted a psychological condition of wanting to flee the plantation. For Cartwright, those of African stock were so obviously ordained to be slaves that such behavior could only be considered evidence of insanity.[7]

INSANITY, RELIGION, AND MORALITY

Insisting that mental illnesses were caused by somatic irregularities had an obvious appeal to physicians drawn to the treatment of insanity, for it helped them in squeezing out their professional rivals for the job of running asylums. With the building of dozens of new asylums from the 1820s onwards, physicians were quick to invoke the biological nature of insanity as a justification for their assertion of control over the asylums. Amariah Brigham, first superintendent of the Utica State Hospital in New York State, explained that because insanity is caused by physical disease, patients must be "assigned to the physician, and treated for corporeal disease."[8] For a time the threat to medicine's monopoly over state asylums was quite real: when a Kentucky asylum opened in 1824, the lay keeper and a physician had to share power.[9] This situation did not last for long. Having so effectively defined mental illness in biological terms, the medically trained soon took over.

Not that antebellum psychiatrists were enemies of religion. In fact, many drew their inspiration for bringing succor to the insane from upbringings in evangelical households. They also defended biological views of madness as a bulwark against the radical doctrine that insanity alters the mind or soul. Leaders of the field like John P. Gray, superintendent of the Utica asylum, realized that if people believed that the mind itself could get sick, then it had to be physical, and therefore there could be no soul. Denying the distinction between mind and body, said Gray, would be to commit the outrage of declaring religion a fraud.[10] In the first half of the 1800s American psychiatrists also realized that their profession could hardly afford to attack religion at a time when its own status was extremely fragile. Standard accounts of the nature of madness were therefore made acceptable to liberal theologians. The religious orthodoxy of psychiatry is apparent in its promotion of moral and religious conventions. The cardinal sins of lust, pride, and envy ranked high among the apparent causes of madness identified by asylum psychiatrists. In keeping with Biblical mandates against nonprocreative sexual behavior, a significant percentage of cases were attributed to masturbation causing nervous irritation.[11] To most psychiatrists the best defense against insanity was to preserve one's moral purity by maintaining a tight control over thoughts and actions.

No-one, said Edward Jarvis, can for long evade the iron-clad "laws of vitality" that "God has stamped upon our frames."[12] Those who fell afoul of the divinely ordained rules of existence could expect to lose their reason.[13]

But the urge to implicate immorality in the onset of mental illness clashed with the desire of many psychiatrists to relieve the insane of responsibility for many of their actions. This tension came to the fore during the famous 1881 trial of Charles Guiteau for assassinating President Garfield. The law in most jurisdictions stipulated that if a person committed a murder knowing that it was wrong to do so, then he or she had to be found guilty of homicide. The insanity defense could only apply if a defendant acted under the clear influence of a delusion or hallucination. So if Guiteau knew that what he planned violated the law and standard morality, then he had to be declared wicked rather than mad. To nobody's great surprise, given the public outrage at the president's coldblooded killing, the court agreed that Guiteau had been aware of the illegality of his actions, and he therefore went to the gallows.[14] A number of psychiatrists, however, vehemently disagreed with the narrow definition of insanity that sent Guiteau to the hangman. They cited patients who were fully capable of reason but who appeared to act insanely due to irresistible emotional impulses. They referred to such cases as "moral insanity." The neurologist Dr. Edward Spitzka, for instance, described Guiteau as a "congenital moral monster" who lacked free will due to a "defective nervous system."[15]

MEDICINE FOR THE INSANE

Prior to the nineteenth century only a tiny minority of the insane had received a doctor's care. Residing in a parental home, almshouse, or poorhouse; confined to a cage; or just left to wander in lonely misery, most of the mentally ill were strangers to medicine. In both Europe and the United States those suffering from mania, delusions, and hallucinations were usually felt to have permanently lost their reason. Violent "lunatics" were therefore liable to be whipped and chained as if they were wild beasts whose aggressive instincts had to be curbed.[16] Few doctors at the start of the century were outraged when they encountered the insane shackled or caged. One Delaware physician in 1802 wrote to a journal about a man who was "chained to the floor" at home with "his hands tied across his breast," virtually naked and with "his feet and elbows bruised considerably." There was no implied criticism: he was simply describing the scene.[17] Many people also considered the antics of the severely mentally ill to be pure entertainment.

An animated Charles Guiteau defends himself on the stand during his trial for the assassination of President James Garfield. The Guiteau trial captivated the United States during 1881–1882 and brought to the fore debates within psychiatry about the nature of mental illness and the legitimacy of the insanity defense. (*Frank Leslie's Illustrated Newspaper*, 1881)

The Pennsylvania Hospital for the insane became a popular Sunday destination to locals who were happy to pay a modest fee for the chance to gawk at and tease the patients. They did not reflect on the possibility that they were inflicting suffering on fellow beings. Their indifference went along with the medical opinion that the mad, like wild animals, did not suffer from cold and pain, a view indicating a seriously deficient knowledge of both zoology and human physiology.

Only with the establishment of asylums during the 1800s did a significant number of the insane fall under the authority of doctors who tried to cure them with standard medical techniques and drugs: bleeding, leeching, cupping, and the liberal use of cathartics and emetics. Benjamin Rush, the leading American student of insanity in the decades following the Revolution, recommended the most vigorous bloodletting for the mentally ill. He also devised methods of trying to reduce the flow of blood to the brain that he reckoned to be the cause of insanity. These included cold showers and a "tranquilizer" chair that enclosed the patient's head in a box so as to reduce stimulation. In addition, Rush deduced that he could transfer the "morbid excitement" of the vessels in the brain to less critical parts of the body by starving his patients. He predicted that the debilitated stomach would somehow

draw off the energies causing irritation of the brain.[18] The next generation of psychiatrists relied on many of the same treatments. Dr. Samuel
B. Woodward, medical superintendent of the asylum of Worcester in
Massachusetts, regarded inflammation as a primary cause of insanity
and accordingly prescribed laxatives, digitalis as a counterirritative,
and plenty of local bleeding. Likewise, Utica asylum's Dr. Amariah
Brigham concluded that bloodletting would "arrest the disease" by
relieving irritation of the brain.[19]

In short, medicine for the insane conformed to the rest of medical
theory and practice: physiological balance had to be restored by regulating the body's intakes and outflows. Psychiatrists had only a few
physical treatments that were tailored to the needs of the asylum populations: agitated or violent patients were calmed or sedated through the
use of cold showers, opium, morphine, hyoscyamine, and chloral
hydrate. But asylum psychiatrists did not feel that their curative
options ended with physical remedies. Instead, they widely adopted a
variety of psychological therapy that had been developed in asylums
in France, Italy, and England in the decades around 1800. They called
the new approach "moral treatment."

"Elevation of state asylum for the insane, Tuscaloosa, on the linear
plan." Originally printed in T. S. Kirkbride, *On the Construction,
Organisation, and General Arrangements of Hospitals for the Insane*, 2nd edition.
Philadelphia: J.B. Lipincott and Co., 1880. This state asylum in Alabama
exemplifies Kirkbride's attempt to use architecture for therapeutic effect: as
patients improved they would be moved closer to the center, where the
superintendent and his family resided. (Wellcome Library, London)

MORAL TREATMENT AND THE RISE OF THE ASYLUM

Moral treatment involved a rethinking of the nature of insanity and the role of the asylum. Its exponents based their practices on two basic principles: First, that violence towards patients and the use of shackles to restrain them had to be stopped for, as the asylum superintendent Samuel B. Woodward put it, "Insanity was rarely cured by whips and dungeons and chains!"[20] Second, that the insane were not hopelessly reduced to the condition of animals but retained sufficient reason for them to be able to resume a meaningful and contented existence if given the right kind of help. In effect, moral treatment depicted the insane as akin to errant children who had succumbed to the mastery of base desires and appetites but were open to the gently corrective influence of wise adults. Between 1811 and 1822 several new asylums were constructed to provide moral treatment to the mentally ill: the McLean Asylum in Belmont in Massachusetts, the Bloomingdale Asylum in New York, the Friends' Asylum in Philadelphia, and the Hartford Retreat in Connecticut. The superintendents of these institutions regarded their role as encouraging the patient to use his or her residual rationality in order to start thinking and behaving normally once again.[21]

To accomplish this task the physician had to assume the role of a kind protector who showed an active interest in the welfare of each patient. The asylum superintendent therefore aimed to develop an intimate relationship with his wards and to provide the encouragement and comfort they needed if they were to face the world. Luther V. Bell, superintendent of the Maclean Asylum in Massachusetts, spoke of the importance of cultivating this "paternal relation" between doctor and patient.[22] In order to make the asylum as much like a real home as possible, superintendents and their staff organized guest speakers, plays, and magic lantern shows and sometimes allowed patients to produce their own newspapers. Patients also had the options of baseball, dancing, billiards, sewing circles, and walking parties. Removed from the domestic settings in which they had broken down, patients were expected to draw sustenance from the ordered homeliness of the asylum and its benevolent patriarch.[23] In addition, the new asylums were equipped with extensive and peaceful gardens to bring comfort to the patients, and the perimeter walls were high but elegant in order to lessen the sense of being incarcerated.

Moral treatment also involved the well-meaning manipulation of the patient to get him or her to practice self-restraint. Superintendents saw kindness as a means of reawakening a patient's desire for respect and esteem. As Samuel B. Woodward put it in 1839, "respect them and they will respect themselves; treat them as reasonable beings, and they will take every possible pains to show you that they are such."[24] To this end the wise and stern father of the asylum used psychological rewards and punishments to retrain the patients in the exercise of self-control. Those who behaved well and conformed to the house rules about tidying their rooms, completing their prescribed chores, displaying correct manners, and showing respect for staff and fellow patients might receive special privileges like being able to visit the nearby town on their own. Those who became unruly and uncooperative were liable to be sent to the lower floors to spend time among the most troubled patients.[25] The standard design of the American asylum, which owed much to the imagination of Dr. Thomas S. Kirkbride, complemented this carrot-and-stick approach. The asylum structure comprised a central section where the superintendent and his family lived and from which wings spread out on either side for males and females. Kirkbride designed these wings with the principles of reward and punishment in mind, for as patients improved they were able to move from the most distant rooms closer to the center.[26]

Early American exponents of moral treatment like Woodward and Kirkbride exuded confidence in the therapeutic power of their new system. If a patient came to the asylum having been insane for a year or less, proclaimed Woodard, he or she had a chance of recovery somewhere between 82 and 91 percent. Most antebellum asylums published equally gratifying data.[27] This belief in the curative power of moral treatment helped to justify the wave of asylum building that began in the early 1800s. As the first humane asylums filled up with patients whose families could afford to pay for their care, several state legislatures voted funds for the construction of state asylums in which moral treatment could be practiced without charge to the patient.[28] Dorothea Dix, a brilliant campaigner born in Maine and raised in Massachusetts, now emerged as the leader of a movement to create enough public mental hospitals that the insane could be rescued from the degradation and misery of prisons and poorhouses.[29]

The opening of the South Carolina Lunatic Asylum in 1828 marked the beginning of this new phase of asylum construction. In 1833 the Worcester Asylum opened in Massachusetts, having received $30,000 from the state legislature. Ohio and Vermont opened asylums in 1840, and fewer than 10 years later Maine, New Hampshire, New York, New Jersey, Indiana, Tennessee, Georgia, and Louisiana all followed suit. At the high point of optimism about moral treatment, the proud superintendent of the new Texas state asylum, Dr. Beriah Graham,

announced in 1857 that "it is well ascertained that a far greater proportion of insane recover in Asylums, where every means of treatment is
provided than at home, where the original exciting causes and associa-
tions continue."[30] In this hopeful spirit the numbers of asylums rapidly
grew. From a mere 18 public and private institutions in 1840, there
were 139 in 1880.[31]

Explaining the Rise of Moral Treatment

For several decades historians and social theorists have debated why,
after centuries of brutality and neglect, doctors and lawmakers began
to think that the insane deserved decent care at the tax-payer's expense.
There is some evidence that the improvement of the care of the insane
formed part of a broader humanitarian movement that led to greater
protections for the people described by Dorothea Dix as "the miserable,
the desolate, the outcast."[32] Historians have highlighted the role of
influential religious groups in nurturing this culture of compassion.
Quakers, who had long been dedicated to social and moral
causes, were clearly instrumental in creating the Friends' Asylum in
Philadelphia. A resurgent evangelical Protestantism also played a part:
the Second Great Awakening's stress on the capacity of humans to better their world could be channeled into a new sense of responsibility
toward the insane and a confidence that they could be cured.[33]

Other historians have rightly emphasized the social factors
that obliged states and cities to accept responsibility for a problem usually handled by families and communities in the rural context.
Urbanization and market capitalism, argues Gerald Grob, fundamentally altered the status of the mentally ill. Families that moved to cities
were less able than before to take care of insane relations because they
were frequently obliged to work outside the home and did not have
the wider kin supports of the rural world. Furthermore, many city
dwellers arrived alone, so if they developed mental illness there was
often no-one at all to take care of them.[34] In this context cities and states
were put under pressure to assume responsibility for the insane as an
alternative to them starving in the streets or creating a public nuisance.
Asylums became a preferred option over poorhouses once it became
clear that many of those judged to be permanently deranged could
actually be cured or at least improved.[35]

Another attempt to explain why the treatment of the insane underwent such a radical change is more controversial. The French social
theorist Michel Foucault argued in his 1961 book *Madness and
Civilization* that moral treatment was a manifestation of the new

compulsion in modern states to force everybody to become a productive citizen. Far from being humane, said Foucault, moral treatment simply replaced physical brutality or neglect with a relentless psychological cruelty. The insane now had to endure the inner turmoil and self-recrimination that came with trying to meet the superintendent's demands and expectations. Those who were released, Foucault went on, were usually not cured. They had merely internalized the values of a capitalist age that could not tolerate unproductive members and would psychologically pressure them into outward conformity.[36] There are major flaws in Foucault's thesis, however. First, he ignored the fact that the mentally ill who retain a level of self-awareness were always subject to acute self-criticism, especially where their incapacity threatened the economic security of their family. Second, Foucault went out of his way to ignore the obvious reality that getting patients back to work or to family life was the only way in which most could hope to experience contentment and security. Prior to the birth of the welfare state, employment was a matter of basic survival rather than a slavish conformity to bourgeois values. Third, detailed studies of asylums usually reveal that superintendents rarely had enough time to see each patient for more than a few minutes a day, hardly sufficient for forging the mental chains that Foucault associated with moral treatment. It is fairer to regard psychiatrists like Kirkbride and Woodward as doing the best they could to restore self-respect to their patients in circumstances that made it extraordinarily hard for them to realize their goals.

The Obstacles to Moral Treatment

State asylums found it impossible to remain the curative havens envisaged by their founders. In its first decade of operation after opening in 1833, Samuel B. Woodward's Worcester asylum discharged 80% of patients at least temporarily cured. In its second 10 years this number had slipped down to just 67% and would fall even further as the century progressed.[37] The same depressing trajectory can be charted for all the state asylums, in large part due to the combination of a lack of money and serious overcrowding. Funds were usually exhausted before the completion of state asylums so that they were often cold, drab, and dark. Medical superintendents were then overwhelmed by numbers of patients far in excess of what they could adequately care for. They also found that they were spending so much of their time dealing with emergencies that they lacked the time for one-on-one therapy with all their patients. Most patients were taken to the asylum by family or ordered there by police and courts because their delusions and hallucinations were extreme or their depressive states profound. A good number were known to be dangerous to themselves or others, and a minority regularly besmeared their beds, rooms, and bodies with excrement. Not surprisingly, physicians struggled to establish therapeutic relationships with these more chronically sick patients. Benevolence and charisma could only stretch so far.[38]

Living in crowded, rowdy, and disturbed institutions seriously undermined the patient's chance of recovery. Woodward and Kirkbride had insisted that they could not perform moral treatment if there were more than 250 inmates. By 1874 the average state hospital had 432 patients. Dozens of patients at the Middletown asylum in Connecticut had to sleep in corridors because there were not enough beds. Hundreds more moldered in poorhouses waiting for spaces to open up in the asylum. Superintendents now had to become managers first and physicians second.[39] Patients who might have had a decent shot at a speedy recovery in a small, intimate asylum suffered by being deposited in these unruly and often frightening environments. The historian Ellen Dwyer describes how patients "could be forced to retire by mid-evening, but not to sleep. Screams, noisy songs and loud obscenities filled the night air, despite vocal complaints from quieter patients."[40] Attendants who had to toil for 10-hour days with the constant threat of violence struggled to maintain their humanity. In some places the working conditions were so notoriously bad that only "criminals and vagrants" would accept the job. By the late 1850s, few state asylums were able to do without the restraints, straitjackets, and padded cells that the architects of moral treatment had hoped to expunge from the mental institution.[41]

The difficulties of overcrowding were to a large extent due to the fact that many patients suffered from chronic and incurable conditions. Sadly typical were cases like that of the Irish domestic worker admitted to New York's Willard Asylum in 1869 who sat for over 10 years in mute misery with her head bent and her eyes closed. Many of these chronic patients were suffering from "general paresis of the insane," the third stage of syphilis that did overwhelming damage to the central nervous system and brain leading to strange behavioral symptoms, convulsions, personality changes, unconsciousness, delusions, and death.[42] As time passed, more beds were occupied by men and women with conditions like paresis for whom no recovery was possible. The superintendent of Middletown Asylum reckoned in 1875 that only 8% of patients were by now curable.[43] The situation worsened in 1890 with the passage of a law that mandated that all insane patients had to be looked after in state asylums. City governments quickly realized that they could save money by sending senile elderly people from poor-houses to the asylums that were paid for by the state. Asylums, says Gerald Grob, became "surrogate old age homes."[44]

Asylum superintendents tried various ways to uphold the standards of moral treatment and avoid becoming merely custodians to the mentally ill. Some argued that separate institutions were needed for the chronic and the curable so that the latter could receive the care they needed. A number experimented with housing the incurably insane within a central building while allowing the more hopeful cases to live in on-site cottages where they did their own washing and cooking and had an outdoor privy. The Kankakee Hospital in Illinois, established in 1880, had plenty of these smaller structures, and as patients improved they were able to move further and further away from the main building and closer to the outside world. But no public institution managed to overcome the twin pressures of overcrowding and straitened finances.[45]

THE RISE OF NEUROLOGY

In the decades after the Civil War, asylum psychiatry came in for bitter criticism from the members of an emergent specialty known as neurology. The neurologists believed that a lot of mental illness could be treated on Main Street more effectively than in secluded asylums. The leading neurologist Silas Weir Mitchell lampooned what he saw as the "superstition ... that an asylum is in itself curative."[46] Neurologists also argued that the asylum system stood in the way of proper scientific research. The most uncompromising opponent of the asylum, the neurologist Edward Spitzka, stereotyped the superintendent as knowing far more about "gardening and farming" than "the diagnosis, pathology and treatment of insanity."[47] Neurologists were convinced that, in brilliant contrast to the asylum superintendent, they were at the leading edge of the biological study of brain disease. And, committed to grounding their science exclusively in an understanding of nerves and cells, they largely abandoned the mind–body distinction that had been so important to early superintendents.

The brash confidence of postwar American neurologists reflected both their own personal experiences and important scientific trends in Europe. American neurologists were often accomplished surgeons who had become familiar with nerve damage caused by bullets during the Civil War, and this led them to believe that they had a superior grasp of what could go wrong with the central nervous system. They were also aware of the decades of effort expended in the laboratories and asylums of Germany on the scientific study of insanity. An entire generation of German psychiatrists had devoted their careers to the patient study of microscopic slices of brain matter in search of lesions that correlated with the symptoms of madness.[48] The American neurologist and ex-army surgeon Charles Beard, extolling their achievements, recommended that his own countrymen be "nursed at the breast" of German science.[49] Even if neurologists in the United States had nothing like the laboratory facilities of their European counterparts, they shared an unflappable conviction that insanity involves actual damage to the nerves or brain. In fact, Americans like Silas Weir Mitchell and Charles Beard were somewhat less cautious in their approach than the Germans they so admired. They were fully convinced, without the need for the formality of laboratory investigations, that mental conditions arose from the nerves being physically exhausted or damaged. In 1869 Beard dubbed the resultant condition "neurasthenia" and confidently asserted that "in time" his theory would be "substantially confirmed by microscopical and chemical examination."[50]

If Beard provided the popular diagnosis, his fellow Civil War surgeon Silas Weir Mitchell offered the most popular treatment. Mitchell's 1877 book *Fat and Blood* made world famous his "rest cure" that combined seclusion, bed rest, a fatty milk diet, and the application of electricity and massage to restore the vitality of the nerves. Mitchell also helped inaugurate a new approach to treating the mentally ill outside of the asylum. No longer was psychiatric practice largely confined to the asylum. The care of the mentally ill had entered the clinic.[51] In practice neurologists spent most of their time treating conditions that were insufficiently severe for their clients to have been sent to asylums: they had opened up a lucrative new market in taking care of men and women with mild forms of mental illness. The managers of some privately owned asylums soon got in on the act by switching to the treatment of men and women who desired residential care but who were neither seriously ill nor a danger to themselves or others. Butler Hospital in Providence, for instance, began to advertise itself as a treatment center for neurasthenia. By 1908 nearly half of Butler's patients were there voluntarily. The patients who benefited from the "rest cure" probably did so because they were given a rare opportunity to rest and because they received the sustained and respectful attention of self-assured physicians. But neurologists like Mitchell insisted that every patient who departed their clinics happier and heavier had had his or her weakened nerves physically strengthened.[52]

In spite of their optimism about curing neurasthenia, most neurologists had a strongly pessimistic view about the possibility of treating more extreme forms of mental illness. They considered mania and deep depression to be virtually incurable and almost always inherited. This heavy emphasis on heredity marks a return to the therapeutic pessimism that had preceded the heady optimism of moral treatment between the 1820s and the 1850s. Low discharge rates from asylums nurtured this grim hereditarianism. In the 1840s asylum psychiatrists had tended to chalk up around 40% of their cases to heredity. Now that recoveries had heavily declined, in 1907 as many as 90% were ascribed to tainted pedigrees.[53] This prevalent belief that some people are foreordained by their ancestry to insanity lent a new credibility to the idea of sterilizing those of allegedly "corrupted" stock. In 1896, the state legislature of Connecticut became the first body to institute an explicit eugenic law, promising to imprison for three years any woman deemed to be eugenically unfit who had sex within or outside of wedlock. Within less than a decade, Washington and California had similar laws on their statute books. In the following century, over 70,000 people would be involuntary sterilized in American prisons and asylums.[54]

NEW AND OLD DIRECTIONS

Psychiatry entered the twentieth century deeply fractured. The superintendents of state asylums were slugging it out against neurologists over where the mentally ill ought to be treated. Neurologists regarded superintendents as mere expert jailors while many of the latter insisted that asylums really could benefit patients if they were not hopelessly overcrowded. Some of the asylum superintendents took the neurologists' criticisms to heart and brought in pathologists to perform autopsies on the brains of deceased patients. Edward Shorter talks of one young asylum pathologist who wrote a scientific article about the bloody welts he kept finding on the outer ears of deceased patients. The pathologist, manacled to a voguish biological paradigm, thought he had found an interesting physiological correlate of late-stage mental illness. He was actually documenting the results of staff brutality.[55] Similarly, when American soldiers succumbed to shell-shock amid the mud and gore of trench warfare in World War I, the biological psychiatrists were quick to ascribe their condition to physical damage caused by bullets and shrapnel.[56] Although only some realized it at the time, neurologists and their allies had overreached themselves at least as much as the early proponents of moral treatment. The followers of Beard and Mitchell had utterly failed to discover anything wrong with the nerves of neurasthenics. Nor were they able to substantiate, to the satisfaction of the rigorous mind, most of their claims about the heritability of mental defects.

Around the turn of the century the shortcomings of neurology provided fertile ground for a very different approach to thinking about mental illness. The domains of thoughts and feelings had been neglected by neurologists partly because they were so hard to study scientifically. As the philosopher and psychologist William James noted, emotions had been considered "the 'unscientific' half of existence."[57] Psychologists and psychiatrists now started to explore anew how factors like familial relationships might gain expression in the form of mental disorders. They even anticipated some of the core ideas developed by Sigmund Freud in late nineteenth-century Vienna, for example using hypnosis and talk therapy to unlock and apparently release long-buried traumatic memories. Not that Freudianism won immediate favor in the United States. Most students of mental illness were scandalized by his discussions of infantile sexual desire. Mitchell picked up one of Freud's books to read one evening, exclaimed "Where did this filthy thing come from!" and consigned it to the fire.[58] By the time the United States entered World War I, however, some psychologists were prepared to regard insanity as due to psychological factors rather than lesions that might one day be observable in a slice of brain or nerve tissue. Rather than feeding traumatized soldiers fatty diets or giving them electric shocks, they encouraged them to talk about the horrors they had experienced. The scene was set for over a century of polarizing conflict between the proponents of biological psychiatry and the advocates of talk therapy.

NOTES

1. Charles E. Rosenberg, *The Trial of the Assassin Guiteau: Psychiatry and Law in the Gilded Age*. Chicago: University of Chicago Press, 1968, chapter 1; Norman Dain, "Madness and the Stigma of Sin in American Christianity," in Paul Jay Fink and Allan Tasman (eds.), *Stigma and Mental Illness*. Washington, DC: American Psychiatric Press, 1992, pp. 73–84; and Norman Dain, *Concepts of Insanity in the United States, 1789–1865*. New Brunswick, NJ: Rutgers University Press, 1964, p. 43.

2. Dain, *Concepts of Insanity*, p. 64.

3. Gerald Grob, *The Mad among Us: A History of the Care of America's Mentally Ill*. New York: Maxwell Macmillan International, 1994, p. 60.

4. Rosenberg, *Trial of the Assassin Guiteau*, chapter 1.

5. Grob, *The Mad Among Us*, p. 69.

6. Grob, *Mad among Us*, p. 87.

7. Samuel Cartwright, "Report on the Diseases and Physical Peculiarities of the Negro Race," *New Orleans Medical and Surgical Journal* 7 (1851), 692–713.

8. Dain, *Concepts of Insanity*, p. 65.

9. Grob, *Mad among Us*, p. 42.

10. Dain, *Concepts of Insanity*, p. 65.

11. Peter Lewis Allen, *The Wages of Sin: Sex and Disease, Past and Present*. Chicago: University of Chicago Press, 2000, chapter 6.

12. Grob, *Mad among Us*, p. 63.

13. Rosenberg, *The Trial of the Assassin Guiteau*, p. 60.

14. Ibid., chapter 7.

15. Grob, *The Mad Among Us*, p. 135.

16. Roy Porter, *Mind-forg'd Manacles: A History of Madness in England from the Restoration to the Regency*. Cambridge, MA: Harvard University Press, 1987.

17. Dain, *Concepts of Insanity*, p. 24.

18. Ibid., p. 19.

19. Grob, *Mad among Us*, p. 65.

20. Dain, *Concepts of Insanity*, p. 59.

21. Grob, *Mad among Us*, pp. 66–67.

22. Ibid., p. 83.

23. Nancy Tomes, *A Generous Confidence: Thomas Story Kirkbride and the Art of Asylum-Keeping, 1840–1883*. New York: Cambridge University Press, 1984.

24. Grob, *Mad among Us*, pp. 66–67.

25. Ibid., p. 68.

26. Nancy Tomes, *A Generous Confidence*.

27. Grob, *Mad among Us*, p. 45.

28. Lawrence B. Goodheart, "From Cure to Custodianship of the Insane Poor in Nineteenth-Century Connecticut," *Journal of the History of Medicine and Allied Sciences* 65 (2010), 106–30, p. 112.

29. Grob, *Mad among Us*, p. 46.

30. Sarah C. Sitton, *Life at the Texas State Lunatic Asylum 1857–1997*. College Station: Texas A&M University Press, 1999, p. 14.

31. Robert Whitaker, *Mad in America: Bad Science, Bad Medicine, and the Enduring Mistreatment of the Mentally Ill*. Cambridge, MA: Perseus Publishing, 2002, p. 34.

32. Grob, *Mad among Us*, p. 41.

33. Ibid., p. 30.

34. Ibid., chapter 2.

35. David J. Rothman, *The Discovery of the Asylum: Social Order and Disorder in the New Republic*. Boston: Little, Brown, 1971.

36. Foucault, *Madness and Civilization*.

37. Whitaker, *Mad in America*, p. 35.

38. Grob, *Mad among Us*; Ellen Dwyer, *Homes for the Mad*; and Sarah C. Sitton, *Life at the Texas State Lunatic Asylum, 1857–1997*.

39. Grob, *Mad among Us*, p. 92.

40. Ellen Dwyer, *Homes for the Mad: Life inside Two Nineteenth-Century Asylums.* New Brunswick, NJ: Rutgers University Press, 1987.

41. Grob, *Mad among Us*, p. 92.

42. Ibid., p. 105.

43. Goodheart, "From Cure to Custodianship," p. 119.

44. Grob, *Mad among Us*, p. 120.

45. Ibid., p. 115.

46. Goodheart, "From Cure to Custodianship," p. 127.

47. Grob, *Mad among Us*, p. 133.

48. Eric Engstrom, *Clinical Psychiatry in Imperial Germany: A History of Psychiatric Practice.* Ithaca, NY: Cornell University Press, 2004.

49. Charles E. Rosenberg, "George M. Beard and American Nervousness," in *No Other Gods: On Science and American Social Thought.* Baltimore, MD: Johns Hopkins University Press, 1976, p. 99.

50. Rosenberg, "George M. Beard," p. 100.

51. Shorter, *A History of Psychiatry*, chapter 4.

52. Dowbiggin, *Keeping America Sane*, p. 63.

53. Nathan G. Hale Jr., *Freud and the Americans; the Beginnings of Psychoanalysis in the United States, 1876–1917.* New York, Oxford University Press, 1971, p. 76.

54. Daniel Kevles, *In the Name of Eugenics: Genetics and the Uses of Human Heredity.* New York: Knopf, 1985, pp. 99–100.

55. Shorter, *History of Psychiatry*, p. 91.

56. Hale, *Freud and the Americans.*

57. Ibid., p. 54.

58. Ibid., p. 62.

CHAPTER 10

The Pharmacopeia

Minerals and plants were central to European-style, African American, and Native American healing practices in the nineteenth century. The United States' indigenous peoples had extensive repertoires of organic remedies that were usually administered in accordance with supernaturalist beliefs in the case of serious internal illnesses and practical experience in the treatment of superficial conditions. African American healers were heavily reliant on the plants that they could harvest from forests, fields, and swamps in the vicinity of where they labored. The pharmacopeia of European-style medicine comprised extracts from native and imported flora but stands out for the harshness of such common remedies as the elements mercury and antimony and the shameless profiteering of many commercial medicine producers. Only a small minority of these drugs worked in a conventional sense, and the medical laboratory had delivered only a few powerful new therapies by the end of the century. But it is important to keep in mind that conventional measures of efficacy are not the only ways of valuing medicines. Nineteenth-century patients undoubtedly benefited from the placebo effects triggered by receiving drugs from trusted healers. No less importantly, medicines formed important parts of the cultures of North American peoples, especially among slaves and their descendants, who strove to uphold a sense of cultural separateness from their masters, and Native Americans, for whom the mysteries of medicine were inseparable from their most fundamental beliefs about the spirit world.

DRUGS IN THE EUROPEAN MEDICAL TRADITION

The Age of Heroic Medicine

Until late in the 1800s regular physicians had few medicines that we know to have been physiologically effective. Genuine remedies like quinine for malaria, digitalis for dropsy, and lime juice for scurvy represent a small fraction of the drugs routinely prescribed. Most physicians of the early nineteenth century judged a plant or mineral substance according to its ability to bring about the evacuation of fluids or to calm the blood flow. As Charles Rosenberg explains, most maladies were associated with the eruption, expulsion, or retention of fluids and feces and so it seemed obvious to doctors and patients alike that hastening their removal would either alleviate or actually get rid of the disease process.[1] Copious bloodletting, cathartics to promote defecation, emetics to cause vomiting, and diaphoretics to increase perspiration were therefore staples of medical practice. Many physicians favored drugs that had the extreme physiological effects of mercury and antimony or the plant derivatives jalap, scammony, rhubarb, and quinine. Benjamin Rush exemplified this heroic approach to therapy.[2] "Always treat nature in a sick room," he advised, "as thou would a noisy dog or cat ... drive her out at the door & lock it upon her."[3] Patient and physician could both draw reassurance from the highly visible effects of heroic doses. The doctor was also expected to be aggressive in treatment where any sign of self-doubt might cause the patient to question his wisdom. Behaving, as historian Steven Stowe puts it, in a "masculine and assertive" way put the client's mind at rest and buttressed the physician's credibility.[4]

The liberal use of "calomel," or mercurous chloride, illustrates just how much physicians expected patients to endure, and how much the sick were willing to undergo, in order to have normal bodily operations restored. Mercurous chloride remained among the most frequently prescribed of all regular medicines until it began to decline in popularity during the 1840s. Even at routine doses it caused violent vomiting and copious salivation. Many patients developed mercury poisoning: their mouths ulcerated, their gums sloughed off, and their teeth fell out. Those given very high doses also risked necrosis to their jaw bones. Some were reduced to sucking gruel and water through straws inserted into holes in the dead and disintegrating bone.[5] Samuel Jackson, chair

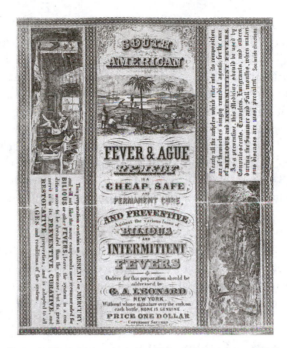

Antiague medicines like this one (ca. 1850–1900) were widely employed in frontier regions and the southern states where malaria struck hardest. Many of these patent remedies contained quinine, derived from the cinchona tree of South America. Although quinine was known to reduce the severity of malarial symptoms, some patent manufacturers diluted it to such an extent that their drugs made little or no difference. Quinine-containing medicines were also used to treat other febrile conditions, including typhoid fever and yellow fever, and as a tonic in an attempt to restore the body's vitality. Patients and physicians did not realize that quinine is only effective against malaria. (Library of Congress)

of physiology at the University of Pennsylvania, felt the need to tell his colleagues in 1853 not to give calomel to children under six. He had seen too many cases of their teeth falling out and gangrene taking grip in the bloody cavity.[6] But serious diseases appeared to require no-nonsense remedies. Rush prescribed heavy doses of calomel, combined with the plant-derived cathartic jalap, to deplete the body of the fluids that he believed to be irritating the blood vessels.[7]

Not all practitioners favored heroic regimens. The healer and midwife Martha Ballard, who practiced in rural Maine between 1785 and 1812, reproved in her diary local doctors who prescribed large quantities of drugs like quinine. Her practice also provides a window into the continuation of magical belief systems during the early nineteenth century.

To treat shingles Martha "bled a Catt & applid the Blood," and she tried
to cure her niece's tuberculosis by taking the "the last milk from the cow"
and squirting it into her mouth.[8] John Mack Faragher has likewise
revealed a thriving folk medicine in the prairies of Illinois at mid-
century. Settlers told of the dangers of witches and evil spirits. Some people also invoked the ancient doctrine of signatures: for instance, the
round-lobe hepatica, of the butter-cup family, was believed to cure "bilious ailments" because its leaves were apparently a similar shape to the
human liver.[9] Such practices were not confined to lay practitioners.
In fact, Martha attributed her occult remedy for tuberculosis to a local
physician called Amos Page. The same physician left behind a remedy
book that suggests a strong preference for gentle remedies. Page treated
dropsy, for example, with parsley roots, horseradish, and mustard seed.[10]
In the glutted medical marketplace of the nineteenth century, a patient
could choose according to his or her tolerance of pain what kind of practitioner to summon. The fear of calomel ensured that physicians with a
reputation for employing kinder regimens were able to stay in business.

New Directions in Chemotherapy

During the middle decades of the century American physicians came to
reply less and less on such heroic depletives as bleeding, calomel, and
antimony. Instead they more often prescribed hearty diets and "tonics"
like quinine, cinchona, iron compounds, and alcohol. Heroic drugs like
calomel did not fall entirely from use but came to be used by a minority
of physicians or in exceptional circumstances. John Harley Warner's
study of hospital treatment shows that just 28.7% of male patients were
receiving calomel by the 1850s, and typhoid fever was much more
likely to be combatted using whiskey, wine, brandy, iron, cod liver
oil, and tincture of cinchona.[11] The prescription book of the Second
North Carolina Military Hospital in Petersburg, Virginia, shows that
over 60% of Civil War prescriptions contained whiskey as a tonic:
patients were on average receiving about a third of a pint of liquor a
day. Another 10% of remedies contained quinine as a tonic.[12] The incli-
nation to assist the body's attempts to heal itself complemented an
increased reliance on palliatives. Over 40% of prescriptions at the
Second North Carolina Military Hospital contained an opiate to quell
the pain of convalescent or dying soldiers. Opium use in hospitals more
generally rose from about 45% of male admissions in the 1830s to over
60% in the 1860s.[13] Hospitals, physicians, and patients also ordered
large quantities of Dover's Powder, which contained opium and the
plant derivative ipecacuanha. Both drugs controlled pain and helped

bring the relief of sleep. Moreover, patients were receiving increasing quantities of morphine, the hypnotic principle of opium isolated by a German chemist in 1805.[14] First used in the United States at Massachusetts General Hospital in the 1830s, as many as a fifth of the hospital's patients were prescribed morphine by the 1870s, not least because it could be easily injected with a hypodermic syringe. Palliative care had become a basic objective of American medicine.[15]

The clinical use of morphine highlights the increasing role of the biological and chemical laboratory in the emergence of new therapeutics after mid-century. A view emerged among many educated physicians that medical discoveries could only be made in laboratories in which a wide range of compounds could be produced and then systematically tested on animals.[16] Occasional breakthroughs like the development of chloral hydrate emboldened these exponents of laboratory research. In the 1860s the German experimental pharmacologists Rudolf Buchheim and Oscar Liebreich correctly predicted that chloral hydrate would have a strongly sedative effect. Liebreich tried it on animals before experimenting on himself to confirm the chemical's potential to bring calm and sleep to the patient. Not long after, chloral hydrate was being used in hospitals and asylums across Europe and the United States. The last year of the century brought another success story in the form of aspirin. The analgesic properties of salicylic acid, derived initially from willow bark, had been known since the 1700s, and a German chemical firm had started to synthesize it during the 1870s. Although this drug proved to be effective in lowering fevers and in reducing the pain associated with rheumatism, headaches, neuralgias, and rheumatism, it often caused severe side effects, especially in the stomach. Eventually the problem was solved by the chemist Felix Hoffman and the pharmacologist Heinrich Dreser, working for the Bayer Company in Germany. Their variant of salicylic acid, called aspirin, was far safer and became a rapid commercial success.[17] But it was the rise of bacteriology that most firmly established the laboratory as the primary site of medical progress. With the success of the diphtheria antitoxin, confidence grew in the possibility of further therapeutic boons.[18] By the end of the century, the best American medical colleges had recognized the power of laboratory medical science, and their salaried scientists were joining the hunt for effective chemotherapies.[19]

Pharmacists and Pharmaceuticals

Early in the century healers could obtain the ingredients for their remedies from several different sources. Herbal medicines they frequently gathered from nearby fields and forests. Martha Ballard, for whom the earth had been bestowed with healing plants by a benevolent God, had to walk only a short distance from her home to collect burdock to treat sore joints and cold water root for scarlet fever. Cow pats and sheep dung for poultices were obviously readily available in the rural United States. In fact virtually the entire armarium for lay healers like Ballard derived from native and introduced plants growing in the immediate vicinity.[20] The same applied to the hundreds of thousands of Americans who were swept up by the enthusiasm for the botanical medicines of the Thomsonians and the Eclectics. The mainstays of Samuel Thompson's regimens, like lobelia and cayenne peppers, could be grown widely across North America.[21]

Mineral drugs like antimony and calomel or harder-to-extract plant derivatives such as quinine usually had to be procured from commercial dealers. Physicians and patients relied on a thriving trade that linked up drug importers, wholesalers, apothecaries, and chemists. Apothecary shops, like Durand's Drug Store on Sixth and Chestnut in Philadelphia, carried extensive ranges of drugs from around the world alongside compounded medicines for the physician.[22] So important were the compounders of drugs to physicians that, as Paul Starr notes, some of the first telephone lines in the United States during the 1870s were set up to connect doctors with their local pharmacies.[23] But the purveyors of drugs differed considerably in expertise. Many druggists just flogged secret nostrums made by patent medicine manufacturers. Those who ran pharmacies, in contrast, were often men with training in chemistry, who knew of the latest research being carried out in Europe and could chemically extract the active components of medicinal plants. Eager to distance themselves from mere shopkeepers, Philadelphia's pharmacists established a College of Pharmacy in 1821. After the Civil War, aspiring pharmacists began to attend college in significant numbers. By 1865 there were only 5 pharmacy schools in the United States. This number stood at 500 at the turn of the century. By then a number of states had passed laws regulating who could set up a pharmacy.[24]

But the compounding pharmacist remained under economic threat from the manufacturers of patent medicines. English imports like Bateman's Pectoral Drops and Hooper's Female Pills flooded the market at the start of the century, but canny American businessmen were quick to get in on the act. Within a few years most nostrums sold in catalogues were being manufactured in the United States.[25] Samuel Lee Jr. marketed "bilious pills," the box emblazoned with the American eagle, to treat yellow fever, jaundice, dysentery, worms, and female complaints. It sold copiously in the expanding frontiers among families with little or no access to medical care. Thomas W. Dyott, an English immigrant who falsely claimed to be a doctor himself and the grandson of a famous Scottish doctor, left an estate worth a massive $250,000 from the proceeds of products like his Robertson's Infallible Worm Destroying Lozenges. The rising incidence of tuberculosis also created a huge commercial opportunity for selling "pulmonic syrups" and "pectoral lozenges."[26]

Manufactures were notorious for the shamelessness of the advertisements with which they crowded the pages of the nation's dailies and weeklies. Shock tactics helped to ensure that hundreds of thousands of men and women parted with a dollar or two just in case the assertions of drug manufacturers were actually true. One typical nostrum container bore a drawing of a man firing a bullet into his head because he had not treated his nervousness with the company's medicine. These products usually contained the kinds of drugs prescribed by orthodox physicians. Piso's Cure for Consumption, Tobia's Derby Condition Powder, and Ayer's Cherry largely consisted of antinomy. Storey's Worm Cakes and Cling's Worm Lozenges were filled with dangerously high levels of calomel, jalap, and scammony, which, when over-liberally prescribed by anxious mothers and fathers, caused many a child to lose teeth or the ability to move the lower jaw.[27] Nevertheless, some patent brands were popular because they induced less extreme physiological effects than the treatments of doctors like Benjamin Rush. As John Harvey Young points out, a pill containing a moderate quantity of calomel caused much less discomfort than Rush's practice of depleting some patients of 80% of their blood.[28]

The makers of patent remedies were always ready to exploit the latest discovery or medical fad. A Prussian immigrant to Texas called William Radam made a personal fortune by selling gallon jugs of his Microbe Killer. By 1890 he ran 17 separate factories. A chemical investigation revealing that his solution was 99.381% water with tiny additions of sulfuric acid did little to hurt his sales.[29] Americans who were just beginning to comprehend the danger of the invisible germ sustained his lavish lifestyle in a mansion on Fifth Avenue overlooking Central Park. Patent medicine producers also seized on the potential offered by the discovery in 1884 that cocaine has local anesthetic properties. Cocaine Toothache Drops enriched manufacturers in Albany, New York, while a Boston doctor happily provided a testimonial to the makers of Liebig Company's Coca Beef Tonic describing his "unfailing success" in using the tonic "among hundreds" of "broken-down and nervous lady patients."[30] Such was the cynical

Advertisements for Horsford's tonic, a phosphoric acid compound, developed by the Harvard chemist Eben N. Horsford and manufactured by the Rumford Chemical Works of Rhode Island, claimed that it "nourishes and invigorates the tired brain and body, imparts renewed energy and vitality, and always enlivens the functions." Horsford's tonic exemplifies the lack of regulation of the patent drug industry in the nineteenth century. Firms had no obligation to demonstrate the safety or efficacy of their products. (Library of Congress)

cleverness of producers and the desperation of the sick that as many as 50,000 different patent remedies were available in the United States in 1905.[31]

But the makers of nostrums faced growing competition from a pharmaceutical industry that produced and sold large quantities of drugs of known quality. German and French chemists led the way in isolating plant alkaloids like morphine, strychnine, quinine, and caffeine. Industrial firms then quickly opened up to supply the medical market. In 1818 John Farr and Abraham Kunzi started an operation in Philadelphia that produced bulk quantities of quinine and other alkaloids. In 1841 Smith, Kline and French opened its manufactory in Philadelphia. By the late 1850s Cincinnati, Detroit, and Baltimore all had firms with substantial laboratories in which they too isolated alkaloids. The pharmaceutical industry managed to grow in size because of a couple of important developments. First, they got better at maintaining the quality of their products. The Detroit firm Parke-Davis, for instance, teamed up with the University of Michigan's chemist Albert Lyons in 1880 in order to find ways to ensure the quality of over 20 widely prescribed chemicals. Second, they created laboratories in which they could supply the huge demand for new biological products including diphtheria antitoxin, antistreptococcus serum, rabies vaccine, and tetanus antitoxin. By 1900 some of the largest pharmaceutical firms in the United States had achieved the necessary scientific expertise to embark on the search for novel biological and chemical therapies.[32]

The sellers of mysterious nostrums were more vulnerable to attack as the educational standards of doctors and pharmacists rose and drug development became more scientific. Late in the century physicians and lawmakers began to realize that high levels of calomel and antimony were often extremely dangerous. Doctors and pharmacists also came to appreciate that the activities of entrepreneurs compromised the reputation of medicine in general. So the American Medical Association led a furious charge against the nostrum sellers as the enemies of public health. The AMA's assaults helped to bring about the Food and Drug Act of 1906 that allowed a government agency to prosecute anyone who sold drugs without making its "strength, quality, or purity" transparently clear. It provided the starting point for subsequent enactments that made medicines in the United States considerably safer as well as more effective.[33]

THE PHARMACOPEIA OF AFRICAN AMERICAN MEDICINE

Plants were the mainstay of medicine as practiced within African American communities. Healing plants were either grown or gathered by slaves prior to abolition. Those like garlic and sage could be cultivated in the small plots of land granted by some masters to their slaves in order to save money on food. Other medicinal plants were collected in the forests or wetlands that bordered plantations. Slaves called it "root en herb gatherin."[34] Dulcinda Baker Martin of Kentucky later explained: "Us uster gather cherry bark, horseradish root, dand'line root, hickory bark, mullen, penny-royal, poke root, en poke berries, en de Lord knows what ... Chicken gizzard skin was saved fer medicine."[35] The historian Herbert Covey has detailed many of the plant species that were used as medicines on plantations: lion's tongue, red oak bark, life everlasting, garlic, chinaberry tea, Jerusalem oak, dogwood, tansy leaves, peach tree leaves, catnip, calamus root, flag root, sage, snakeroot, sage, Indian hemp, sore throat root, sweat root, arrowroot, backache root, raspberry leaves, pine needles, elephant tongue, comfrey, sea myrtle, orange milkweed, wild cherry bark, poke root, mustard weed, may apple, and sweet William roots.[36] Some of these were used because they were similar to West African species, others due to the influence of Native American healers, and some because they were found to induce a desired physiological effect.

Different sicknesses were combated using specific parts and products of the local flora. In southern Appalachia, slaves took black snake root for coughs and colds or as a blood cleaner and buckeye for rheumatism. Sassafras occupied an especially important place in African American medical practice. Its roots and bark were said to clean the blood, especially after winter when impurities were believed to accumulate, as well as to treat venereal diseases and fevers. Many slave children were also made to drink garlic rum on the first sunny day after winter as a "spring tonic."[37] In addition, those with stomach aches might receive flag root or snakeroot; pepper and dogwood tea were given for fevers and jimsonweed for headaches or dropsy; Indian turnip root or jack-in-the-pulpit were expected to cure kidney, liver, and ulcer problems; and bowel problems were treated with yams.[38] There are also accounts of the oil being extracted from castor beans to grease the backs of badly-whipped slaves to prevent their shirts becoming stuck in their scabs.[39] The exact remedies employed depended on the particular ecologies of the plantation region. In some places, like the Georgia and South Carolina Sea Islands, there is also good evidence of the continuity of African cultural practices in the use of herbal remedies.[40] Some of the herbs used had even been transplanted from West Africa and knowledge of how to use them transmitted by oral tradition.[41]

Other African American remedies relied on the use of easily available fauna. For lockjaw, usually caused by tetanus, cockroaches could be ground up and made into a tea. In Alabama slaves were treated for whooping cough, colds, or influenza with teas prepared from the scrapings from hog's feet. A majority of African American medicines were ingested, but they could also be used topically for certain complaints. Toothache was believed to be eased by slicing off skin from the fleshy part of a horse's hoof, crumbling it into ash above a fire, and then applying it to the troublesome tooth.[42] Moreover, remedies often had magical rationales. Later interviews tell us that many slaves wore herbs in the belief that they would ward off illness and promote health. The historian Herbert Covey described how, due to its foul odor, asafetida or "devil's dung" was frequently hung around the necks of children to prevent asthma, mumps, smallpox, diphtheria, and whooping cough. Others carried asafetida, garlic, or potatoes in their pockets to ward off disease.[43]

Slavery profoundly affected the African American pharmacopeia. The degradation of the slave system encouraged African Americans to develop therapies that conflicted with those of the dominant white culture and that drew on African traditions of healing. In this way they maintained a cultural space free from the ideas of their oppressors. Furthermore, slave healers unsurprisingly placed far greater emphasis on the use of herbal remedies that did not cause serious discomfort where the white doctor's vomits and enemas often felt like extensions of the punitive regime of slavery. As the historian Sheila Fett points out, for most slaves there was no clear line between white medicine and the relentless discipline of the slave system.[44]

THE PHARMACOPEIA OF NATIVE AMERICAN MEDICINE

The medicinal use of plant products by Native Americans is a topic of extraordinary complexity for the simple reason that native peoples developed so many different applications for the rich fauna of North America's diverse landscapes and geographical zones. The ethnobiologist Daniel E. Moerman has calculated that indigenous groups employed about 2,564 separate species out of 21,641 types of flora.[45] Parts of plants might be blown on to the body of the sick, ingested as food or drink, inhaled as smoke treatments, released into a river in the hope that they would take away the patient's malady, applied as an ointment or poultice, or laid across wounds in an attempt to stem bleeding. The encyclopedic range of native remedies does not mean that indigenous people were indiscriminate in what flora they gathered or grew. As Moerman also revealed, they used only 11.8% of all available flora for medicines. The majority they considered to have no medicinal value at all.[46] Of course each society made use of only a fraction of the 2,564 plants, but all had very extensive repertoires of plant remedies. The aim of this section is to convey a general sense of the diverse plants identified as medicinal by different native populations and the varied manners in which they were administered.

The limited range and distribution of plants made an obvious difference to what species were used by different native peoples. Populations living close to the Mexican border recognized the psychoactive properties of the indigenous peyote cactus and gave it in the form of decoctions to treat fevers and obviate pain. Several plants that grew widely in California were likewise used to diminish pain or as sedatives. In northern California the Capella Indians prescribed the roots of the red delphinium to promote sleep among children and the sick, and they placed scrapings of the Californian poppy into tooth cavities to relieve toothache. Indian societies of the thickly wooded regions of the North relied more heavily on the barks, leaves, gums, and resins of evergreen trees.[47] The itinerant healer Molly Ockett, among the last of the Pigwacket people of New Hampshire and Maine, treated both her fellow Indians and frontier whites with the inner bark of spruce trees for dysentery. For headaches she combined the bark of birch and hemlock and added the sperm of buck deer, wild onions, garlic, and molasses.[48] The rhizome bloodroot was an especially popular source of medicine in the hardwood forests of the eastern United States. The Rappahannocks of Virginia, for example, considered its bloodlike juice to be a palliative for rheumatism. Those living in the eastern and central regions of the United States also used a number of flowering plants native to this vast region. Indigenous groups living between Kansas in the west and the eastern seaboard drank or smoked lobelia or Indian tobacco as a treatment for asthma, bronchitis, and other respiratory complaints.[49] White and black cohosh, which grew in the eastern woodlands, were employed in an attempt to ease the pains of rheumatism, childbirth, nervous irritability, and spasms. The rare lady's slipper orchid also grew in eastern bogs and woods and was said to alleviate depression and anxiety.[50]

Many of these plants were exploited by native healers simply because they had the desired effect. Herbalists knew what plants were good as diaphoretics, emetics, and cathartics because the bodies of patients responded so visibly to them: it did not take long for native peoples of the Carolinas to realize that a tea made of the leaves of the yaupon tree caused violent puking.[51] Most of these remedies did not benefit patients beyond the triggering of a placebo effect. Other plant-based medicines, however, were prescribed over successive generations because they actually did cure diseases or bring relief to the patient. Through serendipity and keen observation, long before the nineteenth century indigenous peoples had identified genuinely effective remedies. For instance, the peoples of the trans-Mississippi West who ate cranberry berries in cases of scurvy had surely discovered that they cured the receding gums, ulcerations, and lassitude typical of this deadly malady.[52] Similarly, the Potawatomis of the upper Mississippi region learned that jewelweed is effective against the contact dermatitis caused by poison ivy.[53] And it may be that Indian healers like Molly Ockett made poultices out of rotten apples because her forebears had noticed that they work better than anything else. We now know that apples are often spoiled by molds producing penicillin.[54] The historian Virgil J. Vogel points out that "aboriginal knowledge" of "their native flora" was so extensive that "Indian usage can be demonstrated for all but a bare half dozen, at most, of our indigenous vegetable drugs."[55]

Indigenous societies were particularly good at recognizing plants with effects on the nervous system. The ethnobiologist William A. Emboden Jr. has identified scores of native medicines that could give relief from pain, anxiety, and depression or provide a narcotic escape. Red delphinium and the bark and roots of wild black cherry can induce sleep while the Californian poppy root contains potent opiates.[56] The native groups that chewed the bark of willow also ingested the salicylic acid that is the active ingredient of aspirin. Moreover, recent clinical studies indicate that the roots of *Echinacea* species, chewed or made into tinctures by groups like the Cheyenne and Choctaw to treat colds and sore throats, significantly reduce the symptoms and duration of upper respiratory tract infections. There is modern data to suggest that several other widely employed plants may have lessened the chronic inflammation of rheumatoid arthritis.[57]

Most native remedies were selected because they were consistent with a group's spiritual beliefs. Vogel points out that native populations widely subscribed to the doctrine of signatures according to which the appearance of a plant is an indication of the maladies it can cure: wormroot was believed to fight worms due to its appearance, bloodroot was used to stop bleeding because of its red juice, and yellow plants were assumed to be effective against jaundice. Other plants were identified as curative because they smelled or tasted foul or caused the patient to vomit or have diarrhea. Demons and evil spirits were expected to quit the patient's body as it became distasteful or dangerous for them to remain.[58] The role of supernaturalist beliefs is especially apparent in the use of plants without them being ingested or inhaled. Among the Iroquois, for instance, the ears of defective corn plants were wrapped up in the clothing of a sick person and then placed beneath the pillow of the shaman, who was then expected to have a dream revealing the source of the patient's condition.[59] The eastern Cherokee gathered healing herbs and then floated them down rivers in sacred cloth in the hope that sicknesses would be taken with them.[60] In short, a considerable amount of what the shaman did can only be understood in terms of complex sets of religious ideas.

THE THREE TRADITIONS

There is not much to choose among the three broad traditions of healing in terms of efficacy. European-style and Native American healers used a number of natural products that helped to fight specific illnesses or provided relief from pain or anxiety. African American healers, cir-cumscribed by the brutal conditions of slavery, had access to fewer use-ful remedies, but they at least used fewer of the harsh and damaging depletives of early nineteenth-century white medicine. For the most part, however, European-style, Native American, and African American medicines relied on pharmacopeias that did not work by conventional definitions. People took what they were prescribed for a variety of reasons: the desperate optimism of the sick, deference to long tradition or to the authority of the healer, the intuitive plausibility of the overarching medical and religious theories that rationalized their use, the ease with which we assume that just because a patient gets better after taking a drug that he or she recovered because of it, and the powerful placebo effect triggered in some patients. In addition, both African Americans and Native Americans considered upholding their own traditions to be a bulwark against the absolute domination of white culture and power. Only with the rise of laboratory medicine did European-style medicine begin to make significant advances. At first most advances enhanced the ability of scientists to explain and to diagnose disease. But the systematic methods of the laboratory had created the essential conditions in which discoveries could be made. The next century would see the development of a long series of new drugs, massive expenditure on research, and the growth of a vast and highly profitable enterprise of producing and marketing drugs.

NOTES

1. Charles E. Rosenberg, "The Therapeutic Revolution: Medicine, Meaning and Social Change in Nineteenth-Century America," *Perspectives in Biology and Medicine* 20, no. 4 (1977), 485–506.

2. John Harley Warner, *Therapeutic Perspective: Medical Practice, Knowledge, and Identity in America, 1820–1885.* Cambridge, MA: Harvard University Press, 1986, p. 51; and John S. Haller Jr., *American Medicine in Transition, 1840–1910.* Urbana: University of Illinois Press, 1981, p. 72.

3. Warner, *Therapeutic Perspective,* p. 18.

4. Steven M. Stowe, *Doctoring the South: Southern Physicians and Everyday Medicine in the Mid-Nineteenth Century.* Chapel Hill: University of North Carolina Press, 2004, p. 161; and John S. Haller Jr., "The Use and Abuse of Tartar Emetic in the Nineteenth-Century Materia Medica," *Bulletin of the History of Medicine* 49 (Summer 1975), 235–57, p. 253.

5. Haller, *American Medicine in Transition,* p. 86.

6. Ibid., p. 86.

7. Ibid., p. 78.

8. Laurel Ulrich, *A Midwife's Tale: The Life of Martha Ballard, Based on Her Diary, 1785–1812*. New York: Knopf, 1990, p. 51.

9. John M. Faragher, *Sugar Creek: Life on the Illinois Prairie*. New Haven, CT: Yale University Press, 1986, p. 93.

10. Ulrich, *A Midwife's Tale*, p. 54.

11. Warner, *Therapeutic Perspective*, p. 130.

12. Ibid., p. 140.

13. Ibid., p. 30.

14. John P. Swann, "The Evolution of the American Pharmaceutical Industry," *Pharmacy in History* 37, no. 2 (1995), 76–86.

15. Warner, *Therapeutic Perspective*, p. 36.

16. Harry Marks, *The Progress of Experiment: Science and Therapeutic Reform in the United States, 1900–1990*. New York: Cambridge University Press, 1997, p. 21.

17. Charles C. Mann and Mark L. Plummer, *The Aspirin Wars: Money, Medicine, and 100 Years of Rampant Competition*. New York: Knopf, 1991.

18. Warner, *Therapeutic Perspective*, p. 278.

19. Kenneth Ludmerer, *Learning to Heal: The Development of American Medical Education*. New York: Basic Books, 1985.

20. Ulrich, *A Midwife's Tale*, chapter 1.

21. Haller, *The People's Doctors*.

22. Swann, "The Evolution of the American Pharmaceutical Industry," p. 77.

23. Paul Starr, *The Social Transformation of American Medicine*. New York: Basic Books, 1982, p. 69.

24. Gregory J. Higby, "Professionalism and the Nineteenth-Century American Pharmacist," *Pharmacy in History* 28, no. 3 (1986), 115–24, p. 121.

25. James Harvey Young, *The Toadstool Millionaires: A Social History of Patent Medicines in America before Federal Regulation*. Princeton, NJ, Princeton University Press, 1961, p. 47; and Young, *The Toadstool Millionaires*, p. 16.

26. Ibid., pp. 16–20.

27. Haller, *American Medicine in Transition*, p. 86.

28. Young, *The Toadstool Millionaires*, pp. 36–7.

29. Ibid., p. 148.

30. J. Worth Estes, "The Pharmacology of Nineteenth-Century Patent Medicines," *Pharmacy in History* 30, no. 1 (1988), 3–18, p. 13.

31. Young, *The Toadstool Millionaires*, p. 111.

32. Swann, "The Evolution of the American Pharmaceutical Industry," pp. 75–79.

33. Philip J. Hilts, *Protecting America's Health: The FDA, Business, and One Hundred Years of Regulation*. New York: Alfred A. Knopf, 2003.

34. Herbert C. Covey, *African American Slave Medicine: Herbal and Non-Herbal Treatments*. Lanham, MD: Lexington Books, 2007, p. 77.

35. Covey, *African American Slave Medicine*, p. 77.

36. Ibid., p. 78.

37. Kenneth F. Kiple and Virginia Himmelsteib King, *Another Dimension to the Black Diaspora: Diet, Disease, and Racism*. New York: Cambridge University Press, 1981, p. 170.

38. Covey, *African American Slave Medicine*, pp. 76–78.

39. Fett, *Working Cures*, p. 129.

40. Ibid., p. 7.

41. Peter Wood, *Black Majority: Negroes in Colonial South Carolina from 1670 through the Stono Rebellion*. New York: W. W. Norton & Co., 1974, p. 12.

42. Covey, *African American Slave Medicine*, p. 128.

43. Ibid., p. 75.

44. Fett, *Working Cures*, p. 148.

45. Daniel E. Moerman, "An Analysis of the Food Plants and Drug Plants of Native North America," *Journal of Ethnopharmacology* 52 (1996), 1–22.

46. Moerman, "An Analysis of the Food Plants and Drug Plants."

47. Virgil J. Vogel, *American Indian Medicine*. Norman: University of Oklahoma Press, 1970, p. 95.

48. Bunny McBride and Harald E. L. Prins, "Walking the Medicine Line: Molly Ockett, a Pigwacket Doctor," in Robert S. Grumet (ed.), *Northeastern Indian Lives, 1632–1816*. Amherst: University of Massachusetts Press, 1996, p. 333.

49. Wayland D. Hand (ed.), *American Folk Medicine: A Symposium*. Berkeley: University of California Press, 1976, p. 163.

50. Ibid., p. 164.

51. Vogel, *American Indian Medicine*, p. 53.

52. Ibid., p. 109.

53. Ibid., p. 387; and Vicki Abrams Motz, Christopher P. Bowers, Linda Mull Young, and David H. Kinder, "The Effectiveness of Jewelweed, *Impatiens capensis*, the Related Cultivar *I. balsamina* and the Component Lawsone in Preventing Post Poison Ivy Exposure Contact Dermatitis," *Journal of Ethnopharmacology* 143 (2012), 314–18.

54. McBride and Prins, "Molly Ockett," p. 334.

55. Vogel, *Native American Medicine*, p. 6.

56. William A. Emboden Jr., "Plant Hypnotics among the North American Indians," in Hand (ed.), *American Folk Medicine*, pp. 157–68, p. 163.

57. Andrea T. Borchers, Carl L. Keen, Judy S. Stern, and M. Eric Gershwin, "Inflammation and Native American Medicine: The Role of Botanicals," *Journal of Clinical Nutrition* 72 (2000), 339–47.

58. Vogel, *Native American Medicine*, p. 33.

59. James W. Herrick, *Iroquois Medical Botany*. Syracuse, NY: Syracuse University Press, 1995, p. 20.

60. Lee Irwin, "Cherokee Healing: Myth, Dreams, and Medicine," *American Indian Quarterly* 16 (Spring 1992), 237–57.

CHAPTER 11

War and Health

Walt Whitman aptly described the U.S. Civil War as "about nine hundred and ninety-nine parts diarrhea to one part glory."[1] His words could be fittingly applied to most human conflicts prior to the twentieth century's staggering advances in surgery and therapeutics. American soldiers who fought the British between 1812 and 1815, the Mexican army in 1846–1847, one another in the Civil War of 1861–1865, and the Spanish in Cuba and the Philippines in 1898 perished in terribly high numbers as a result of both camp sicknesses and battlefield wounds. This century of warfare revealed with tragic repetitiveness not only the limitations of the medical art but also the rank amateurishness with which the government and army prepared for the inevitable casualties of armed conflict. The fortunes of American soldiery did gradually improve. Basic medical innovations and the efforts of many thousands of civilians and individual medical officers eventually increased their survival chances. At the end of the century, more soldiers than ever were able to recover from bullet wounds due to a combination of knowledge of bacteriology, changes to the velocity of bullets, and the use of the X-ray machine. Even so, strategic blunders, inadequate resources, and the obstructionism of line officers meant that thousands of men were still dying unnecessarily of camp diseases.

MILITARY MEDICINE AT THE START OF THE CENTURY

During the late eighteenth century the American government began to accept some responsibility for the health and well-being of soldiers and sailors. It did so for obvious pragmatic reasons: outbreaks of infectious disease in military camps could seriously compromise an army's fighting potential, the sick could sometimes be returned to action after a period of medical convalescence, and sections of the citizenry disapproved of seeing disabled soldiers or sailors starving in the streets. In 1798 the federal government passed an Act for the Relief of Sick and Disabled Seamen that instructed customs collectors to collect from shipmasters 20 cents a month for each serving seaman. The Treasury spent the funds on building naval hospitals or paying for sailors to stay in general hospitals.[2]

The federal government also made tentative steps towards improving the health of its infantry. The Second Continental Congress of 1775 established the Hospital Department for the Army, responsible for ensuring the provision of bedding and medicines as well as for evaluating regimental and volunteer surgeons for their fitness to serve. Unfortunately, the department languished after the Revolution as the military declined to just a few regiments, garrisons, and fighting ships. In consequence, the physicians recruited to perform battlefield surgery in the War of 1812 were often woefully ignorant about how to carry out swift amputations. The regimental surgeon William Beaumont described how he "cut and slashed for 48 hours without food or sleep." In this age before anesthesia and strict rules of hygiene, medical officers like Beaumont did at least recognize the importance of speed for reducing the risks of physiological shock and infection. But a soldier's chances were significantly lowered by the antique dictum that pus is a positive sign of healing unless it becomes copious, thick, and yellow. Allowing "laudable pus" to accumulate just facilitated the growth of bacteria.[3]

THE AMERICAN–MEXICAN WAR AND ITS AFTERMATH

The war against Mexico that began in the spring of 1846 to establish control over Texas highlights how little thought the government and the military gave to the health of soldiers. As American troops fought their way into the Mexican capital and took control of the vast territories of California, they left behind over 10,000 of their own dead and sent home a larger number of the wounded, sickly, and permanently debilitated. A staggering 110 out of every 1,000 American combatants perished in the Mexican War, and seven died of disease to every one who succumbed to battlefield injuries.[4] Even before hostilities began the inadequacy of the army's preparations were obvious. Short of wood, decent provisions, and hygienic precautions, dysentery and fever laid low a sixth of General Zachary Taylor's men, and as much as half of his army was said to be unwell in some fashion.[5] The worst off were the young men who had volunteered from the farms scattered across the lands of the Midwest. Less likely to have been exposed to diseases like measles, mumps, chickenpox, whooping cough, scarlet fever, and diphtheria, to which city dwellers had acquired immunity in childhood, their chances of surviving camp life were grim.[6] "They die like sheep," one observer remarked.[7] The logistical nightmares of taking an army through vast deserts then ensured that fatality rates would soar. Everywhere the regiments camped became fouled by the fecal waste of man and beast. Conditions grew worse as the supply chains were stretched across the desert sands of the Rio Grande.[8] Soldiers in Mexico scooped up into their parched and blistered mouths water from buffalo wallows, puddles "perfumed with dead mules," and ponds on which floated the corpses of Mexican soldiers and rotting horses.[9]

Those who sustained battlefield injuries were usually condemned to inadequate surgical care because at the start of the war the Army Medical Department comprised a measly 20 surgeons and 50 assistant surgeons. Even applicants from well-known medical colleges had barely any experience of surgery, and quite a few displayed the same level of ignorance as the young physician who thought that castor oil was harvested from a beast called a castor.[10] Some army surgeons were undoubtedly courageous: one Dr. E. K. Chamberlain left a vivid account of the assault on Monterey during which he had operated "upon a poor fellow, whose foot was shot off by a cannon-ball and in a place where twelve and eighteen-pounders were tearing the ground."[11] But even brave surgeons unwittingly caused deadly infections by groping around in bloody and lacerated flesh in search of bullets and shattered bones. The army's failure to construct hospitals with adequate numbers of beds, nurses, orderlies, cooks, or matrons exacerbated this dire situation. Barna Upton of the 3rd U.S. infantry described how "The wounded, both friend and foe, were collected on the bank of the pond." As the thinly stretched surgeons amputated in the open air, he added, "The dead lay in a heap beside."[12]

Medicines for camp diseases met the standards of the day but were almost invariably useless or harmful. Acetate of lead or opium could not help those prostrated by diarrhea and dysentery. Bleeding, calomel, quinine, and enemas were just as useless in treating yellow fever. Doctors did prescribe quinine for malaria, and yet the doses they handed out were probably insufficient to bring about a real cure.[13] Samuel Curtis, the American military governor of the city of Matamoros, recorded his regular self-dosing with quinine, but he left Mexico describing malaria as a "dull memento" of his campaign. One solitary medical achievement stands out from this short but miserable war: soldiers as well as many Mexican civilians were vaccinated against smallpox.[14]

The capitulation of Mexico handed to the United States an additional 1.2 million square miles of territory but without the resources to safeguard the health of those sent out to defend it. A tiny army had to be spread across the prairie and the plains, the Colorado Plateau and far Southwest, the Pacific coast, and the distant Northwest.[15] Disease flourished in the newly constructed and widely scattered forts. Although U.S. troops were fighting Native Americans in Texas, New Mexico, California, Oregon, the Washington Territories, and across the vast lands stretching between the Mississippi and the Rocky Mountains, far more soldiers fell sick to dysentery, respiratory infections, venereal diseases, and malaria than succumbed to wounds, accidents, or injuries.[16] Diarrheal diseases were inevitable where the pit toilets of frontier forts, usually just holes in the ground covered with planks of wooden housing, were too often dug close to the water supply.[17] Poor diets and overcrowding also encouraged respiratory infections. Soldiers even succumbed to scurvy due to severe dietary deficiencies among some garrisons. At Fort Rice in Sioux country between 1864 and 1865, 37 soldiers died of scurvy and just 8 during skirmishes with Native Americans.[18]

THE CIVIL WAR YEARS

Unsanitary Camps and the Sanitary Commission

"Medicine," observed the historian Richard Shyrock in 1961, "seems the least apt to lend itself to centennial celebrations."[19] Both sides in the war of 1861–1865 suffered catastrophic losses due to disease. We do not have exact numbers for the scale of mortality: according to the standard figures around 94,000 Confederate soldiers died of battle injuries and 164,000 succumbed to sickness while the Union side lost roughly 110,000 men to bullets and shells and a massive 225,000 to sickness.[20] But, more recently, historians have suggested that these numbers are underestimates. Allen C. Guelzo, for instance, points out that as many as 200,000 northern soldiers died as a result of wounds and disease in the decade after the war.[21] In addition, something like 50,000 civilians were butchered during the conflict.[22]

The deaths of many of the Civil War soldiers were unavoidable. Once again, young men from remote farmsteads were arriving at camps to be exposed for the first time to the diseases to which their urban brethren had acquired immunity as children. Soldiers from Midwestern states suffered a disease mortality 43 percent higher than those from the urban states of the Northeast.[23] It did not help that many patently unfit soldiers were allowed to enter the ranks. One observer talked of legion "feeble boys, toothless old men, consumptives, asthmatics, one-eyed, one-armed men."[24] Conversely, large numbers of perfectly able men managed to evade service: one disgusted surgeon wrote of men coming to his selection office "fortified with elaborate certificates from sympathizing friends, kind-hearted family physicians, stupid quacks, and the learned homoeopathist who has testified to the appalling infirmity of 'paralysis of the scrotum'."[25] Intestinal diseases, malaria, and respiratory maladies were the chief agents of death. On the Union side diarrhea killed nearly 45,000 men, typhoid another 30,000, malaria an additional 10,000, and measles about 4,300. The bacteria and viruses that cause diarrhea flourished amid military camps in which scant attention had been given to disposing of human and animal excreta. Over half of Union soldiers had at least one serious bout of intestinal disorder, as did nearly all Confederate troops. The pathogens responsible for typhoid fever and the mosquito vectors that spread malaria likewise thrived amid the pools of filth that collected alongside privies and tents. A shortage of fresh vegetables, exacerbated by officers seizing most of the supply for their own benefit, condemned another 30,000 Union soldiers to the acute discomfort and psychological distress of scurvy.[26] The escaped slaves who made it to Union lines suffered the highest relative death toll from camp disease. They arrived famished and exhausted, broken down by the rigors of slavery, many with abdominal hernias brought on by decades of overwork. At the camps they were given inferior, bug-infested tents, threadbare clothing, and poorly made shoes. About 18.5% of African Americans died in the Union army compared to 13.5% of whites.[27] The high rates of camp sickness had profound implications for the prosecution of the war. As James McPherson points out, the incapacity of large numbers of his men contributed to the failure of General Robert E. Lee's West Virginia campaign of 1861. The sickness of over 50% of Union soldiers and sailors likewise stymied the first Union attempt to capture Vicksburg in July 1862.[28]

Nurses and officers of the U.S. Sanitary Commission in Fredericksburg, Virginia, ca. 1864. The Sanitary Commission was a private agency formed to lessen the mortality and suffering of Union troops during the Civil War. Arising out of a meeting of concerned women held in New York in April 1861, it grew into a major organization that arranged for the staffing of hospitals, provided decent food to military camps, supplied clothes and bedding, administered homes for convalescing and disabled soldiers, and highlighted the unsanitary conditions in which soldiers were forced to live. Many women, like Louisa Mary Alcott, who served as a nurse in the Union Hospital at Georgetown, D.C., and Mary Livermore, who visited army posts and hospitals, were instrumental in the success of the Sanitary Commission. (Library of Congress)

In spite of the military wisdom of minimizing levels of infectious disease, the authorities on both sides remained paralyzed in the early stages of the war. One critic not unreasonably condemned the surgeon general, Clement Finley, as a "self-satisfied, supercilious, bigoted block-head." With the situation deteriorating, thousands of northern civilians felt the patriotic call to do something. The result was the founding of the U.S. Sanitary Commission in June 1861 during a meeting of the New York's Women's Central Relief Association.[29] Despite being rebuffed by President Lincoln and a proprietorial Army Medical Department, the commission still became a major operation. Within months it had elicited a huge outpouring of donations. Half a million dollars alone came from over the Rockies in the fall of 1862, sent by men who had made it big in the Gold Rush.[30] The commission paid for sanitary inspectors to visit Union army camps; sent vital medical supplies to military hospitals that often lacked the most basic equipment; worked with the Women's Central Relief Association to coordinate the efforts of tens of thousands of volunteers in stockpiling and delivering blankets, warm clothing, and good food to the soldiers; dispatched women to serve as nurses and to run kitchens in army camps; took charge of hospital ships and homes for recuperating and disabled soldiers; and relentlessly lobbied the government for rational reforms to the Army Medical Department.[31] These efforts were complemented by a Colored Women's Sanitary Commission, funded by wealthier African Americans in cities like Philadelphia, to ensure that ex-slaves and black northern volunteers also received proper clothing and bedding.[32]

Treating the Wounded Early in the War

If the men wounded in battle were to stand a decent chance of survival, they had to be carried quickly from the field to an operating facility and then to a hospital where they could convalesce. Speed was critical where the chances of surviving a limb amputation fell from 75% in the first two days to 65% after day three.[33] At the outset of the war these conditions were rarely met. Untold numbers of men with gunshot wounds died in agony because of the military's failure to create an efficient ambulance corps or hospital system. Nor did the government quickly step up to the challenge. General in Chief Henry W. Halleck and Secretary of War Edwin M. Stanton at first rejected appeals to introduce a professional ambulance corps. Some generals, like Don Carlos Buell of the Army of the Ohio, were flatly indifferent to the torments of men left in the field.[34] Due to Buell's lack of empathy and foresight, at the Battle of Bull Run in 1861 the injured lay for days on the battlefield, thirsty and in pain, many dying from their wounds or choking on their own vomit. At the Second Battle of Bull Run a year later the Union army still had only 45 ambulances. Many of these broke down, and the ill-qualified civilians hired to operate them frequently fled the action. Several days after the firing of the last shot, about 3,000 men still lay where they had fallen.[35]

Those soldiers in the early stages of the war who reached the surgical table then stood a high probability of receiving inadequate care in the most unsanitary of conditions. In 1861 the U.S. Army had just

114 surgeons, 24 of whom decamped to the Confederate side at the start of hostilities. Few of the contract physicians who joined up in the following months were at all suitable. Once again the Army Medical Department found that most had never had to perform an amputation or tackle a gunshot wound, and even regimental surgeons often held their posts due to the favoritism of medically ignorant colonels or medical boards under pressure from state governors. Talented surgeons expressed contempt for the bungling ignorance of colleagues who spent their days botching amputations and ligating arteries so ineptly that they hemorrhaged shortly after.[36] And yet there had never been so urgent a need for competent surgeons. The United States was fighting the largest war in its history, and recent technological developments had made bullet wounds more devastating than ever. In 1841 gunsmiths had begun to groove the barrels of muskets so as to make them more accurate. They also introduced a devastating kind of shot. Civil War muskets fired conical balls with hollow bases that travelled at low velocity, made large holes as they flattened on impact, shattered two or three inches of bone, and carried with them particles of skin and clothing into the wound. The probability of infection was appallingly high. Nearly two-thirds of gunshot wounds to the chest led to death as did almost 90% of abdominal wounds. Those shot in the limbs were more likely to survive but usually only if they underwent amputation. In consequence as many as 75% of all Civil War operations, around 60,000 in total, involved the removal of limbs in whole or part.[37]

Even the most skilled surgeons had to become inured to high levels of postoperative mortality because they did not understand the supreme importance of surgical hygiene. One of the many misfortunes of the war was that it occurred only about 20 years before doctors began to recognize the role of bacteria in causing gangrene, septicemia, and erysipelas.[38] Surgeons and their assistants therefore unwittingly passed on deadly germs via their hands, aprons, tools, dressings, and sponges. "We operated in old blood-stained and often pus-stained coats," William Williams Keen recalled, "We used undisinfected instruments from undisinfected plush-lined cases, and still worse, used marine sponges which had been used in prior pus cases and had only been washed in tap water."[39] Amputated limbs were flung into large piles a few feet away where they attracted flies and gave off a nauseating stink. The leading New York surgeon, Frank Hamilton, told of operating late into the night, with only the feeble light of tallow candles, and his hands "stiff with blood." Patients were then sent to recover in hospitals aptly described by one visitor as "simply disgusting." And although a good number of surgeons experimented with pouring bromine or carbolic acid on infected wounds, they often left it too late because they were yet to abandon the antique doctrine of laudable pus. Once tissues had started to turn grey disinfectants were not likely to work. As a result, many surgeons concluded that antiseptics were a waste of time.[40]

Advances in Medical Treatment

The quality of surgeons and the conditions in which they worked did improve. Surgeons became more skilled as they gained in practical experience. The Sanitary Commission also achieved the coup of the appointment of Dr. William Hammond as surgeon general of the U.S. Army. Having been revolted during his visits to the military hospitals of Maryland and Virginia, in 1862 Hammond started to oversee a vast plan for the building of hospitals that observed the hygiene principles adopted by the British nurse Florence Nightingale during the Crimean War. His commodious pavilion-style hospitals were everything that their predecessors were not: clean, well-ventilated, generously supplied with medicines, staffed by dedicated nurses, and equipped with wards for the isolation of infectious patients. By June 1863 Hammond had presided over the construction of 182 hospitals with 84,000 beds and a mortality rate among the convalescent as low as 10%.[41]

The task of demonstrating the value of professional ambulance corps fell to Jonathan Letterman, a Pennsylvanian surgeon appointed medical director of the Army of the Potomac by Hammond in June 1862. General George B. McClellan happily cooperated with Letterman in the supply of sufficient wagons and trained personnel. As a result, at the Battle of Antietam, fought in September 1862, the injured were rescued from the battlefield with unprecedented efficiency. Having been triaged, the wounded were treated in mobile field hospitals by surgeons of proven ability. They were then dispatched to nearby hospitals or by train to new pavilion hospitals in Baltimore, Philadelphia, and Washington. Before the Battle of Fredericksburg in December 1862, Letterman's staff had assembled 500 hospital tents, 254 medical knapsacks, and nearly 1,000 ambulances. Only the 200 men who had fallen close to Confederate lines were not quickly recovered from the field. So effective had Letterman's system proved that the Ambulance Corps Act of 1864 forced all Union armies to adopt it. In readiness for General Ulysses Grant's spring offensive of 1864, the Army Medical Department had 600 ambulance vehicles with 60 officers and 2,300 men to operate them, nearly 700 medical officers, and almost 300 field hospital tents.[42]

Nurses also made a significant impact on the quality of care received by the wounded. The roughly 20,000 recruited during the war were socially highly diverse: female slaves, Catholic sisters, working-class women, upper-class ladies, and the wives of injured or fighting men. The famous New England humanitarian Dorothea Dix recruited 3,200 with the stipulation that they be over 30, plain looking, and free from such vanities as curls and bows, criteria that excluded highly qualified candidates like Esther Hill Hawks who had been educated at Samuel Gregory's New England Female Medical College but was felt to be too young, good-looking, and strong-minded.[43] The selected nurses were mandated to keep patients clean, to prepare and serve their food, to give them medicines, and to relieve the boredom of convalescence. Sometimes they assisted in operations, and regimental nurses accompanied soldiers to the battlefield, where some drove ambulance wagons under fire and helped with amputations. It took time for surgeons to get used to the presence of women in their wards, especially when they were not always subservient. But, as the historian Jane Schultz notes, nurses were not only medically indispensable but brought a tenderness to patients quite out of character for most surgeons. While to be wounded in this bitter conflict remained terrifying and agonizing, a nurse's human touch was profoundly valued.[44]

Many soldiers continued to receive unnecessarily poor treatment in spite of improved hospitals and ambulances. Margaret Humphreys shows that African American regiments tended to be assigned the fewest and the least qualified surgeons. Aware that black patients died in hospitals more often than their white counterparts, medical commentators insisted that African Americans lacked the robustness of whites. The army physician Ira Russell cleverly put this theory to the test. In one hospital for black soldiers a Dr. James Martin with a reputation for entering "heart and soul" into his duties had an excellent recovery rate. The surgeon on another ward, who reckoned it to be "useless to doctor a sick negro, for he was sure to die," had far inferior levels of postoperative survival. So Russell had Dr. Martin transferred to the latter surgeon's ward. The result: the rate of recovery there went up once the patients had a surgeon willing to make an effort. Having seen a typically filthy hospital for African American patients, one observer raged: "Had these men been white soldiers, think you this could have been their condition? No! And yet the Black fell side by side of the white with their faces to the Foe."[45]

Trauma and Disability

The hardships of war extended far beyond the battlefield and into the postwar era. Terrible numbers of civilians found themselves in the way of advancing or retreating troops and were often subjected to vicious attacks. Many soldiers did not care to distinguish too sharply between combatants and civilians. There are many recorded cases of atrocities. Confederate soldiers gunned down 15 men and boys in a raid on Shelton Laurel in North Carolina.[46] "We looked upon South Carolina as the cause of our woe," said one of the Union soldiers marching with General William Tecumseh Sherman, "she thoroughly deserved extirpation." As they proceeded south, Sherman's men massacred livestock, ruined fields of crops, and brutalized civilians.[47] Furthermore, the carnage of the Civil War also unleashed the misery of grief on an unimaginable scale. "I care very little for anybody or anything," wrote the bereaved Abbie Brooks of Georgia.[48] Henry Wadsworth Longfellow's poem "Killed at the Ford" tried to capture the horror of the bereft mother. It tells with poignant simplicity of a bullet that kills a Union soldier and then flies on:

> Till it reached a town in the distant North
> Till it reached a house in a sunny street
> Till it reached a heart that ceased to beat
> Without a murmur, without a cry.[49]

Many soldiers sustained emotional as well as physical scars. One soldier wrote home about a colonel who rode off one morning, wearing clothes saturated in diarrhea, and returned a few days later shaking and acting "like a little child." Private William Leeds was repeatedly found "strolling about in the woods" and ended up being sent to an asylum. Others who experienced intolerable levels of trauma and fled the field of battle were shot as cowards and deserters. Those who returned home with deep psychological wounds presumably buried or hid their symptoms as best they could. Many probably found succor in the oblivion of booze or opium. Horace B. Day's 1868 book *The Opium Habit* talked of "Maimed and shattered survivors from a hundred battle-fields" as well as "anguished and hopeless wives and mothers, made so by the slaughter of those who were dearest to them," depending on drugs to make life bearable.[50]

The men who returned with one of more missing limbs, 21,753 from the Union army alone, often adapted well back into civilian life. Many

refused to wear prosthetics, preferring to sport empty sleeves and trou-
ser legs as honorable scars.[51] For the politically ambitious, a missing
arm could prove an asset on the hustings: governors of Wisconsin,
Louisiana, and Arkansas had all lost arms in the war. In response to
the difficulty many amputees faced in performing their old jobs,
Union soldiers were made eligible for pensions, and a good number
received federal jobs or plots of land to farm. How amputees fared in
the marriage market is harder to ascertain. Louisa May Alcott advised
her sex to "admire the honorable scar," though one wonders how many
single women heeded her advice.[52] The only unambiguous beneficiar-
ies of the high rate of amputation were the entrepreneurs responsible
for a 290% increase in patients for prosthetics and assisting devices
between 1861 and 1873.[53]

SICKNESS AND THE SPANISH–AMERICAN WAR OF 1898

Just over 30 years after the end of the Civil War, American soldiers
were sent once again into combat situations on a large scale. Fighting
in Cuba, Puerto Rico, and the Philippines against a tottering Spanish
Empire, infantrymen suffered from the same fatal errors as in previous
wars but also benefited from medical breakthroughs.

Superficially it might have looked in 1898 as if the lessons of the Civil
War had been properly digested. Under the leadership of Surgeon
General Dr. George Sternberg, the Army Medical Department had
spent years working out ways of preventing sanitary disasters and giving army physicians a state-of-the-art education in military hygiene. On
the day that Spain declared war on the United States, Sternberg issued
Circular No. 1 with strict guidelines about how to maintain the cleanliness of troops and camps, including the digging of sinks before setting
up camp, the pouring of quicklime over fecal matter, the punishment of
soldiers who did not keep clean, and the treatment with disinfectant of
anything discharged from the body of a febrile patient. Unfortunately
these rules were virtually unenforceable.

Inadequate funds and personnel combined with a lack of cooperation from the army stood firmly in the way of the implementation
of Circular No. 1. The federal government had allotted a paltry $20,000
to the Army Medical Department, and only 100 medical officers were
available at the start of the war, with the result that the army had to hire
civilian physicians who had no idea how to enforce strict standards of
camp hygiene. In addition, the line officers who ran the military camps
were typically hostile to what they saw as the wanton interference of
men with medical training. Officers characterized medicine as a form

During the Spanish–American War of 1898, thousands of American troops fell prey to diseases ranging from measles to yellow fever. The U.S. Army Medical Corps administered to them under often primitive conditions. This war did, however, witness significant advances in the treatment of gunshot wounds. (National Museum of the United States Army)

of pampering for men who ought to toughen up rather than allowing themselves to be molly-coddled. New recruits do not need "feather beds and lamb chops," said one officer.[54] As a result, the campsites where recruits gathered in Texas and Florida were soon heavily contaminated with feces. Typhoid quickly took hold and left more than 20,000 seriously sick and 1,500 dead. About 87% of American deaths from disease in the war were caused by typhoid fever in unnecessarily filthy camps.[55]

The disasters accumulated with the dispatch of troops to Cuba and the Philippines. The government ignored Sternberg's sensible advice not to invade Cuba in the middle of the rainy season. In consequence, the invasion party was hit by yellow fever with predictable severity.[56] The Fifth Corps had so many cases that barely had victory been achieved when it had to be quarantined.[57] In the Philippines, General Wesley Merritt's force bore the brunt of the endemic fevers of the monsoon season. In brutal fighting, 600 of his soldiers lost their lives, but 700 succumbed to disease. Nor should one forget that about 700,000 Filipinos died in combat or during the epidemics of cholera, typhoid, smallpox, tuberculosis, beriberi, and plague that flared up as millions were displaced by the war, and others were forced into concentration camps in which sickness spread with terrible rapidity.[58]

Military Surgery in the Spanish–American War

In one key respect the Spanish–American War did mark a significant advance on the experience of the Civil War. For all the problems encountered in getting the wounded to hospitals, an extraordinary 95% of those wounded on the battlefield recovered. This gave soldiers in 1898 a 4.3-fold greater probability of living than their predecessors who came under the knives and saws of Union and Confederate surgeons. Operators in the late 1890s were able to accomplish this feat for two basic reasons. First, they knew that bacteria cause infection and can be either killed with disinfectants or prevented from entering the wound through aseptic surgery. Second, only two-fifths of operations were amputations, compared to three-quarters in the Civil War, meaning that surgeons could further reduce the risks of infection by carrying out much more conservative surgery.[59]

Concerted efforts were made to reduce the risk of death from wounds by having medical officers provide prompt treatment on the battlefield. In the Philippines, prior to being sent to hospitals, men with bullet wounds had elastic bandages or traditional tourniquets applied so as to prevent hemorrhage while antiseptics were applied to kill germs.[60] The best hospitals in Cuba and the Philippines were equipped with state-of-the-art sterilizing chests, clean instruments, operating tables, and fresh dressings. Surgeons also strove to practice antiseptic and aseptic surgical techniques. Having scrubbed their hands as best they could and sterilized their instruments, they sought to remove anything from the patient's wounds that might carry harmful bacteria.[61] "One speck of filth, one shred of clothing, one strip of filthy integument left in ever so small a wound," explained one surgeon, "will do more harm, more seriously endanger life, and much longer invalid the patient, than a wound half a yard long of the soft parts, when it is kept aseptic."[62]

Knowing the importance of eliminating bacteria in the wound, surgeons in the Spanish–American war could also treat wounds to the limbs more conservatively than in previous wars. Even if a bullet had fractured bone, surgeons in 1898 did not usually consider it necessary to amputate. Kept clean with antiseptic occlusive dressings and then left alone, such wounds tended to heal without the need for further intervention. It also helped that many Spanish soldiers were firing the same metal-jacketed, high-speed, and small-caliber bullets as the Americans. These travelled at such a speed as to be virtually aseptic at the point of entry, and if they struck hard bone they often passed through without causing shattering. Only when bullets had caused a lot of damage to the soft tissue and bones, and especially where infection had set in, did surgeons favor amputation. The availability of X-ray technology in the Cuban theater then came to their aid. Surgeons had once had to probe open wounds with hands or instruments to ascertain the extent of damage and the location of the bullet and bone fragments.[63] The X-rays installed aboard the hospitals ships *Relief, Missouri,* and *Bay State* in the Cuban harbor of Siboney dramatically lessened the need to dig around in raw and bloody wounds and allowed operators to accurately assess the level of damage and so avoid amputation wherever possible.[64] In many cases wounded soldiers still received inferior care in hospitals that would have been appallingly filthy and poorly equipped had it not been for the efforts of the American Red Cross, founded in 1881 through the efforts of Clara Barton. Even so, it made a significant difference to the survival rate that military surgeons knew in principle how to reduce the risk of infections before and after surgery.[65]

MILITARY MEDICINE IN TRANSITION

Military medicine had reached a transitional stage by the time of the Spanish–American war of 1898. The filth of camps and the depredations of typhoid harked back to disasters of the past. In contrast, the military had more quickly accepted the value of decent hospitals, well-trained ambulance corps, and skilled nurses. Furthermore, the acceptance of germ theory had created the conditions for a dramatic reduction in the death rate among wounded soldiers. Bacteriology taught camp medical officers that even apparently clean objects could carry bacteria and that the sputum, feces, and saliva of the sick were vehicles for the transmission of deadly disease. When they were listened to they were able to slash rates of mortality. Germ theory also made surgeons realize that they had to apply antiseptics to wounds prior to evacuating the wounded and that hospitals, operating rooms, and surgical instruments had to be disinfected as thoroughly as possible. The enormous technological advance of the X-ray machine further reduced the likelihood of surgeons contaminating wounds when probing blindly for bullets with ungloved hands. Medicine could now make an unprecedented difference to the survival chances of the American soldier.

NOTES

1. Vincent J. Cirillo, *Bullets and Bacilli: The Spanish–American War and Military Medicine*. New Brunswick, NJ: Rutgers University Press, 2004, p. 33.

2. James H. Cassedy, *Medicine and American Growth, 1800–1860*. Madison: University of Wisconsin Press, 1986, p. 16.

3. Basil A. Pruitt Jr., "Combat Casualty Care and Surgical Progress," *Annals of Surgery* 243, no. 6 (June 2006), 715–29, p. 716.

4. Richard Bruce Winders, *Mr Polk's Army: The American Military Experience in the Mexican War*. College Station: Texas A&M University Press, 1997, p. 139; and M. McCaffrey, *Army of Manifest Destiny: The American Soldier in the Mexican War, 1846–1848*. New York: New York University Press, 1992, p. 53.

5. Paul Foos, *A Short, Offhand, Killing Affair: Soldiers and Social Conflict during the Mexican-American War*. Chapel Hill: University of North Carolina Press, 2002, p. 18.

6. McCaffrey, *Army of Manifest Destiny*, p. 52.

7. Winders, *Mr Polk's Army*, p. 146.

8. Foos, *A Short, Offhand, Killing Affair*, p. 85.

9. Winders, *Mr Polk's Army*, p. 142; McCaffrey, *Army of Manifest Destiny*, p. 58.

10. McCaffrey, *Army of Manifest Destiny*, p. 56.

11. Christopher D. Dishman, *A Perfect Gibraltar: The Battle for Monterrey, Mexico, 1846*. Norman: University of Oklahoma Press, 2010, p. 123.

12. Winders, *Mr Polk's Army*, p. 163.

13. Margaret Humphreys, *Malaria: Poverty, Race, and Public Health in the United States*. Baltimore, MD: Johns Hopkins University Press, 2001, p. 123.

14. John Mckiernan-González, *Fevered Measures: Public Health and Race at the Texas-Mexico Border, 1848–1942*. Durham, NC: Duke University Press, 2012, p. 28.

15. Durwood Ball, *Army Regulars on the Western Frontier, 1848–1861*. Norman: University of Oklahoma Press, 2001.

16. Robert Marshall Utley, *Frontier Regulars: The United States Army and the Indian, 1866–1891*. New York: Macmillan, 1974, p. 86.

17. David A. Clary, "The Role of the Army Surgeon in the West: Daniel Weisel at Fort Davis, Texas, 1868–1872," *The Western Historical Quarterly* 3, no. 1 (January 1972), pp. 53–66, p. 60.

18. Ron Field, *Forts of the American Frontier 1820–91: Central and Northern Plains*. Oxford, England: Osprey Publishing, 2005, p. 40; Utley, *Frontier Regulars*, p. 87; and James O. Breeden, "Health of Early Texas: The Military Frontier," *The Southwestern Historical Quarterly* 80, no. 4 (April 1977), 357–98, p. 369.

19. Richard Shyrock, "A Medical Perspective on the Civil War," *American Quarterly* 14, no. 2 (Summer 1962), 161–73, p. 161.

20. Gerald Grob, *The Deadly Truth: A History of Disease in America*. Cambridge, MA: Harvard University Press, 2002, pp. 147–8.

21. Allen C. Guelzo, *Fateful Lightning: A New History of the Civil War and Reconstruction*. Oxford, UK: Oxford University Press, 2012, p. 515.

22. Drew Gilpin Faust, *This Republic of Suffering: Death and the American Civil War*. New York: Alfred A. Knopf, 2008, p. xii.

23. James McPherson, *This Mighty Scourge: Perspectives on the Civil War*. New York: Oxford University Press, 2007, p. 119.

24. Laurann Figg and Jane Farrell-Beck, "Amputation in the Civil War: Physical and Social Dimensions," *Journal of the History of Medicine and Allied Sciences* 48, no. 4 (1993), 454–75, p. 472.

25. Richard H. Kohn, "The Social History of the American Soldier: A Review and Prospectus for Research," *The American Historical Review* 86, no. 3 (June 1981), 553–67, p. 560.

26. Richard F. Selcer, *Civil War America, 1850 to 1875*. New York: Infobase Publishing, 2006, p. 394.

27. Margaret Humphreys, *Intensely Human: The Health of the Black Soldier in the American Civil War*. Baltimore, MD: Johns Hopkins University Press, 2008, pp. 7–10.

28. James M. McPherson, *The Illustrated Battle Cry of Freedom: The Civil War Era*. New York: Oxford University Press, 2003, p. 417.

29. Ira M. Rutkow, *Bleeding Blue and Gray: Civil War Surgery and the Evolution of American Medicine*. New York: Random House, 2005, p. 9.

30. Margaret Humphreys, *The Marrow of Tragedy: The Health Crisis of the American Civil War*. Baltimore, MD: Johns Hopkins University Press, 2013, p. 107.

31. Humphreys, *The Marrow of Tragedy*, p. 106; and Judith Ann Giesberg, *Civil War Sisterhood: The U.S. Sanitary Commission and Women's Politics in Transition*. Boston: Northeastern University Press, 2000.

32. Ibid., p. 109; and Forbes, *African American Women during the Civil War*. New York: Garland, 1998, p. 94.

33. Figg and Farrell-Beck, "Amputation in the Civil War," p. 474.

34. Rutkow, *Bleeding Blue and Gray*, p. 193.

35. Richard H. Shyrock, "A Medical Perspective on the Civil War," *American Quarterly* 14 (1962), 161–73, p. 162.

36. John Duffy, *From Humors to Medical Science: A History of American Medicine*. Urbana: University of Illinois Press, 1993, chapter 5.

37. Figg and Farrell-Beck, "Amputation in the Civil War," p. 474.

38. Shyrock, "A Medical Perspective."

39. Rutkow, *Bleeding Blue and Gray*, p. 64.

40. Ibid., p. 24 and pp. 235–6.

41. Ibid., pp. 161–2.

42. Ibid., pp. 206–7 and p. 302.

43. Jane E. Schultz, "The Inhospitable Hospital: Gender and Professionalism in Civil War Medicine," *Signs* 17, no. 2 (Winter 1992), 363–92, p. 368.

44. Schultz, "The Inhospitable Hospital," p. 378.

45. Humphreys, *Intensely Human*, p. 76.

46. Faust, *This Republic of Suffering*, pp. 137–38.

47. J. Edward Lee and Ron Chepesiuk (eds.), *South Carolina in the Civil War: The Confederate Experience in Letters and Diaries*. Jefferson, NC: McFarland, 2000, p. 3.

48. Faust, *This Republic of Suffering*, p. 145.

49. Faust, *This Republic of Suffering*, p. 143.

50. John Talbott, "Combat Trauma in the American Civil War," *History Today* 46 (1996), 41–7. David T. Courtwright, "Opiate Addiction as a Consequence of the Civil War," *Civil War History* 24, no 2 (June 1978), 101–111.

51. Frances Clarke, " 'Honorable Scars': Northern Amputees and the Meaning of Civil War Injuries," in Paul A. Cimbala and Randall M. Miller (eds.), *Union Soldiers and the Northern Home Front: Wartime Experiences, Postwar Adjustments*. New York: Fordham University Press, 2002, p. 361.

52. Figg and Farrell-Beck, "Amputation in the Civil War," p. 470.

53. Rutkow, *Bleeding Blue and Gray*, p. 255.

54. Cirillo, *Bullets and Bacilli*, p. 28, p. 54.

55. Ibid., pp. 1–8, 37.

56. Ibid., p. 12.

57. Ibid., p. 95.

58. Warwick Anderson, *Colonial Pathologies: American Tropical Medicine, Race, and Hygiene in the Philippines*. Durham, NC: Duke University Press, 2006, p. 14.

59. Cirillo, *Bullets and Bacilli*, p. 37.

60. Anderson, *Colonial Pathologies*, p. 32.

61. Ibid., p. 16.

62. Anderson, *Colonial Pathologies*, p. 23.

63. Vincent J. Cirillo, "The Spanish-American War and Military Radiology," *American Journal of Roentgenology* 174 (2000), 1233–39, p. 1230.

64. Ibid., pp. 1237–39.

65. Cirillo, *Bullets and Bacilli*, p. 16.

CHAPTER 12

Institutional Facilities

Of all the many changes to the American medical landscape in the nineteenth-century it is the birth of the hospital that stands out most boldly. Starting as little more than receptacles for the urban poor, they came to symbolize the success and promise of medical science. Without any difficulty a patient in 1800 could grasp how the word *hospital* had come to be constructed from the words "hospice," meaning an asylum for the needy, and "spital," translated as a foul and stinking place.[1] So deeply stigmatizing was it to enter an antebellum hospital that the majority of the lower social classes who fell ill vastly preferred to rely on the free advice and drugs provided by the outpatient dispensary. Contrast this grim image of the hospital with the situation just 100 years later when many boasted clean wards presided over by trained nurses in spotless uniforms, laboratories containing the latest diagnostic equipment, and sterile surgical theaters run by highly skilled personnel. Once the hospital could promise a high level of care as well as considerable comfort for those able to pay, members of the middle and upper classes began to go there for surgery and for the treatment of acute conditions. The institutional response to sickness and disability also extended to the establishment of new asylums for the insane; schools for the deaf, dumb, and blind; and foundling hospitals for the orphan. If these developments did not immediately have a major impact on longevity, they marked a crucial turning point in the way in which medicine would be delivered in the following century.

THE ANTEBELLUM HOSPITAL

The first hospitals in the United States were private or "voluntary" institutions overseen by boards of lay trustees and exclusively devoted to treating members of the lowest social classes. The philanthropists who established Philadelphia's Pennsylvania Hospital in 1751, New York Hospital in the 1790s, and Boston's Massachusetts General Hospital in 1821 shared the view that the urban poor needed institutions in which to receive free medical care as well as food and shelter while recuperating. Not everyone was considered worthy of their charity. Before being admitted, desperate applicants had to furnish testimonials from respectable members of the community to say that they belonged to the ranks of the miserable but morally worthy poor.[2] Drunkards, prostitutes, and those afflicted with syphilis or gonorrhea were forbidden access to general hospitals while unmarried pregnant women were turned promptly away from charitable lying-in hospitals. As late as 1888 New York Hospital's executive committee stipulated that "All persons applying for free service must bring a note from some well-known citizen, or present other evidence that their inability to pay does not arise from improvidence or dissipation."[3] The ideal patients were deemed to be widows of unimpeachable character and injured workmen with reputations for perfect sobriety and regular worship in the "right" churches. These judgments reflected not only the stern moralities of the trustees but their pragmatic awareness that upper-class donors and church societies would withhold their cash if they felt that private hospitals were providing succor to the lascivious and irresponsible. The innocent victims of accidents or sickness alone could jolt the sympathies of the donor.[4]

Admittance to a voluntary hospital also depended on satisfying strict medical criteria. These were not acute care facilities. Those with incurable or contagious conditions were denied entry, and patients who contracted transmissible maladies while in the hospital were shown the door. Trustees accepted patients suffering from semichronic conditions who were expected to recover from their ailments. So when the trustees visited Massachusetts General in October 1876 they were able to record that the patients were "comfortable and not one very sick; Marcus Jones had walked out; and John Baptiste gone home."[5] These admission criteria were only relaxed for patients who had money to offset some of the costs of their inpatient care. Hospitals nearly always had private rooms, some of which had damask drapes and heavy cherry furniture, that contrasted strikingly with the somberness of the regular wards.[6] These "pay-patients," usually small shopkeepers, successful artisans, and sailors benefiting from early federal insurance schemes, were exempt from performing chores in the hospital and were off-limits to the medical students who, when they had the chance, took liberties with the destitute sick. Pay patients might even be alcoholics or afflicted with venereal disease. Cash alone could assuage the moral disgust of the trustee.[7]

The Shame of the Almshouse Ward

The poor sick who were refused admission to a private hospital had the unenviable choice of either perishing on the streets or gritting their teeth and enduring the humiliation of entering the almshouse. In these degrading institutions the aged, insane, disabled, and blind shared their misery with poor men and women suffering from a wide range of contagious, chronic, curable, and incurable maladies. They had in common extreme poverty and desperate need.[8] Almshouses were seen to be receptacles for the most "depraved and miserable" members of the community, fittingly grim institutions in which drunks, idlers, and "blasted, withered" prostitutes went to die, often two to a bed, surrounded by filth and vermin.[9] One almshouse chaplain presented a succinct formula: "Like brutes they live, like brutes they die."[10] Indeed, one of the main arguments presented in favor of setting up private hospitals is that the respectable poor who fell ill should not be forced to bear the permanent moral odium of having been in an almshouse. The already meager sympathy of the propertied classes deteriorated with a steep rise in the proportion of inmates from Catholic Ireland. In 1851 one rich Bostonian suggested that the Irish be confined to a separate and inferior ward because "They cannot appreciate & do not really want, some of those conveniences which would be deemed essential by most of our native citizens."[11]

For all their horrors the almshouses were destined to become more and more important receptacles for the sick. Where private hospitals had insufficient beds and rejected many patients on moral or medical grounds, in the later 1700s it had already fallen to the almshouse to make up the shortfall in beds. Urbanization in the nineteenth century imposed still greater demands on these institutions. The concentration in towns and cities of hundreds of thousands of migrants from rural areas and overseas meant that more and more working people were falling sick without family supports. Even where kin were close by they

"Alms House in Spruce Street, Philadelphia, 1800." A sense of the degradation of entering an almshouse is conveyed by the brick walls that confined inmates within the almshouse grounds. Discipline inside this almshouse proved difficult to maintain, in part because of the grog shops lining Spruce Street. The almshouse did, however, contain an infirmary. Over the following decades such institutions would slowly turn into municipal hospitals. (Library of Congress)

usually did not have the time or the resources to care for a sick relative. Almshouses were expected to take up the slack. By the early 1800s those in large cities like Boston, New York, and Philadelphia had effectively turned into municipal hospitals. In 1870 the private Massachusetts General Hospital had only 137 patients when fully occupied compared to the 1,000 accommodated in New York's public Bellevue Hospital.[12]

Not that medicine was a fundamental feature of life in the almshouse or private hospital prior to the Civil War. These institutions were managed by laypersons rather than physicians, and not until 1869 did a medical school, the University of Michigan, gain control over a hospital for teaching purposes.[13] The trustees of private hospitals not unreasonably feared that members of the worthy poor would stay away if they felt they might be handed over to young doctors who wanted to test out drug regimens or procure their bodies for autopsy. And there is plenty of evidence of physicians being too socially distant from the patients to be capable of treating them with basic respect. Hospital internships gave physicians who had just completed their apprentice-ships or were fresh out of college such valuable clinical experience they were usually sold to well-heeled applicants who could afford to pay a substantial fee. Hailing from the upper classes, these men were the most inclined to regard the hospitalized sick as akin to kenneled brutes.[14] The records of institutions like the New Orleans Charity Hospital resonate with the dehumanization of the patient. One poor Irish woman was described as having borne her oviarotomy "as a pig does spaying," and a 13-year-old prostitute inspired the puerile case note from a young doctor: "By the way, She would make a very nice go."[15] New York physicians refused to visit the wards of African Americans and patients with venereal diseases. Not that this made much difference to their well-being. White patients seldom saw a doctor, and hospital surgery rarely extended beyond setting fractures and lancing ulcers.[16]

Life on the Hospital Ward

Harsh and unsanitary conditions ensured that antebellum hospitals were dysfunctional and unhealthy places. Patients received poor diets and substandard clothing, and wards were dirty and often vermin-ridden. Nursing care also left a lot to be desired: most nurses were either ambulatory patients or men and women who had recovered from their illnesses but had no job or home to which to return. A typical advertisement in a Boston newspaper of 1874 ran: "Wanted, a nurse at Boston Lying-in Hospital ... Experience not required."[17] The career of Mary Falconer of the Blockley almshouse in Philadelphia is quite typi-cal. Having been for "3 years a patient," she spent "near two years Matron, and about 18 years a nurse in the house." Only a minority of these staff members displayed skill or tenderness.[18] Often they were brutal or incompetent. One drunk nurse who killed two patients with an overdose was merely suspended for a week.[19] In their defense, hos-pital staff did not have an easy job. They bemoaned the difficulty of enforcing rules about smoking, drinking, card-playing, "impertinence," and fighting. Since most patients were mobile, they were able to test the limits of their freedoms. Sailors were notorious for causing trouble and for covertly bringing whisky into the wards. Many more patients had to be upbraided for clumsily emptying bedpans or spitting wherever they chose.[20]

Patients behaved badly in part due to the hardness and tediousness of their daily lives. "I visited the almshouse today," recorded one young Bostonian visiting Philadelphia in 1806, "where I saw more collective misery than ever before met my eye."[21] All except for the bedbound were expected to toil hard. One unfortunate Philadelphian girl was put to work on a sewing machine at the almshouse just hours after she had given birth and been thrown out of her home by her stepfather.[22] The venereal patients on New York's Blackwell Island labored as patients and then for an additional period of time after regaining their health in order to repay the costs of their care. Syphilitics were also often given bed sheets of a different color that maximized their shame, and they were forbidden access to the hospital library.[23] African American patients usually had it worse: they were made to live in attics that were freezing in the winter and roasting in the summer. But all categories of hospital patient in the antebellum United States perished at elevated rates. Infection spread terribly fast in wards in which bacteria-laden blood, sputum, and feces easily passed from patient to patient. Beaten down by lives bereft of comforts and opportunities, some inmates reaching an inner breaking point and took their own lives.[24]

Even though the far better designed and managed hospitals of the Civil War played a vital role in saving the lives of soldiers, their success did not lead to an immediate rethinking of the potential of civilian hospitals and almshouses. For at least a decade after the end of hostilities, most private and public hospitals remained appallingly unsanitary and unhealthy. In 1872 New York's Bellevue Hospital was the subject of devastating exposes about the "unspeakable" dirt and smells in its wards. In 1862 the surgeon Samuel Gross remarked that scurvy was endemic in the Blockley Almshouse.[25] To say that hospitals were not yet places of therapeutic excellence would be a massive understatement.

THE AMERICAN DISPENSARY

Outpatient institutions known as dispensaries provided most of the free medical care received by the poor throughout the nineteenth century. These were self-standing facilities, supported by charitable contributions, and they usually had a single full-time staff member who might be an apothecary or a physician. Dispensary staff were responsible for the provision of a range of therapeutic duties to the worthy poor, such as performing minor surgery, administering vaccines, and dispensing drugs. The first dispensary appeared in Philadelphia in 1768, followed by ones in New York in 1791, Boston in 1796, and then Baltimore in 1800. Thereafter, as Charles E. Rosenberg has documented, the movement gathered momentum. By 1874 New York alone had 29 dispensaries, and they were treating an extraordinary 876,000 people a year by 1900. As the demand for dispensary care grew in large urban areas they also evolved into more complex institutions. By the 1850s most had both a resident physician and a druggist-apothecary. Moreover, some dispensaries began to specialize: New York already had specialist dispensaries for treating eye and ear disorders in the 1820s, and most cities followed suit after 1850 with outpatient clinics focused on one or a few regions of the body.[26]

Rosenberg explains that the dispensary thrived during the nineteenth century because it had so much to offer patients, doctors, and donors. Patients benefited from free vaccinations and access to clinicians who knew how to treat fractures and lacerations. The fact that young dispensary doctors often visited patients in their own beds was an additional boon to those who desperately wished to avoid being hospitalized. Physicians and medical colleges also had much to gain. Doctors fresh out of college were often more than happy to volunteer their time in exchange for the intensive experience they acquired. Indeed, serving as a dispensary physician became highly important for doctors who wished to rise into the medical elites. As medical schools began to improve, the dispensary also assumed a key role in providing aspiring doctors with opportunities for clinical instruction. Some colleges actually set up their own dispensaries, called cliniques, where students gained experience in diagnosing and prescribing.[27] Wealthy philanthropists had equally pragmatic reasons for supporting dispensaries over hospitals, for morally worthy patients could be treated more cheaply in their own homes than in hospitals and were less likely to contract additional maladies. This meant that injured and sickly laborers could be returned to work more quickly, and everyone knew that a city's economy depended on keeping its most conscientious workers in the factory, workshop, or warehouse.[28] The dispensary, concluded one official report of 1856, is "cheapness and utility combined."[29]

THE TRANSFORMATION OF THE HOSPITAL

In the last decades of the century the American hospital underwent a transformation that turned it from a place of dependency and degradation to "the most visible embodiment of medical care in its most technically sophisticated form."[30] This shift is indicated by a massive boom in hospital building: just 178 general hospitals in 1873 grew to more than 4,000 by 1910, containing a total of 421,065 beds.[31] Even members of the middle and upper classes by 1900 were going to hospitals in order to receive expert care. Both social and medical factors were responsible for this dramatic reshaping of the medical landscape.

The acceleration of urbanization and industrialization after the Civil War gave enormous impetus to the establishment and expansion of hospitals. Some physicians quickly appreciated that proprietary hospitals could be made economically viable because in an urban context large numbers of patients lived within a short walk, ride, or electric tram journey. The hospital clinician could now see considerably more patients each day by saving the time once spent travelling from house to house. The city environment proved still more conducive to making hospitals profitable because it gave rise to both high levels of sickness and a decent number of people who could afford to pay for medical services. As the number of people needing inpatient care increased, so did the incentive for doctors to pool their skills and set up hospitals.[32] At the same time the breakdown of community supports in the city prompted state governments to try to protect the vulnerable by establishing humanitarian and therapeutic institutions. The unmet needs of many thousands of mentally ill men and women, many of them living hellish lives in almshouses or prisons, spurred a massive program across the country for building public and private mental asylums. Vulnerable children too became the recipients of government and private support. The Connecticut Asylum for the Education and Instruction of Deaf and Dumb Persons opened in 1817 in Hartford, Connecticut. After the Civil War more special schools were founded to teach the Braille system to blind children. The many thousands of infants and children who were orphaned by the death of parents to disease were increasingly taken to newly constructed foundling homes and asylums.[33]

The hardships and social dislocations of the urban world played a vital role in opening up the purses of large numbers of wealthy philanthropists who bankrolled the construction of private hospitals, dispensaries, and asylums. Although elite donors were often motivated by ideologies of Christian stewardship, philanthropy towards the vulnerable also broadcast their enormous wealth and gave them kudos for appearing to be genuinely benevolent.[34] Even the sons of textile tycoons got into the act of philanthropy. The established elites welcomed arrivistes into their ranks so long as they adopted and touted traditional genteel values. Risen men were sometimes eager to contribute toward charitable efforts like the construction of asylums in order to assert their fitness to be invited into the highest social ranks.[35] As urbanization transformed the United States they also perceived the social and political value of supporting charitable efforts directed at obviating the worst sufferings of the lowest social classes. The postwar elites were often justifiably disturbed by the breakdown in the vertical social ties between masters and men that had once served as guarantors of social cohesion. The United States in which rich and poor knew one another personally had disappeared from large parts of the country to be replaced by growing antagonism between the propertied class and an underclass comprising large numbers of immigrants of alien faith and customs. Easing the resentments of the poor by providing institutional care for the sick and disabled was now regarded as an essential means of lessening class tensions. As one Boston newspaper put it in 1879, "The only way to reconcile labor to capital is to show the laborer by actual deeds that the rich man regards himself as the steward of the Master," meaning that the lowest classes had to be convinced that the rich were their divinely appointed protectors.[36] Fearful of the potential volatility of the masses of poor men and women, they tried to win their loyalty through a selective generosity. Backed by the financial clout of the "rich man" seeking to smooth over social cleavages, doctors were able to realize their ambitions of setting up proprietary hospitals.

The progress of the hospital also depended on middle- and upper-class patients accepting them as desirable places in which to receive medical care. They had to be persuaded that the hospital could offer services and a quality of care hard to achieve in their own homes. This important shift in attitudes rested above all else on major advances in the safety and the scope of surgery in the last two decades of the century. Strict aseptic principles meant that hospital patients could undergo invasive surgery in the thorax, abdomen, and skull from which they could realistically expect to survive. Although it took decades to fully erode centuries of negative connotations about the hospital, the dissemination of the germ theory of disease meant that patients eventually came to appreciate the importance of hospital surgeons being about to create relatively sterile environments. It also helped that well-heeled patients could stay in elegantly-furnished private rooms that were entirely separate from the general wards of the impoverished sick.[37]

The new and reformed hospitals of the later 1800s had several other attractions for the middle and upper classes. First, economies of scale allowed managers to invest in state-of-the-art equipment such as X-ray machines and to create diagnostic laboratories, staffed by teams of expert technicians, for testing a person's sputum, blood, or urine for indications of specific pathologies.[38] Second, women of means could also now go to the hospital to deliver babies under the care of obstetricians and in environments far cleaner than their own bed-rooms.[39] And, third, hospitals were in a position to take on consultants who could limit themselves to taking care of patients with problems affecting specific organs or body parts, whether the bones, eyes, skin, or reproductive organs.[40] The largest of cities could sustain hospitals dedicated entirely to a particular class of patient, like New York City's Nursery and Child's Hospital and Boston Children's Hospital. People of all social classes were coming to recognize the value of consulting a clinician with profound knowledge of particular conditions, genders, and phases of life.

INVENTING THE PROFESSIONAL NURSE

The provision of quality hospital care also depended on what Susan Reverby has called the "invention of the trained nurse."[41] After the experience of the Civil War, during which about 20,000 women of diverse backgrounds had volunteered as nurses, an argument gained ground that the "thinking physician" ought to be assisted by educated nurses.[42] This call for the introduction of professional nursing came at a propitious time. A rapid growth in educational opportunities for middle-class women after the Civil War had created a sizeable demand for meaningful employment. Many chose nursing as a career and, by enrolling in training colleges attached to hospitals, turned their voca-tion into a professional occupation. A mere 15 nursing schools in 1880 had proliferated to 432 in 1900 and 1,129 a decade later as clinicians came to appreciate the virtues of the knowledgeable and highly compe-tent nursing staff.[43] The trend soon extended to municipal hospitals. In 1883 the Philadelphia Hospital, once the Blockley Almshouse, created its own nurse training school and then hired the English nurse-administrator Alice Fisher to run the school and manage nurses on the hospital wards.[44]

Professional nursing became a viable career option for the daughters of respectable families because they were able to clearly distinguish themselves from the traditionally lower-class hospital nurse. Middle-class nurses derived kudos from their work in several ways. Nursing was presented as a reflection of the respectable woman's maternal and spiritual qualities.[45] Many a nurse came from a strongly religious background and regarded her work as a "secular ministry."[46] Isabel Hampton Robb, first superintendent of the Johns Hopkins Hospital nursing school, referred to nursing as "consecrated service."[47] Male doctors endorsed this view. The "nurse business" is ideal for the woman of good family, agreed the neurologist Silas Weir Mitchell, because it requires exactly the same aptitudes for loving and obedience as "the wife business."[48] Some nurses eschewed these statements as misogynistic platitudes. But all skilled nurses could agree that womanly virtues were an insufficient basis for a nursing career. They knew that they could not always afford to be highly empathetic: one commented that "affection, however warm, will not qualify a sick-nurse."[49] If we fail to keep an emotional distance from patients, said another, we should "be used up and we should die." They were not on the ward to provide mere tenderness.[50]

Most nurses by the 1880s and 1890s also grounded their sense of occupational prestige in the exacting practical and intellectual demands of the job. The new cadres of nurses had studied the sciences of physiology, chemistry, and bacteriology. Once on the ward they were responsible for knowing how to use diagnostic technologies and what signs to look for in a patient's condition. Far from slavishly following the physician's instructions, they had to know how to respond if a patient started to deteriorate and there was no time to await the doctor's arrival. A keen knowledge of drugs and physiology as well as an ability to make independent decisions in a crisis were essential aspects of their daily work. Indeed, the obvious abilities of ward nurses caused some physicians to worry lest they try to usurp the authority of the male doctor or even "open offices and practice medicine."[51] This is why they so often tried to browbeat graduating nurses into remembering their inferior position in the hospital hierarchy. "What error can be more stupid," one physician opined, "than the nurse attempting to impress the doctor with her knowledge?"[52] The concern of doctors is indicative of the fact that by the late 1800s nurses had turned a career once notorious for drunkenness and neglect into a respectable middle-class occupation. Hospital surgeons and physicians had grown to be so dependent on them that the famous Philadelphia surgeon Samuel Gross could refer to the nurse as the doctor's "lieutenant."[53] Patients too came to appreciate the professionalism and competence of the trained nurses who significantly enhanced the quality of hospital care.

THE HOSPITAL AND MEDICAL EDUCATION

The rise of the hospital is intimately bound up with improvements to the quality of medical education as well as medical care. As we have seen, from the mid-1840s onwards the nation's better medical colleges, starting with Harvard University and the University of Michigan, had their pupils spend long hours on hospital wards learning palpation, auscultation, and percussion on actual patients and observing specific conditions and complications. It was not easy for these colleges to transition from a system in which medical students never or hardly ever entered a hospital to one in which ward visits lay at the heart of their education. Colleges had to fight hard to overcome the opposition of lay trustees who felt it to be their duty to protect patients from the prodding and probing of students. But the professors of elite medical colleges, in their determination to raise the standard of their graduates and medicine more generally, succeeded in integrating the classroom into the ward. Proprietary colleges that did not forge close ties with hospitals were in steep decline by the end of the century. The remainder would fade into oblivion over the next 20 years. And, as the hospital became a central component of medical treatment, teaching, and research, physicians now assumed most of the authority over how they were run. Even in the old almshouses-turned-municipal hospitals the power of the lay trustee gave way to the expertise and professional kudos of the clinician.

INSTITUTIONAL CARE AT THE END OF THE CENTURY

The nineteenth-century hospital had undergone a dramatic change. From the humblest beginnings it had become the flagship of scientific medicine. This tremendous growth in the hospital sector had the effect of weakening the position of the dispensary during the early twentieth century. The ambitious young doctor who had once clamored for dispensary experience now preferred to learn in hospitals containing the latest diagnostic technologies and the funds to build aseptic surgical theaters. Dispensaries that had always done a lot with very little simply could not compete with the capital- and labor-intensive hospital. In addition, argues Charles Rosenberg, far fewer young doctors in the late 1800s relished working among poor populations, not least because the tenements of major cities like New York, Boston, and Philadelphia were home to large populations of immigrants from southern and eastern Europe. Nor did the medical profession at large mourn the declining significance of the dispensary. Private practitioners fumed that many of their own would-be patients were receiving free care when they could perfectly well afford a doctor's fees. There was probably little truth in this claim, but many a physician nevertheless agitated for the complete abolition of the dispensary. In the event, the dispensary survived into the 1920s, when it was eclipsed by hospital outpatient clinics that offered more comprehensive diagnostic and therapeutic services.[54]

If the future lay with the hospital, we need to be careful not to exaggerate how much difference the institution had made to the longevity of Americans by 1900. Without antibiotics to contain infections, hospitals often had the effect of hastening the spread of deadly germs.[55] Substandard conditions and heightened death rates also persisted in many almshouses-turned hospitals. Perhaps most shocking, in 1896 about 96% of babies taken to New York's chronically underfunded Infant Hospital perished. The *New York Times* described the unfortunate infants sent there as "mere skeletons with a bit of blue-black skin drawn over them."[56] Furthermore, although hospitals now could save lives, rural populations were mostly denied their benefits. In 1920 Hermann Biggs, the health commissioner of New York, talked of the millions "cut off absolutely from all kinds of laboratory and X-ray services ... from all assistance of specialists." Biggs proposed a solution: the setting up of private rural health centers that would combine the services of hospitals and public health agencies. The leaders of the medical profession smothered the idea not because they did not think it would work but because it might entail ceding authority to mayors and lay administrators. Convinced that the prestige of medicine depended on the absolute freedom of the individual doctor to practice and to charge as he saw fit, they would not tolerate any possibility of physicians becoming salaried employees or being subject to the oversight of civil authorities. American doctors were just entering the long struggle to keep government as much out of medical practice as possible.[57]

NOTES

1. Susan M. Reverby, *Ordered to Care: The Dilemma of American Nursing, 1850–1945.* New York: Cambridge University Press, 1987, p. 22.

2. Charles E. Rosenberg, *The Care of Strangers: The Rise of America's Hospital System.* New York : Basic Books, 1987, p. 18.

3. Charles E. Rosenberg, "And Heal the Sick: The Hospital and the Patient in the 19th Century America," *Journal of Social History* 10, no. 4 (Summer 1977), 428–47, p. 430.

4. Rosenberg, *Care of Strangers*, p. 19.

5. Rosenberg, "And Heal the Sick," p. 431.

6. Reverby, *Ordered to Care*, p. 24.

7. Rosenberg, "And Heal the Sick," p. 439.

8. John Harley Warner, "Power, Conflict, and Identity in Mid-Nineteenth-Century American Medicine: Therapeutic Change at the Commercial Hospital in Cincinnati," *The Journal of American History* 73, no. 4 (March 1987), 934–56, p. 944.

9. Rosenberg, *Care of Strangers*, p. 16.

10. Ibid., pp. 17, 45.

11. Rosenberg, "And Heal the Sick," p. 438.

12. Reverby, *Ordered to Care*, p. 24.

13. Atwater, "Touching the Patient," p. 134.

14. Rosenberg, "And Heal the Sick," p. 438.

15. Steven M. Stowe, *Doctoring the South: Southern Physicians and Everyday Medicine in the Mid-Nineteenth Century*. Chapel Hill: University of North Carolina Press, 2004, p. 60; and Warner, "Power, Conflict, and Identity," p. 944.

16. Rosenberg, *Care of Strangers*, p. 36.

17. Reverby, *Ordered to Care*, p. 27.

18. Rosenberg, "And Heal the Sick," p. 438.

19. Charles E. Rosenberg, "From Almshouse to Hospital: The Shaping of Philadelphia General Hospital," *Explaining Epidemics and Other Studies in the History of Medicine*. New York: Cambridge University Press, 1992, pp. 178–213, p. 196.

20. Rosenberg, "And Heal the Sick," p. 433.

21. Rosenberg, "From Almshouse to Hospital," p. 179.

22. Ibid., p. 198.

23. Rosenberg, "And Heal the Sick," p. 432.

24. Ibid., p. 434.

25. Reverby, *Ordered to Care*, p. 27; and Rosenberg, "From Almshouse to Hospital," p. 192.

26. Rosenberg, "The Rise and Fall of the Dispensary," p. 156.

27. Atwater, "Touching the Patient," p. 134.

28. Rosenberg, "The Rise and Fall of the Dispensary," p. 162.

29. Ibid., p. 162.

30. Paul Starr, *The Social Transformation of American Medicine*. New York: Basic Books, 1982, p. 145.

31. Rosenberg, *Care of Strangers*, p. 5.

32. Ibid., chapter 4.

33. Janet Golden, "Children's Health: Caregivers and Sites of Care," in Janet Golden, Richard A. Meckel, and Heather Munro Prescott (eds.), *Children and Youth in Sickness and in Health: A Historical Handbook and Guide*. Westport, CT: Greenwood Press, 2004, pp. 67–84.

34. Frederic Cople Jaher, *The Urban Establishment: Upper Strata in Boston, New York, Charleston, Chicago, and Los Angeles*. Urbana: University of Illinois Press, 1982, p. 57.

35. Ibid., p. 60.

36. Reverby, *Ordered to Care*, p. 24.

37. Rosenberg, *Care of Strangers*, p. 245.

38. Bettyann Holtzmann Kevles, *Naked to the Bone: Medical Imaging in the Twentieth Century*. Reading, MA: Addison-Wesley, 1998.

39. Judith Walzer Leavitt, *Brought to Bed: Childbearing in America, 1750 to 1950*. New York: Oxford University Press, 1986.

40. Rosenberg, *Care of Strangers*, p. 172.

41. Reverby, *Ordered to Care*, p. 39.

42. Patricia D'Antonio, *American Nursing: A History of Knowledge, Authority, and the Meaning of Work*. Baltimore, MD: Johns Hopkins University Press, 2010, p. 8.

43. D'Antonio, *American Nursing*, p. 29.

44. Rosenberg, "From Almshouse to Hospital."

45. Siobhan Nelson, *Say Little, Do Much: Nursing, Nuns, and Hospitals in the Nineteenth Century*. University of Pennsylvania Press, 2001.

46. Reverby, *Ordered to Care*, p. 3.

47. D'Antonio, *American Nursing*, p. 51.

48. Ibid., p. 33.

49. Ibid., p. 20.

50. Ibid., p. 43.

51. Ibid., p. 21.

52. Reverby, *Ordered to Care*, p. 51.

53. D'Antonio, *American Nursing*, p. 17.

54. Rosenberg, "Rise and Fall of the Dispensary," p. 174.

55. Rosenberg, "From Almshouse to Hospital," p. 149.

56. John Duffy, *The Sanitarians: A History of American Public Health*. Urbana: University of Illinois Press, 1990, p. 181.

57. Starr, *Social Transformation*, p. 195.

CHAPTER 13

Disease, Healing, and the Arts

Literary and artistic reflections on disease and medicine in the nineteenth century fell into three basic categories. First, novelists, photographers, and painters responded creatively to the horrendous levels of death and suffering unleashed by epidemics and warfare. These works ranged from painfully realistic images of Civil War casualties to the genre of consolatory literature written for parents who had lost children to sickness. Second, American novelists reflected on the themes of health and disease in the context of addressing fundamental questions about the character of the urban poor and the condition of the African American slave. Finally, novelists offered a variety of literary renderings of the medical practitioner: wise or incompetent physicians, unfeeling surgeons, medical scientists willing to sacrifice their humanity in pursuit of secular truths, and female doctors who either lacked the stomach for medicine or succeeded due to their masculine personas. Although a few famous surgeons were celebrated in oils and statuary, the overall impressions from these diverse works of artistic creativity are that sickness seemed omnipresent and that relatively few regarded the medical profession as likely to be able to turn back the tide of pain and death.

DEPICTING SICKNESS AND DEATH

Confronting Loss

The conspicuous place of dying and disease in American literature obviously owed a lot to the terrible frequency of premature death. Families across the United States lived in the knowledge that children or spouses might be claimed suddenly by any of a wide range of fatal maladies. Some novelists were deeply affected by their own experiences of disease. Charles Brockden Brown witnessed the early stage of the devastating yellow fever outbreak in Philadelphia in 1793. Six years later his novel *Arthur Mervyn* dramatized the "unspeakable perturbation" caused by the threat of the fever in Philadelphia and vividly described it scything its way through the city and his list of characters.[1] Mark Twain addressed the appalling disease burden of his age in both his fictional and nonfictional writings. Twain never left behind the chronic anxiety about epidemics that he had felt growing up in a small town near Hannibal in Missouri. In reporting on June 3, 1847, that only half of all local children reached the age of 21, the *Hannibal Gazette* lent precision to what everyone already knew: that childhood in frontier states was highly precarious. Decades later Twain told of the descent of yellow fever onto the population of Hannibal in 1849–1850 and the "alarming slaughter" of a measles epidemic when he was 12, and he recalled his brother's account of steamboat crews in 1849 "burying their passengers" who had perished from cholera "at every wood yard, both from cabin and deck." Hardly surprisingly, novels like *Huckleberry Finn* are replete with maladies that impair senses, cripple bodies, and leave behind scores of young corpses. This was the stuff of real life in an age prior to the development of adequate systems of sanitation, effective chemotherapies, and our modern array of vaccinations.[2]

Americans who took up the pen to write about disease and death were often motivated by the personal experience of bereavement. Writing about real losses, especially those of children, could be both profoundly cathartic and a means of keeping alive the memory of a cherished loved one. The manuscript volume known as *Harriet Gould's Book* is a poignant example of how the bereaved sought what comfort could be gained from composing heartfelt poetry. This book contains a series of poems by parents living in Dover, Vermont, from 1837 onwards who were reflecting on the deaths of their own children who were buried in the local cemetery. These poems capture in honest if not necessarily brilliant or original language the malignant agony of loss with which their authors were burdened. One father spoke of his "speechless gloom" at the death of one of his children, and a bereaved mother wrote these intensely loving lines:

Oh can it be that Wayland's dead
My lovely darling son
Oh can it be his soul has fled
To its eternal home.

But deeper sadder is the gloom
That rests on all around
As one by one the days move on
In their appointed rounds.[3]

Such poems usually adopted the consolatory belief that deceased children were now in the happy embrace of God. The bereaved mother of Wayland concluded her poem with the following uplifting lines:

And if to God we faithful prove,
And act the Christian part
We'll join them in that world above
Where we shall never part.

And another of Harriet's poets concluded:

I know my boy though lost to me
Has reached the blissful shore.[4]

Memorializing the dead child in this way required a general shift in American culture away from the harsher theologies of the past. Convinced of the inherent sinfulness of humankind, Puritan leaders had preached not only that children can end up in hell but that the bereaved must accept with pious equanimity God's decision to take away their children. Following the American Revolution, this unconsoling doctrine steadily made way for more reassuring set of practices and beliefs as rival denominations gained the freedom to practice. In this more competitive religious climate, many clergymen grasped the virtue of issuing a message that offered comfort to worshippers. This involved abandoning pure forms of Calvinist predestination and instead offering up sermons, books, and hymns that eased the pain of the bereaved. Americans also adopted increasingly complex rituals of mourning, and parents commissioned elaborate statutory, often in the form of weeping female figures, to adorn the graves of their children.

And they created a new "cult of mourning literature" that provided a soothing conceptualization of the deceased child as so pure and sensitive that a kind God had unquestionably allowed him or her to ascend to a pain-free heaven.[5]

Although pious writers of mourning literature are now mostly forgotten or regarded as painfully sentimental, their works sold in large volumes because they brought much-needed comfort amid high levels of child mortality. Book stalls in the decades either side of the Civil War, says the literary scholar Ann Douglas Wood, were stocked full of accounts of "death bed scenes and celestial communications."[6] Lydia Huntley Sigourney became one of the most revered authors in the United States for her emotionally wrought renderings of the deaths of innocent children.[7] Sigourney encouraged parents to feel that the dead were still a real part of their worlds, looking down on them from heaven, even sometimes crossing briefly back into the corporeal world. The genre is epitomized by the 1868 bestseller *The Gates Ajar* by Massachusetts-born Elizabeth Stuart Phelps. Inspired in part by the death of her fiancé during the Battle of Antietam, this novel takes the form of a prolonged discussion in which a young woman called Mary reflects on the death of a much-loved brother. It culminates in the dramatic rejection of the stern and comfortless Calvinism of old. Mary comes to see that her brother is always with her, watching and waiting for her from a heaven free from the cares and injustices of Earth. Authors like Phelps, as Ann Douglas Wood points out, portrayed the afterlife as a carefree version of the domestic sphere in which all would be well again after the brief interlude of earthly existence.[8]

Romanticizing deadly disease acted as another kind of analgesic for those left behind. Tuberculosis received the most extensive romantic makeover. Understood by many as a disease of overtaxed bodies and minds, it could be interpreted as the price of heightened sensitivity and highly refined sensibilities. Novelists perpetuated an older cultural association between consumption and creative genius: the sensitive artist was depicted as suffering for his work and so exhausting his stock of nervous energy that tuberculosis eventually took hold. Well-born women and children who died of consumption were presented as being of such refined sensitivity that they could not withstand the shocks of normal life.[9] A few authors went to extravagant lengths to romanticize tuberculosis. In his story "Metzengerstein," Edgar Allen Poe described the death from consumption of a female character as "gentle" and "glorious" in spite of the fact that his own mother had died from the disease when he was just three years old. It took his wife's first pulmonary hemorrhage, in 1842, for Poe to face up to the true horribleness of this disease.[10]

Death, Art, and War

The artwork produced in response to the U.S. Civil War broke new ground in the veracity with which is showed the hell of conflict. Artists had conventionally depicted war in the form of romanticized battle scenes that extolled the derring-do of military heroes or celebrated their deaths as acts of sublime self-sacrifice. One thinks immediately of the heroism and pathos conveyed by John Trumbull's 1776 *The Death of General Warren at the Battle of Bunker's Hill, June 17, 1775* or Emanuel Gottlieb Leutze's 1851 *Washington Crossing the Delaware*. The war fought between 1861 and 1865 did inspire some of these stylized artistic responses. Firms like New York's Currier and Ives produced thousands of hand-colored "Cheap and Popular Prints" showing the opposing armies marching in orderly fashion towards one another. The images sold by Currier and Ives had all the hallmarks of having been created in Manhattan according to convention, not observation. As one veteran put it, Civil War soldiers did not stride into battle shoulder to shoulder, for "God don't make men who could stand that."[11] This lack of realism may explain why none of these artistic renderings won acclaim during the war or in its aftermath. The most emphatic praise instead went to paintings, engravings, and photographs that related the true experiences of the common soldier.

Photography allowed artists to record scenes of conflict with raw and poignant honesty. The finest Civil War photographers, Matthew B. Brady, Alexander Gardner, Timothy H. O'Sullivan, and George N. Barnard, conveyed the true misery of war with breathtaking immediacy.[12] Alexander Gardner compiled a particularly chilling record. His photographic series *Confederate Dead, Antietam* shows hundreds of corpses lying discarded in tangled heaps or lined up ready to be interred in hastily dug graves, their contorted faces, often bloated by decay, staring directly back at the viewer. Dr. Oliver Wendell Holmes, who had rushed to Antietam in search of his combatant son, spoke of such photographs as almost unbearably close to "visiting the battlefield."[13] New York's George N. Barnard shared Gardner's commitment to recording the destructiveness of the conflict, photographing the ruins of southern cities like Charleston and Colombia which General William Sherman had ordered destroyed in order to weaken the South's fighting resolve. His images of shattered cityscapes

Confederate soldier killed during the Battle of Antietam, September 21, 1862. Photographed by Alexander Gardner. Having emigrated to the United States from Scotland in 1856, Gardner emerged as one of the foremost photographers of the Civil War. Few captured so brilliantly the true horror of the conflict. (© Medford Historical Society Collection/ Corbis)

introduced northerners to the systematic ferocity of Sherman's campaign. Photography had for the first time in the United States been deployed to show the pitiless ugliness of war.[14]

Painters shared the photographer's determination to show a war defined by fear and death as well as boredom and homesickness rather than by the acts of a few valiant men. Winslow Homer, the most admired of Civil War–era artists, painted soldiers in the humble hues of ordinary men involved in a tragic conflagration. In doing so, wrote one critic, he tells us "truth about the war."[15] One of Homer's most moving paintings, the *circa* 1865 *Trooper Meditating beside a Grave*, shows a Union soldier gazing forlornly at a crucifix atop the burial site of a fallen friend. It contains neither heroes nor meaningful self-sacrifice. Homer's painting is simply an exquisitely captured scene of human loss. Nor is it hard to understand why artists such as Homer, Gardner, and Barnard broke with the traditions of heroic military art. They were striving to represent a war on which it was hard to impose the easy dichotomies of the Revolutionary War. Although they might accept that the Civil War had to be fought, artists recognized it to be an absolute catastrophe to a young nation that had seemed destined for uninterrupted progress. Americans slaughtering fellow Americans could not be celebrated with the simpleminded bravado of patriots sticking it to redcoats. The Civil War also involved death on a scale that horrified and sickened. Artists who spent time at the front articulated the conflict's moral ambiguities and found in the daily hardships experienced by soldiers the only truths worth recording.[16]

THE POLITICS OF HEALTH

Novelists and the Urban Slum

Grasping the true scale of disease in the nineteenth century required that a novelist recognize the hazards of life in the urban slum. American novelists mostly preferred to set their stories in more salubrious settings: towns of the colonial past, homesteads of the present, the cultural capitals of Europe, or the drawing rooms of the East Coast upper crust. Even so, some novelists from the 1840s found a muse in the wretched moral and physical condition of slum dwellers. Several adopted the trope of the naïve country boy or girl who experiences a painful collision with the sordidness of the city and its inhabitants. Walt Whitman's *Franklin Evans* (1842) tells of a young man who leaves a peaceful Long Island, journeys to New York, slips into desperate alcoholism, and only just manages to regain his self-control after a series of tragedies. Herman Melville's novel *Pierre* (1852) likewise contrasts the bucolic bliss of "Saddle Meadows" in upstate New York, where Pierre is raised, to the crowded Babylon of Manhattan where he flees having been thrown out of his natal home.[17] After the Civil War, as urbanization and industrialization accelerated, more novelists expressed the visceral disgust that most members of the middle classes felt on entering tenement districts. Edward Townsend's 1895 *Daughter of the Tenements* painted a gothic picture of filthy, claustrophobic, and diseased tenements for middle-class readers who would never dream of entering the slums themselves.[18]

Few novelists were able to work out quite why urban poverty and disease were becoming such chronic problems in an apparent land of plenty and opportunity. Most could agree that children growing up in slums became habituated to vice, but rarely did they pursue this sociological insight with great depth. Novelists were usually more interested in indulging a variety of armchair tourism in which readers vicariously entered the slums, felt a surge of fascination for the exotic underworld, and then finished the book with a reassuring sense of pride in their own comfortable respectability.[19] When they were not muck-raking, novelists were constructing pleasing fictions for middle-class readers who warmed to the message that they need feel no moral responsibility towards the lower classes. No matter how terrible life could be for the poverty-stricken worker, writers insisted that men and women are to blame when they fall into misery and sickness. In some ways, *Life in the Iron Mills* (1861), a novella by Rebecca Harding Davis, offers a bravely realistic portrait of the lives of factory operatives. Davis evoked some sympathy among well-to-do readers for the main protagonist, Hugh Wolfe, who has clear talent but cannot escape the drudgery of factory work. Yet *Life in the Iron Mills* culminates in Hugh having to decide whether or not to keep a wallet of cash stolen by a friend. He makes the "wrong" decision, and soon after takes his own life in his prison cell. The novel ends with a typically conservative moral judgment: Wolfe had failed a critical moral test and so no longer had claims on the reader's pity. No amount of deprivation could justify his criminal act.[20]

Some American novelists did arrive at a more sophisticated account of the effects of slum existence on an individual's character and health. Revolted by what he viewed as the false and un-Christian doctrine that the poor are responsible for their own misery, Melville wrote in *Pierre* of the "unequal toil and poverty" that left countless men deformed.[21] To Melville, the urban poor were limping indictments of an unjust world in which rich men absolved themselves of any blame by twisting the Gospels into justifications of rank selfishness.[22] In refusing to censure the lower classes for their poverty and mortality, Melville anticipated the assertions of later writers like Jacob Riis, whose nonfiction exposé *The Children of the Poor* (1892) argued that tenements were "nurseries of pauperism and crime" and bred "moral contagion" because brutal "conditions" were the "parents of corresponding habits and morals."[23] Melville and Riis believed that the richer sections of society needed to show greater sympathy for the lower classes. They could not be allowed to find shelter from the truth in ignorance or time-worn myths about the undeserving poor.

With the slums becoming a permanent feature of U.S. cities, late nineteenth-century writers were more willing to acknowledge the awesome power of the environment to shape character but lacked Melville's desire to trigger the reader's sympathy. In his 1893 novella *Maggie: A Girl of the Streets*, Stephen Crane documented an entire tenement family, brutalized by their surroundings and neighbors, "Goin to deh devil." Crane hoped to show "that environment is a tremendous thing in the world, and frequently shapes lives regardless."[24] *Maggie* is an exemplar of the naturalistic style of writing that expressed a deepening pessimism about the possibility of eradicating extreme urban poverty and its associated diseases.[25] Where Crane had emphasized the force of the environment others wrote of the inescapable power of heredity. As families from southern and eastern Europe crowded into the tenements of cities like New York and Boston, novelists played cheaply on fears of immigrants who threatened to overwhelm "true" American stock, subvert the nation's values, and spread deadly diseases. In their own small way these writers contributed to a growing belief among turn-of-the-century Americans that only immigration restriction or eugenics could prevent the swamping of the northern European races.[26]

Literature, Race, and Sickness

The subject of the health of slaves assumed tremendous importance to novelists in the decades either side of the Civil War. Literary accounts that described the physical and emotional sufferings of plantation life were written with the explicit aim of galvanizing the North against slavery. Of all antislavery writers, Harriet Beecher Stowe furnished the most powerful critique of slavery as a deadly and degrading institution. In several scenes of *Uncle Tom's Cabin* (1852), the best-selling novel of the century, Stowe describes the terrible suffering and anguish of the slave's life: the slave Prue, who falls into depression and alcoholism after her child's death; Cassy's severe mental distress at her children being sold; and the fatal beating of Tom on the orders of the slave owner Simon Legree. *Our Nig: Sketches from the Life of a Free Black* (1859), by the African American author Harriet E. Wilson, reminded northerners that even free blacks were vulnerable to vicious exploitation. An autobiographical novel, it tells of a young black woman in the North whose health is ruined by the demands placed on her by a white mistress. Although born free, the heroine of *Our Nig* is treated like a slave because of her color. The novel sold few copies for the obvious reason that northern abolitionists were reluctant to accept that virulent racism, called the "shadow of slavery" by Wilson, thrived in northern as well as southern states.[27]

Novelists in the slave-owning states of the South tried to refute the devastatingly negative image of slavery in novels like *Uncle Tom's Cabin*. The literature scholar Scott Romine points out how southern novelists crafted an iconic view of the South as a land of genteel benevolence in which slavery was maintained because slaves were not physically or mentally equipped for lives of freedom.[28] Caroline

In this scene from Harriet Beecher Stowe's *Uncle Tom's Cabin*, Uncle Tom saves Eva from a watery grave. The first book by an American author to have an African American hero, *Uncle Tom's Cabin* was published serially in 1851 and 1852 in the Washington, D.C., antislavery paper *National Era* and later in book form in 1852. The novel brilliantly dramatized the physical and psychological traumas of slavery. (Library of Congress)

Hentz's 1854 *The Planter's Northern Bride* is typical of this lucrative genre. The novel presents the unlikely scenario of the daughter of a northern abolitionist marrying a planter. She slowly learns about the "true" South in which slaves are content and dutifully taken care of by their masters in old age.[29] Such novels continued to find eager readers after the Civil War among those who looked back nostalgically on what they recalled as an age of joyful harmony. "Dem wuz good ole times, master—de bed Sam ever see!" exclaims one ex-slave in Thomas Nelson Page's 1884 novel *Marse Chan*.[30] Readers were eager to pay for these gross misrepresentations of reality. It made the present more bearable to believe that black Americans had once been happy and healthy under their care.

REPRESENTATIONS OF DOCTORS AND SURGEONS

Positive and Negative Images

Depictions of medical men and women in nineteenth-century literature drew on both a traditional cynicism about the motives and abilities of physicians and a growing confidence in the power of scientific medicine. The laments of American doctors that their work lacked prestige are certainly borne out by the harsh verdicts of popular writers. In his 1894 short story *The Extraordinary Twins*, Mark Twain sent up the doctor's use of jargon to dazzle the credulous. In a delightful passage, the story's physician explains to his sick client the implications of him not agreeing to undergo a particular intervention: "exudation of the aesophagus is nearly sure to ensue," the doctor asserts, "followed by ossification and extradition of the maxillaris superioris, which must decompose the granular surfaces of the great infusorial ganglionic system, thus obstructing the action of the posterior varioloid arteries and precipitating compound strangulated sorosis of the valvular tissues. . . ."[31] Twain's ability to camouflage criticism with good humor allowed him to get away with an amazingly biting attack when receiving an honorary degree in from the New York Postgraduate Medical College in 1909. Pretending to be a physician, he said:

> I was once a sharpshooter, but now I practice a much higher and equally as deadly a profession. . . . When I settled on my farm in Connecticut in June I found the community very thinly settled—and since I have been engaged in practice it has become more thinly settled.[32]

A serious distrust underlay Twain's rudeness about medicine. He suspected that one of his brothers had been killed by inexperienced medical students who administered too much morphine. He also blamed the death of his cherished eldest daughter from meningitis on the ineptitude of her physicians. Kindred experiences convinced many other Americans that doctors got things wrong too often to deserve much credit. "It seems a stupid idea," Twain wrote in a letter of September 1902, "to keep a student 4 years in a medical college to merely learn how to guess—and guess wrong. . . . Let me die a natural death."[33]

The cocksure commitment of some physicians to voguish theories inspired one of the most brilliantly disturbing short stories of the century. Charlotte Perkins Gilman, the Connecticut-born feminist, writer, sociologist, and poet, had been experiencing bouts of depression for some time before she decided to consult the world-famous neurologist Silas Weir Mitchell. Convinced that neurasthenics were the victims of nervous overexertion, Mitchell prescribed for her plenty of rest, insisted that she not touch pen and paper, and allowed her only two hours of mental work a day.[34] Gilman complied with the doctor's instructions with disastrous effects. Later she wrote that it had brought her "near the borderline of utter mental ruin." Using her "remnants of intelligence," in 1892 Gilman retaliated by writing "The Yellow Wallpaper," the story of a woman's descent into insanity due to the terrible isolation of the rest cure. Her protagonist is being treated for postpartum depression by her doctor-husband. Following Mitchell's stipulations to the letter, he keeps his wife isolated in the nursery with nothing to do and puts her on a strict regimen of phosphates, tonics, and food. Eventually her mind starts to fixate on the yellow wallpaper, and she imagines that a woman is moving behind its patterns who must be liberated. Eventually she tears all the paper from the wall and announces to her husband "I've got out at last." Her descent into madness is complete. She has gained her freedom at the expense of her sanity.[35] In an article of 1913 Gilman talked of the "noted specialist in nervous diseases" who had caused her such misery—obviously Mitchell himself—and explained that she wrote the "Yellow Wallpaper" "to save" other "people from being driven crazy."[36]

Some novelists did present physicians in a more positive light as combining the insights of both scientist and sage.[37] The 1861 *Elsie Venner*, by the writer, poet, and Harvard medical professor Oliver Wendell Holmes tells of two doctors who try to care for a young woman called Elsie who has the wildness of a serpent due to a rattlesnake having bitten her mother when pregnant. In one passage a Dr. Kittredge impugns the knowledge of which the local clergyman boasts: "God opens one book to physicians," he patronizingly explains to the minister, "that a good many of you don't know much about,— the Book of life."[38] Although Holmes's account of medical expertise is self-congratulatory, later in the century novelists were more willing to regard the doctor as possessing "sagacity and skill." In this manner, Sarah Jewett's Dr. John Leslie in *A Country Doctor* (1884) describes a physician who not only treats sick bodies but also has the "great knowledge of human nature" to "help many of his patients whose ailments were not wholly physical."[39] Jewett's novel may reflect the rising status of medicine as educated physicians were increasingly able to lay claim to esoteric scientific knowledge.

Surgery received the most adulation because its practitioners had so dramatically enhanced the safety and scope of their profession. Large memorials appeared in prestigious parks and streets to celebrate the finest surgeons. In 1893 Alexander Stirling Calder produced a statue of Samuel Gross that stood in the mall of Washington, DC, and James Marion Sims was memorialized in New York City, at Jefferson Medical College in Philadelphia, and in the capitals of both South Carolina and Alabama. In addition, leading artists selected surgeons as fitting subjects for heroic portraiture. When Thomas Eakins decided to produce a "big painting" in 1875 that might win him recognition at the U.S. Centennial Exposition in Philadelphia, he chose to paint Samuel Gross at work. In 1889 Eakins returned to the same theme and painted the University of Pennsylvania's Dr. David Hayes Agnew as he and his staff performed a mastectomy. Both *The Gross Clinic* and *The Agnew Clinic* depict accomplished surgeons in the most heroic of hues. Critics condemned Eakins for vulgarity because he unblushingly included so much nudity and blood. No-one questioned, however, the appropriateness of an artist celebrating surgical excellence: viewers simply preferred more sanitized images.[40]

The critical responses to *The Gross Clinic* and *The Agnew Clinic* draw attention to how medical achievements could disturb and repel. Many a writer feared that surgeons were prone to becoming soulless and inhumane. In his 1850 story *White-Jacket*, Herman Melville relied on a stereotype of the surgeon as cruelly dispassionate. Cadwallader Cuticle MD, surgeon of the fleet, is a heartless butcher who remains "almost supernaturally calm" as he slices through limbs heedless of the "moans and shrieks" of his unfortunate patients. Stripped of human feeling, Cuticle fills his stateroom with grotesquely morbid objects that would make a normal man's "whole heart burst with sorrow." Cuticle's appearance, "withered, shrunken, one-eyed, toothless, hairless," reflects his cold indifference to suffering. Melville included another ship's surgeon, in his brilliant story *Billy Budd, Sailor*, who takes obvious pride in the "scientifically conducted" onboard hangings that he directs.[41]

Melville's depictions of Cadwallader Cuticle borrowed from the literary trope of the mad scientist driven to sacrifice all in the pursuit of knowledge. Cuticle is not innately wicked but has been corrupted by science's immoderate lust for truth. Nathaniel Hawthorne expressed similar fears for where the scientific will to know might lead. In the 1843 "The Birth-Mark" a scientist's love of science becomes intertwined with his love for his beautiful wife who has a birthmark on her cheek. Her slight imperfection then becomes the object of his scientific curiosity. At the end of the story the birthmark is gone, but his wife has been killed in the process. Hawthorne's point is that as the scientist's narrow obsession with individual tissues and organs blinds him to interconnectedness of the whole and to the "angelic spirit" that is in "union with the mortal frame."[42] The physician, writer, and suffragist Mary Putnam Jacobi's 1869 "A Martyr to Science" presents the same trope of the mad scientist with a clever variation. Her scientist is so obsessed with the importance of vivisection that he tries to arrange for his own thorax to be opened to reveal his beating heart. Before he can execute his plan, his students have him confined to an asylum. In Jacobi's story, as in Hawthorne's "The Birth-Mark," it is not just cold logic that drives the scientist into murderous lunacy. The human traits of ambition and vanity whip them on until they destroy themselves or those whom they love. Underlying such stories lay an anxiety about the power of science to undermine faith. They feared a culture in which medical science imagined life to comprise a soulless series of mechanical functions.[43]

Women Doctors in the American Novel

A rapid increase in the number of female doctors after the Civil War gave American writers an opportunity to engage in debates about the real or imagined differences between men and women. Were the sexes innately fitted to occupy separate spheres so that female doctors could never rival their male counterparts? Could women ever be as rational as men? Many male physicians and medical students were horrified at the prospect of female practitioners. The University of Pennsylvania's Dr. Agnew once melodramatically resigned for a brief period over the suggestion that female students be admitted. Female surgeons, he warned, will lose "all those qualities now the glory of the sex." Dr. Elizabeth Blackwell rejoined that women were born with a facility for the "subordination of the self to the welfare of others." Lacking the selfishness of the male, said Blackwell, she brings a kindness to the bedside that few men could provide.[44]

The arguments of Agnew and Blackwell were played out in dozens of postwar novels and short stories. Novelists who denied the suitability of women for medicine had a guaranteed audience of readers who were averse to any attack on the sexual division of labor. William Dean Howell's *Dr Breen's Practice* (1881) depicts a jilted woman who turns to medicine but finds that she lacks the stomach to enjoy her work. Ultimately her innate femininity prevails. She marries, jettisons medicine, and devotes herself to looking after sick children at her husband's factory more in the manner of a mother than a clinician. The profoundly unfeminist way in which Howell has Dr. Breen declare her love, "with the beautiful artless action of a shame-smitten child," epitomizes his view that women are not born to be physicians. In contrast, Rebecca Harding Davis' 1878 *A Day with Doctor Sarah* is consistent with Blackwell's belief in the special gifts of the woman for healing. Dr. Sarah's talent for bringing succor to the needy, as "a born mother," makes her a good physician.[45]

Novelists who challenged Howell's assumption that women do not make good doctors could adopt the alternative argument that a minority are specially fitted for the profession because they lack feminine qualities. Dr. Prance in Henry James's *The Bostonians* (1885–1886) is a competent woman physician who is accordingly presented as lacking in emotion. She even has the curveless body of a man.[46] Likewise, Elizabeth Stuart Phelps's 1882 *Dr Zay* tells of a female doctor who is so good at her job that she commands an annual salary of $5,000 but is "unwomanly" by the conventional standards of the age.[47] To be an effective doctor apparently required a woman to transcend the norms of her gender. Few successful novelists tried to construct female characters who excelled at both healing and motherhood.

Search for the Hero

One of the most striking features of artistic and fictional accounts of medicine in the nineteenth century is that they contain so few heroes. Not until Sinclair Lewis's 1925 *Arrowsmith* would the United States have a great novel that celebrated the achievements and potential of medical science.[48] This is not surprising. Although sanitary engineers and public health reformers had saved tens of thousands of lives, the individual physician could still turn to only a handful of obviously effective drugs. Lewis wrote *Arrowsmith* in a dramatically different medical landscape in which Americans were benefiting from such fruits of laboratory research as the first antibiotic, Salvarsan, and had every reason to expect that medical scientists would shortly provide a bumper harvest of treatments. Few artists or novelists in the nineteenth century could anticipate this coming age of curative medicine.

NOTES

1. Charles Brockden Brown, *Arthur Mervyn; or, Memoirs of the Year 1793*. Philadelphia: Printed and published by H. Maxwell, 1799.
2. K. Patrick Ober, *Mark Twain and Medicine: "Any Mummery Will Cure."* Columbia: University of Missouri Press, 2003, 37, pp. 21, 46.

3. Mary Louise Kete, *Sentimental Collaborations: Mourning and Middle-Class Identity in Nineteenth-Century America.* Durham, NC: Duke University Press, 2000, p. 4.

4. Kete, *Sentimental Collaborations,* p. 5.

5. Ann Douglas Wood, "Heaven Our Home: Consolation Literature in the Northern United States, 1830–1880," *American Quarterly* 26, no. 5 (December 1974), 496–515, p. 512.

6. Wood, "Heaven Our Home," p. 503.

7. Martha V. Pike and Janice Gray Armstrong, *A Time to Mourn: Expressions of Grief in Nineteenth Century America.* Stony Brook, NY: Museums at Stony Brook, 1980.

8. Wood, "Heaven Our Home" and Philippe Ariès (ed.), *Death in America.* Philadelphia: University of Pennsylvania Press, 1975, p. 67.

9. Clark Lawlor and Akihito Suzuki, "The Disease of the Self: Representing Consumption, 1700–1830," *Bulletin of the History of Medicine* 74, no. 3 (2000), 458–94, p. 463.

10. Arthur Hobson Quinn, *Edgar Allen Poe: A Critical Biography.* Baltimore, MD: Johns Hopkins University Press, 1998, p. 97.

11. David E. Shi, *Facing Facts: Realism in American Thought and Culture, 1850–1920.* New York: Oxford University Press, 1995, p. 60.

12. Eleanor Jones Harvey, *The Civil War and American Art.* New Haven, CT: Yale University Press, 2012, p. 74.

13. Ibid., p. 76.

14. Ibid., pp. 99–101.

15. Shi, *Facing Facts,* p. 59.

16. Steven Conn, "Narrative Trauma and Civil War History Painting, or Why Are These Pictures so Terrible?" *History and Theory* 41, no. 4 (December 2002), 17–42.

17. Leslie A. Fiedler, *Love and Death in the American Novel.* New York: Anchor Books, 1992, p. 484.

18. Keith Gandal, *The Virtues of the Vicious: Jacob Riis, Stephen Crane and the Spectacle of the Slum.* New York: Oxford University Press, 1997, p. 43.

19. Gavin Jones, *American Hungers: The Problem of Poverty in U.S literature, 1840–1945.* Princeton, NJ: Princeton University Press, 2008, p. 26.

20. Gandal, *The Virtues of the Vicious,* p. 41.

21. Herman Melville, *Pierre; Or, the Ambiguities.* New York: Harper & Brothers, 1852, Book 6, Chapter 1.

22. Brian Higgins and Hershel Parke, *Reading Melville's Pierre; Or, the Ambiguities.* Baton Rouge: Louisiana State University Press, 2006, p. 15.

23. Jacob Riis, *How the Other Half Lives: Studies among the Tenements of New York.* New York: Charles Scribner's Sons, 1914, p. 4.

24. Stephen Crane, *Maggie, a Girl of the Streets: A Story of New York.* New York: Newland Press, 1893.

25. Malcolm Bradbury, "Sociology and Literary Studies: II. Romance and Reality in 'Maggie'," *Journal of American Studies* 3, n. 1 (July 1969), 111–21,

p. 113; Susan Laura Mizruchi, *The Rise of Multicultural America: Economy and Print Culture, 1865–1915.* Chapel Hill: University of North Carolina Press, 2008, p. 184; and Gandal, *The Virtues of the Vicious*, p. 39.

26. Gandal, *The Virtues of the Vicious*, p. 39.

27. John Ernest, "Economies of Identity: Harriet E. Wilson's *Our Nig*," *Proceedings of the Modern Language Association* 109, no. 3 (May 1994), 424–38.

28. Scott Romine, *The Narrative Forms of Southern Community.* Baton Rouge: Louisiana State University Press, 1999, p. 65; Elizabeth Moss, *Domestic Novelists in the Old South: Defenders of Southern Culture.* Baton Rouge: Louisiana State University Press, 1992; and Gretchen Martin, "Overfamiliarization as Subversive Plantation Critique in Charles W. Chesnutt's *The Conjure Woman* and Other Conjure Tales," *South Atlantic Review* 74, no. 1 (Winter 2009), 65–86.

29. Elizabeth Moss, *Domestic Novelists*, p. 116.

30. Matthew R. Martin, "The Two-Faced New South: The Plantation Tales of Thomas Nelson Page and Charles W. Chesnutt," *The Southern Literary Journal* 30, no. 2 (Spring 1998), 17–36, p. 20.

31. Ober, *Mark Twain and Medicine*, p. 15.

32. Ibid., p. 2.

33. Ibid., pp. 78–80.

34. Charlotte Perkins Gilman, "Why I Wrote the Yellow Wallpaper," *The Forerunner*, October 1913.

35. Elaine Showalter, *The Female Malady: Women, Madness, and English Culture, 1830–1980.* New York: Pantheon Books, 1985.

36. Perkins, "Why I Wrote the Yellow Wallpaper."

37. Stephanie Browser, "Doctors, Bodies, and Fiction" in Shirley Samuels (ed.), *A Companion to American Fiction 1780–1865.* Malden, MA: Blackwell, 2004, 216–27, p. 217.

38. Cynthia J. Davis, *Bodily and Narrative Forms: The Influence of Medicine on American Literature, 1845–1915.* Stanford, CA: Stanford University Press, 2000, p. 42.

39. Chester R. Burns, "Fictional Doctors and the Evolution of Medical Ethics in the United States, 1875–1900," *Literature and Medicine* 7 (1988), 39–55, p. 47.

40. Amy Werbel, *Thomas Eakins: Art, Medicine, and Sexuality in Nineteenth-Century Philadelphia.* New Haven, CT: Yale University Press, 2007.

41. Stephanie P. Browner, *Profound Science and Elegant Literature: Imagining Doctors in Nineteenth-Century America.* Philadelphia: University of Pennsylvania Press, 2005, pp. 85–99.

42. Browner, *Profound Science*, p. 47.

43. Carla Bittel, *Mary Putnam Jacobi and the Politics of Medicine in Nineteenth-Century America.* Chapel Hill: University of North Carolina Press, 2009, p. 123.

44. Browner, *Profound Science*, pp. 138, 146.

45. Ibid., pp. 159–60.

46. Ibid., p. 169.

47. Burns, "Fictional Doctors," p. 45.

48. Sinclair Lewis, *Arrowsmith.* New York: Harcourt Brace & Company, 1925.

Bibliography

Adams, Henry. *Eakins Revealed: The Secret Life of an American Artist*. New York: Oxford University Press, 2005.

Adler, Jeffrey S. "Streetwalkers, Degraded Outcasts, and Good-for-Nothing Huzzies: Women and the Dangerous Classes in Antebellum St. Louis." *Journal of Social History* 25, no. 4 (1992): 737–55.

Aldrich, Mark. *Death Rode the Rails: American Railroad Accidents and Safety, 1828–1965*. Baltimore, MD: Johns Hopkins University Press, 2006.

Aldrich, Mark. *Safety First: Technology, Labor, and Business in the Building of American Work Safety, 1870–1939*. Baltimore, MD: Johns Hopkins University Press, 1997.

Allen, Peter Lewis. *The Wages of Sin: Sex and Disease, Past and Present*. Chicago: University of Chicago Press, 2000.

Anderson, Jeffrey E. *Conjure in African American Society*. Baton Rouge: Louisiana State University Press, 2007.

Anderson, Warwick. *Colonial Pathologies: American Tropical Medicine, Race, and Hygiene in the Philippines*. Durham, NC: Duke University Press, 2006.

Anonymous, "Practical Essays on Medical Education and the Medical Profession, in the United States." *The Western Journal of the Medical & Physical Sciences* 3 (April, May, and June 1829): 14.

Apple, Rima D. *Mothers and Medicine: A Social History of Infant Feeding, 1890–1950*. Madison: University of Wisconsin Press, 1987.

Ariès, Philippe, *Death in America*. Philadelphia: University of Pennsylvania Press, 1975.

Aronowitz, Robert A. *Unnatural History: Breast Cancer and American Society*. New York: Cambridge University Press, 2007.

Atwater, Edward C. "Touching the Patient: The Teaching of Internal Medicine in America." In *Sickness and Health in America: Readings in the History of Medicine and Public Health*, edited by Judith Leavitt and Ronald L. Numbers, 129–147. Madison: The University of Wisconsin Press, 1985.

Ball, Durwood. *Army Regulars on the Western Frontier, 1848–1861*. Norman: University of Oklahoma Press, 2001.

Beaumont, William. *Experiments and Observations on the Gastric Juice and the Physiology of Digestion*. Edinburgh, Scotland: Maclachlan & Stewart, 1838.

Berger, Peter L. *The Sacred Canopy: Elements of a Sociological Theory of Religion*. Garden City, NY: Doubleday, 1967.

Bergquist, James M. *Daily Life in Immigrant America, 1820–1870*. Westport, CT: Greenwood Press, 2008.

Berlin, Ira. *Generations of Captivity: A History of African-American Slaves*. Cambridge, MA: Belknap Press of Harvard University Press, 2003.

Berlin, Ira. *Many Thousands Gone: The First Two Centuries of Slavery in North America*. Cambridge, MA: Belknap Press of Harvard University Press, 1998.

Bittel, Carla. *Mary Putnam Jacobi and the Politics of Medicine in Nineteenth-Century America*. Chapel Hill: University of North Carolina Press, 2009.

Bledstein, Burton J. *The Culture of Professionalism: The Middle Class and the Development of Higher Education in America*. New York: Norton, 1976.

Borchers, Andrea T., Carl L. Keen, Judy S. Stern, and M. Eric Gershwin. "Inflammation and Native American Medicine: The Role of Botanicals." *Journal of Clinical Nutrition* 72 (2000): 339–47.

Borst, Charlotte G. *Catching Babies: The Professionalization of Childbirth, 1870–1920*. Cambridge, MA: Harvard University Press, 1995.

Bradbury, Malcolm. "Sociology and Literary Studies: II. Romance and Reality in 'Maggie'." *Journal of American Studies* 3, no. 1 (July 1969): 111–21.

Breeden, James O. "Health of Early Texas: The Military Frontier." *The Southwestern Historical Quarterly* 80, no. 4 (April 1977): 357–98.

Brieger, Gert H. "Sanitary Reform in New York City: Stephen Smith and the Passage of the Metropolitan Health Bill." In *Sickness and Health in America: Readings in the History of Medicine and Public Health*, edited by Ronald Numbers and Judith Leavitt, 437–50. Madison: University of Wisconsin Press, 1985.

Brieger, Gert H. "Therapeutic Conflicts and the American Medical Profession in the 1860s." *Bulletin of the History of Medicine* 41, no. 3 (1967): 215–22.

Brodie, Janet Farrell. *Contraception and Abortion in Nineteenth-Century America*. Ithaca, NY: Cornell University Press, 1994.

Brown, Charles Brockden. *Arthur Mervyn; or, Memoirs of the Year 1793*. Philadelphia: H. Maxwell, 1799.

Brown, David and Clive Webb. *Race in the American South: From Slavery to Civil Rights*. Gainesville: University Press of Florida, 2007.

Browner, Stephanie P. *Profound Science and Elegant Literature: Imagining Doctors in Nineteenth-Century America*. Philadelphia: University of Pennsylvania Press, 2005.

Browser, Stephanie. "Doctors, Bodies, and Fiction." In *A Companion to American Fiction 1780–1865*, edited by Shirley Samuels, 216–27. Malden, MA: Blackwell, 2004.

Bruce, Henry Clay. *The New Man: Twenty-Nine Years a Slave, Twenty-Nine Years a Free Man*. York, PA: P. Anstadt, 1895.

Buchan, William. *Domestic Medicine, or, A Treatise on the Cure and Prevention of Diseases by Regimen and Simple Medicines*. London: A. Strahan, T. Cadell and W. Davies, 1798.

Bullough, Vern and Martha Voght. "Women, Menstruation, and Nineteenth-Century Medicine." *Bulletin of the History of Medicine* 47, no. 1 (1973): 66–82.

Burk, William. "Puffball Usages among North American Indians." *Journal of Ethnobiology* 3, no. 1 (1983): 55–62.

Burnham, John C. "Medical Inspection of Prostitutes in the Nineteenth Century: The St. Louis Experiment and Its Sequel." *Bulletin of the History of Medicine* 45, no. 3 (May–June 1971): 203–18.

Burns, Chester R. "Fictional Doctors and the Evolution of Medical Ethics in the United States, 1875–1900." *Literature and Medicine* 7 (1988): 39–55.

Bynum, W. F. *Science and the Practice of Medicine in the Nineteenth Century*. New York: Cambridge University Press, 1994.

Camazine, Scott M. "Traditional and Western Health Care among the Zuni Indians of New Mexico." *Social Science and Medicine* 14 (1980): 73–80.

Campbell, Malcolm. *Ireland's New Worlds: Immigrants, Politics, and Society in the United States and Australia, 1815–1922*. Madison: University of Wisconsin Press, 2008.

Cartwright, Samuel. "Report on the Diseases and Physical Peculiarities of the Negro Race." *New Orleans Medical and Surgical Journal* 7 (1851): 692–713.

Cassedy, James H. "The Flamboyant Colonel Waring." *Bulletin of the History of Medicine* 36 (March and April 1962): 163–68.

Cassedy, James H. *Medicine and American Growth, 1800–1860*. Madison: University of Wisconsin Press, 1986.

Castañeda, Antonia I. "Engendering the History of Alta California, 1769–1848: Gender, Sexuality, and the Family." *California History* 76, no. 2/3 (Summer–Fall, 1997): 230–59.

Cathell, D. W. *Physician Himself*. Philadelphia: F. A. Davis Co., 1896.

Cayleff, Susan. *Wash and Be Healed: The Water-Cure Movement and Women's Health*. Philadelphia: Temple University Press, 1987.

Cheney, Rose A. "Seasonal Aspects of Infant and Childhood Mortality: Philadelphia, 1865–1920." *The Journal of Interdisciplinary History* 14, no. 3 (1984): 561–85.

Chesler, Phyllis. *Women and Madness*. Garden City, NY: Doubleday, 1972.

Child, Brenda. "Homesickness, Illness, and Death: Native-American Girls in Government Boarding Schools." In *Wings of Gauze: Women of Color and the Experience of Health and Illness*, edited by Barbara Bair and Susan E. Cayleff, 170–80. Detroit, MI: Wayne State University Press, 1993.

Chireau, Yvonne. *Black Magic: Religion and the African American Conjuring Tradition*. Berkeley: University of California Press, 2003.

Chireau, Yvonne. "Conjure and Christianity in the Nineteenth Century: Religious Elements in African American Magic." *Religion and American Culture: A Journal of Interpretation* 7 (Summer 1997): 225–46.

Cirillo, Vincent J. *Bullets and Bacilli: The Spanish-American War and Military Medicine*. New Brunswick, NJ: Rutgers University Press, 2004.

Cirillo, Vincent J. "The Spanish-American War and Military Radiology." *American Journal of Roentgenology* 174 (2000): 1233–39.

Clarke, Frances. " 'Honorable Scars': Northern Amputees and the Meaning of Civil War Injuries." In *Union Soldiers and the Northern Home Front: Wartime Experiences, Postwar Adjustments*, by Paul A. Cimbala and Randall M. Miller, 361–93. New York: Fordham University Press, 2002.

Clary, David A. "The Role of the Army Surgeon in the West: Daniel Weisel at Fort Davis, Texas, 1868–1872." *The Western Historical Quarterly* 3, no. 1 (January 1972): 53–66.

Clement, Priscilla Ferguson. *Growing Pains: Children in the Industrial Age, 1850–1890*. New York: Twayne Publishers, 1997.

Condran, Gretchen A. and Eileen Crimmins-Gardner. "Public Health Measures and Morality in US Cities in the Late Nineteenth Century." *Human Ecology* 6, no. 1 (1978): 27–54.

Condran, Gretchen A., Henry Williams, and Rose A. Cheney. "The Decline of Mortality in Philadelphia from 1870 to 1930: The Role of Municipal Services." In *Sickness and Health in America: Readings in the History of Medicine and Public Health*, edited by Ronald Numbers and Judith Walzer Leavitt, 422–438. Madison: University of Wisconsin Press, 1985.

Cook, Sherburne Friend. *The Conflict between the California Indian and White Civilization*. Berkeley: University of California Press, 1976.

Cooter, Roger. *The Cultural Meaning of Popular Science: Phrenology and the Organization of Consent in Nineteenth-Century Britain*. New York: Cambridge University Press, 1984.

Corn, Jacqueline. "Protective Legislation for Coal Miners, 1870–1900: Response to Safety and Health Hazards." In *Dying for Work: Workers' Safety and Health in Twentieth-Century America*, edited by David Rosner and Gerald E. Markowitz, 67–82. Bloomington: Indiana University Press, 1987.

Courtwright, David T. "Opiate Addiction as a Consequence of the Civil War." *Civil War History* 24, no. 2 (June 1978): 101–111.

Covey, Herbert C. *African American Slave Medicine: Herbal and Non-Herbal Treatments*. Lanham, MD: Lexington Books, 2007.

Crane, Stephen. *Maggie, A Girl of the Streets: A Story of New York*. New York: Newland Press, 1893.

Cutler, David and Grant Miller. "The Role of Public Health Improvements in Health Advances: The Twentieth Century United States." *Demography* 42, no. 1 (2005): 1–22.

Dain, Norman. "Madness and the Stigma of Sin in American Christianity." In *Stigma and Mental Illness*, edited by Paul Jay Fink and Allan Tasman, 73–85. Washington, DC: American Psychiatric Press, 1992.

Dain, Norman. *Concepts of Insanity in the United States, 1789–1865*. New Brunswick, NJ: Rutgers University Press, 1964.

D'Antonio, Patricia. *American Nursing: A History of Knowledge, Authority, and the Meaning of Work*. Baltimore, MD: Johns Hopkins University Press, 2010.

Dary, David. *Frontier Medicine: From the Atlantic to the Pacific, 1492–1941*. New York: Alfred A. Knopf, 2009.

Davies, John D. *Phrenology: Fad and Science, a 19th-Century American Crusade*. Hamden, CT: Archon Books, 1971.

Davies, Wade. *Healing Ways: Navajo Health Care in the Twentieth Century*. Albuquerque: University of New Mexico Press, 2001.

Davis, Cynthia J. *Bodily and Narrative Forms: The Influence of Medicine on American Literature, 1845–1915*. Stanford, CA: Stanford University Press, 2000.

Davis, David Brion. *Inhuman Bondage: The Rise and Fall of Slavery in the New World*. New York: Oxford University Press, 2006.

Degler, Carl N. "What Ought to Be and What Was: Women's Sexuality in the Nineteenth Century." *The American Historical Review* 79 (December 1974): 1467–90.

Delaporte, Francois. *The History of Yellow Fever: An Essay on the Birth of Tropical Medicine*. Translated by Arthur Goldhammer. Cambridge, MA: MIT Press, 1991.

Dishman, Christopher D. *A Perfect Gibraltar: The Battle for Monterrey, Mexico, 1846*. Norman: University of Oklahoma Press, 2010.

Dixon, Edward. *Woman, and Her Diseases, from the Cradle to the Grave*. New York, 1847.

Douglass, Frederick. *Narrative of the life of Frederick Douglass, an American slave*. London: H. G. Collins, 1851.

Dowbiggin, Ian R. *Keeping America Sane: Psychiatry and Eugenics in the United States and Canada, 1880–1940*. Ithaca, NY: Cornell University Press, 1997.

Downs, Jim. *Sick from Freedom: African-American Illness and Suffering during the Civil War and Reconstruction*. New York: Oxford University Press, 2012.

Duffy, John. *From Humors to Medical Science: A History of American Medicine*. Urbana: University of Illinois Press, 1993.

Duffy, John. *The Sanitarians: A History of American Public Health*. Urbana: University of Illinois Press, 1990.

Duffy, John. "Social Impact of Disease in the Late Nineteenth Century." *Bulletin of the New York Academy of Medicine* 47, no. 7 (July 1971): 797–810.

Dusinberre, William. *Them Dark Days: Slavery in the American Rice Swamps.* New York: Oxford University Press, 1996.

Dwyer, Ellen. *Homes for the Mad: Life inside Two Nineteenth-Century Asylums.* New Brunswick, NJ: Rutgers University Press, 1987.

Dye, Nancy Schrom, and Daniel Blake Smith. "Mother Love and Infant Death, 1750–1920." *The Journal of American History* 73, no. 2 (September 1986): 329–53.

Emboden, William A., Jr. "Plant Hypnotics among the North American Indians." In *American Folk Medicine,* edited by Wayland D. Hand, 157–68. Berkeley: University of California Press, 1976.

Engstrom, Eric. *Clinical Psychiatry in Imperial Germany: A History of Psychiatric Practice.* Ithaca, NY: Cornell University Press, 2004.

Ernest, John. "Economies of Identity: Harriet E. Wilson's Our Nig." *Proceedings of the Modern Language Association* 109, no. 3 (May 1994): 424–38.

Espinosa, Mariola. *Epidemic Invasions: Yellow Fever and the Limits of Cuban Independence, 1878–1930.* Chicago: University of Chicago Press, 2009.

Estes, J. Worth. "The Pharmacology of Nineteenth-Century Patent Medicines." *Pharmacy in History* 30, no. 1 (1988): 3–18.

Faragher, John M. *Sugar Creek: Life on the Illinois Prairie.* New Haven: Yale University Press, 1986.

Faust, Drew Gilpin. *This Republic of Suffering: Death and the American Civil War.* New York: Alfred A. Knopf, 2008.

Fett, Sharla M. *Working Cures: Healing, Health, and Power on Southern Slave Plantations.* University of North Carolina Press, 2002.

Fiedler, Leslie A. *Love and Death in the American Novel.* New York: Anchor Books, 1992.

Field, Ron. *Forts of the American Frontier 1820–91: Central and Northern Plains.* Oxford, UK: Osprey Publishing, 2005.

Figg, Laurann and Jane Farrell-Beck. "Amputation in the Civil War: Physical and Social Dimensions." *Journal of the History of Medicine and Allied Sciences* 48, no. 4 (1993): 454–75.

Fogel, R. W. "Economic Growth, Population Theory, and Physiology: The Bearing of Long-Term Principles on the Making of Economic Policy." *American Economic Review* 84 (1994): 369–95.

Fogel, R. W. "Health, Nutrition, and Economic Growth." *Economic Development and Cultural Change* 52, no. 3 (April 2004): 643–58.

Fogel, R. W. and Stanley L. Engerman. *Time on the Cross: The Economics of American Negro Slavery.* Boston: Little, Brown, 1974.

Forbes, Ann. *African American Women during the Civil War.* New York: Garland, 1998.

Foucault, Michel. *Madness and Civilization: A History of Insanity in the Age of Reason*. Translated by Richard Howard. New York: Vintage Books, 1965.

Fox-Genovese, Elizabeth. *Within the Plantation Household: Black and White Women of the Old South*. Chapel Hill: University of North Carolina Press, 1988.

Fraser, Gertrude Jacinta. *African American Midwifery in the South: Dialogues of Birth, Race, and Memory*. Cambridge, MA: Harvard University Press, 1998.

Freedman, Estelle B. "Sexuality in Nineteenth-Century America: Behavior, Ideology, and Politics." *Reviews in American History* 10, no. 4 (December 1982): 196–215.

Freemon, Frank R. *Gangrene and Glory: Medical Care during the American Civil War*. London: Associated University Presses, 1998.

Gandal, Keith. *The Virtues of the Vicious: Jacob Riis, Stephen Crane and the Spectacle of the Slum*. New York: Oxford University Press, 1997.

Giesberg, Judith A. *Civil War Sisterhood: The U.S. Sanitary Commission and Women's Politics in Transition*. Boston: Northeastern University Press, 2000.

Genovese, Eugene D. *Roll, Jordan, Roll: The World the Slaves Made*. New York: Pantheon Books, 1974.

Genovese, Eugene D. *The World the Slaveholders Made: Two Essays in Interpretation*. Middletown, CT: Wesleyan University Press, 1988.

Gilman, Charlotte Perkins. "Why I Wrote the Yellow Wallpaper." *The Forerunner*, October 1913.

Goffman, Erving. *Stigma: Notes on the Management of Spoiled Identity*. New York: Simon & Schuster, 1963.

Golden, Janet. "Children's Health: Caregivers and Sites of Care." In *Children and Youth in Sickness and in Health: A Historical Handbook and Guide*, edited by Janet Golden, Richard A. Meckel, and Heather Munro Prescott, 67–84. Westport, CT: Greenwood Press, 2004.

Golden, Janet. *A Social History of Wet Nursing in America: from Breast to Bottle*. New York: Cambridge University Press, 1996.

Golden, Janet, Richard A. Meckel, and Heather Munro Prescott (eds). *Children and Youth in Sickness and in Health: A Historical Handbook and Guide*. Westport, CT: Greenwood Press, 2004.

Gollaher, David. *Circumcision: A History of the World's Most Controversial Surgery*. New York: Basic Books, 2000.

Gollaher, David L. "From Ritual to Science: The Medical Transformation of Circumcision in America." *Journal of Social History* 28, no. 1 (Autumn 1994): 5–36.

Goodheart, Lawrence B. "From Cure to Custodianship of the Insane Poor in Nineteenth-Century Connecticut." *Journal of the History of Medicine and Allied Sciences* 65 (2010): 106–130.

Gorn, Elliott J. "Folk Beliefs of the Slave Community." In *Science and Medicine in the Old South*, edited by Ronald L. Numbers and Todd L. Savitt, 295–326. Baton Rouge: Louisiana State University Press, 1989.

Graham, Sylvester. *A Lecture to Young Men on Chastity*. Boston: George W. Light, 1840.

Grob, Gerald. *The Deadly Truth: A History of Disease in America*. Cambridge, MA: Harvard University Press, 2002.

Grob, Gerald. *The Mad among Us: A History of the Care of America's Mentally Ill*. New York: Maxwell Macmillan International, 1994.

Groneman, Carol. "Nymphomania: The Historical Construction of Female Sexuality." *Signs* 19, no. 2 (Winter 1994): 337–67.

Groneman, Carol. "Working-Class Immigrant Women in Mid-Nineteenth-Century New York: The Irish Woman's Experience." *Journal of Urban History* 4 (May 1978): 257–71.

Grossberg, Michael. *Governing the Hearth: Law and the Family in Nineteenth-Century America*. Chapel Hill: University of North Carolina Press, 1985.

Guelzo, Allen C. *Fateful Lightning: A New History of the Civil War and Reconstruction*. Oxford: Oxford University Press, 2012.

Gunn, John C. *Gunn's Domestic Medicine: Or, Poor Man's Friend; Describing, in Plain Language the Diseases of Men, Women, and Children*. Pittsburgh, PA: J. Edwards & J. J. Newman, 1839.

Haber, Samuel. *The Quest for Authority and Honor in the American Professions, 1750–1900*. Chicago: University of Chicago Press, 1991.

Hacker, David J. and Michael R. Haines. "American Indian Mortality in the Late Nineteenth Century: The Impact of Federal Assimilation Policies on a Vulnerable Population." *Annales De Démographie Historique* 2 (2005): 17–45.

Haines, Michael R. "The Population of the Unites States, 1790–1920." In *The Cambridge Economic History of the United States*, edited by Stanley L. Engerman and Robert E. Gallman, 145–60. Cambridge, UK: Cambridge University Press, 2000.

Haines, Michael R. and Richard H. Steckel (eds.). *A Population History of North America*. New York: Cambridge University Press, 2001.

Hale, Nathan. *Freud and the Americans: The Beginnings of Psychoanalysis in the United States, 1876–1917*. New York: Oxford University Press, 1971.

Haller, John S. *American Medicine in Transition, 1840–1910*. Urbana: University of Illinois Press, 1981.

Haller, John S. *Medical Protestants: The Eclectics in American Medicine, 1825–1939*. Carbondale: Southern Illinois University Press, 2013.

Haller, John S. *The People's Doctors: Samuel Thomson and the American Botanical Movement*. Carbondale: Southern Illinois University Press, 2000.

Haller, John S. "The Use and Abuse of Tartar Emetic in the Nineteenth-Century Materia Medical." *Bulletin of the History of Medicine* 49 (Summer 1975): 235–57.

Hand, Wayland D. *American Folk Medicine: A Symposium*. Berkeley: University of California Press, 1976.

Harrington, Judith M. and Robert L. Blakely. "Bones in the Basement: Bioarcheology of Historic Remains in Nonmortuary Contexts." In *Bodies of Evidence: Reconstructing History through Skeletal Analysis,* edited by Anne L. Grauer, 105–119. New York: Wiley-Liss, 1995.

Harvey, Paul. *Freedom's Coming: Religious Culture and the Shaping of the South from the Civil War through the Civil Rights Era.* Chapel Hill: University of North Carolina Press, 2005.

Hautaniemi, Susan I., Alan C. Swedlund and Douglas L. Anderton. "Mill Town Mortality: Consequences of Industrial Growth in Two Nineteenth-Century New England Towns." *Social Science History* 23, no. 1 (Spring 1999): 1–39.

Herndl, Diane Price. "The Invisible (Invalid) Woman: African American Women, Illness, and Nineteenth-Century Narrative." In *Women and Health in America: Historical Readings,* edited by Judith Walzer Leavitt, 131–45. Madison: University of Wisconsin Press, 1999.

Herrick, James W. *Iroquois Medical Botany.* Syracuse, NY: Syracuse University Press, 1995.

Higby, Gregory J. "Professionalism and the Nineteenth-Century American Pharmacist." *Pharmacy in History* 28, no. 3 (1986): 115–24.

Higgins, Brian and Hershel Parke. *Reading Melville's Pierre; Or, the Ambiguities.* Baton Rouge: Louisiana State University Press, 2006.

Higgs, Robert. "Cycles and Trends of Mortality in 18 Large American Cities, 1871–1900." *Explorations in Economic History* 16, no. 4 (1979): 381–408.

Hilts, Philip J. *Protecting America's Health: The FDA, Business, and One Hundred Years of Regulation.* New York: Alfred A. Knopf, 2003.

Hirata, Lucie Cheng. "Free, Indentured, Enslaved: Chinese Prostitutes in Nineteenth-Century America." *Signs* 5, no. 1 (Autumn 1979): 3–29.

Hoffman, Steven J. *Race, Class and Power in the Building of Richmond, 1870–1920.* Jefferson, NC: McFarland & Co., 2004.

Holmes, Oliver Wendell. *Puerperal Fever as a Private Pestilence.* Boston: Ticknor and Fields, 1855.

Holt, Marilyn Irwin. *Indian Orphanages.* Lawrence: University Press of Kansas, 2001.

Hultkrantz, Åke. *Shamanic Healing and Ritual Drama Health and Medicine in Native North American Religious Traditions.* New York: Crossroad, 1992.

Hultkrantz, Åke and Robert Holland. *Soul and Native Americans.* Woodstock, CT: Spring Publications, 1997.

Humphreys, Margaret. *Intensely Human: The Health of the Black Soldier in the American Civil War.* Baltimore, MD: Johns Hopkins University Press, 2008.

Humphreys, Margaret. *Malaria: Poverty, Race, and Public Health in the United States.* Baltimore, MD: Johns Hopkins University Press, 2001.

Humphreys, Margaret. *The Marrow of Tragedy: The Health Crisis of the American Civil War.* Baltimore, MD: Johns Hopkins University Press, 2013.

Hyson, John M. *A History of Dentistry in the US Army to World War II.* Washington, DC: Borden Institute, Walter Reed Army Medical Center, 2008.

Ignatiev, Noel. *How the Irish Became White*. New York: Routledge, 1995.

Imber, Jonathan B. *Trusting Doctors: the Decline of Moral Authority in American Medicine*. Princeton, NJ: Princeton University Press, 2008.

Irwin, Lee. "Cherokee Healing: Myth, Dreams, and Medicine." *American Indian Quarterly* 16 (Spring 1992): 237–57.

Jackson, Robert H. and Edward Castillo. *Indians, Franciscans, and Spanish Colonization: The Impact of the Mission System on California Indians*. Albuquerque: University of New Mexico Press, 1997.

Jaher, Frederic Cople. *The Urban Establishment: Upper Strata in Boston, New York, Charleston, Chicago, and Los Angeles*. Urbana: University of Illinois Press, 1982.

Johnson, Wallace W. "The History of Prosthetic Dentistry." *The Journal of Prosthetic Dentistry* 9, no. 5 (1959): 841–46.

Jones, David S. "The Persistence of American Indian Health Disparities." *American Journal of Public Health* 96, no. 12 (December 2006): 2122–34.

Jones, David S. *Rationalizing Epidemics: Meanings and Uses of American Indian Mortality*. Cambridge, MA: Harvard University Press, 2004.

Jones, Gavin. *American Hungers: The Problem of Poverty in U.S literature, 1840–1945*. Princeton, NJ: Princeton University Press, 2008.

Jones, Jacqueline. *Labor of Love, Labor of Sorrow: Black Women, Work and the Family, from Slavery to the Present*. New York: Basic Books, 2010.

Jones, Mary E. *Daily Life on the Nineteenth Century American Frontier*. Westport, CT: Greenwood Press, 1998.

Joyner, Charles. *Down by the Riverside: A South Carolina Slave Community*. Urbana: University of Illinois Press, 2009.

Katz-Hyman, Martha B. and Kym S. Rice (eds.). *World of a Slave: Encyclopedia of the Material Life of Slaves in the United States*. Santa Barbara, CA: Greenwood Press, 2011.

Kellogg, John Harvey. *Plain Facts for Young and Old*. Burlington, IA: I. F. Segner, 1892.

Kete, Mary Louise. *Sentimental Collaborations: Mourning and Middle-Class Identity in Nineteenth-Century America*. Durham, NC: Duke University Press, 2000.

Kevles, Bettyann H. *Naked to the Bone: Medical Imaging in the Twentieth Century*. Reading, MA: Addison-Wesley, 1998.

Kevles, Daniel. *In the Name of Eugenics: Genetics and the Uses of Human Heredity*. New York: Knopf, 1985.

Kiple, Kenneth F. and Virginia Himmelsteib King. *Another Dimension to the Black Diaspora: Diet, Disease, and Racism*. New York: Cambridge University Press, 1981.

Kohn, Richard H. "The Social History of the American Soldier: A Review and Prospectus for Research." *The American Historical Review* 86, no. 3 (June 1981): 553–67.

Kraut, Alan M. *Silent Travelers: Genes, Germs and the "Immigrant Menace."* New York: BasicBooks, 1994.

Kusmer, K. L. "The Homeless Unemployed in Industrializing America, 1865–1930: Perception and Reality." *Amerikastudien* 40, no. 4 (1995): 667–94.

LaVeist, Thomas A. *Minority Populations and Health: An Introduction to Health Disparities in the U.S.* San Francisco, CA: John Wiley & Sons, 2011.

Lawlor, Clark, and Akihito Suzuki. "The Disease of the Self: Representing Consumption, 1700–1830." *Bulletin of the History of Medicine* 74, no. 3 (2000): 458–94.

Leavitt, Judith Walzer. *Brought to Bed: Childbearing in America, 1750 to 1950.* New York: Oxford University Press, 1986.

Leavitt, Judith Walzer. *The Healthiest City: Milwaukee and the Politics of Health Reform.* Princeton, NJ: Princeton University Press, 1982.

Leavitt, Judith Walzer. *Typhoid Mary: Captive to the Public's Health.* Boston: Beacon Press, 1996.

Lee, J. Edward and Ron Chepesiuk (eds.). *South Carolina in the Civil War: The Confederate Experience in Letters and Diaries.* Jefferson, NC: McFarland, 2000.

Leone, Mark P. and Gladys-Marie Fry. "Conjuring in the Big House Kitchen: An Interpretation of African American Belief Systems Based on the Uses of Archaeology and Folklore Sources." *The Journal of American Folklore* 112 (Summer 1999): 372–403.

Levenstein, Harvey. " 'Best for Babies' or 'Preventable Infanticide'? The Controversy over Artificial Feeding of Infants in America, 1880–1920." *Journal of American History* 70, no. 1 (1993): 75–94.

Licht, Walter. *Working for the Railroad: The Organization of Work in the Nineteenth Century.* Princeton, NJ: Princeton University Press, 1983.

Lingenfelter, Richard E. *The Hardrock Miners: A History of the Mining Labor Movement in the American West, 1863–1893.* Berkeley: University of California Press, 1974.

Long, Gretchen. *Doctoring Freedom: The Politics of African American Medical Care in Slavery and Emancipation.* Chapel Hill: University of North Carolina Press, 2012.

Loudon, Irvine. *Childbed Fever: A Documentary History.* New York: Garland, 1995.

Louis P. Cain. "Raising and Watering a City: Ellis Chesbrough and Chicago's First Sanitation System." In *Sickness and Health in America: Readings in the History of Medicine and Public Health*, edited by Ronald Numbers and Judith Walzer Leavitt, 531–41. Madison: University of Wisconsin Press, 1985.

Ludmerer, Kenneth. *Learning to Heal: The Development of American Medical Education.* New York: Basic Books, 1985.

Maines, Rachel P. *The Technology of Orgasm: "Hysteria," the Vibrator, and Women's Sexual Satisfaction.* Baltimore, MD: Johns Hopkins University Press, 1999.

Mann, Charles C. and Mark L. Plummer. *The Aspirin Wars: Money, Medicine, and 100 Years of Rampant Competition.* New York: Knopf, 1991.

Markel, Howard. "For the Welfare of Children." In *Formative Years: Children's Health in the United States, 1880–2000*, edited by Alexandra Minna Stern and Howard Markel, 47–65. Ann Arbor: University of Michigan Press, 2002.

Marks, Harry. *The Progress of Experiment: Science and Therapeutic Reform in the United States, 1900–1990*. New York: Cambridge University Press, 1997.

Martin, Gretchen. "Overfamiliarization as Subversive Plantation Critique in Charles W. Chesnutt's *The Conjure Woman* & Other Conjure Tales." *South Atlantic Review* 74, no. 1 (Winter 2009): 65–86.

Martin, Matthew R. "The Two-Faced New South: The Plantation Tales of Thomas Nelson Page and Charles W. Chesnutt." *The Southern Literary Journal* 30, no. 2 (Spring 1998): 17–36.

May, Elaine Tyler. *Barren in the Promised Land: Childless Americans and the Pursuit of Happiness*. New York: BasicBooks, 1995.

McBride, Bunny, and Harald E. L. Prins. "Walking the Medicine Line: Molly Ockett, a Pigwacket Doctor." In *Northeastern Indian Lives, 1632–1816*, edited by Robert S. Grumet, 321–47. Amherst: University of Massachusetts Press, 1996.

McCaffrey, M. *Army of Manifest Destiny: The American Soldier in the Mexican War, 1846–1848*. New York: New York University Press, 1992.

McClain, Charles J. *In Search of Equality: The Chinese Struggle against Discrimination in Nineteenth-Century America*. Berkeley: University of California Press, 1994.

McGregor, Deborah Kuhn. *From Midwives to Medicine: The Birth of American Gynecology*. New Brunswick, NJ: Rutgers University Press, 1998.

Mckiernan-González, John. *Fevered Measures: Public Health and Race at the Texas-Mexico Border, 1848–1942*. Durham, NC: Duke University Press, 2012.

McPherson, James. *The Illustrated Battle Cry of Freedom: The Civil War Era*. New York: Oxford University Press, 2003.

McPherson, James. *This Mighty Scourge: Perspectives on the Civil War*. New York: Oxford University Press, 2007.

Meckel, Richard A. *Save the Babies: American Public Health Reform and the Prevention of Infant Mortality, 1850–1929*. Baltimore, MD: Johns Hopkins University Press, 1990.

Meeker, Edward. "The Improving Health of the United States, 1850–1915." *Explorations in Economic History* 9, no. 4 (1972): 353–70.

Melosi, Martin V. *Garbage in the Cities: Refuse, Reform, and the Environment*. Pittsburgh, PA: University of Pittsburgh Press, 2005.

Melville, Herman. *Pierre; Or, the Ambiguities*. New York: Harper & Brothers, 1852.

Miller, Kerby A. *Emigrants and Exiles: Ireland and the Irish Exodus to North America*. New York: Oxford University Press, 1985.

Miller, Kerby A. and Paul Wagner. *Out of Ireland: The Story of Irish Emigration to America*. Niwot, CO: Roberts Rinehart, 1997.

Minges, Patrick. *Far More Terrible for Women: Personal Accounts of Women in Slavery*. Winston-Salem, NC: John F. Blair, 2006.

Mizruchi, Susan Laura. *The Rise of Multicultural America: Economy and Print Culture, 1865–1915*. Chapel Hill: University of North Carolina Press, 2008.

Moerman, Daniel E. "An Analysis of the Food Plants and Drug Plants of Native North America," *Journal of Ethnopharmacology* 52 (1996): 1–22.

Montgomery, David. *Citizen Worker: The Experience of Workers in the United States with Democracy and the Free Market During the Nineteenth Century*. New York: Cambridge University Press, 1993.

Mooney, James. "Cherokee Theory and Practice of Medicine." *The Journal of American Folklore* 3, no. 8 (1890): 44–50.

Morantz, Regina Markell. "The Connecting Link: The Case for the Woman Doctor in 19th-Century America." In *Sickness and Health in America: Readings in the History of Medicine and Public Health*, edited by Ronald Numbers and Judith Walzer Leavitt, 213–34. Madison: University of Wisconsin Press, 1985.

Moss, Elizabeth. *Domestic Novelists in the Old South: Defenders of Southern Culture*. Baton Rouge: Louisiana State University Press, 1992.

Motz, Vicki Abrams, Christopher P. Bowers, Linda Mull Young, and David H. Kinder. "The Effectiveness of Jewelweed, *Impatiens Capensis*, the Related Cultivar *I. Balsamina* and the Component Lawsone in Preventing Post Poison Ivy Exposure Contact Dermatitis." *Journal of Ethnopharmacology* 143 (2012): 314–18.

Nelson, Siobhan. *Say Little, Do Much: Nursing, Nuns, and Hospitals in the Nineteenth Century*. Philadelphia: University of Pennsylvania Press, 2001.

Northup, Solomon. *Twelve Years a Slave: Narrative of Solomon Northup, a Citizen of New-York*. New York: Miller, Orton & Mulligan, 1855.

Novak, William J. *The People's Welfare: Law and Regulation in Nineteenth-Century America*, Chapel Hill: University of North Carolina Press, 1996.

Numbers, Ronald L. "Sex, Science, and Salvation: The Sexual Advice of Ellen G. White and John Harvey Kellogg." In *Right Living: An Anglo-American Tradition of Self-Help, Medicine and Hygiene*, edited by Charles E. Rosenberg, 206–226. Baltimore, MD: Johns Hopkins University Press, 2003.

Numbers, Ronald L. and John Harley Warner. "The Maturation of American Medical Science." In *Sickness and Health in America: Readings in the History of Medicine and Public Health*, edited by Ronald L. Numbers and Judith Walzer Leavitt, 113–28. Madison: University of Wisconsin Press, 1985.

Ober, K. Patrick. *Mark Twain and Medicine: "Any Mummery Will Cure."* Columbia: University of Missouri Press, 2003.

Oppenheim, Janet. *"Shattered Nerves": Doctors, Patients, and Depression in Victorian England*. New York: Oxford University Press, 1991.

Osterud, Nancy Grey. *Bonds of Community: The Lives of Farm Women in Nineteenth-century New York*. Ithaca: Cornell University Press, 1991.

Pernick, Martin S. *A Calculus of Suffering in 19th-Century Surgery: Pain, Professionalism, and Anesthesia in Nineteenth-Century America.* New York: Columbia University Press, 1985.

Perrin, Liese M. "Resisting Reproduction: Reconsidering Slave Contraception in the Old South." *Journal of American Studies* 35 (2001): 255–74.

Pike, Martha V. and Janice Gray Armstrong. *A Time to Mourn: Expressions of Grief in Nineteenth Century America.* Stony Brook, NY: Museums at Stony Brook, 1980.

Plane, Ann Marie. "Childbirth Practices among Native American Women of New England and Canada, 1600–1800." In *Women and Health in America: Historical Readings,* edited by Judith Walzer Leavitt, 38–47. Madison: University of Wisconsin Press, 1999.

Porter, Roy. *Mind-forg'd Manacles: A History of Madness in England from the Restoration to the Regency.* Cambridge, MA: Harvard University Press, 1987.

Powers, Ramon and James N. Leiker. "Cholera among the Plains Indians: Perceptions, Causes, Consequences." *The Western Historical Quarterly* 29, no. 3 (Autumn 1998): 317–40.

Prescott, Heather Munro. "Stories of Childhood Health and Disease." nI, *Children and Youth in Sickness and in Health: A Historical Handbook and Guide,* edited by Janet Golden, Richard A. Meckel, and Heather Munro Prescott, 123. Westport, CT: Greenwood Press, 2004.

Preston, Samuel and Michael Haines. *Fatal Years: Child Mortality in Late Nineteenth-Century America.* Princeton, NJ: Princeton University Press, 1991.

Pritchett, Jonathan B. and Insan Tunali. "Strangers' Disease: Determinants of Yellow Fever Mortality during the New Orleans Epidemic of 1853." *Explorations in Economic History* 32, Issue 4 (1995): 517–39.

Pruitt, Basil A. Jr. "Combat Casualty Care and Surgical Progress." *Annals of Surgery* 243, no. 6 (June 2006): 715–29.

Quinn, Arthur Hobson. *Edgar Allen Poe: A Critical Biography.* Baltimore, MD: Johns Hopkins University Press, 1998.

Reagan, Leslie J. *When Abortion was a Crime: Women, Medicine, and Law in the United States, 1867–1973.* Berkeley: University of California Press, 1997.

Reiser, Stanley. *Medicine and the Reign of Technology.* New York: Cambridge University Press, 1978.

Reverby, Susan M. *Ordered to Care: The Dilemma of American Nursing, 1850–1945.* New York: Cambridge University Press, 1987.

Riis, Jacob. *How the Other Half Lives: Studies among the Tenements of New York.* New York: Charles Scribner's Sons, 1914.

Rogers, Naomi. *An Alternative Path: The Making and Remaking of Hahnemann Medical College and Hospital of Philadelphia.* New Brunswick, NJ: Rutgers University Press, 1998.

Romine, Scott. *The Narrative Forms of Southern Community.* Baton Rouge: Louisiana State University Press, 1999.

Ronald L. Numbers, "The Rise and Fall of the American Medical Profession." In *Sickness and Health in America: Readings in the History of Medicine and Public Health*, edited by Judith Walzer Leavitt and Ronald L. Numbers, 185–96. Madison: University of Wisconsin Press, 1985.

Rosen, George. "Urbanization, Occupation and Disease in the United States, 1870–1920: The Case of New York City." *Journal of the History of Medicine and Allied Sciences* 43, no. 4 (1988): 391–425.

Rosen, Ruth. *The Lost Sisterhood: Prostitution in America, 1900–1918*. Baltimore, MD: Johns Hopkins University Press, 1982.

Rosenberg, Chaim M. *Child Labor in America*. North Carolina: McFarland and Company, 2013.

Rosenberg, Charles E. "And Heal the Sick: The Hospital and the Patient in the 19th Century America." *Journal of Social History* 10, no. 4 (Summer 1977): 428–47.

Rosenberg, Charles E. "The Bitter Fruit of Heredity: Heredity, Disease, and Social Thought." In *No Other Gods: On Science and American Social Thought*, edited by Charles Roseberg, 25–53. Baltimore, MD: Johns Hopkins University Press, 1976.

Rosenberg, Charles E. *Care of Strangers, The Rise of America's Hospital System*. New York: Basic Books, 1987.

Rosenberg, Charles, *The Cholera Years: The United States in 1832, 1849, and 1866*. Chicago: University of Chicago Press, 1987.

Rosenberg, Charles E. "From Almshouse to Hospital: The Shaping of Philadelphia General Hospital." *Explaining Epidemics and Other Studies in the History of Medicine*, 178–213. New York: Cambridge University Press, 1992.

Rosenberg, Charles E. "George M. Beard and American Nervousness." *No Other Gods: On Science and American Social Thought*. Baltimore, MD: Johns Hopkins University Press, 1976.

Rosenberg, Charles. "Pietism and the Origins of the American Public Health Movement: A Note on John H. Griscom and Robert M. Hartley." *Journal of the History of Medicine and Allied Sciences* 23 (1968): 16–35.

Rosenberg, Charles E. "Sexuality, Class and Role in 19th-Century America." *American Quarterly* 25 (May 1973): 131–53.

Rosenberg, Charles. "The Therapeutic Revolution: Medicine, Meaning and Social Change in Nineteenth-Century America." *Perspectives in Biology and Medicine* 20, no. 4 (1977): 485–506.

Rosenberg, Charles E. *The Trial of the Assassin Guiteau: Psychiatry and Law in the Gilded Age*. Chicago, University of Chicago Press, 1968.

Rothman, David J. *The Discovery of the Asylum: Social Order and Disorder in the New Republic*. Boston: Little, Brown, 1971.

Rothman, Sheila M. *Living in the Shadow of Death: Tuberculosis and the Social Experience of Illness in American History*. New York: Basic Books, 1994.

Rothstein, William G. *American Physicians in the Nineteenth Century: From Sects to Science*. Baltimore, MD: Johns Hopkins University Press, 1972.

Rugh, Susan S. *Our Common Country: Family Farming, Culture, and Community in the Nineteenth-century Midwest.* Bloomington: Indiana University Press, 2001.

Rush, Benjamin. *An Account of the Bilious Remitting Yellow Fever ... of Philadelphia ... 1793.* Philadelphia: Thomas Dobson, 1794.

Rutkow, Ira M. *Bleeding Blue and Gray: Civil War Surgery and the Evolution of American Medicine.* New York: Random House, 2005.

Rutkow, Ira M. *Surgery: An Illustrated History.* St. Louis, MO: Mosby-Year Book and Norman, 1993.

Savitt, Todd L. "Black Health on the Plantation: Masters, Slaves, and Physicians." In *Sickness and Health in America: Readings in the History of Medicine and Public Health*, edited by Judith Walzer Leavitt and Ronald L. Numbers, 351–68. Madison: University of Wisconsin Press, 1985.

Savitt, Todd L. "Four American Proprietary Medical Colleges: 1888–1923." *Journal of the History of Medicine and Allied Sciences* 55 (July 2000): 203–55.

Savitt, Todd L. *Medicine and Slavery: The Diseases and Health Care of Blacks in Antebellum Virginia.* Urbana: University of Illinois Press, 2002.

Savitt, Todd L. "The Use of Blacks for Medical Experimentation and Demonstration in the Old South." *The Journal of Southern History* 48, no. 3 (August 1982): 331–48.

Scholten, Catherine M. *Childbearing in American Society, 1650–1850.* New York: New York University Press, 1985.

Schultz, Jane E. "The Inhospitable Hospital: Gender and Professionalism in Civil War Medicine." *Signs* 17, no. 2 (Winter 1992): 363–92.

Schwarz, Marie Jenkins. *Birthing a Slave: Motherhood and Medicine in the Antebellum South.* Cambridge, MA: Harvard University Press, 2010.

Selcer, Richard F. *Civil War America, 1850 to 1875.* New York: Infobase Publishing, 2006.

Shepard, Ben. *War of Nerves: Soldiers and Psychiatrists in the Twentieth Century.* Cambridge, MA: Harvard University Press, 2001.

Shoemaker, Nancy. *American Indian Population Recovery in the Twentieth Century.* Albuquerque: University of New Mexico Press, 1999.

Shortt, S. E. "Physicians, Science, and Status: Issues in the Professionalization of American Medicine in the Nineteenth Century." *Medical History* 27 (January 1983): 51–68.

Showalter, Elaine. *The Female Malady: Women, Madness, and English Culture, 1830–1980.* New York: Pantheon Books, 1985.

Shyrock, Richard H. "A Medical Perspective on the Civil War." *American Quarterly* 14 (1962): 161–73.

Simmons, Marc. *Witchcraft in the Southwest: Spanish and Indian Supernaturalism on the Rio Grande.* Lincoln: University of Nebraska Press, 1980.

Sims, James Marion. *The Story of My Life.* D. Appleton and Company, 1888.

Sitton, Sarah C. *Life at the Texas State Lunatic Asylum 1857–1997.* College Station: Texas A&M University Press, 1999.

Slater, Peter Gregg. *Children in the New England Mind in Death and in Life.* Hamden, CT: Archon Books, 1977.

Smith, Christian (ed.), *The Secular Revolution: Power, Interests, and Conflict in the Secularization of American Public Life.* Berkeley: University of California Press, 2003.

Smith-Rosenberg, Carroll and Charles Rosenberg. "The Female Animal: Medical and Biological Views of Woman and Her Role in Nineteenth-Century America." *The Journal of American History* 60, no. 2 (September 1973): 332–56.

Starr, Paul. *The Social Transformation of American Medicine.* New York: Basic Books, 1982.

Steckel, Richard H. "A Dreadful Childhood: The Excess Mortality of American Slaves." *Social Science History* 10 (1986): 427–65.

Steckel, Richard H. and Joseph M. Prince, "Tallest in the World: Native Americans of the Great Plains in the Nineteenth Century." *The American Economic Review* 91, no. 1 (March 2001): 287–94.

Stevenson, Brenda E. "Distress and Discord in Virginia Slave Families, 1830–1860." In *Joy and in Sorrow: Women, Family, and Marriage in the Victorian South, 1830–1900,* edited by Carol Bleser, 103–24. New York: Oxford University Press, 1991.

Stowe, Steven M. *Doctoring the South: Southern Physicians and Everyday Medicine in the Mid-Nineteenth Century.* Chapel Hill: University of North Carolina Press, 2004.

Swann, John P. "The Evolution of the American Pharmaceutical Industry." *Pharmacy in History* 37, no. 2 (1995): 76–86.

Szreter, Simon. "Rethinking McKeown: The Relationship between Public Health and Social Change." *American Journal of Public Health* 92, no. 5 (2002): 722–25.

Tadman, Michael. "Class and the Construction of 'Race': White Racism in the American South." In *The State of US History,* edited by Melvyn Stokes, 327–46. Oxford, UK: Berg, 2000.

Takaki, Ronald. *A Different Mirror: A History of Multicultural America.* New York, Little, Brown, and Co., 2008.

Thoreau, Henry David. *Walden.* Boston and New York: Houghton, Mifflin and Company, 1892.

Thornton, Russell. *American Indian Holocaust and Survival: A Population History since 1492.* Norman: University of Oklahoma Press, 1987.

Trattner, Walter I. *Crusade for the Children: A History of the National Child Labor Committee and Child Labor Reform in America.* Chicago: Quadrangle Books, 1970.

Tomes, Nancy. "Feminist Histories of Psychiatry." In *Discovering the History of Psychiatry,* edited by in Mark S. Micale and Roy Porter, 348–82. New York: Oxford University Press, 1994.

Tomes, Nancy. *A Generous Confidence: Thomas Story Kirkbride and the Art of Asylum-Keeping, 1840–1883.* New York: Cambridge University Press, 1984.

Trennert, Robert A. *White Man's Medicine: Government Doctors and the Navajo, 1863–1955*. Albuquerque: University of New Mexico Press, 1998.

Troesken, Werner. *Water, Race, and Disease*. Cambridge, MA: MIT Press, 2004.

Ulrich, Laurel. *A Midwife's Tale: The Life of Martha Ballard, Based on her Diary, 1785–1812*. New York: Knopf, 1990.

Urban, Andrew. "Irish Domestic Servants, Irish Domestic Servants, 'Biddy' and Rebellion in the American Home, 1850–1900." *Gender & History* 21, Issue 2 (August 2009): 263–86.

Utley, Robert Marshall. *Frontier Regulars: The United States Army and the Indian, 1866–1891*. New York: Macmillan, 1974.

Valenčius, Conevery Bolton. *The Health of the Country: How American Settlers Understood Themselves and Their Land*. New York: Basic Books, 2002.

Vogel, Virgil J. *American Indian Medicine*. Norman: University of Oklahoma Press, 1970.

Vretto, Athena. *Somatic Fictions: Imagining Illness in Victorian Culture*. Stanford, CA: Stanford University Press, 1995.

Waller, John. *The Discovery of the Germ: Twenty Years that Changed the Way We Think about Disease*. New York: Columbia University Press, 2002.

Waller, John. " 'The Illusion of an Explanation': The Concept of Hereditary Disease, 1770–1870." *Journal of the History of Medicine and Allied Sciences* 57, no. 4 (October 2002): 410–48.

Ward, Thomas J. *Black Physicians in the Jim Crow South*. Fayetteville: University of Arkansas Press, 2003.

Warner, John Harley. *Against the Spirit of the System: The French Impulse in Nineteenth-Century American Medicine*. Princeton, NJ: Princeton University Press, 1998.

Warner, John Harley. "The Fall and Rise of Professional Mystery: Epistemology, Authority, and the Emergence of Laboratory Medicine in Nineteenth-Century America." In *The Laboratory Revolution in Medicine*, edited by Andrew Cunningham and Perry Williams, 310–41. Cambridge, UK: Cambridge University Press, 1992.

Warner, John Harley. "The Idea of Southern Medical Distinctiveness: Medical Knowledge and Practice in the Old South." In *Science and Medicine in the Old South*, edited by Ronald L. Numbers and Todd L. Savitt, 179–205. Baton Rouge: Louisiana State University Press, 1989.

Warner, John Harley. "Power, Conflict, and Identity in Mid-Nineteenth-Century American Medicine: Therapeutic Change at the Commercial Hospital in Cincinnati." *The Journal of American History* 73, no. 4 (March 1987): 934–56.

Warner, John Harley. *The Therapeutic Perspective: Medical Practice, Knowledge, and Identity in America, 1820–1885*. Cambridge, MA: Harvard University Press, 1986.

Webb, James L. A., Jr. "On Biomedicine, Transfers of Knowledge, and Malaria Treatments." In *Indigenous Knowledge and the Environment in Africa and*

North America, edited by David M. Gordon and Shepard Krech III, 53–68. Athens: Ohio University Press, 2012.

Werbel, Amy. *Thomas Eakins: Art, Medicine, and Sexuality in Nineteenth-Century Philadelphia.* New Haven, CT: Yale University Press, 2007.

Whitaker, Robert. *Mad in America: Bad Science, Bad Medicine, and the Enduring Mistreatment of the Mentally Ill.* Cambridge, MA: Perseus Publishing, 2002.

White, Deborah G. *Ar'n't I a Woman? Female Slaves in the Plantation South.* New York: Norton, 1999.

White, Richard. *The Roots of Dependency: Subsistence, Environment, and Social Change among the Choctaws, Pawnees, and Navajo.* Lincoln: University of Nebraska Press, 1983.

Whorton, James C. *Nature Cures: The History of Alternative Medicine in America.* New York: Oxford University Press, 2002.

Whorton, James C. "Patient, Heal Thyself: Popular Health Reform Movements as Unorthodox Medicine." In *Other Healers: Unorthodox Medicine in America,* edited by Norman Gevitz, 52–81. Baltimore, MD: Johns Hopkins University Press, 1988.

Wilkie, Laurie A. "Medicinal Teas and Patient Medicines: African-American Women's Consumer Choices and Ethnomedical Traditions at a Louisiana Plantation." *South-eastern Archeology* 15, no. 2 (1996): 119–31.

Williams, James C. "The American Industrial Revolution." In *A Companion to American Technology,* edited by Carroll Pursell. Malden, MA: Blackwell Pub., 2005.

Winders, Richard Bruce. *Mr Polk's Army: The American Military Experience in the Mexican War.* College Station: Texas A&M University Press, 1997.

Wolf, Jacqueline. *Don't Kill Your Baby: Public Health and the Decline of Breastfeeding in the 19th and 20th Centuries.* Columbus: Ohio State University Press, 2001.

Wolf, Jacqueline. "Low Breastfeeding Rates and Public Health in the United States." *American Journal of Public Health* 93, no. 12 (December 2003): 2000–2010.

Wood, Ann Douglas. "'The Fashionable Diseases': Women's Complaints and Their Treatment in Nineteenth-Century America." *The Journal of Interdisciplinary History* 4, no. 1 (Summer 1973): 25–52.

Wood, Ann Douglas. "Heaven Our Home: Consolation Literature in the Northern United States, 1830–1880." *American Quarterly* 26, no. 5 (December 1974): 496–515.

Wood, Peter. *Black Majority: Negroes in Colonial South Carolina from 1670 through the Stono Rebellion.* New York: W. W. Norton & Co., 1974.

Young, James Harvey. *The Toadstool Millionaires: A Social History of Patent Medicines in America before Federal Regulation.* Princeton, NJ: Princeton University Press, 1961.

Young, Jeffrey Robert. "Ideology and Death on a Savannah River Rice Plantation, 1833–1867: Paternalism amongst 'a Good Supply of Disease and Pain.'" *Journal of Southern History* 59, no. 4 (November 1993): 673–706.

Index

Abortion, 80

African American healers: conjure, 5–6, 28–29, 61–63; hostility of planters to slave medicine, 6–7; practicing "regular" medicine, 29, 30–31; rejection of white medicine, 201; slave midwives, 4, 5, 28, 78; treating both black and white patients, 6–7, 78

African American medical schools, 29–31

Alcott, William A., 52, 53

Alternative medicine: chiropractic, 22; Christian Science, 22–23; competition against regular healers, 38, 39–40; Eclectics, 17–18; homeopaths, 18–19; hostility of "regulars" toward naturopaths, 18–19; hydropathy, 18; osteopathy, 22; overview, 16–19; reasons for popularity, 16, 17, 40; Thomsonians, 17, 40, 196

American Medical Association, 36, 39, 83, 199

Apache medicine: healing rituals, 66; treatment of wounds, 8

Army Medical Department, 75, 209, 212, 213–14, 218

Augusta, Alexander (physician), 29

Bacchus, Josephine (ex-slave), 5

Bacteriology: acceptance in United States, 44, 56, 58, 77, 195; opposition to, 21, 43, 77; overview, 19, 21, 41, 54, 129, 164, 169, 207, 221

Ballard, Martha (midwife), 77, 79, 193, 196

Bambara, 6, 61

Battle Creek Sanitarium, 59

Beach, Wooster (alternative practitioner), 17

Beaumont, William (physician), 10, 36, 208

Bigelow, Charles (physician), 83

Blackwell, Elizabeth (physician), 52,
    88, 89, 160, 254, 255
Bliss, Sally, 81
Bloodletting, 14, 15–16, 178,
    192, 194, 209
Bosque Redondo reservation, 75
Breast cancer, 158
Bright's disease, 19
Brisbane, Jimmy (conjurer), 62
Broussais, Francois
    J. V. (physician), 13
Brown, John (settler), 12
Bruce, Henry Clay (ex-slave), 5
Brunson, Vinnie (ex-slave), 28
Bubonic plague, 19, 118, 220
Buchan, William (physician), 13
Butterworth, Rebecca (settler), 36
Byford, Henry (physician), 84

Calomel (mercurous oxide): decline,
    15, 16, 194, 199; effects, 192–93,
    197, 199; popularity, 5, 14, 192
Campbell, Marie (slave midwife), 28
Cancer, 22, 23, 145, 158
Castor oil: as cathartic, 5; to lessen
    infection among slaves, 200
Cathell. D. W. (physician), 21, 43
Cerebrospinal meningitis, 19, 96, 251
Chandler, Lizzie (ex-slave), 5
Cherokee: healing practices, 65–66,
    203; medical theories, 9, 63, 65;
    mortality of Trail of Tears, 120
Childbed fever. *See* Puerperal fever
Children's health: child mortality,
    95–111; coping with loss, 105–7,
    242–44; among Native
    Americans, 99; overview,
    95–111, 237; school health
    visitors, 109–11; among slaves,
    138; working children, 139, 150
Chiropractic, 22
Cholera: association with urban
    poverty, 11–12, 53–54, 107;
    death toll, 11, 242; debates
    about cause, 10, 11–12, 15;

decline debates about
    contagiousness, 11–12; impact
    on Native Americans, 99;
    incidence, 2, 11, 117, 118, 119,
    242; increasing public
    skepticism about physicians, 37;
    public health initiatives, 55, 123,
    125, 126; quarantine, 122;
    theological responses to, 53–54
Christian Science, 22, 59–60
Cinchona bark. *See* Quinine
Civil War medicine: artistic
    depictions, 244, 245–47; camp
    hygiene, 210, 211; civilian
    casualties, 217; deaths to
    disease, 210–11; effects on
    African American health, 101–2;
    hospitals, 215, 230; introduction
    of ambulance corps, 213,
    215–16; medicinal drugs,
    194–95; nurses, 216, 234;
    overview, 163, 210–18;
    prosthetics, 218; psychological
    trauma, 217–18; surgery,
    163–64, 213–14; U.S. Sanitary
    Commission, 211–13
Clarke, Edwin C. (physician), 85, 89
Climate, 1, 2, 12, 115–16
Collins, Harriet (ex-slave), 5
Comstock Law (1873), 83–84
Comstock, Anthony, 83
Conjurers, 5–6, 28–29, 61–63
Cooke, John Esten (physician), 13–14
Cottonwood (contraceptive), 81
Cree, 67

Darkas, Aunt (slave healer), 60
Davis, Anne, 75
Davis, Nathan (physician), 34, 39
Diagnostic tools: instruments, 19, 41,
    42, 107, 109, 128, 129, 225, 233;
    role in enhancing doctor's
    authority, 41
Diarrheal disease: association with
    milk substitutes, 104; due to

insanitary conditions, 3, 101;
mortality, 2, 3, 11, 13, 14, 76,
101, 104, 108, 115, 116, 119, 129,
130, 203, 207, 209–10, 211, 218
Diphtheria: antitoxin, 20, 21, 107,
109, 128, 199; decline, 130; killer
of children, 95, 96; opposition to
free provision of antitoxin, 109;
overview, 2, 86, 95, 118;
remedies on plantations, 200;
susceptibility of rural recruits in
Civil War to, 209
Dispensaries: decline of, 236–37;
opposition from physicians,
109; rising importance of,
230–31
"Doctor's Riot," 34
Douglass, Frederick
(ex-slave), 28, 141
Dysentery, 2, 3, 10, 12, 99, 108,
115–16, 121, 125, 196,
202, 209, 210

Earheart, Amelia, 59
Eastern Shoshoni: healing rituals, 66;
theories of disease, 31
Eclectics, 17, 18, 38, 45, 46, 196
Eddy, Mary Baker (alternative
practitioner), 22, 60
Eliot, Charles (physician), 35
Emancipation, health of former
slaves after, 28, 121
Emetics: in Native American
medicine, 202; in Thomsonian
medicine, 17; use by regular
physicians, 5, 14, 17,
177, 192, 202
Experts, rise of, 41, 43, 44,
214, 236, 252

Family as healers, 38, 78
Family limitation: among African
Americans, 81; contraception,
73, 82, 84; among Native
Americans, 80–81; opposition

to, 83–84; rising trend,
75, 80–83
Feaster, Gus (ex-slave), 29
Fett, Sheila, 29, 201
Field, Justice Stephen, 44–45
Finlay, Carlos (physician), 21,
42, 129
Fitzbutler, William Henry
(physician), 30
Ford, Henry, 59
France: laboratories, 19; treatment of
insanity, 178
Frontier, health conditions, 96,
99–100, 150, 193, 210, 242

Gaffney, Mary (ex-slave), 81
Geography, 2, 116, 117
Germany: introduction of aseptic
surgery, 165; level of industrial
accidents, 143, 151; rise of
laboratories, 19, 36, 103, 195;
study of insanity, 185
Gonorrhea, 19, 107, 226
Graham, Sylvester (alternative
practitioner), 18, 56
Grant, President Ulysses S., 22
Graves, Mildred (slave
midwife), 78
Gregg, Josiah, 67
Griscom, John H. (physician), 55
Guerard, Arthur (physician), 58
Guiteau, Charles J., 176
Gunn, John C. (physician), 36

Hahnemann, Samuel (alternative
practitioner), 17
Hall, G. Stanley (psychologist), 56
Hammond, William (surgeon
general): on female sexuality,
85; pavilion-style hospitals, 215
Hartley, Robert (physician), 55
Harvard Medical School, 34,
35, 42, 105
Heredity, 10, 174, 186, 249
Heroic medicine, 192–93, 197

Holmes, Oliver Wendell (physician),
    14, 77, 164, 245, 252
Homeopathy, 16, 17, 38, 45, 46
Hospitals: almshouses, 176, 227–34,
    236, 237; asylums, recovery
    rates in, 179–84; building new
    asylums, 179–81; building new
    hospitals, 64, 127, 166, 226, 227,
    232; Civil War hospitals, 215,
    230; laboratories in hospitals,
    225, 233; need for mental
    asylums, 181; nursing schools,
    234; professional nursing, 43,
    225, 234–36; surgery in hospitals,
    43, 165–66, 229, 233–34;
Humoral theory, 13, 14, 15
Hurons, 64
Hurston, Zora Neale, 28
Hydropathy, 18
Hysteria, 85–86, 87

Igbo, 6, 61
Immigrants: Chinese prostitutes,
    148; exploitation of, 140–43, 152,
    160–61; Famine Irish, 11, 122;
    hostility towards, 122, 125,
    141–43, 174, 233, 249; immigrant
    populations, 12, 58, 79, 80, 83,
    97, 117–18, 119, 125, 128, 233;
    use for anatomy instruction,
    160–61
Industrial accidents, 142–48
Industrialization: increased rate of
    accidents, 1, 3, 142–45; cause of
    respiratory diseases, 144;
    attempts to regulate, 150–51
Infant mortality: attempts to reduce
    mortality, 107–11, 129; causes of
    death, 96–98; coping with loss,
    105–7, 242–44; malnutrition,
    100–102, 102–5; among Native
    Americans, 99; slavery and, 138
Iroquois, 66, 203
Irregular practitioners.
    See Alternative medicine

Jackson, President Andrew, 54
Jim Crow: decline in African
    American physicians, 31; effects
    on health, 31, 130
Johns Hopkins Medical School, 42,
    43, 161, 169, 234

Kellogg, John Harvey (physician and
    Seventh-Day Adventist),
    56, 58, 59
Knowlton, Charles, 82, 83
Koch, Robert (bacteriologist), 19, 20,
    21, 41, 164
Kongo, 6, 61
Kwakiutls, 8, 66

Laboratories: diagnostic laboratories,
    42, 107, 109, 128, 129, 225, 233;
    for formula feed production,
    105; in hospitals, 225, 233; in
    study of insanity, 184–85;
    introduction into medical
    education, 42, 46; lack of
    laboratory research in United
    States, 36–37; overview, 19–23,
    41, 191, 195–96, 204, 255;
    pharmaceutical firms, 198–99;
    skepticism about their role, 23
Laennec, René-Théophile-Hyacinthe
    (physician), 14
Lincoln, President Abraham,
    29, 140, 212
Littlejohn, Reverend Abram
    Newkirk, 57
Louisville National Medical College,
    30–31
Ludmerer, Kenneth, 43

Malaria: avoidance of wet lowlands,
    4, 131; decline, 4; mortality, 2–3,
    4, 12, 15, 17, 99, 116, 120, 121,
    131, 139, 192, 193, 210, 211;
    treatment with quinine, 14–15,
    38, 131, 193
Manifest Destiny, 1

Martin, David, 57
Massachusetts Institute
    of Technology, 44
Masturbation: attempts to remedy,
    56–57, 169; belief in danger of,
    18, 55–57, 59, 84, 169, 175;
    naturopaths, 18, 38, 56
Medical College of Georgia,
    34, 39, 161
Medical colleges: African American
    colleges, 29–32; closure of low-
    standard colleges, 34–36, 236;
    development of proprietary
    colleges, 34; early colleges,
    34–35; improving curricula,
    42–44, 235–36; obstacles to
    improvement, 39, 40; women's
    and co-educational
    colleges, 38, 89
Medical licensing, 35, 40, 44–46, 80
Medicine lodges (Native American),
    32–33
Medicine men or women.
    See Shamans
Meharry Medical College, Nashville,
    30–31
Meigs, Charles (physician), 77
Mercurous oxide. *See* Calomel
Mesmer, Franz (alternative healer),
    22, 60
Mesmerism, 22, 60
Miasma theory, 11, 12, 14,
    128, 144, 164
Michigan Indians, 8
Michigan Medical Society, 45
Michigan State Board of Health, 44
Micmacs, 74
Mississippi River, 2, 110,
    117, 131, 210
Mohegans, 8
Mohr, James, 82, 83, 84
Moore, William H. (senator), 62

Native American childbirth
    practices, 74, 78

Native Americans: adoption of
    native treatments by white
    healers, 10; attempts to destroy
    Native practices, 10, 67–68, 120;
    breastfeeding, 102; childbirth
    practices, 74, 79; contraception
    and abortion, 80–81; death of
    children, 99; destruction of
    means of subsistence, 3; effects
    on health of warfare, 4, 75;
    exposure to pathogens from
    white settlers, 117, 119–20;
    immunological vulnerability, 2;
    infectious disease, 1, 2, 3–4,
    74–76, 81, 100, 107–8, 111, 115,
    119–20, 131, 132; infectious
    disease in boarding schools,
    100–101, 107; influenza, 2, 100,
    118, 200; medicines and drugs,
    196, 200, 201–5; pregnancy and
    childbirth, 74; reduced fertility,
    75; relative longevity, 115;
    reservations, 3, 75, 89, 100, 102,
    111, 120, 131, 132; selection of
    healers, 31–33; sexual assault by
    colonists, 81; shamanic healing,
    66–68; smallpox vaccination,
    131; theories about disease,
    7–10, 63–68; tuberculosis,
    75, 89, 99, 100
Navajo: healing rituals, 66; shamans,
    32, 66; susceptibility to disease,
    75; theories of disease, 63, 64;
    training of shamans, 32
Neurasthenia, 85–86, 185, 186, 252
New York Association for
    Improving the Condition of the
    Poor, 55
New York: asylums, 179, 183;
    corruption of city government,
    54–55; dispensaries, 231, 236;
    hospitals, 226, 228–30, 234, 236,
    237; mortality in slums, 53;
    public health initiatives, 55–56,
    108, 109, 123, 125, 126, 128, 129

Nursing: almshouse nurses, 229–30; in wartime, 163, 212, 213, 215–16, 221; involvement in public health initiatives, 128–29; nursing schools, 234; overview, 107, 128, 212, 213, 215, 216, 229–36; professional nursing, 43, 225, 234–36; relationship with surgeons, 33, 235

Ohio River, 2
Ojibwa medicine: diagnosis, 65; medical theories, 8, 9, 63–64; medicine lodges, 33; selection of healers, 31–32; treatment, 67; wound repair, 8
Osteopathy, 16, 22

Palmer, Bartlett Joshua (alternative practitioner), 22
Palmer, Daniel David (alternative practitioner), 22
Paris Medicine, 14, 16, 33, 88
Parvin, Theophilus (physician), 77
Pasteur, Louis (bacteriologist), 19, 21, 41, 54, 129, 164
Patent medicines, 10, 193, 196–98
Physicians: African American, 28–31; apprenticeships, 33–34; attempts to regulate, 35, 39–40, 45–46; campaign against abortion, 83; care of the insane, 175–76, 179; Civil War, 163–65, 208–16; competition for patients, 36, 38–39, 78, 104–5, 109–11; contraception, 82; debates about contagion, 3, 12, 77, 122, 126; debates about germ theory, 20, 21, 22, 41–42, 77, 128, 130, 126; decline of heroic remedies, 15, 16, 195–96, 199; education, 33–35, 39–40, 42–43, 160–61, 228–29; financial difficulties, 37–38, 63, 109–11, 236; growing credibility, 39,

40–42, 43–44, 58; involvement in dispensaries, 230–31; involvement in public health reforms, 44, 55–56, 126–27, 130; misogyny, 73, 84–87, 87–89; performing abortions, 84; popular distrust, 36, 37, 121–22, 251–53; promoting breast-milk substitutes, 104–5; relations with alternative practitioners, 45–46; relationship to nurses, 234–35; relationship with religion, 52–54, 56–57, 57–58; setting up hospitals, 232; specialization, 80, 166; taking over midwifery, 76, 77, 79–80; theories of diseases, 10–16, 52–56; training overseas, 14, 16, 41; treatments, 15–16, 192–96, 199; use of heroic remedies, 15–16, 192–93; women entering the profession, 38, 87–89, 254–55
Pneumonia, 2, 10, 19, 96, 108, 118, 151
Postpartum depression, 76
Potawatomis, 8, 202
Preston Retreat, Pennsylvania, 77
Price, Joseph, 77
Prostitutes: attempts to regulate, 149–50; denied access to voluntary hospitals, 226; as patients in almshouses, 228–29
Pure Food and Drug Act (1906), 44, 199

Quakers, 55, 181
Quarantine: during Spanish–American War, 219; for prostitutes with venereal disease, 150; on Native American reservations, 131; opposition to quarantine, 3, 117, 122; overview, 3, 12, 37, 118, 122; during Spanish–American War, 219

Quinine: as a 'tonic', 16, 193, 194–5; efficacy, 4, 210; as patent remedy, 38, 193, 194; efficacy, 4, 210; as a tonic, 16, 193, 194–95; to treat ague, 4, 14–15, 52, 131, 210

Race suicide, 186, 249
Reed, Major Walter (major and physician), 21, 42, 129
Reid, Hugo, 81
Restell, Madame (abortionist), 83
Rosenberg, Charles, 14, 192, 230–31, 236
Rush, Benjamin (physician), 9–10, 13–14, 34, 169, 176, 192–93

Salmonella, 2, 121
Sanitary reform: clean water supply, 2, 55, 97–98, 108, 125–26, 111, 127, 128; importance in mortality decline, 129–31, 132, 255; obstacles to, 54, 55, 109, 122–23, 130; overview, 107–11, 121–32, 231; public health activism, 44, 55, 56–56, 108, 119, 125–26, 127, 231; regulation of milk, 111, 129; school health visitors, 110; street cleaning sanitation, 2, 108, 125–26, 127, 128, 231
Scarlet fever, 2, 10, 19, 80, 95–96, 118, 130, 196, 209
Schwartz, Marie Jenkins, 28
Sedgwick, William T. (physician), 44
Self-treatment, 38
Seventh-Day Adventists, 56, 59
Shamans (Native American): medical practices, 9, 32–33, 63, 65–67, 203; medicine bundle, 9, 65
Shine, Polly (ex-slave), 6
Sickle-cell anemia, 2
Sims, J. Marion (surgeon), 35, 159, 160, 165, 169, 253

Sioux: selection of healers, 32; susceptibility to infectious disease, 99, 100, 120
Slavery: breastfeeding, 100–101; Christianity and conjure, 62; Civil War, 101, 211–12; conjure, 5–6, 28–29, 61–63; drugs used by healers, 62, 199–201; early weaning, 101; effect on physical health, 2, 62, 74, 89, 100–102, 115, 120–21; elevated rates of infectious disease, 101, 120–21, 137–39; Emancipation, 102, 115; exploitation by surgical pioneers, 160–61; health of infants and children, 100–102; in literature, 249–51; nutrition, 101; physical abuse, 101, 138; psychological trauma, 62–63, 101; rates of stillbirth, 74; relative longevity, 89; religio-medical beliefs, 29, 60–63, 68; selecting healers, 27–29; separation of families, 101; slave midwives, 27–28; training of healers, 29
Smallpox: devastating Native Americans, 99–100, 119–20; incidence of, 4, 10, 96, 99–100, 109, 117, 119–20; vaccination, 107, 117, 123, 131
Smith-Rosenberg, Carroll, 78
Solidism, 13, 14–15
Starr, Paul, 40, 196
Still, Andrew Jackson (alternative practitioner), 16, 22
Stillbirth: among Native Americans, 75; among slaves, 74
Storer, Horatio (physician), 83
Stowe, Steven, 35, 192
Streptococcus, 75, 199
Stroyer, Jacob (ex-slave), 62
Supernaturalist medical beliefs: African Americans, 60–63; Native American, 9–10, 63–68, 203; white Americans, 51–60

Surgery: abortions, 83–84; advances, 159–60, 161–63, 221–22, 233–34; amputations, 36, 163, 208, 213–14, 220, 221; anesthesia, 79, 89, 161–63, 167, 197; celebration of leading surgeons, 253; circumcision, 169–70; dispensaries, role of, 128; exploitation of African Americans, 160–61; in hospitals, 43, 165–66, 229, 233–34; hygiene standards, 158, 163–66, 220–21, 233; Native American techniques, 7, 8–9, 32, 33, 63, 201; problem of pain, 159, 160–63, 253; reputation of, 166, 253–54; techniques, 157–58, 169, 233; theory of "laudable pus," 158; wartime, 163, 208–21

Syphilis: cause of stillbirths, 75; among Native American women, 75, 89; neurosyphilis (general paresis of the insane), 85, 183; among prostitutes, 149; sufferers denied entry to voluntary hospitals, 226

Tammany Hall, 122
Taylor, President Zachary, 54, 209
Telfair, Alexander (slave owner), 4
Tetanus, 19, 101, 158, 199, 200
Thomson, Samuel (alternative practitioner), 17, 38, 40, 196
Thomsonianism. *See* Alternative medicine
Tocqueville, Alexis de, 40
Trade: facilitating disease transmission, 2, 117–18, 119
Tuberculosis: in children, 96, 108, 151; discovery of bacterial cause, 19; genital tuberculosis, 75; indigenous peoples, 75, 89, 99, 100, 120; in literature, 244–45; measures to combat, 128, 129, 194; mortality, 2, 11,

22, 33, 95, 118, 149; slavery, 121; theories about cause, 11–12; transmission via milk, 129
Twain, Mark (writer), 39, 242, 251
Tweed, Boss, 54
Typhoid fever: among children, 116; decline, 130; on frontier, 99, 116; mortality, 2, 3, 12, 15, 19, 23, 99, 108, 116, 125–26, 130, 139, 193, 194, 211, 219, 221; racial disparity in incidence, 130; during war, 211, 221

University of Michigan Medical College, 30, 42, 44, 199, 228
Urbanization: creation of an urban underclass, 121–22, 232; decline of wet-nursing, 103; increasing the affordability of physicians, 40–41; infant and child mortality, 97–99; infectious disease, 1, 2, 4, 12, 41, 43, 54, 57–58, 81, 82, 97, 99, 103, 107, 115, 118, 119, 122, 126–27, 132, 166, 181, 226–27, 231–32, 247–49; need for mental asylums, 181; promoting the building of hospitals, 64, 127, 166, 226, 227, 232; public health initiatives, 2, 107; rise of the urban dispensary, 231; secularization, 57–58; urban fertility decline, 81–82; urban slums in literature, 247–49

Vaccination: free provision by dispensaries, 107, 109, 128, 131, 231; Native Americans, 131; opposition to, 117, 123; overview, 107, 109, 123, 210, 231; smallpox, 107, 123
Valenčius, Conevery Bolton, 38
Virchow, Rudolf (physician), 15

Wabanaki, 65
Walker, Clara (slave healer), 28, 78

Walker, John (slave owner), 6

Waring, Colonel George E., 58, 127, 129

Welch, William (physician), 42

Whitcomb, H. (physician), 80

White, Ellen (Seventh-Day Adventist), 59

White, George (slave healer), 60

Wied-Neuwied, Prince Maximilian of, 64

Witchcraft beliefs: in Native American medicine, 9, 64, 65; among white Americans, 194

Women's health: childbirth, 73–80; childbirth complications, 74, 75–77, 102–3, 159; female midwives, 74–78; gynecological surgery, 159–60; increasing standards of hygiene, 164, 234; Native Americans, 74, 78; obstetric anesthesia, 89; obstetricians, 77, 79, 80, 83, 159, 234; physicians replace midwives, 79; pregnancy rates, 73–76, 80; puerperal (childbed) fever, 75–77, 99, 164

X–ray machine, 19, 165, 207, 221, 233, 237

Yellow fever: death toll, 110, 116, 117, 219; ideas about cause, 12, 58, 129; medicines, 193, 210; Memphis epidemic (1878), 127; mosquito vector, 21, 42, 116; overview, 2, 34, 58, 110, 118, 242; public health responses, 123, 125, 127, 129; quarantine, 37, 112, 118

YMCA, 83

Yoruba, 6, 61

Zunis, 33, 78

About the Author

JOHN C. WALLER is an associate professor of the history of medicine at Michigan State University and director of the Social Science Scholars Program. He has written five books on various aspects of the history of medicine, science, and child labor, including *Einstein's Luck* (2002), *The Discovery of the Germ* (2004), and *A Time to Dance, a Time to Die* (2009). He is currently completing a study of ideas of innate difference from classical antiquity into the modern age.